PAUL McCARTNEY

PAUL McCARTNEY
A LIFE

PETER AMES CARLIN

BOOKS

Other titles by Peter Ames Carlin

*Catch a Wave: The Rise, Fall and Redemption
of the Beach Boys' Brian Wilson*

Beyond the Limits

Brave New Bride

First published in Great Britain in 2009 by
JR Books, 10 Greenland Street, London NW1 0ND
www.jrbooks.com

A catalogue record for this book is available from the British Library.

ISBN 978-1-906779-64-1

1 3 5 7 9 10 8 6 4 2

Printed by MPG Books, Bodmin, Cornwall

For Ralph Berkowitz

PAUL McCARTNEY

I

Paul McCartney is almost home.

He's in Liverpool, the city where he was born and raised. Not just that, but he's in Anfield, the section of Liverpool where his father grew up, where his grandfather lived and worked and raised his family, way back in the nineteenth century. No wonder Paul is beaming. He is only weeks from celebrating his sixty-sixth birthday, and at this moment he is right where his people have always been. In the midst of his family. Surrounded by friends. Right in the middle of a party. Joe McCartney would have been doing this, too, not a mile away, in 1908. Jim Mc-Cartney did it his way in 1928. And now, nearly a decade into the twenty-first century, Jim's son is doing the same thing.

His cheeks glow. His eyes sparkle. His mouth opens wide as he tilts his head back and lets out a high-pitched howl of delight. *Ahhhhhhh!*

Tens of thousands of voices scream back.

Paul is wearing a dark suit with its collar turned up and a loose white shirt on underneath. His hair is preternaturally brown, which makes him look young, but in a kind of surreal way. But more impor-tant, he has his Höfner bass strapped around his neck, and this makes him look—and almost certainly feel—ageless. As he knows, it's the instrument you see him holding when you close your eyes. If rock 'n' roll has any iconic symbols, Paul's violin-shaped Höfner bass is one of them. It is his Rosebud, his Excalibur. It's not the key to his past, exactly. But that he still has it, and wields it so frequently in public, tells you something.

The Höfner is light in his hands and moves easily on his waist as he turns around and plucks a few notes. Behind him the drummer taps the hi-hat cymbal gently, establishing a rhythm. Paul spins on his heel, steps up to the microphone, and barks out a greeting to the one hundred thousand faces arrayed before him.

Faw goodness' sake—I got that hippy hippy shake . . .

An explosion of drums and guitars and keyboards meets the roar from the crowd, and this is the instant when Paul really comes home. He didn't write this song, but he made it his own nearly fifty years ago, playing with some friends in a dank basement filled with kids from the neighborhood. Nobody talked about history then, nobody thought in terms of icons or legends. But what would any of that have mattered? They had three chords, drums, and some wild nonsense about shaking it to the left, then shaking it to the right, and doing a hippy shake-shake with all of your might. And that was really all they needed, really all that could possibly matter.

That's where it began for Paul and his friends. And then it was everywhere else. A bigger basement, then a beer-splattered nightclub in Hamburg, Germany. A dance hall, then an auditorium, then more auditoriums. Then they were in London, then Paris, then New York City. Then they were all around the world. And then the other three were gone, and it was just him and Linda. And he made sure she came with him now, out onstage to ride that wave of energy. Then there was life, too. Home and kids and all that, but still the lights and the cameras and the music in the studios. And always the pure electric blast of guitars and drums and keyboards and his own sweet, clear, piercing voice.

He's standing up there now, his body coiled like a spring, his fingers dancing on the frets of the Höfner, his voice wailing, because he wants to tell you his story. Not in words, exactly. Certainly, Paul likes to talk about himself, organizing and reorganizing facts and ideas to fit his evolving sense of reality. But the man's heart is in his music, so this is where his truth resides. Listen. He's done with "Hippy Hippy Shake" now, and so much more is to come. It's his whole life up there, flashing before your, and his, ears.

Now it's "Jet" and Paul and Linda at their height. Young, in love, with children and dogs at their feet, stoned out of their sweet, goofy gourds. Flash back now to "Drive My Car," and it's John and Paul huddled by the piano, weaving a slim idea and a bit of attitude into a wickedly slinky rocker about lust, money, and power. *I got no car and it's breaking my heart / But I found a driver, and that's a start!* The entire writing of the song took, what, two hours? And that included a tea break. Next jump thirty years to "Flaming Pie," and a look back at that same fated partnership, with a flicker of resentment for anyone who thought he might have been the junior partner: *I'm the man on the flaming pie!* And just to prove Paul's still on top of it, here's his new single, "Dance Tonight," perhaps the most gloomy invitation to boogie that has ever been issued.

Oh, but now a moment to remember George with a ukulele-led version of "Something." This is sweet and yet strange. A ukulele? Paul plays it far more straight with his own classics "Penny Lane" and "Hey Jude." Even straighter with "Yesterday," that gift from the subconscious whose melancholy seems to spring straight from the loss that devastated him as a teenager, that made him grip his guitar so tightly he never let it go. "Let It Be" tells another version of the same story—here mother Mary takes her own form—then comes another tribute, this one far more emotionally complex given all that happened, and all that didn't, and where he's singing this, and how he knows full well that Yoko Ono is out there in the audience watching his every move.

I read the news today, oh boy . . .

He's never tried this before, a live take on "A Day in the Life," perhaps the most complicated recording the Beatles ever committed to tape. It is, in many ways, the true apex of his collaboration with John Lennon, the seamless marriage of one man's existential gloom with another's surreal prankishness. The cameras find Yoko in the crowd, a black top hat perched elegantly on her jet-black hair, and she's smiling and nodding even as the live music fades to make room for a taped sample of the famous orchestral anarchy, building to a slightly underwhelming climax in the stadium's speakers. Then there's a quick pivot and the band lurches into full-throttle anthem mode for the chorus of "Give Peace a Chance." *All we are saying . . .* And now Yoko is beaming and clapping along, and Paul is waving his hands to get the crowd going even louder. And the Liverpudlians are ecstatic, bellowing and waving their tribute to a fallen hero, a sainted man, a martyr to the cause. Which is exactly what Paul intended, even if it's also what drives him a little berserk.

So dry your eyes and blow your nose, because now we're going back to the basements of our youth. Coming full circle to those sweaty young boys, so full of life and joy and not even suspecting where all of this is about to take them.

A-one, two, three—fah!

It's time for the show to end, so we're going back to the very beginning, back to the four working-class kids with nothing but a few chords, cheap instruments, and a dream about not getting real jobs. *How could I dance with another?* Paul's got a new band now, the latest in a succession of them but the massive video screens behind them show the Beatles again, back in their prime, running and leaping and dancing together, spinning madly in and out of one another's arms. They were so young then, so in love with one another, and so swept up in the joyful noise that came so easily to them. Paul's wailing as hard as he can, the place is rocking, the walls literally shaking with the beat. But it's that old film that everyone is staring at, and Paul can't resist a glance over his shoulder, either. The way he looked then, the way they sounded—well, it was way beyond compare.

Many years earlier it had just been the four of them. Jim and Mary and their pair of rambunctious young boys, Paul and Michael. Jim and Mary were older than you'd expect. Jim was already past forty when Paul had been born, and Mary was well into her thirties when Michael entered the scene two years later. Maybe this, along with some of the clouds the elder McCartneys knew were lurking on the horizon, made them treasure their family time that much more. Besides, the McCartney clan had always been close, and when a winter afternoon turned dark and cold, the family would settle into their sit-

ting room and Jim would pull out the piano bench and let his fingertips settle on the cool, smooth keys.

He wasn't a terrific pianist; trumpet had been his instrument, back
in the day. But Jim had a good set of ears and nimble fingers that
could locate the rhythm and melody in a popular song and pound it
out until the top of the piano rattled against the frame. Ragtime songs,
big-band hits. Mary wasn't musical herself—she was a nurse who
looked at the world through dark, though sweet-natured, eyes—but
she loved her husband's way with a song. She especially enjoyed seeing Paul gazing up at his dad from the floor, his soft brown eyes alight,
his chubby cheeks split open with a smile. He'd chime in with re-
quests, sometimes for "Lullaby of the Leaves," but always for his favorite among his dad's party pieces: George Gershwin's "Stairway to
Paradise." *Play it again, Dad! Play it!*

So of course Jim would, a smile on his own wide cheeks, his fingers
tracing the upward progression of the chords (Hear that? Just like a
stairway!), and his own pleasant voice belting out the cheery words
about how feeling bad was madness, when you could follow the steps
straight up to gladness.

I'll build a stairway to paradise with a new step every day!

Young Paul loved the song, just as much as he loved his dad playing it, and the way the old man would look over his shoulder when he
was done and give a little wave, as if acknowledging an appreciative
crowd. He'd seen a few of those in his day, which is why Paul never
thought to question the advice Jim always gave after his spontaneous
musicales: "You should learn an instrument. Once you do, you'll always be invited to the party."

The boy took the lesson to heart, just as Jim had followed the
same advice from his father, Joe. They took each other seriously, the
McCartneys did. Maybe because they had always been too poor for
anyone else to extend them the same courtesy. It had been that way
ever since the first McCartneys came to Liverpool from their native
Ireland, arriving as most immigrants do, carrying little more than the
clothes on their backs, their hopes for the future, and whatever muscle
and brainpower they might apply to propel themselves out of the past
and into a future of their own devising.

We can only imagine what inspired the McCartneys to start their journey, but it's far easier to describe what they found when they arrived: a thriving northwestern port, its position near the mouth of the river Mersey (which is actually a long inlet from the Atlantic) making it the veritable threshold for all of England, and Europe beyond. The docks stretched down the riverbank, all of them crowded with ships delivering sugar, rum, tobacco, and cotton, taking away textiles, packaged food, and durable goods. Liverpool also served nicely as a stopping point for slave vessels en route from Africa to the United States, thus nurturing a cultural and economic bond that prompted the government of the American Confederacy to place an unofficial embassy in the city.

Some immigrants flooded in while others flooded back out, departing for the untrammeled shores of the New World or sunny, empty Australia. The ones who remained built careers, and sometimes fortunes, in Liverpool's trades, particularly as its shipping-based economy prospered into the early years of the twentieth century. Visitors marveled at the city's neoclassical architecture, its elevated railway and distinctly cosmopolitan feel. Aromas from the Indies, Asia, Africa, wafted through restaurant doors. The Adelphi Hotel, the jewel of the Georgian section above the City Centre on Lime Street, honed a worldwide reputation for its luxurious rooms and the turtle soup in its restaurant. Charles Dickens called it the best hotel in the world.

What seemed exotic or flat-out bizarre in London barely caused a ripple on Merseyside. African men walked arm in arm with fair-skinned local ladies and no one batted an eye. The jazz age arrived early, shipped straight from the funkiest precincts of New Orleans and New York City, and took permanent residence. One jazz club called itself Storyville, after the Crescent City's red-light district. American country music also flourished, the folk-music revival struck a chord, too, with its mix of plainspoken storytelling, musical simplicity, and socialist ambitions. Music came naturally to Liverpool. It's "more than a place where music happens," wrote native son Paul Du Noyer. "Liverpool is a reason *why* music happens."

It certainly happened in the McCartney family's house. Every song had a story, and every story came with a song. Remember old Joe

McCartney, the bass horn–playing patriarch? He was born right here in Liverpool in 1866—in Everton, to be exact. Just imagine life in those days. Horses and buggies, endless work and hardly any money at all. And you think Everton's a bit down-at-heels now, but back then everyone knew it was the worst slum in all of England. Still, Joe got himself a job at Cope's tobacco warehouse and labored there for years, cutting tobacco leaf, stoving it down, rolling it out. Sometimes catching fairly significant amounts of it in his pant cuffs. Who knew how it got there (wink-wink), but there it was, and so he'd collect it at home, and at the end of the week there might be enough to roll a cigar or two he could sell to a friend on the corner, pulling in a few more pennies for the family.

It was quite a family. Joe had married Florrie Clegg in 1896, and before long the babies started showing up. Joe and Florrie had nine kids, seven of whom lived past the cradle, which meant a lot of little McCartneys were running around Everton. Not being quiet about it, either. No matter how crowded their house was, the McCartney family's door was usually open, and when it was, the music was always playing. Joe played his horn in the territorial army brass band, too, so friends and bandmates were always dropping in for a bit of a play or a cup of tea. Or maybe something stronger, if they really got going. Joe preferred lemonade, but he never got in the way of anyone else's good time. Florrie would be leading the charge in the kitchen, calling out the welcomes and handing around pots of tea and platters of Welsh rarebit to keep everyone going. By the end of the evening the doors would be wide-open, the music in full cry, friends and neighbors out in the yard, dancing in the streets.

This was the McCartneys of Solva Street, Everton. Maybe every McCartney man was destined to spend his life as a laborer or as an anonymous drudge scraping away in the lower reaches of someone else's factory. But maybe, with a bit of luck and hard work, they could find their way to something better. And maybe it didn't hurt to enjoy yourself along the way, either.

Such was the wisdom that Joe McCartney tried to teach his children, and his second-oldest, born James McCartney on July 7, 1902, took it all to heart. He was a handsome, charming boy, graced with an aquiline nose and thin brows whose prominent arch made him appear to be perpetually delighted, which the fun-loving lad often was. James—or Jim, as he was called—paid attention to his lessons at Everton's Steer Street School and followed the old man's musical lead by taking up the trumpet. When a neighbor gave the family a battered, old spinet piano from the Epstein family's NEMS music store, Jim felt drawn to its keyboard, too, teaching himself enough notes and chords to be of some use when the doors opened and the family musicale began. When the time came for the schoolboy to find a way to carry his weight financially, Jim took a job at the nearby Theatre Royal vaudeville house, selling programs before the show, then scampering up to the balcony to operate the limelight during the performance. After the show the boy would troll the aisles for abandoned programs, which he would take home and refurbish (a quick wipe and iron did the trick) to resell them at the next show.

Jim left school at fourteen and hired on with A. Hannay & Co., Cotton Merchants, running samples of cloth from market to warehouse and back for a weekly salary of six shillings. Donkey work, they called it, but Jim McCartney pursued it with a diligence and creative energy that made his bosses look twice. Maybe this cheeky lad was cut out for something beyond the company's lowest rungs. Jim kept up his end, grinding his way up the ladder until, after fourteen years, Hannay's management rewarded him with a rare promotion from the warehouse into the suit-and-tied ranks of the salesmen. It was quite a leap for a lower-class kid without much formal education. And the family was most pleased.

Every mickle makes a muckle! Moderation and toleration! To Jim, the secret of life came down to two simple notions: common sense and uncommon good cheer. He did his job, lived up to his obligations, and enjoyed himself as much as possible. He was sharp and funny and enjoyed being the center of attention. Indeed, Jim McCartney was a bit of a legend in Everton, where local jazz-age gadabouts knew him as the raffish leader of Jim Mac's Band. This loosely constructed musical outfit, a bit rough around the edges, was more than able to fill a neighborhood ballroom or labor hall with the day's jauntiest pop and ragtime numbers.

Jim McCartney could clearly be a rascal. He enjoyed a drink, particularly when he was playing the horses ("a little flutter on the gee-

gee's" was Jim's proto-psychedelic expression for placing a bet). But Jim could also tell when the time had arrived for him to get serious. So once Jim ascended into the suit-and-tie ranks of Hannay's salesmen, Jim Mac's Band (and also the Masked Melody Makers) soon played their last dance.

But when would the charming Mr. McCartney find himself a wife and settle down? For most of his adult life Jim had been happy to be the man-about-town. But by the end of the thirties the atmosphere had changed. The gloomy shadow of World War II was descending upon Liverpool, and the fear and promise of destruction was everywhere. Jim's relatively advanced age (he was pushing forty) and a ruptured eardrum from a childhood accident kept him out of the service. But the cotton industry had been nationalized for the duration, leaving Hannay's shuttered and Jim out of a job. He ended up with a low-paying defense-industry job turning a lathe in the Napiers engineering works. Then the bombs started to fall on Liverpool.

The raids began in August 1940 and continued through the early weeks of 1942, killing more than two thousand six hundred of the city's residents, and sending nearly as many into the hospital with serious wounds. More than ten thousand homes were destroyed, with far more suffering serious damage. This they withstood day after day. The descent of night, the sirens, the planes, the perpetual knowledge that the only thing standing between you and a sudden, fiery death was fate, and maybe luck.

Jim spent his days at the Napiers works, and his nights volunteering as a lookout for the local fire brigade. One day, he knew, Hannay's would be back in business and he would resume his prewar career. But was that really all that lay ahead of him? Jim had started to notice the new generation of apple-cheeked McCartneys running around the family parties. He'd watch them play and hear their little voices call out to their parents. Somewhere in the back of his mind, Jim wondered what he had done with his life. Would he ever have a son of his own to pick up and hold in his lap when the hour got late and the songs turned slow and sweet?

It's easy to imagine these thoughts playing through Jim's mind that night in June 1940 when he came whistling up the walk and knocked on the door of the home his sister Jin had just moved into with her new husband, Harry. The couple had set up housekeeping on a tree-lined block in suburban West Derby, so now they were having the traditional open house, inviting friends and family in to admire the new place, have a drink, and put their troubles aside, if only for a few hours. On this fine evening, the suburban air full of sweet spring blossoms and freshly cut grass, Jim glimpsed a dark-eyed, quiet woman, Mary, sitting in the living room.

Maybe that's as far as it would have gone. The party was supposed to be an early-evening affair, a casual dinner not intended to trail into the night. But then the sirens came wailing over the rooftops. The entire party ran for Jin and Harry's cellar—turn out the lights, and don't forget to bring the champagne!—and hunkered down in the darkness. Most often the all-clear sounded within minutes, certainly no more than an hour or two. But this time the alert went on deep into the night. So they sat there, the McCartneys and their friends. Jim was next to Mary the entire time, chatting and joking, lighting her cigarettes, helping to keep things relaxed. He made her laugh. He seemed entirely charming, and also, she said later, delightfully "uncomplicated." They were married at St. Swithins' Roman Catholic chapel in West Derby on April 15, 1941, and moved into some furnished rooms on Sunbury Road in the Anfield section of Liverpool.

The first boy arrived in the evening of June 18, 1942, born in relative luxury, thanks to Mary's professional connections, in a private ward of Walton Hospital. Her friends in the hospital also bent the rules far enough to afford Jim a glance at his son just moments after his birth. Unfortunately, no one had thought to warn Jim about how vestiges of the womb and of the birthing can alter a newborn's appearance. What he saw in those moments left the new father shocked and horrified. "He looked like a horrible piece of red meat," Jim recalled. "He had one eye open and just squawked all the time." A bath (for the boy) and a good night's sleep (for his father) improved things markedly, and by the time James Paul McCartney came home to his parent's furnished rooms in Anfield, Jim saw things more clearly. "He turned out a lovely baby in the end."

The addition of Paul sent the family first to a Liverpool council-subsidized house in Wallasey, a neighborhood on the Wirral Peninsula just across the Mersey from the city center. The family moved back to central Liverpool a year later, but the arrival of another boy, Peter Michael McCartney (who would also be known by his middle name), in January 1944, qualified them for a larger flat in a modern complex in Knowsley. They headed to a new council development in Speke, on Liverpool's southern fringe, two years later. The neighborhood was still being built, so the McCartney boys rode their bikes down muddy, unfinished streets, chasing their friends past vacant lots and half-framed houses to open pastures and thickets of trees.

The end of the war sparked the city's spirit, just as the reprivatization of the cotton industry, and subsequent reopening of Hannay's, restored Jim's job on the cotton market. But Liverpool was still pocked with the scars of war, and its economic structure remained a shambles. The once-thriving cotton import trade had fallen to half its prewar levels, reducing Jim's income by nearly as much. Mary had traded regular hospital work for the more flexible—if less dependable—hours of a visiting midwife, but her job came with a guaranteed salary and benefits (such as access to the council's better subsidized-housing projects) that far outstripped her husband's weekly income. Between the two of them Jim and Mary did well enough to keep their family fed and clothed, and to even provide the occasional luxury.

For Jim and Mary, both of whom grew up in families grasping to the lowest rungs of the working class, the life they had attained was, if not the culmination of a dream, a solid step in the right direction. Sometimes, when they took the boys off for a day on the beach in New Brighton, or for their annual week at holiday camp in Wales, or at yet another song-filled McCartney family get-together, it could all seem heavenly. And it would have been, if they hadn't known what was looming in the distance.

Soon after Mike was born in 1944, painful swelling in her breasts sent Mary to the hospital. She was treated for mastitis, an illness that commonly affects new mothers. But as doctors know now, its symptoms can also be an indicator of breast cancer. Though the swelling subsided, Mary's health was never quite the same again. A visit to the doctor in 1948 led to a much more serious diagnosis—breast cancer. Though the disease was in its earliest stages, Mary knew enough about medicine to know that her time on earth, and with her family, would be limited.

She and Jim simply followed the old McCartney dictum and soldiered on. When things seemed dire, he'd hold out a hand and whisper another family saying: *Put it there, if it weighs a ton.*

So their lives went on. The young McCartney brothers thrived, growing quickly into a pair of energetic lads whose mischievous ways soon inspired a whole new series of family legends. The grade-school-aged boys once got caught stealing apples and ended up locked in one of the farmer's outbuildings until Jim—summoned by the mates who got away—came to apologize. Or, more scarily, one time they both ignored paternal commands to avoid a water-filled lime pit, and both fell in. They couldn't climb out on their own, the walls being too steep and slick and acidic to grip. So they tread water helplessly until a construction worker happened by and pulled them out.

"The McCartney boys were like a circus," noted their cousin John Mohin. But they were also sweet and smart, and both had inherited the twinkle in their father's eye. Paul, in particular, was the image of the younger Jim, from the graceful arch of his eyebrows to the slim line of his nose and the soft, almost feminine lips. He had also taken on his dad's winning smile and ingratiating wink, both of which came in handy when he was talking his way into, or out of, some kind of trouble. "He was a charmer, even then," recalls Tony Bramwell, who grew up nearby in Speke and ran in the same crowd of kids. "He was always the diplomat, always very nice." And certainly conscious of his appeal, and how to apply it as a social emollient, particularly when his antics had carried him into trouble. "He could charm the skin off a snake," one relative recalled.

Paul also had an introspective side, and a persistent appetite for solitude. When the shouts of his friends began to grate, he'd hop on his bike and make for the nearby woods, where he'd lose himself in the shadows, examining the wildlife and consulting his well-thumbed *Observer Book of Birds* when an interesting creature fluttered through the dense green canopy. If he heard other people nearby, he'd find a strong-looking tree and shin his way up to find a perch where he could silently sit, watching the world pass beneath him. "I'd be like a super-spy, the silent observer, the sniper," he recalled.

Paul also kept a careful watch when he was in the streets of Speke, hoping to avoid the knots of young thugs who patrolled such working-class neighborhoods. Thus, Paul made a point of keeping his eyes focused down the street, perpetually on the lookout for the telltale signs of the hard lads. Better to cross the street or even take the long way around the block than to end up on the receiving end of a street-corner thumping. Nevertheless, bad boys caught up to the McCartney brothers on the Mersey banks one day, and the scene soon spiraled into the inevitable shakedown. *Whaddaya got? A watch? I'll have that, son.* They sent Paul and his brother running tearfully for home, but that's not where it ended. Paul knew exactly who the thugs were—if only because they lived around the corner, in a house with an adjoining yard. Once Jim got home, Paul lost no time telling him the whole story. Jim provided the information to the local constable, and the heat descended soon thereafter. When the boys came to trial a few weeks later the key witness was Paul, whose testimony helped convict his antagonists. "Dear me, my first time in court," Paul said.

It was as much a lesson for Paul as it was for the neighborhood bullies: *you work hard and keep your word, and if someone tries to take something that belongs to you, fight back.* Jim did not take material things lightly. He had worked hard and made a point of keeping his word along the way. This was bedrock for Jim, and he made sure Paul and Mike understood what it meant: get an education, pay attention to what you're told, work hard, and value what you get in return.

From his earliest days at Stockton Wood Road Primary School, Paul established himself as an enthusiastic, well-behaved student. Transferring to Joseph Williams Primary in 1949, Paul impressed headmistress Muriel Ward as an unusually neat boy whose pressed trousers and tightly knitted tie were as striking as his gently prankish sense of humor. Paul also stood out in the classroom as a focused student who listened to directions and completed assignments with dispatch. His most striking achievement in primary school came near the end of his time at Joseph Williams, when he won his age division's prize in a citywide essay contest pegged to the coronation of Queen Elizabeth II in June 1953. His prize included a gift certificate for a book. What he opted for seems particularly intriguing, given his age and background: a book on modern art. "Lots and lots of pictures; people like Victor Pasmore, Salvador Dalí, Picasso, and a lot of artists I hadn't heard of."

Paul's performance on the eleven-plus examinations—the standardized test eleven-year-olds took to set the course of the rest of their academic lives—was even more significant. Students who scored well gained access to the upper rank of the city's schools, and Paul was one of four students, out of the ninety Joseph Williams students who sat for the examination, who scored well enough to be offered a seat at the Liverpool Institute, commonly accepted as the city's best grammar school. For Jim and Mary, it was impossible to overstate the importance of their elder son's achievement. Until recently a privately funded school with a steep tuition, the institute not only drew the most promising students from all over Liverpool, but also propelled them into social and professional orbits that no previous McCartney could have dreamed of entering.

2

Perched on a hill above the city center, the Liverpool Institute was an imposing stone structure, its Greek revivalist facade contrasting nicely with the vast Liverpool Cathedral looming around the corner on Hope Street. The students' day was rigidly structured, with an emphasis on strict discipline and intellectual rigor. The morning began at an all-student assembly in the school chapel, where balding, hawkish headmaster J. R. Edwards recited prayers and cued music teacher Les "Squinty" Morgan to play the morning's hymn on the school's vast pipe organ. From there the children climbed spiraling stone staircases to the classrooms to sit for compulsory lessons in English, mathematics, world history, music, and foreign language.

Nearly from the moment Paul McCartney first stepped through the school's side door in the fall of 1953 (only sixth-formers could enter through the majestic front door), the young student made a strong impression on his instructors and fellow students. Arthur Evans, who taught German, pegged the young student as "eminently likable," the sort of boy who was "always armed with very ready quips, but [wasn't] impertinent." Frequently tapped by his classmates to be "head boy" in their classes, Paul would take attendance at the start of the hour and serve as a kind of ambassador between students and their teachers. "He was responsible for organizing the class," literature teacher Alan "Dusty" Durband recalled. "But never in any boot-licking way—he was just a good executive."

So good that Paul's teachers tended to ignore the stream of wise-cracks he whispered to his neighbors during class. When he did raise his voice beyond sotto voce, the cheerful boy could maneuver the conversation so gracefully the teachers didn't realize they were being manipulated at all. When history got boring, Paul would put up his hand and ask the teacher, Cliff Edge, something about his coming holidays. Where did he say he was going, again? That was good for fifteen minutes right there, and when German got tiresome, Paul could always make an offhand reference to an interesting bus he'd seen rumbling down Mather Avenue that morning—at which point Norman Forbes would forget all about conjugating verbs. And if Paul thought to bring up the German teacher's ongoing campaign to lobby the Liverpool council for pedestrian rights, well, that could be the rest of the class right there. To Evans, who saw Paul in class and during the weeklong summer scout camp, the charismatic student presented an engaging paradox. He was, in Evans's words, "a conformist rebel," an icono-clast whose gentle teasing was intended in part to mask his innate be-lief in the institutional structure. At least to the extent that it didn't get in his way.

"A lot of people don't like school," Paul recalled in the early nine-ties. "I didn't like it very much, but I didn't dislike it. And I quite liked parts of it. What I didn't like was being told what to do."

Most often things seemed to go Paul's way. In 1955 Jim and Mary moved their boys into a new house in a newly constructed working-class development on Forthlin Road in Allerton, a suburb just north-west of Speke on the road to Liverpool. The government-subsidized rent came to £1 6s. a week, which was more than reasonable for a tidy brick row house that offered three bedrooms, a sitting room with sunny eastern windows, and a modern kitchen with enough room for a washing machine. The crowning luxury was upstairs: the indoor toilet, located just across the hall from the bath. Jim planted his laven-der bushes in the front courtyard (he would dry the leaves for Mary to sew into bags that she would hide around the house to give their home a nice scent), and the afternoon sun visited the grassy backyard with its pair of sling chairs for reading and relaxing. They moved in late spring, just when news arrived that Mike had passed his eleven-plus examination in unexpectedly fine form. Now both of the McCartney boys would be attending the Liverpool Institute.

The McCartneys must have seemed blessed. They were still working-class—the cotton industry would never again find the momentum to elevate Jim back onto the arc he had once felt assured to him. But Mary made a good income, and they had a cozy home and a pair of sons on the same upwardly mobile path. Yet the darkness had stalked Mary for a decade, and during the summer of 1956 she felt the pain clawing into her again.

She felt it deep inside now, sometimes so sharply that she would pause and double over, her hands pressed against her aching breast. One afternoon, just after he'd started his studies at the Liverpool Institute, Mike ran up the stairs to his room, only to see his mother crying softly on her bed, a crucifix clutched in one hand and the portrait of a relative who served as a Catholic priest in the other.

"What's up, Mum?" he asked.

Mary looked up quickly, wiping tears from her eyes. "Nothing, love."

A visit to the clinic and a set of X-rays revealed that the cancer had spread beyond her breast, moving its roots into other vital organs. Nothing could be done now except to forestall the inevitable. A mastectomy would keep the illness at bay for a while—weeks, maybe a few months. Would she see the spring? Possibly, but only if she had the procedure immediately.

They set the operation for the afternoon of October 30, giving Mary a day to prepare herself for the ordeal. She made the boys their breakfast, then spent the rest of the morning cleaning the house from top to bottom. She washed the dishes, swept the floors, made the boys' beds, and washed and then pressed their school clothes for the next morning, leaving them, as usual, on the foot of their beds. Her sister, Dill, came to take her to the hospital that afternoon and sighed when she saw how hard Mary had been working, despite doctors' orders to rest up for her surgery. Mary simply shrugged. Everything had to be ready, she sighed, "in case I don't come back."

Later that evening Mary was taken into the operating room. The doctors worked for hours, then pronounced the procedure a success.

But the disease had already taken too large a toll on her body; she no longer had the strength to recover. Mary woke up the next morning, but the hollowness around her eyes was unmistakable. By the next afternoon her blood pressure was slipping; the doctors knew her time was drawing short.

The family—McCartneys and Mohins—gathered at her bedside. Jim went home to Forthlin Road and told the boys they could visit their mother, but first they had to wash their hands and faces and put on their school uniforms. Jim knew what was happening, it was all he could do to keep himself together on the drive back to the hospital. When they got there, he called his sister-in-law, Dill Mohin, aside and asked her to do a final check of the boys' fingernails and ears. Judged acceptable, Paul and Mike were walked down the corridor and led through the door and into Mary's room. She leaned up on one elbow to greet them.

Mike leaped up on her bed to give her a hug, and she tried to smile. Both boys kissed her face, and she reached out for their hands. But Paul glimpsed a gruesome red stain on the white sheets, and a darker truth began to dawn on him. "It was terrible," he recalled.

Mary tried not to cry. They talked for a while, a few minutes. There were more kisses, a quick good-bye. Paul and Mike touched their lips to their mother's face one last time and were taken home. An hour later the priest who had run the clinic where she worked wrapped a strand of rosary beads around her hand and began to recite the last rites. Mary turned to her sister and whispered, "I would have liked to have seen the boys growing up."

What Paul remembered most vividly about that day was saying the worst possible thing at the worst possible moment. The words flew out of his mouth and there was no taking them back. They just hung there in the air, smoldering like the grief in the pit of his stomach.

He hadn't mean it. He hadn't known what to say. What could anyone say? His mother was dead. The rest was a blur: his uncles and aunts pale and tearful, his father not even able to face them, he was so torn apart.

Your mum . . . the doctors did what they could . . . I'm afraid she passed last night. She's in heaven now, with God . . .

Neither boy cried out or wept. They blinked, perhaps, and nodded. They understood. They would be staying with Uncle Joe and Aunt Joan for a few days, their dad needed some time alone. Did they want to go to school today? Yes, they did, that would be fine. What had their father always told them about tough breaks? *Just soldier on.* So this is precisely what they did. Tucking in their shirts, smoothing the wrinkles in their pants, reaching for their coats, and preparing to get moving. Somewhere in there, Paul thought of something to say.

What are we going to do without her money?

Did anyone hear? Did anyone notice? Possibly not. The only person who even remembered hearing those words that morning was Mike. The shock of the moment had hit the youngest McCartney so hard he spent years thinking he was the one who had said it. "It was a silly joke," he recalled a decade later. "We both regretted it for months."

There was so much to regret. So much to miss. Mary's absence made the little house on Forthlin Road feel cavernous. The rich smell of her scones no longer filled the morning air. The reassuring clatter of dishes in the sink, the perfume of her tea and ciggies, the melody of her voice calling up the stairs. It was all gone, along with her cuddles, the secretly proffered treats, the gentle strength of her arms when she pulled them close.

The tragedy shook the foundations of everything they had once taken for granted. Their father, once the model of quiet, working-class strength, now faltered visibly. "That was the worst thing for me," Paul said. "You expect to see women crying . . . but when it's your dad, then you know something's really wrong, and it shakes your faith in everything."

The worst thing was, Paul *wanted* to believe. No matter how cheeky he could be, he had always paid attention in class, always respected his elders. He remembered what they told him and took it to heart. Like Mike, Paul saved his tears for the darkness of his room, lying in bed and feeling the emptiness closing in around him. At first he tried praying, hands clasped tight as he implored God to fix everything; swearing that he'd do anything, he'd be good forever, if only He could send her back. Anything. *Anything!* After he'd grown up, the memory curdled on his tongue. "See, the prayers didn't work!" he noted acidly. "When I really needed them to, as well."

Paul was back in school the next morning, walking straight into Alan "Dusty" Durband's literature classroom, number 32, and taking his usual desk near the window. Still, Paul's schoolwork tailed off in the next few weeks. At first the fourteen-year-old student seemed preoccupied, prone to staring out the window. Then as November went on, his assignments went undone, test results sagged. The jokes became more jagged, Paul's tone more strident. "He did go through a bit of a rough patch there," Durband recalled. "I think it shattered him a lot." Nevertheless, Paul did his best to go on as if nothing had happened. Once the initial shock wore off, he realized that the loss had left him feeling older, and tougher. "I was determined not to let it affect me," he said of his mother's death. "I learned to put a shell around me."

He also learned to keep his coat on when he and Mike got back to their empty house in the afternoons. These were the most heartbreaking hours, finding a home that had once been so full of light and warmth, now dark and cold and void of life. The chores started immediately. Paul would sweep out the ashes in the grate, set a new fire, and light the flame. Mike would already have put on the kettle, and when its whistle blew, Paul and Mike sat for tea together at the family's small dining-room table, warming their fingers over steaming cups. Refreshed, the boys stacked their dishes on the drainer, took a stab at homework, then turned their attention to their comic books, or perhaps turned on the TV to see the adventure serials and "Jennings at School" on the BBC's daily *Children's Hour* at 5 p.m.

Months passed, and a new kind of normal settled on the McCartney home. Jim came home from the cotton market in the late afternoon, and the three of them settled in for their evening, the aroma of cooking sausages and mash blending with the clink of glasses and the McCartneys' indefatigable wit and wisdom. Tell a bad joke and Jim would wink and give the old vaudevillian's promise: *It'll go better second house.* Then there was the other family favorite, delivered with just the right note of mock-confidence colliding with mock-panic: *Here we are . . . where are we?* Still at home, despite everything. "I had a very nice warm family," Paul said. "There was a lot of security there."

•   •   •

For all of his combed-and-pressed demeanor at school, Paul felt a deep attraction to its more outlandish characters. The most significant of these friendships turned out to be the one he shared with Ivan Vaughan, a classmate who came from Woolton, the leafy stretch of detached and semidetached homes not far from the McCartney's council house in Speke. Ivan was an average-looking guy with protruding ears and curly, dark hair that he wore thick on top and tight on the sides. His most striking features were the gleam in his eyes and the cockeyed smile that lit his face when he was amused. Which was often, because Ivan was usually up to something strange. He lived with his mother on a quiet street just a few feet from the back wall of the Salvation Army's Strawberry Field estate. Their house was relatively large and comfortable, but that didn't stop Ivan from painting his name across his bedroom windows in three-foot letters. Another time, he showed up at school with his regulation black shoes painted an electric, canary yellow. "It was Ivan who stood out," an institute schoolmate named Peter Sissons (who grew up to become a prominent TV news anchor in the UK) told the *Sunday Mirror* in 1997. "What an original article he was."

For the authority-conscious Paul, Ivan was a revelation. They had met early in their institute careers and discovered that they had the same birthday, June 18, 1942. They became friends, sharing enthusiasms for poetry, humor—particularly the *Goon Show*—and then rock 'n' roll music.

Where did Paul hear it first? By the winter of 1957 the new, raw sound from America, rock 'n' roll, had been seeping into his consciousness for months, pushed along by Britain's own Lonnie Donegan, the leading figure in skiffle, the rock/folk/jazz hybrid that first rattled up the British charts in early 1956, dragged along by Donegan's arrangement of the American standard "Rock Island Line." Still, this homegrown sound was merely an echo of the real thing, which was harder to find, and nearly impossible to hear on the airwaves. Rock 'n' roll. The name itself could send a shiver up your spine. *Rock 'n' roll!* You didn't even have to get the sexual allusion (the phrase came from Trixie Smith's 1922 rhythm-and-blues song "My Man Rocks Me with One Steady Roll," which would have been banned if anyone in power had ever bothered to hear it) to have a visceral understanding of that allusion.

No wonder the music ignited the flames behind fourteen-year-old Paul's eyes. Just the *sound* of it. The borderline hysteria of "Tutti Frutti" and "Long Tall Sally." The barrelhouse piano in "Whole Lotta Shakin' Going On." The herky-jerky rhythm of "Twenty Flight Rock." Paul had grown up listening to music—Jim's jazz and ragtime 78s, his enthusiastic piano thumping. But this was something different. It was *fun*. More than that, it was youth and action. Rock 'n' roll was the sound of girls, parties, and *life*. This music was wild and dangerous, just like Elvis Presley, who not only sounded like a sexed-up riot, but actually looked like one, too. Paul and Mike would peer at his picture on record covers, gaping at his motorcycle leathers, piled-up hair, and that hip-cocking, open-lipped leer. Whenever his records came on, you'd see kids dancing and screaming, shirts coming untucked, school ties flying. No one could believe it. Except for Paul, who had found the one thing he could believe in. "It's him! It's him!" he thought. "The messiah has arrived!"

Not that the BBC was eager to recognize the new deity and his acolytes. Already restricted from playing much recorded music, Britain's sole broadcaster stuck with big bands and light jazz combos. If they'd even heard of rock 'n' roll, the aged masters of the Beeb, as the BBC was called, were not going to beam it into the quiet living rooms of the empire.

So people with a hankering for rock had to find it for themselves. Maybe this was half the fun—the beat was just as elusive as it was riveting. For most serious fans, the real homing signal could be found after dark on their radio's medium wave at 208 meters, where the signal for Radio Luxembourg crackled. The English-language broadcasts of popular music only played at night and were always subject to the quirks of meteorology and the airwaves. Still, Paul and Mike became obsessed with the nightly broadcasts, the both of them hunkering close to the radio speaker until long after Jim had started badgering them to go to bed. Finally, the elder McCartney wired the boys two sets of rudimentary headphones, with extension cords leading up to their bedrooms, so they could listen beneath the covers, the distant sound of guitars, drums, and wailing vocals the bridge between their days and their dreams. "It was music that I loved," Paul recalled once, thinking back to those early Elvis-fired days. "If we were feeling lousy, we'd go back and play 'Don't Be Cruel,' and we'd be right up there again. It could cure any blues."

He couldn't just listen. Paul wanted to hold the music in his hands, to make that sound himself and feel it vibrating in his bones. This was where the little guitar he'd got for his birthday the summer before came in. It was a cheap acoustic, a factory-made Zenith with a high-strung bridge and a rickety neck that always seemed to be on the verge of snapping off. At first Paul found it nearly impossible to play; the fingers on his left hand kept getting tangled on the instrument's neck and refused to develop the muscular acuity required to form even the most basic chords. He was stymied until he came across a magazine with a picture of country musician Slim Whitman, who held his guitar the opposite way from every other player on the stage. *Of course!* He was left-handed, too! Paul realized he had to reverse everything—restring the instrument in opposite order and flip it over so he could form chords with his right hand—in order to master the guitar. From that moment the Zenith became the gravitational center of his life. Paul cradled the thing for hours, head bent over the curving edge as he ran his fingertips over the strings, finding notes and fitting them into chords. He'd be singing to himself, a song he'd heard on the radio, and try to navigate the distance between what he could hear in his head and the noise coming from the Zenith's strings. This would go on for hours, and nothing else mattered. Schoolwork went undone. Comics ignored. "He was lost," Mike recalled. "He didn't have to eat or think about anything else."

Look for Paul, and you'd see the Zenith, too. On his lap while he watched the telly in the sitting room. Lying across his chest in his bedroom. It echoed from the toilet and the bath, the chords gradually getting clearer, the melodic runs becoming longer and more assured. Eventually the sounds from the record player began to emerge from Paul's guitar, and in his own clear, increasingly strong voice, too. *Well, I've got a girl with a record machine, when it comes to rockin' she's the queen . . .* This was magic! Listening to a record was one thing, but being able to summon it with your own fingers was like jumping inside the music and becoming the song. All that joy, excitement, defiance—they become yours, too. When Paul's own feelings seemed unspeakable, he could always pick up the guitar and use the music to either push them out of his head or else project them into his hands, into the rhythm, then out into the air around him.

One afternoon he hunched over his guitar, strumming a few chords over and over. G, G-7, C. Nothing to it, the simplest of progressions. When he set it to a country shuffle kind of rhythm, it reminded him of a song Buddy Holly might write—a sprightly tune about an ordinary girl whose winsome glance might break your heart right in two. That could be a whole song, right there! So he kept at it, kept strumming the chords, singing the words he'd thought of, humming the ones he hadn't. "Something was making me make it up, whether I knew how to do it or not."

I woke up this morning, my head was in a whirl . . .

Paul played it over and over, first singing the verse with the melody going up, then with the melody going down. Which worked better? He couldn't decide, so he used one on the first verse and the other on the second. What else could he toss in? Paul thought about his favorite records. The stop/start rhythm of "Twenty Flight Rock," Buddy Holly's wordless vocal sighs. Those became part of the song, too, and though he never quite got around to writing a full chorus (the verses climax by repeating the title, then pausing for a four-beat vocal swoon), when it was done, he knew he had something. Not much, perhaps. But *something*.

"It's a funny, corny little song," Paul said many years later. But he never forgot it and, even decades later, made a point of including it among the many classic songs he'd perform on stages around the world. It was a nostalgic gesture, to be sure, and he made certain to play up his own ironic distance from his immature self. "Her hair wouldn't *curl*?" he'd say, shaking his head. But these repeated visits to his compositional debut also brought the man back to his emotional headwaters, back to the moment when a bereaved boy first tried to weave his feelings into music. No matter how airy the song, it's impossible to miss the significance of its plaintive title: "I Lost My Little Girl."

Like so many big things, it all started with a small, offhand idea. Ivan Vaughan suggested Paul come to a party and take a look at his friend's band. It wasn't far away, the stone walls of St. Peter's Parish Church were just up the hill and around the corner from Ivan's house in Woolton. He'd been going to the church's Saturday Garden Fetes for years, playing the carnival games, watching the parade, feasting on the sweets and the lemonade they sold out in the churchyard. But the fete also held a distinct appeal for the older boys, too. There would be girls, obviously, swarms of them, and also music. Including, he added, a skiffle band fronted by his backyard neighbor, John Lennon. Did Paul know him? The band was called the Quarrymen, named for the Quarry Bank grammar school most of its members attended. Ivan played with them, on occasion, taking up the bass when Len Garry, the usual guy, couldn't make it. (*Jive with Ive,* he wrote on his strap. *The Ace on the Bass.*) So how about it, then?

Paul always liked a party—that was another trait he had picked up from the erstwhile leader of Jim Mac's Band—especially if there might be girls afoot. The prospect of meeting some other aspiring musicians made it even better. The Quarrymen were set to play their first set at 4:15, so Paul started preparing himself by midafternoon, setting off his extratight, black "drainpipe" trousers with a white sport coat that had sporty flaps over the pockets and a weave with reflective, silvery threads that shimmered in the light. Paul gave his hair an extra dollop of grease to guard against the heat, then steered his three-speed Raleigh bike down Forthlin Road to Mather Avenue, past Calderstones Park, then up the hill to St. Peter's. He was a bit late—the Quarrymen were already playing on the outdoor stage (actually the back of a flatbed truck) when Paul arrived. As he blended into the crowd, he was struck less by the band itself, whose members were something other than accomplished musicians, than by the charisma of the teenager who stood front and center, taking the stage's sole microphone for himself.

So *that* was John Lennon! Paul recognized him, though they'd never actually met. He was the tough-talking older guy he'd seen around the fringes of Allerton and Woolton—laughing on the bus with a friend, strutting down Mather Avenue—the kind of noisy, unruly guy Paul had learned to steer away from during his schoolboy days in Speke. And no wonder: John looked like a teddy boy, one of the vaguely Edwardian-dressed young toughs you'd see slouched against a wall somewhere, going out of their way to menace anyone who walked past. Only he was a friend of Ivan's, which meant he couldn't be all bad. And here John was in a checked shirt and dark trousers, a stray lock of chestnut hair falling across his damp forehead as he strummed his acoustic guitar and sang into the stand-up microphone.

The other Quarrymen—another guitar player, a tea-chest bass, a washboard player, a drummer, and a guy on banjo—followed along. All were competent enough, but Lennon was the one you had to look at. He wasn't a great guitar player, by any stretch. In fact, his playing was downright strange; his fingering was off, he played three-finger chords that Paul didn't recognize from his own guitar studies. And the words he was singing were off, too. Now the guy in "Come Go with Me" was inviting his love to a penitentiary. Another song veered into a reference to someone named Mimi coming up the path, which seemed to be directed to the stern-looking, older woman he was grinning at on the fringe of the crowd. But no matter what he sang in his raw, powerful voice—"Puttin' On the Style," "Maggie Mae," "Railroad Bill," "Be-Bop-A-Lula"—Lennon projected an anarchic, yet prankish, glee.

The band played for a while, maybe thirty minutes, then moved quickly to gather up their things and clear the stage. An announcement about the church-hall dance that night, with the Quarrymen playing two sets, echoed across the grass. Paul met up with Ivan, who patted him on the back and gestured toward the little wooden Scout hut where the Quarrymen, along with the day's other performers, were storing their things between shows. *Let's go say hi, then.* Ivan led Paul in a beeline for the hut, and once they ducked inside, they found the group in one corner, slightly away from a pair of Boy Scouts who were bleating on their trumpets. The Quarrymen drummer, Colin Hanton, looked up from his drums and nodded. "I saw Ivan coming in with this other lad," he says. "Just this guy we didn't know. And then they were talking to John."

At first the head Quarryman projected little beyond disdain. He shrugged, he didn't say much, he noted how young Paul looked—the last vestiges of early-adolescent flab only made him look younger than his fifteen years. Later, Paul recalled that John was drunk (eventually he'd decide he himself was "a little sloshed," too). But Rod Davis, the Quarrymen banjo player, dismisses this as a "highly colorful" version of events. "There's no way [St. Peter's reverend] Pryce-Jones would have let us anywhere near his fete if we'd been smelling of beer, let alone drunk." And where would they have got the beer? None of them had enough money to stand rounds at a pub. And which Woolton pub would have served a gang of local teenagers? "They all knew us, so that's impossible. The best [washboard player] Pete Shotton and I can figure is that someone might have given John a bottle of beer."

Ivan kept on, telling John what a great guitar player Paul was, and how many songs he could play from memory. They talked about guitars, and John said that he kept his guitar in an open-G tuning, just like a banjo. His mother had taught him that, and he'd never learned the proper guitar tuning. They talked songs, comparing what they knew, what they were still hoping to figure out. When Paul mentioned Eddie Cochran's "Twenty Flight Rock," John's eyes flickered with interest—he really knew it? Chords, words, and all? Paul beamed. *Sure!* He gestured at John's guitar. *D'ya mind?* John shrugged. Paul took up the guitar, then reached for the pegs and quickly readjusted the strings to the standard tuning. That achieved, he flipped the instrument around, found a G chord, and—playing with the strings wrong-side-up for his hands—ripped into the first verse. *Oh well, I gotta girl with a record machine . . .*

The Quarrymen were impressed. "It was uncanny," Eric Griffiths, the other guitar player recalled. "He had such confidence, he gave a real *performance.*"

Ivan beamed. Even John seemed impressed. Delighted to have an audience, Paul kept on. He took a run at "Be-Bop-A-Lula"—a gutsy move, seeing how the Quarrymen had just played the song onstage—then a variety of Little Richard hits: "Tutti Frutti," "Long Tall Sally," "Good Golly Miss Molly." Paul had fallen in love with Richard's rollicking bass lines and powerful, high-pitched vocals, and he had spent hours learning how to mimic his every *Wop-bop-a-loo-bop* and piercing falsetto whoop.

"He could play and sing in a way none of us could, including John," Griffiths went on. "We couldn't get enough of it." John was clearly thrilled, too, laughing and clapping along. But when Paul was done, John stopped short of inviting the new boy to join his group. "I'd been kingpin up to then," he recalled to Hunter Davies in 1967. "It went through my head that I'd have to keep him in line if I let him join. But he was good, so he was worth having." They went their separate ways that evening with no promise that they'd ever be seeing one another again. But John floated the idea by his best friend and bandmate, Pete Shotton, when they were walking home that night, and Pete agreed immediately: that Paul guy would be a fine addition to the band. So when Pete saw Paul riding his Raleigh up to Ivan's house a few days later, he waved him over and delivered the invitation: would he like to join the Quarrymen? Paul shrugged, nodded. *Well, yeah, sure. Sounds fun.* So, Shotton went on, could he come to practice for their next show, downtown at the Cavern jazz club on August 8? Paul grimaced. Oh, aye, that's when he'd be off on holiday. But he'd be home not long after, would that be okay? Shotton nodded, and they went their separate ways. Pete walked down Menlove Avenue toward his house, while Paul pedaled off on his bike. "I went off in a completely new direction from then on," he told Davies. "Once I got to know John, it all changed."

3

He had a softness about him in those days. He was still a little chubby, for one thing—the layer of baby fat that saw Paul into early adolescence had stuck with him, thanks in part to the cakes and treats supplied to the motherless McCartney boys from their loving aunts. This weakness proved useful to younger brother Mike, who realized early on that he could always provoke an explosion from Paul with a well-timed catcall of *fatty*. But just beneath his pudgy cheeks and soft brown eyes was a steely resolve and an assurance that was particularly striking in such a young adolescent.

"He was a born leader, so gregarious, so popular," said modern-languages teacher Jack Sweeney. "And yet there was also this toughness. He would hold the class entranced." More than anything, Sweeney recalled, Paul projected a deep-seated belief in himself. "He had this extraordinary faith in his own star."

Paul's self-assurance came with him for the week he spent with Mike and a few dozen of their Liverpool Institute compatriots at Boy Scout camp a few days after the Woolton fete. The days passed quietly—except for the part where Paul instigated a cliff-hanging experiment that ended with Mike breaking his arm and being shipped to the Sheffield Infirmary. Beyond that mishap, Scout leader Arthur Evans recalled being most impressed with Paul's enthusiastic showmanship while leading the Scouts' nightly campfires. He'd brought his guitar, of course, so once the Scouts gathered and the flames rose, the evenings would become full-blown McCartney concerts, complete with jokes and a setlist split between rock 'n' roll favorites and what Evans recalled as a few McCartney originals. "And he displayed no qualms about entertaining the whole camp—thirty or forty boys."

The guitar also came on the family's vacation at the Butlin's holiday camp in North Wales a few weeks later. The Butlin's camps were designed as full-service leisure environments that provided their working-class campers with slates of activities to carry them from waking to bedtime. Legions of professionally genial red-coated staffers were on hand to run everything from the croquet tournaments to the art classes to the camp-only radio station. A pair of McCartney cousins—Bett and her husband, Mike Robbins—worked as redcoats. In fact, the raffish, mustachioed Mike Robbins organized and emceed the camp's nightly entertainment shows, including the week-ending talent show. Paul signed up immediately and spent hours polishing his rendition of Little Richard's "Long Tall Sally." But sensing the heart-tugging potential of a fraternal harmony act, he turned to his still-battered younger brother to join in for a go at the Everly Brothers'"Bye Bye Love." They'd been singing it together in the family sitting room for months, so of course they could do it. How hard could it be?

"No way," Mike responded. His arm was still in a sling, for heaven's sake. He didn't feel well. More to the point: he had no intention of walking onstage and singing in front of a thousand strangers.

Paul enlisted Jim, and the erstwhile bandleader sided with his older, stagestruck son. "It's only a bit of fun. What have you got to lose?"

Paul smiled. "You'll come with me, won't you?"

Mike gave in reluctantly, and the McCartney Brothers gave their first, and last, performance as a duo. Paul closed the set as a solo artist with his much honed "Long Tall Sally," and though they were too young to compete for the £5,000 in prize money, they did emerge with a fan—a teenaged girl named Angela, who followed up her summer-camp flirtations with a series of lovelorn letters. All of which were addressed to Mike, though he didn't see them for years. His jealous older brother had snuck them all out of the family's mailbox to read, and keep, for himself.

•   •   •

Paul's first rehearsal as a Quarryman came on a Saturday afternoon near the end of the summer. The band usually got together at Eric Griffiths's house because his father had died in the war and his mother, who worked, was often out. This afforded the boys plenty of room not just for their instruments and music, but also for the friends who came to listen and cheer them on. Whether they were at Griffiths's house, Colin Hanton's, or at John's isn't clear—memories vary. At the time there was some confusion about whether Paul was showing up to play or just watch. "John told me he was a mate of Ivan and had come to watch us practice," Rod Davis recalls. But Paul definitely had his guitar with him this time, and once he had it in his hands, he was bursting to play, and to show the other musicians, and particularly John, how many songs he knew.

"He was very nice, very polite. Very clean, too, always very well turned-out," Colin says, recalling the view from behind his drum kit. "He got John and Eric playing guitar chords, tuning their guitars properly. He taught them both how to play, I'm pretty sure." Eventually they also started practicing in the sitting room of the McCartney home on Forthlin Road, often with Jim McCartney perched next to the piano, alternately keeping young Mike from getting underfoot, and waving his hand when he thought the thump and bang might disturb the neighbors on the other side of the sitting-room wall.

Rehearsing in the Forthlin Road sitting room also gave Paul a chance to show his new bandmates his chops on the piano, further establishing his credentials as something of a musical prodigy. His expertise didn't end there, as Colin soon discovered. "Paul was very intent on telling me how to play things," he says, recalling how Paul would stand next to his drum kit, using his fingers to pound the snare drum in the rhythm he wanted the Quarrymen drummer to emulate. A habit that soon grated on the drummer's nerves. "I was not best pleased by that."

When they looked to their leader, John just nodded his approval: *Do what he says*. The entire experience was a little jarring, both because the relatively young Paul was so confident in his abilities, and also because John had always made clear, the Quarrymen were *his* band. He chose the members, he assigned the parts, he sang the songs.

Anyone who dared challenge him soon learned the errors of his ways. "John did have a mean streak," Rod Davis says. "He was brilliant and funny, but he could be unpleasant."

Paul's arrival signaled a change. "If John didn't like him, he never would have let him near the microphone," Colin Hanton says. "But when Paul joined, he was more than happy to share and let Paul sing his songs. There was a lot of respect. Mutual respect. You could see the friendship developing. And they harmonized from day one."

Which was fortunate, because Paul had so many ideas: about the clothes the band should wear onstage, how they should stand with a solid line of guitars up front and the others arrayed behind them, and how they should present themselves as a sleek, professional outfit. "So from this scruffy bunch of skifflers, we became this sort of sharply dressed kind of rock band," Colin says.

Paul's first performance with the band was on October 18, at a Conservative Club dance held in a hall in the middle-class Liverpool suburb of Norris Green. Paul practiced relentlessly for the show, particularly on the solo he was to take as the centerpiece to "Guitar Boogie." The hours of practice eventually paid off—by showtime Paul had the piece down perfectly, including a note-for-note rendition of the tune's guitar solo. He had the band dressed in their matching shirts and string ties, with the two front men, Lennon and McCartney, set apart by the cream-colored blazers they wore. They played their first few songs, all featuring John's vocals, with no problems. But when John introduced the group's newest member, calling Paul out to play his big featured solo on "Guitar Boogie," the fifteen-year-old's nerves got the better of him, and he not only missed his cue for the solo, but then tried to rush through it to catch up, succeeding only in botching most of the notes. The incident proved so humiliating ("John was howling with laughter," Hanton recalls), Paul forgot to call for his big solo shot on "Twenty Flight Rock." Nevertheless, the show's promoter was impressed by the band's new harmony-fired sound. So impressed, he invited the Quarrymen to become a regular attraction at the Saturday-night dances he was booking in neighborhood halls all across the city that fall.

They were on their way.

• • •

The two teenagers were, on so many levels, mirror images of one another. Most immediately, when John and Paul sat across from one another, the necks of their guitars—one right-handed, the other
left-handed—pointed in the same direction, while two sets of fingers
danced across the frets in direct accordance with one another. Their
personalities mirrored one another, too, the fiery, often intemperate
older boy balanced by his smiling, ingratiating younger partner. But if
they seemed unlikely choices for one another, John and Paul could
also sense how they shored up one another's weaknesses. John admired Paul's cheery showmanship, both on and off the stage, while
Paul basked in John's withering intelligence, and his willingness—no,
eagerness—to blurt out all the brutal things Paul was secretly thinking, but couldn't bring himself to say.

What both understood, particularly as they came to talk about
their lives and share their secrets, was that their distinct personalities
had been fueled by the same kind of unspeakable loss. For just as Paul
had lost his mother, John's parents had divorced when he was young,
then abdicated their roles in his life—a less permanent, if far more
hurtful, kind of abandonment. John had been raised in relative comfort, living with his stern, but loving, aunt Mimi in the leafy, suburban
comfort of Woolton. But his disconnection from his parents, and an
overwhelming feeling of rejection, haunted John in a palpable way.

"John was caustic and witty out of necessity, and underneath, quite
a warm character," Paul said. "I was the opposite: easygoing, friendly,
no necessity to be acerbic. But I could be tough if I needed to be."

John surely sensed the steely resolve beneath his new friend's warm
exterior. But more than anything, John was thrilled by Paul's musical
skill: by his uncanny ability to figure out the chords and melodies of
songs he'd heard on the sitting-room record player, or even as a fleet-
ing wisp on Radio Luxembourg's nightly broadcasts. That Paul had
actually written songs of his own, "I Lost My Little Girl" and now a
few others, made him even more appealing, just as John's ability to
project his anarchic energy into rock 'n' roll songs, often by applying
his own absurdist words into holes he hadn't been able to fill with the
real lyrics, fired Paul's imagination.

They intuited one another's strengths, and the overwhelming need
that elevated rock 'n' roll into the central focus of their lives. It was

like a physical impulse, a drive that originated from the same churning core that fueled the sexual desire that nearly, but not quite, rivaled their shared appetite for music. In fact, Paul's memories of those early days with the Quarrymen come bound closely with memories of sexual experimentation, sometimes with John and his other bandmates. They would fantasize about girls and masturbate together, Paul recalled, a group of boys sitting in armchairs and imagining their way through the mysterious worlds of pleasure that lay ahead. "Then somebody, probably John, would say, 'Winston Churchill!'" Paul recalled. "It would completely ruin everyone's concentration."

John kept his disruptive impulses in check when it came to their shared drive to unveil the mysteries of music. When Colin Hanton heard about a guy across town who knew how to play a B-dominant seventh chord—a crucial element to any twelve-bar blues played in the key of E—John and Paul grabbed their guitars and took the forty-minute bus trip to get to the guy's doorstep. They took an even longer trip, with not one but two transfers, to chase down (and purloin) a copy of the Coasters'"Searchin'." This was the sort of dedication, Paul realized later, that separated the Beatles from other bands. Just as it separated John and Paul from all of the other Quarrymen.

Soon, their lives revolved around one another's, in ways that were both deliberate and accidental. John was just starting art school, which might have moved him well beyond a grammar school student's social reach. But the school he was attending, the Liverpool Art College, was not only on Mount Street, but literally right next door to the Liverpool Institute. This made it easy for the bandmates to meet up, either after school or—as months passed—in the middle of the day, when they'd sag off together to either listen to records and drink coffee, or else head back to Paul's house to play their guitars and turn their hand toward writing an original song or two. Fueled with fried eggs, toast, and tea (some of which they would smoke in one of Jim's pipes when they couldn't scrounge a ciggie or two), they'd perch on the sitting-room sofa, near the record player and the fireplace, and flail at their guitars until a snatch of melody would lead to a chord progression. Words came next, most of them spinning obviously from the Buddy Holly or Elvis song that had set them off in the first place. When they had come up with something that seemed worth remembering, or even when it didn't, Paul would open a lined school note-book, pen *Another Lennon-McCartney Original* at the top, and write out what they had in his neat, schoolboy's hand. The first songs were rudimentary, at best. "Too Bad About Sorrows," "In Spite of All the Danger," and a particularly egregious teen love ballad called "Just Fun." Then they started to improve. "Like Dreamers Do," written with Paul on the piano, had an ascending chord pattern similar to "Stairway to Paradise." The straight-up rocker "One After 909" had a chugging rhythm and clever lyrics that projected a blues lament to a kind of farcical tale of mixed messages and misread directions.

"We saw ourselves as very much the next great songwriting team," Paul said many years later. "Which, funnily enough, is what we be-came." Still, at the time they were just trying to harness their energy and find their voices. At one point they even tried writing a play, sketching out a modernist fable about a Christ-like figure named Pil-chard who may or may not be the Messiah, but his acolytes can't tell for sure because he never quite descends from an upstairs room. The outline has since been lost, but even Paul's description reveals a crush-ing debt to Samuel Beckett's *Waiting for Godot*. No one ever accused Lennon and McCartney of being great dramatists.

Music was what mattered to them; everything else barely regis-tered. The Quarrymen had begun as a hobby—"a laugh," in the words of Rod Davis—the band's membership dictated more by friend-ship than by musical fixation, let alone skill. But as John fed off Paul, and Paul's influence became more entrenched, the Quarrymen became a very different band. The sound moved away from skiffle and closer to straight-up American rock 'n' roll. Thus, someone had to invest in an electric bass guitar. Eric Griffiths was the obvious candidate—no need for him to serve as a third guitarist, now that John and Paul were both up front playing guitar. Griffiths balked, and so he was out. Not that they told him that in so many words; they just scheduled a re-hearsal and never mentioned it to Griffiths. Other members left for reasons of their own. The tea-chest bass player, Len Garry, contracted a near-deadly case of viral meningitis, landing in the hospital for months. Sometime-member-slash-manager Nigel Walley ended up in the hospital, too, then moved on. Banjo and guitar player Rod Davis left, too, ostensibly to focus on his studies, though his distaste for rock 'n' roll, particularly Elvis Presley ("I thought he was a complete idiot," he says), played a role, too. When the time came for washboard player Pete Shotton to leave, John simply smashed the instrument over his friend's head. The hysterical laughter this provoked was as much from shock as hysteria, but Shotton took it more or less philosophically. "It wasn't the life for me," he told Beatles biographer Hunter Davies in 1967. "I didn't like standing up there. I was too embarrassed."

For John and Paul playing music meant moving *beyond* embarrassment; it was the way to express the feelings that could never emerge in spoken conversation. Soon their connection, formed on those mirrored guitars, was so profound they didn't have to speak to know what the other was thinking. By the end of the winter they were so in touch with one another's thoughts and feelings, one friend noticed, they often finished one another's sentences.

Music also defined the friendship Paul shared with another Liverpool Institute student, a younger guy from Speke, a bus driver's son named George Harrison. They had actually met years earlier, back when the McCartneys lived an easy walk from the Harrisons' house on Upton Green. Back then Paul was merely another face in the mob of kids playing hide-and-seek and pretending to be cowboys or pirates in the bomb sites and vacant lots that dotted the neighborhood. They met more formally on the 86 bus, which carried them from the southern suburbs to the Liverpool Institute, and though George—whose hair was piled higher and pants tailored tighter than Paul ever dared—presented himself as a full-on teddy boy, he was also a serious rock 'n' roll fan whose tastes ran to the same rhythm-and-blues obscurities Paul and John liked. Better yet, he had a guitar. And best of all, he could play the instrument with a fluidity Paul had never before seen amid his generally thick-fingered mates. George was a year behind Paul at the institute, which meant they didn't see one another in classes. But in the schoolyard (George was a regular in Smoker's Corner, the hidden patch of concrete behind an outbuilding where naughty boys could sneak a ciggie beyond the glare of the yard supervisors) and on the bus, they could talk the fanatic's language of chords and solos.

Paul knew George would be a perfect addition to the Quarrymen, particularly after his own "Guitar Boogie" debacle, but since George, at fourteen, was even more baby-faced than Paul made John pause. There was no way a seventeen-year-old college student could have a kid *that* small in his band. Still, Paul knew what he had heard and figured John would know it, too, once he sat long enough to listen to George play. Thinking strategically, Paul concocted a seemingly spontaneous meeting on the upper deck of a bus, where Paul's introduction led quickly to George whipping out his guitar and performing, as Paul had promised, a note-for-note rendition of Bill Justis's cowboy-rock instrumental "Raunchy." John was wowed, but still unconvinced. Paul was undeterred, and a few weeks later he made sure George was in the house when the Quarrymen attended a party held at the Morgue, an off-the-books club run in an abandoned mortuary by the local musician who went by the name Rory Storm.

"A *terrible* dump," Colin Hanton recalls. "It was a condemned building so they ran the wires in from the light post outside. There was a tiny stage in the corner of the living room, and then this tiny guy came out with this big guitar, and someone said, 'That's George.' So this little kid with this huge guitar started playing 'Raunchy,' and he was very good." Maybe John picked up on how impressed his bandmates had been by young George's performance. When Hanton bumped into Nigel Walley three days later, he heard the news—John had decided to let George into the band.

Paul had another addition in mind, too. He had suffered through the institute's required music class with a boy named John Lowe, and though they barely spoke for most of the term, that changed one day when the instructor left the room long enough for Duff, as Lowe was known, to sit at the piano. A veteran of years of lessons, Duff had also taught himself to play boogie-woogie. When he whipped off a few bars of a Jerry Lee Lewis number, Paul's eyes widened. They started to chat, and a few weeks later Paul invited his new friend to become the newest member of the Quarrymen. "Paul gave me a list of numbers they were doing, and the key they were doing them in. I remember 'Boney Maroney' was on it, probably a couple of Everly Brothers numbers. 'That'll Be the Day,' 'Twenty Flight Rock,' 'Mean Woman Blues.' Probably about twelve songs, total." Duff attended his first rehearsal at Paul's house on a Sunday afternoon not long after, and after a few casual introductions they were off, blazing away on "That'll Be the Day" with an anxious Jim McCartney sitting at the side of the keyboard, waving his hands to keep the volume down. Duffs played his first show with them a week or two later, when the group did a few songs in the interval between the other, bigger bands on the bill. The Quarrymen didn't have much of a following, but when they got a shot at the Cavern club one evening that winter, the dank, little basement sprang to life.

"The girls usually sat in the chairs at the front, and the sides were cleared out for dancing," Colin Hanton recalls. "And one night we were playing, really rocking. But people kept getting up. John was upset because he thought they were all leaving." What they couldn't see, of course, was the action taking place on the other side of the stone pillars that divided the basement into three sections. "But later Pete and Nigel came running up and said, *'That was great! Everyone was jiving! They all got up and were jiving!'* And so that was it. We were making some headway, weren't we?"

With the lineup solidified as John, Paul, and George on guitars, the fleet-fingered Duff on piano, and the steadfast Colin on drums, the Quarrymen had started making music that could take a cellarful of uninterested kids, such as the ones they faced at an early Cavern-club gig in the first weeks of 1958, and propel them from their seats to romp madly on the dance floor. It might not have been in the sound, exactly—all three guitarists were still playing the cheap, rattly acoustics that so many teenagers picked up hoping to find the way to a G chord. And they didn't have a lot of chops on those, either. "They hardly knew how to play, truthfully," Duff says. But all those hours of singing and playing together had created a kind of heartbeat communication between John and Paul. No matter what they were playing, it seemed one could always intuit the other's moves, even before he had realized what he was about to do. When they sang, their voices slid naturally together, with John's deeper, rougher voice on the melody line and Paul's higher, smoother harmony soaring gracefully above.

But as the world kept reminding them, the Quarrymen hadn't quite yet made the transition to being a professional band. At one audition to entertain at a Labour club near the Liverpool football ground, the

Quarrymen's blend of rock 'n' roll hits and the occasional skiffle tune lost out to an odd middle-aged man whose entire act involved eating glass, then stuffing newspaper into his mouth to stanch the bleeding. At a school dance a few weeks later the piano the venue supplied for Duff not only wasn't on the stage, it wasn't even in the *auditorium*. "They were on the platform," Duff recalls. "I was playing down the hall."

Hoping that even a vanity-produced record might set their skills in a more impressive context, the band spent weeks working on their rendition of Buddy Holly's "That'll Be the Day," polishing up Paul's jaunty if derivative rewrite of a variety of rhythm-and-blues tropes he called "In Spite of All the Danger" as a B-side. They booked a session at a semiprofessional studio (actually a side room in an electronics shop owned by a fellow named Percy Phillips) and knocked out both tunes in a single take. The group emerged an hour later with a freshly pressed shellac disc, and a new manifestation of their fondest desires. Just having it to hold in their hands was a thrill. Being able to put it on their own record players and hear their own voices and instruments coming out of the same speakers that projected Elvis and Buddy and all their other heroes—*that* was even better. "We agreed to trade it off between us," Duff remembers. "I was the one who ended up with the disc, somehow. And it was years before I ever bought another Beatles record."

Duff left the Quarrymen a few weeks later. He had a new girlfriend, and the one time he took her to a rehearsal at Forthlin Road, the expression on her face radiated something besides joy at what she was hearing. "It was a dreadful noise, in that small room," he says. "She just wanted to take a walk on the sand, really. So I stopped going, and it was as simple as that."

Perhaps it was even simpler than that. By the time Duff escaped to walk on the beach with his girlfriend, just weeks after their heady visit to Percy Phillips's recording studio, the Quarrymen had all but ceased to exist.

It all came crashing down on the evening of July 15, the day after they had made their leap into the nearly big-time world of recorded music. That night John had gone to his mother's house, where he was waiting with her live-in boyfriend and their daughters for Julia to come home. He had grown close to her in the last few months, establishing a bond that never quite seemed maternal—Julia chatted and goofed with her son as if they were close, even flirty, friends. But the relationship assuaged the hurt John had always felt about his childhood, and so he visited often and didn't mind waiting.

Julia, as it turned out, was at his house, visiting with her older sister, Mimi. She said her farewells to Mimi at about 9 p.m., paused briefly to speak with Nigel Walley, who had come looking for John, then set out across the street to wait for the bus home. Julia only made it halfway across Menlove Avenue. Stepping out of the hedge that traced the edge of the grassy median dividing Menlove Avenue in two, Julia was struck by a speeding car. Her body flew one hundred feet down the road. Walley, who witnessed the entire accident, sprinted to her side. By the time he reached out to touch her, he knew she was dead.

John, still scarred from losing his mother the first time around, was devastated. He was too distraught to even discuss the tragedy with Paul, though he knew full well that Paul had suffered precisely the same loss less than two years earlier. Instead, he retreated to his room and shut the door. If he left the house at all, it was to go to a pub, where he'd drink until he could turn his grief into a weapon, snapping at his friends and picking fights with strangers. "The underlying chip on my shoulder that I had as a youth got really big then," John told *Playboy* magazine many years later.

John's guitar—another symbol of his bond to Julia—gathered dust in the corner. Band practice wasn't an option. It took weeks for Paul to get him to even open the door, let alone sit with him and try to write a song or two. Once John was willing to take that step, Paul organized rehearsals, setting them all at John's house to make it convenient for his stubbornly indifferent bandmate. Paul kept it up through the fall, as he and John returned to their respective schools. John's friends at the Art College were dismayed to see what had happened to their classmate over the summer. His mourning for Julia continued into the fall and winter, leading to increasingly decadent, hostile behavior, his lashing out at strangers and friends for no reason other than to vent his fury at the world.

Bill Harry, an aspiring writer who had befriended John early during their first year at college, recalls, "A lot of people lost their patience with John." So many young people in Liverpool had lost parents to the war, or disease, it was actually a fairly common experience. And hardly anyone responded quite as violently as John. "None of us had gone into this big, self-pitying thing. The feeling was—just get on with it."

But Paul seemed to have limitless patience for John, sneaking away from his classes to drink coffee at the Jacaranda coffeehouse, or else spend the afternoon nursing pints and punching rock 'n' roll songs on the jukebox at Ye Cracke pub. Certainly, Paul preferred hanging out with his friend to grinding through lectures and assignments at his schoolboy's desk at the Liverpool Institute. But the hours they spent together held an emotional significance, too. For even if they rarely spoke about the pain of losing their mothers, the mutual feelings of loss—and the rawness of John's wound—gave them a connection that was as vital as it was unspoken. It was, Paul said later, a "special bond for us, something of ours, a special thing." To see the other's eyes, even as they sat silently nodding their heads to Elvis's "All Shook Up" or Gene Vincent's "Blue Jean Bop," was to glimpse the soul of someone who knew how those songs, and so many others, could help fill the worst kind of silence. "We could look at each other," Paul said, "and know."

Paul made a habit of spending most of his lunch hours in the Art College cafeteria, eating and smoking with John and his community of older, more independent art-student friends. Eventually George began to accompany Paul to the Art College cafeteria, and if someone had a guitar (as George and Paul most often did), they'd pull it out and harmonize on a song or two. If it seemed odd at first for the college students to find their cafeteria overrun by kids in grammar-school blazers and ties, no one complained about the music they made. Eventually, Lennon and his baby-faced mates just became part of the scene. "They were there so often I just called them the College Band," Harry says.

One bandmate who never turned up at the lunchtime sessions was Colin Hanton, the drummer, who had already left school to apprentice as an upholsterer. He had a girlfriend, too, and had by early 1959 already figured that the Quarrymen had reached a logical conclusion.

"I never felt we were going to get anywhere. I certainly had no ambitions like that. I was in it for the fun and the Guinness," he says. Still, when Paul managed to book a gig at a busman's social club that winter, Hanton loaded up his drums and came out to play. The band's first set went so well the club owner pointed them to the bar to enjoy a free pint during their break. Unfortunately, they didn't stop with one. "By the time we got to the second set John, Paul, and myself were quite pissed. And the whole thing deteriorated into a drunken disaster."

Bad turned to worse when a manager who had come to the show to scout the Quarrymen for a regular engagement playing the intervals at bingo games marched to the band's dressing room afterward to explain why he wouldn't be hiring them, after all. Thoroughly dejected, but still drunk, the band found their way to the bus stop and were riding home when Paul began to talk with the distinctive slur of a deaf person. This was their new routine, a cruel bit of mimicry he knew would crack up John, who always took perverse glee in making fun of the handicapped. What neither of them knew was that Hanton had a friend at work with precisely that disability, and thus that speaking voice. Given the humiliations of the night, and probably months of being hectored by Paul for his drumming, Hanton finally snapped.

"I rounded on Paul and told him to bloody well shut up," Hanton says. "He looked shocked. He wasn't expecting that. I knew he wasn't imitating anyone in particular, it was just a voice. But between that and the guy from the [bingo hall], that was it for me. I put the drums on top of my wardrobe, and that was the last time I saw them."

4

Sometimes after school Paul would peel away from his friends and wander down Lime Street, toward the city center. Alone in the grownup world of office workers, he'd turn up the collar of his jacket and pull out one of the serious books he'd taken to reading. The works of Tennessee Williams, Oscar Wilde, and George Bernard Shaw, maybe one of the more weighty newspapers . . . Paul usually had at least one of them tucked into his shoulder bag, and when he was off on his own, he'd settle down and read a few pages. Thinking about the words, of course, but also about the faces of the men and women around him. Where did they come from? What were they thinking? He'd listen to their conversations and gauge the feelings behind their jokes, laughs, and sighs. It was all drama to him, another scene in the play he was forever composing in his head.

"I was very conscious of gathering material," Paul said. "I really fancied myself as an artist. I was preparing. I didn't know how the hell I was ever going to achieve it from my background . . . but my mind was full of it, it was an intoxication."

Paul's sense of his intellectual potential, and the horizons it might open for him, grew throughout his years at the Liverpool Institute. He had been particularly fired up by the literature classes of "Dusty" Durband, a bright-eyed, young instructor who spurred his students' appreciation for Chaucer by pointing out the dirty bits in "The Miller's Tale," as well as the bloody, adventure-movie-like aspects in *Hamlet* and Shakespeare's other dramas. Durband was satisfyingly down-to-earth—always an important attribute for a working-class kid like Paul. But just as significantly, given Paul's impulse toward middle-class culture, Durband also came with impressive credentials. He'd studied at Cambridge with the influential literary critic F. R. Leavis and had also written a play that had been produced for BBC radio. Decades later Paul described Durband as "the greatest teacher ever of English literature."

Durband recognized something unique in Paul's eyes, too, and frequently sent him away with recommendations for books other grammar-school students wouldn't have dreamed of reading for fun—that's where Paul's affection for Williams, Wilde, and Shaw originated. But even more important, Durband helped his baby-faced student identify the bond between art, intellectualism, and rebellion.

Entranced by visions of academe, Paul took on the look and habits of a real collegian, collecting books, attending lectures on art at Liverpool University, and buying himself student tickets to the dramas being staged downtown at the Royal Court and Liverpool Playhouse. "I was trying to prepare myself to be a student," he said. When schooling met the stage, he was doubly interested. Paul made a serious bid for a leading role in the school production of George Bernard Shaw's *Saint Joan,* but lost out to the older, more stage-ready Peter Sissons and had to make do with a nonspeaking part as an assessor.

Still, when it came to strict academic terms, Paul was only moderately successful. His commitment to the guitar and the Quarrymen—or to just playing and singing with John—often eclipsed his interest in completing, or even starting, his homework. When the next round of General Certificate of Education exams, the O levels, came around, he took them over two years, passing only Spanish the first time, then passing five more subjects the next time around. He attempted only two of the advanced, or A level, exams the next year, passing only in English.

Generally, Paul did the best in subjects that required as much, or more, natural abilities as they did hard work. Fortunately, he proved a quick study in a wide range of topics. An unusually inspired visual

artist, his drawings and paintings most often earned Paul top marks
and usually the most prominent placings in school art exhibitions. He
won a special prize for art at the institute's illustrious annual Speech
Day awards in December 1959. Still, his unwillingness to actually put
in the hours of study most of his classes required kept Paul from scoring the grades and test results he'd need to propel himself into a topflight university. So as he approached the final two years of his career
at the institute, Paul's teachers, along with his father, urged him to
consider applying next for a position at a teachers college.

It wasn't exactly the ivory-tower fantasy he'd been harboring. That
patched tweed jacket he liked to wear, the neat crewneck sweaters,
and all those weighty paperbacks he toted around were the hallmarks
of a university man, the sort of fellow bound for a career in academe
or the law or even medicine. But while Paul saw the allure of a de-
pendably middle-class route, and even applied to, and was accepted
by, a teachers college in Hereford, he couldn't resist focusing his ener-
gies in another direction.

"I ruined Paul's life, you know," John Lennon said to the journalist
Ray Connolly years later. "He could have gone to university. He could
have been a doctor. He could have *been* somebody!"

But of course Paul already knew whom he wanted to be, and who
he figured would help him reach his goal. He was going to be a songwriter and musician, and his partner in both pursuits would be John
Lennon. Everything else might change, but as long as he could hold on
to this partnership, nothing else mattered.

John, however, had other things on his mind. Through the fall of 1958
and well into 1959, John was far too busy engaging in art-school life—
if not exactly his studies—to think much about playing in a rock 'n'
roll band. He had started dating another student, a quiet blonde from
the relatively posh Hoylake district on the Wirral, named Cynthia
Powell. She proved a warm, stabilizing influence, which helped miti-
gate John's ongoing grief and rage. He had also grown particularly
close to one of the school's most promising students, a blazingly talented painter named Stuart Sutcliffe, whose emotional portraits and
densely wrought abstracts had already caught the eye of the university's
instructors, along with the gallery owners, artists, and critics who or-

bited the bohemian section that bordered the campus. John had been drawn to Stu's talent, too, and when his classmate invited John to move into his large, if downtrodden, flat around the corner from the college in a row of once-elegant homes on Gambier Terrace, the two art students became even closer. The flat became a hub for their college friends, a reliable address for drinking bouts and all-night parties.

Nevertheless, Paul made certain not to be a stranger. He was a regular around Gambier Terrace, often toting his guitar to spur a little playing and singing, and if circumstances permitted, a bit of songwriting. John remained an eager music fan, and a generally enthusiastic partner for playing and singing. But his disinterest in the band, prompted at least in part by his deepening friendship with Stu, frustrated Paul. How could he get John to focus on the Quarrymen when he was so involved in the Liverpool Art College scene, and all the friends he'd found there? Paul was also leery of John's new interest in Benzedrine, along with the other drugs the art students used to fuel their all-night parties. It was, Paul figured, one thing to have a pint or three at the pub. Everyone did that. But John's new habit of tearing apart Vicks inhalers and separating out the trace amounts of amphetamine in order to speed through the night . . . well, that just struck Paul as dangerous and wrong.

John was moving on, and not in a promising direction. George, for his part, had grown sick of waiting and joined the jazz-and-skiffle centered Les Stewart Quartet, though he made it clear to Paul that he'd be back with the Quarrymen whenever they resumed playing. Paul, on the other hand, wasn't interested in playing with anyone else. For whatever combination of emotional and visceral reasons, he couldn't seem to imagine a musical life that didn't include John Lennon as his primary partner. So he persisted, dragging his guitar to Gambier Terrace, making himself a fixture amid the empty beer bottles, overflowing ashtrays, shattered Vicks inhalers, and paint-splattered clothes. If John didn't evince any interest in being in a band, Paul would simply wait, guitar at the ready, until he did.

Eventually, George got the band back together. In search of gigs for the Les Stewart Quartet, he and fellow guitarist Ken Brown had heard rumors of a new all–rock 'n' roll club starting in a most unlikely place—the basement of a large house in West Derby. This was the home of the Bests, a family of boys whose warm, if somewhat domineering, mother, Mona, was an entrepreneurial sort who had come to recognize the demand for an all-ages nightclub that would cater to her sons' generation of music fans. The Bests lived in a sprawling house (purchased courtesy of a racetrack windfall to Mona's husband, Johnny Best), and its basement was vast enough to accommodate hundreds of visitors at once. Seizing on an opportunity to make a profit while also entertaining her sons and their friends, Mo, as everyone called her, set them to work cleaning out the cellar and then decorating it. They were still in the midst of that when George and Ken came around, hoping to score an engagement for their group. They pitched in enough hard labor to earn the opening-night gig, but when they brought that news to Les Stewart, he announced that he had no intention of playing at the Casbah, or any other rock 'n' roll club. Realizing they now had a gig, but no band, George called in his two fellow Quarrymen. Did they want to come out and play? Indeed, they did.

So much, in fact, that both Paul and John showed up to help finish painting the Casbah's walls and ceilings. The opening night was set for August 29, 1959, and when the Quarrymen—who now included Ken Brown as a fourth guitarist, but no drummer—showed up with their instruments, a line literally hundreds long snaked from the Bests' home and down the otherwise quiet, residential block. The crowd packed the large basement to overflowing, and when the band finally stepped to the front of the room with their instruments, the ovation was overwhelming.

"Welcome to the Casbah!" John shouted. "We're the Quarrymen and we're going to play you some rock and roll!"

Paul shrieked the opening line of "Long Tall Sally," and off they went, swinging and swaying through their hardest-rocking material. Whatever the band lacked in drums and bass, their rock-starved crowd made up for with their stomping and clapping. The boys played nonstop for forty-five minutes, ran into a side room to regroup, then came back to a thunderous chant of *We want the Quarrymen!* Back at the microphone, a sweating, glowing Paul leaned into the microphone.

"Are you all *enjoying* yourselves?" A huge roar came back, but he shook his head. "I can't hear you! *Do you want some more?*"

The next ovation all but drowned out the opening riff to Chuck Berry's "Roll Over Beethoven." When they finally left the stage, soaked with sweat and electric with excitement, John, Paul, George, and Ken gaped at one another in disbelief. *Did that really just happen?* And more important, how soon could they make it happen again?

Very soon, as it turned out. Mo Best offered the Quarrymen a weekly engagement; for headlining the Casbah every Saturday night, she would pay the band three pounds in cash, and as many Cokes and bags of crisps as they could consume. They agreed to the deal on the spot. From that moment, the Quarrymen were back in business.

The members of Derry and the Seniors were an established band, and serious musicians, and thus not the least bit interested in the Quarrymen. Or Johnny and the Moondogs, or whatever the hell they were calling themselves in the early weeks of 1960. Sure, they had heard about the new scene out at the Casbah, and the hundreds of kids who had been lining up to see the Saturday-night shows. They'd got in on that, too, particularly after the Quarrymen had gone stomping out of the club in October, so irked by Mo Best's insistence on paying Ken Brown his share of their three-pound fee on a night when he had been too sick to play that they had ended their association with the club and Ken Brown, all in one red-faced stroke. They'd mostly been woodshedding since then, rehearsing and playing the odd party, but Derry and the Seniors were a working band, with all the professionalism that implied. "We looked down on them, at first," recalls Brian Griffiths, the Seniors' guitarist. "They were okay, but definitely not a top band. They didn't even have a drummer."

The rhythm's in the guitars, the Quarrymen liked to proclaim, and now Stuart Sutcliffe, on the strength of the £60 he'd unexpectedly earned for selling a painting, was on the bass. No problem if he couldn't play, John and Paul had assured him. They'd teach him, and how hard could it be? Much less difficult, it seemed, than resisting the combined will of Lennon and McCartney, so Stu went out and bought himself a Höfner bass and became an official Moondog. They had found a new rehearsal spot, playing in the basement of their favorite coffeehouse, the Jacaranda. This was where Griffiths saw them, walking toward the door just as he, singer Derry Wilkie, and sax player Howie Casey were walking out to go to the pub next door. They all chatted for a few minutes, and as John, Paul, George, and Stu continued inside, the other musicians stayed outside in the misty rain, finishing their conversation with Casey, who had decided not to go to the pub after all. He walked away, and they were just stepping toward the pub when the music started. "It's so vivid to me, even now," Griffiths says. What he heard was the opening riff to Chuck Berry's "Roll Over Beethoven," then the urgent bray of John's voice, linking effortlessly to Paul's piercing harmony on the chorus.

"It was amazing," Griffiths continues. With three electric instruments in the lineup (only Paul still played an acoustic), they'd found an entirely new sound. "It was Lennon's tune and he had this great, chunky Chuck Berry–like rhythm pattern. I couldn't believe it, so I turned to Derry and said, 'Is that *them*?' He looked down through the grate and said, 'Yeah, it is!' And I said, 'Fucking hell, does that sound *good*!' And I always remembered that moment."

Something was gelling. Stu may have been a rudimentary bassist, but his presence proved catalytic. He kept John focused on the group, for one thing. And when John mentioned, late one night in February, that they really needed to come up with a better name than Johnny and the Moondogs, Stu helped John pivot from musing about the simple beauty of Buddy Holly's *Crickets* to hitting on *Beetles,* and then—per John's perpetually twisted way with words—*Beatals.* That evolved into *Beatles,* then, per the style of the day, to *Johnny Silver and the Beatles,* then just the *Silver Beatles.* Or sometimes the *Silver Beetles,* depending on who was doing the spelling and, seemingly, what day it was.

When the Jacaranda's owner, a pugnacious thirty-year-old named Allan Williams, had a hankering to expand his current holdings (the Jac, a bar, and a strip club) into an entertainment empire including bands and concert halls, John asked him to manage them. Williams agreed, and tasked with finding the group a drummer, he came back with Tommy Moore, an experienced player who also worked as a laborer in a bottle factory. Moore was alarmingly old (at thirty-six, he was more than twice the age of Paul and George), and his usual repertoire tilted toward jazz and show tunes, but he was available and came with his own drum set, so he was welcomed with open arms. Which he would almost certainly come to regret when he was nearly killed during the band's first tour, a dismal ten-day jaunt backing up a largely unknown young singer named Johnny Gentle for his tour of Scotland's most damp and grim dance halls.

This was the band's big break. Or it would have been if the Beatles/Silver Beatles/Silver Beetles had played well enough to earn the summer-long residency backing up Billy Fury in the summer-resort town of Blackpool for which they had actually been auditioning. Instead, they landed the consolation prize of the Scottish tour, a low-paying, low-profile gig. But the band set out with the highest hopes. Only Tommy didn't adopt a stage name (Paul became Paul Ramon, thinking it sounded wonderfully *mysterious*), and all reveled in the feeling of being a band on the road, moving from town to town, laying down an hour or two of their hottest rock 'n' roll, chatting up a local girl or three, then vanishing with the dawn in the battered van that carried the band, Johnny Gentle, and all their gear. One such journey nearly ended in disaster, as a momentary lapse on the part of the driver (Mr. Gentle, aka John Askew) resulted in a collision with another car. Drummer Tommy bore the brunt of the impact, breaking his nose and a few teeth. He made the show that night in Aberdeen, but the experience soured Tommy on the rock 'n' roll life. Back in Liverpool a few days later, the band played another show or two, then found themselves on the hunt for another drummer.

Still, with the taste of the future still fresh on their tongues, they persisted. A time-filling gig backing up a stripper at Williams's newest club took them through a few weeks in July. "Not an important chapter in our lives," Paul decreed later. "But an *interesting* one." What they didn't know, while strumming their guitars in the shadows behind the stripper, was that they were on the verge of starting an even more interesting, and far more important, chapter. For by the end of the summer they would be headed for the German city of Hamburg, and here a band of enlightened amateurs from the southern suburbs of Liverpool would transform themselves into something else altogether.

The offer came through Williams, who had cultivated a friendship with a thuggish, yet charming German club owner, Bruno Koschmider, he had met through some other shirttail acquaintances. Koschmider, who ran a couple of clubs in Hamburg's sex-, booze-, and crime-laced Reeperbahn district, needed rock music to draw people to his bars. British bands offered an allure that locals didn't, so this joined the two club owners' interests into one: if Williams could channel his Liverpool bands to Koschmider's clubs, the bands would have regular work, Williams's commissions would skyrocket, and Koschmider's bars would funnel rivers of beer and booze into the mouths of thirsty, rock-crazed clubgoers. So the shuttle service began, first with Derry and the Seniors, whose high-energy rhythm-and-blues-style act lit up the Kaiserkeller club in July. The upswing in business was so significant that Koschmider decided to convert another of his clubs, the Indra, from a strip club to a music venue. Which meant he would need another band, preferably British, to fill its postage stamp-size stage. Williams tapped the Beatles (who had finally dropped the *Silver*), but with a condition: they needed to find a full-time drummer first.

Easier said than done. The group had only weeks earlier lost their most recent drummer, a hard-hitting twenty-year-old named Norman Chapman, to Britain's compulsory National Service. Where could they find their third drummer in as many months? The answer came from a familiar direction: Pete Best, the sweet-natured, if taciturn, son of Casbah owner Mona Best, had been drumming for a young band called the Blackjacks. But that group was about to break up, so Paul picked up the phone and tendered the offer to Pete, point-blank: the Beatles had a four-week engagement in Germany. Did he want to join them on drums? He was certainly interested, so they all agreed to meet at the Wyvern Club, where Pete played five or six rock standards, the only one of which he could clearly remember was "Ramrod." They were still talking about his playing when Williams walked into the club. "This is Pete, the new drummer," they announced.

That resolved one problem. But Paul still had another, far more daunting hurdle to clear: getting Jim McCartney to let his oldest son abandon home and, more important, his schooling to pursue his rock dreams to Germany. Not surprisingly, Paul considered the task ahead at some length, eventually realizing that it would be far easier if he wasn't the only one trying to do the convincing. Thus, he moved stealthily to draft younger brother Michael into the effort.

"I've had some amazing news," Paul mused airily while the brothers were riding the 86 bus home from Liverpool's city center. "But I don't know whether I can tell you."

Mike nearly leaped out of his seat as his big brother let him in on his big secret: a monthlong engagement in Germany; big money; maybe even a chance to get famous—as in, *really* famous.

"And I can buy you lots of things, too, but there's just one thing . . . *Dad.*"

Fortunately, Mike dreamed up the solution Paul had undoubtedly been intending him to propose: they could convince their father *together*. Still, Jim wasn't convinced. Wasn't Paul on the verge of going to university? Hadn't he been working his entire life to launch himself out of the working classes and into something a bit more grand? No way was Jim going to let Paul go. Realizing he needed a bigger gun in this fight, Paul called in Allan Williams, who paid a special visit to Jim to chat, man-to-man, about the opportunity that awaited his clearly levelheaded son in Germany: steady employment; nearly twenty pounds a week in take-home pay. Which was, Jim knew, quite a bit more than he was earning each week on the cotton exchange. This last fact, along with Jim's memories of his own showbiz aspirations, did the trick. Given permission, Paul wrote a letter to the Liverpool Institute's headmaster informing him of his decision not to return to school, taking care to mention how much he'd be earning. "It was a 'that's more than you earn' kind of letter," he admitted later. No matter, the headmaster saw to it that the school's handwritten ledger reflected the boy's departure. *School Leaving Age,* someone wrote, noting that J. P. McCartney had fulfilled his legal obligation to become educated. The same hand squeezed in a further explanation: *Working in Hamburg.*

At first it seemed like a disaster. The drive to Hamburg, all of them crammed into a small van with Allan Williams, his wife, Beryl, and a somewhat shady business-partner-slash-wingman known only as Lord Woodbine, had been long and cramped. Only when they crossed into Germany did the British youngsters first realize they might need the official work papers no one had thought to procure for them. They pretended to be students and kept driving, arriving at length in the

Reeperbahn district, then at the address Koschmider had instructed them to find. A tiny, Indian-themed club called the Indra. Just look for the large, neon elephant outside. Inside it got worse: heavy crimson drapes to deaden the sound; a half dozen beer-stained tables, all of them deserted. The band's lodgings, also provided by Koschmider, were a windowless storage room behind the screen of a third-rate movie theater called the Bambi. Bunk beds, cement walls, and the nostril-searing aroma of a fitfully tended ladies' room, right next door.

Back at the Indra for their first night on its small, wooden stage, the Beatles—all but Pete dressed nattily in black trousers and shirts and matching lilac blazers—confronted an empty club. They actually had to take their guitars out into the street to draw passing fun-seekers through the door. "We were like carnival barkers," Paul recalled. "We'd grab two people and do whatever they wanted—our whole repertoire . . . we'd do all the jokes and try to be marvelous and make them want to come back."

Koschmider, appraising his newest employees from the back of the room, thought they were hopeless. The music was okay, perhaps. But why did they seem so meek? Why were they just standing there when rock 'n' roll was supposed to be so exciting?

Mach Schau! he'd shout at them. Make a show! Move to the music! Act like you're having *fun*! So they began to move. Not with the cool, choreographed steps that Cliff Richard and the Shadows had made so popular—who had the time or patience to learn that sort of routine?—but with a loose abandon that grew wilder as the night went on and the empty beer pitchers lined up at their feet. John would pogo with the beat. Paul flailed at his guitar, thrusting its neck up and down as even Stu danced uneasily with his bass, his features impassive as the lights flashed on the lenses of the dark glasses he always wore. The beat propelled the dancing, which fed the volume, which kicked the beat even further into overdrive. Complaints from the Indra's neighbors prompted Koschmider to bring the comparatively quiet strippers back to the Indra's stage, so he pointed the Beatles down the street toward the Kaiserkeller and put them into rotation with Derry and the Seniors, having the bands trade sets from dusk until dawn. Given a bigger crowd, a better stage, and now direct, if friendly, competition with another Liverpool band, the Beatles played even harder. Hipped to the restorative effects of German diet pills, particularly when washed down with beer, the band turned the Kaiserkeller stage into a kind of neon-lit crucible. They didn't all gobble pills with John's heedless enthusiasm (always cautious, Paul barely took them at all, at first), but they all consumed oceans of beer, and the accrued effects of the intoxicants, along with the wild energy of the all-night sessions, launched them into an entirely new orbit.

They moved at such a frantic pace, spinning so fast through such an alien land, that the five boys merged naturally into one. They played on the same tiny stage all night, drinking and speeding to the dawn, when they would eat together, drink (more) together, attract, meet, and then cavort with the same women, often in the same room at the same time. They dressed alike, walked alike, spoke in the same exaggerated Scouse accent. When the hands of the clock spun them again toward the stage, they strapped on their instruments, counted themselves into unison, and flat out *rocked,* Paul screaming "Long Tall Sally" and "Lucille" until his vocal cords seemed to blister, John stepping up to match him scream for scream with "Johnny B. Goode" and "Rock 'n' Roll Music." And more: "Your Feet's Too Big," "Memphis," "That's All Right, Mama." George's solos soared higher than before, Pete went after his drums with two-fisted fury. The nights on stage stretched on and on, so the band grew accordingly, extending their repertoire with every song they'd ever heard of—obscure R & B tunes—the flip sides of American singles they'd bought in Liverpool; Paul recalled Jim's favorite romantic show tunes; they all knew cowboy songs from camp; whatever. Anything could be lashed to that stomping, four-in-a-bar beat and, when necessary, patched together with solos and made-up verses until the tunes went on for thirty minutes, forty-five minutes, an hour, all night long if need be.

Watching from the bar as he cooled off from another set playing sax with Derry and the Seniors, Howie Casey was impressed. "We'd scoffed at them in Liverpool, but they'd obviously been practicing. We saw a *helluva* difference," he says. Casey, a trained musician who had played in a British army band before getting out and turning professional, took particular notice of how the Beatles' left-handed guitar player drove the band musically. "You can always tell which one is the most creative, and Paul obviously had that drive. He was so good at getting chords and figuring out songs. And vocally he was incredible. I know John was the leader in a way, but musically Paul was always in charge."

When the shows were over, Paul often cooled down backstage with the Seniors' guitarist, Brian Griffiths, talking about music and working out the chords for songs he wanted to add to the act. Griffiths, who had already been impressed by the Beatles' musicality, now began to sense how far Paul's tastes ranged, from the rawest rock tunes all the way to jazz and show tunes. "He could play for more than anyone else, right into Gershwin and those guys," Griffiths says. "He had a great ear for progressions and knew diminished chords and like that. I remember thinking, 'Why doesn't he do that onstage?' But they were a rock band."

This became especially clear to Griffiths one morning after a long night of trading sets for the Kaiserkeller crowds. He and John had gone out to breakfast together with the dawn, and when they got back to the Kaiserkeller an hour or so later, they walked through the door to the sound of Paul alone at the piano, working on a cover of Elvis's melodramatic version of "It's Now or Never." Singing through the house microphone, his version of Elvis's vocal histrionics echoed through the empty, half-dark club. John stood with Griffiths in the doorway for a few moments, until John grimaced and elbowed his fellow musician in the ribs. "I hate this shit!" he snapped. "This guy's tryin' to be like Elvis. But it's not rock 'n' roll, then, is it?"

Griffiths got John's point. But he also couldn't help being wowed by Paul's performance. ("I was thinking . . . what a *voice* on that guy!") Just as he found himself consistently impressed with his fellow musician's commitment to professionalism. Even in the hysterical, drunken melee of the Reeperbahn nightclub scene, Paul took care to get things right. "If he was going to do a song onstage, he wanted to do it right. He'd *work* on it. I never saw him quake or crack, he could always pull things off. And that was because he rehearsed, he prepared."

John rarely had the patience for such perfectionism. Still, he was a propulsive rhythm guitarist and a spellbinding singer who could inject new life into the most threadbare rock hits. Often, it was the tension between the two front men that made the Beatles such a compelling band amid the often-generic cover bands flailing away in the Reeperbahn clubs. Any given performance might begin with Paul using his schoolboy German to welcome the crowd, thanking them for coming and heralding the next song. On some nights he'd even play schoolteacher, attempting to teach his rough crowd a few handy words of English. But as the night wore on, and the scene picked up momentum, John would take over, jabbering at the increasingly rowdy throng in purposefully incomprehensible gabble. When the pills and booze really kicked in, he'd go completely over the top. "Clap yer hands yer fuckin' Nazis!" he'd scream, leading the British sailors in the crowd to roar with glee. But so, too, would the Germans, who either didn't understand and just assumed he was saying something encouraging, or else just got off on his craziness.

If the Germans wanted craziness, the Beatles were more than happy to provide it, and for far longer than their original monthlong engagement, now that their contract kept getting extended. As the weeks turned into months, and the nights became a spotlighted blur of booze, diet pills, and screaming sailors, their antics edged toward the inspired lunacy of performance art. John performed one night with a toilet seat around his neck. Paul matched him by playing a set dressed only in a bedsheet. John came back another night dressed only in a swimsuit and punctuated the set by dropping his guitar, spinning in place, and whipping down his trunks to reveal his pale British ass to the cheering crowd.

While it was the echoes of blistering rock 'n' roll that drew a young German art student named Klaus Voormann into the Kaiserkeller one night that fall, it was the anarchic undercurrent running beneath the music that compelled him to return the next night, and the night after that. Eventually he urged his girlfriend, an inspiring photographer named Astrid Kirchherr, to come with him. At first she didn't want to go. "It wasn't a good thing to go to the Reeperbahn," she says. "It took Klaus some days to persuade me to go." But once she did allow him to lead her through the neon-lit streets and into the smoky, beer-splattered pit of the Kaiserkeller, Astrid, too, was transfixed by what she saw. And her hauntingly beautiful eyes cast the Beatles into an entirely new light.

Astrid was even more intrigued by the Beatles than Klaus had been. "I loved them. They were very powerful on the stage. Very powerful. And of course they were absolutely, terribly good-looking." By now the Beatles had traded their ridiculous lilac jackets for black leather suits, which they wore with black T-shirts. But Astrid saw through the biker gear, and the whiff of violence that permeated the smoky air every night at the Kaiserkeller, and recognized the sweetness and intelligence glimmering just beneath the leather. She and Klaus introduced themselves to the group, and though she and Klaus barely spoke English and Paul was the only Beatle who knew more than a few words of German, they grew friendly. After a while she grew comfortable enough to ask if they might allow her to take some photographs of the band. They agreed readily, so she led them to an abandoned fairground, posing the pale, guitar-clutching musicians against the bleak remnants of carnival rides and cast-off buses. "They did anything I told them to do," she recalls. "And because my English wasn't all that good, I just went over and grabbed their faces and put their hands on the right way to hold the guitar. But they were very charming, very well-mannered, and just lovely. You could tell them what to do and they acted absolutely professional."

The images Astrid created that chilly autumn morning, still among the most striking and influential portraits taken of any artists in the modern era, established the Beatles as something more than a traditional rock band. What she captured, between the defiance in their postures and the exhausted melancholy in their eyes, was the raw essence of the group's artistry. An eruption of life against a backdrop of death; the persistence of joy even in the face of heartbreaking loss.

Maybe that was the morning she fell in love with Stuart. They fell into a passionate affair, and the merging of the two communities, the leather-clad British rockers and the avant-garde German students, would transform all of them.

The Hamburg trip ended abruptly, and badly. Wooed to sign a contract to open in the competing Top Ten Club, the Beatles underestimated the wrath of Koschmider, who not only got George deported—he was shocked, *shocked* to learn that the guitarist was only seventeen and thus not of legal nightclub-working age—but also maneuvered to have Paul and Pete arrested for allegedly trying to torch the Bambi cinema while they were packing their clothes to move to the digs arranged by the Top Ten's owner. They were quickly deported, leaving John, who came home soon afterward, and Stu, who opted to stay for a while with Astrid, who was by then his girlfriend.

Back in Liverpool just in time for Christmas, Paul walked through the door of 20 Forthlin Road with the same smile, but a newly whittled-down frame. "There stood an emaciated skeleton that was once my brother," Mike wrote. Paul showed off his new watch, boots, and electric razor, presented his brother with a "gear" blue raincoat, and declared the entire trip an enormous success. "But nothing could detract from the fact that when he sat down, the ankles showing above the winklepicker shoes were as thin and white as Dad's pipe-cleaners," Mike noted.

Paul caught up on his sleep for a day or two, then fell under the stern eye of Jim, who began to wonder, aloud, when his once-promising elder son would either go back to school or roll up his sleeves and get to work. Paul acquiesced, sort of, by finding the lowest-rung job he possibly could—driving a delivery van for a few days, then taking another job as a custodian at the Massey and Coggins electrical plant. But when after a few days his supervisors gleaned something about his years at the Liverpool Institute, they led him into an entry-level job on the management track, winding electrical coils. For a time the simple rhythms of workaday life appealed to Paul. Up in the morning, into his overalls, and off to the factory, just like a regular bloke! This, after all, was another version of the life his father had been living for so many years, just as he had taken on another version of *his* dad's life. Surely it made sense for Paul to take his place in the grand tradition of McCartney workingmen.

But then days passed, maybe a week, and John and George appeared in the work yard. Paul greeted them warily, unsure where they had left things, where it might be headed. John, as usual, got to the point: they'd just got a couple of gigs at the Casbah, others were in the wind, so how's about shaking off this lot and getting back to playing some rock 'n' roll? Paul shook his head. He had a steady job now, earning more than seven pounds a week. And they were training him for management! "That's pretty good. I can't expect more," he insisted.

He was either kidding himself or playing hard to get, waiting for his friends to beg him to come back. Or at least ask nicely. And maybe that's what they did. Or maybe John just stuck a finger in Paul's chest and told him, again, that he was a big boy now and thus needed to tell his dad to fuck off and start living his own life, his own way. One way or another, Paul took a look around at the other men in overalls, all of them busily hunched over machines, or pushing pallets or winding coils, and came to a quick decision. "I bunked over the wall," he recalled, "and was never seen again by Massey and Coggins."

At the Casbah the kids didn't know what to expect. They had seen the Quarrymen back in the late summer of 1959. But that was sixteen months earlier, and the posters promoting this show—put up by Pete's friend Neil Aspinall, then an accountancy student and a roomer at the Best house—promised a group called the Beatles, who were "straight from Hamburg." So a German group, it seemed. Then the band came out, guitars at the ready, and a wave of recognition—Cor, that's the Quarrymen!—gave way to surprise. Look at the black leather suits! Then Paul turned to the others, counted off the first song and . . . *boom!* Chas Newby, a friend of Pete's sitting in for the still-absent Stu on bass, knew the tunes and could play along easily enough. But even from where he was standing, he could barely believe the sound he was hearing. "We all knew that George could play guitar, Paul could sing like Little Richard, and John could do the gravelly-voiced stuff," he says. "But now they were so tight, so fiery . . . they were simply better than everybody else. By far."

They played a similarly hot set at the Grosvener Ballroom a week later, then three days after that, on December 27, dragged their amps to the Litherland Town Hall to play a set in the middle of a bill with the Deltones and the Searchers. The house was full of kids, teenagers mostly, all of them primed to blow off some steam in the dead days between Christmas and New Year's Eve. The Deltones kicked things off with a competent set, and after a brief break the evening's compere, Bob Wooler, took the microphone to introduce the next act. The Beatles, with Newby still on the bass, stood behind the curtain, instruments at the ready. Paul could hear the crowd buzzing beyond the curtain. Wooler was doing his DJ thing, building anticipation. *Ladies and gentlemen*... Paul gripped the neck of his guitar with his right hand, took a step toward the microphone. *Direct from Hamburg*... He held his left hand over the strings, pick at the ready. *The band you've been waiting for—*

"He never got it out," Newby recalls. "Paul just launched into 'Long Tall Sally,' and it caused this *sensation*." The kids had been scattered around the hall talking to one another, scattered in knots smoking ciggies and drinking Cokes, doing what kids do. But Paul's shrieking vocal rattled the windows, and by the time George launched into the song's first guitar break, Newby was watching a veritable stampede of youth headed in his direction. "People were crowding the stage to see this gang of rockers."

From there the evening became a blur—a head-spinning tumult of rock 'n' roll, ecstatic cries from the crowd, and a riot of leaping and dancing. The Beatles were on fire—John screaming out his Chuck Berry songs, George positively shredding his leads, Pete thundering the beat. But Paul was unhinged. He spun like a dervish, he whipped his guitar neck to and fro. A few girls near the front were actually screaming at him, their eyes like saucers, their cheeks flushed crimson. Newby was thrilled ("Well, it was a great gig. Unbelievable"), but it was all he could do to keep up. When it was over, sitting in the dressing room while the promoter moved quickly to book the Beatles for as many shows as they could possibly commit to, Newby realized that he could barely stand up. "My feet were killing me, I'd been stamping the stage so hard," he says. "That had never happened before."

It would never happen to him again, either. A week later Newby was back at Manchester University, studying for his degree in chemistry. The Beatles were headed in an entirely different direction.

5

There could be nothing else. The guitar Paul had wrapped himself around when he was fourteen, the rock 'n' roll music that had merged with the rhythm in his chest, was now the central organizing principle of his entire existence. It was the bond he shared with his best friends, the magnet that drew the attention he craved, the most potent vehicle for all the feelings—wildness, sorrow, love, fear—that he found so difficult to express in words. Nothing could matter more, nothing even came close. There would be no talk of getting a job, no real reason to head off to teachers college.

If only because there was no time for anything else. Through the first three months of 1961 the Beatles played shows nearly every day in and around Liverpool. With Mona Best serving as an ad hoc booking agent, the group often found themselves performing multiple shows in a single day. On February 28, for instance, they began their day with a lunchtime session at the Cavern Club on Mathew Street in the city center, dispatched their gear for an early-evening set at the Casanova Club, then packed up and hauled the gear out to the Litherland Town Hall for a late-night set. This unrelenting schedule kept up until April 1, when the group decamped to Hamburg for another three months of all-night sessions, this time at the larger, shinier Top Ten Club.

During this visit the group finally found their way into a professional recording studio, backing their fellow Briton Tony Sheridan (a white-hot guitarist from England notorious for his mercurial personality) on a variety of sides, including his own hard-rocking arrangement of "My Bonnie." The Beatles got a shot at fronting a couple of tunes themselves, the most successful of these featuring John's raucous vocal on "Ain't She Sweet." Paul ended up playing the bass for the session, underscoring the tension that had been building between John's two closest friends.

Paul had always felt ambivalent about having John's best art-school pal in the band. At first they just needed a bass player, and though Stu had never played the instrument before, his presence in the band, along with his growing enthusiasm for performing, kept John present and focused. But the crucible of Hamburg, and the increasingly profound bonds it had cast within the band, had clarified Paul's visceral sense that Stu had no place in the band. If he never said it directly, he made it as clear as he could with every word he did say. "Paul sometimes freaked out and said, 'You've got to practice! You've played the wrong note!'" Astrid Kirchherr, by then engaged to Stu, recalls. "John said, 'It doesn't matter! He looks good!' But of course Paul was furious. Stuart really never did bother to practice."

But other observers never saw the conflict as strictly musical. Bill Harry, a schoolmate and friend of both John's and Stu's at the Liverpool Art College, and on the way to founding a regional music newspaper he would call *Mersey Beat,* says the other Beatles were actually impressed by their neophyte bassist's progress. "I've got cards from Paul talking about how good a guitarist Stu was," Harry says. Tony Sanders, drummer for Billy Kramer and the Coasters, points out that most of the songs in the Beatles' repertoire were fairly simple rock tunes—three chords, a good beat, and a lot of energy. But even when they took on songs with more complicated progressions—"Three Cool Cats," "Your Feet's Too Big"—Sanders says the bass player always kept up. "I don't remember Stu struggling over that."

The real struggle seemed to be the one Stu was having with Paul over John. "He and I used to have a deadly rivalry," Paul admitted years later. Indeed, Stuart could capture and hold John's attention like no one else. He was a brilliant artist, and sophisticated in a way Paul could only aspire to become, with a sense of style, an artsy panache, that was as breathtaking as it was effortless. "Stu wore dark glasses, and this gabardine mac he wore onstage as a cloak, with the top button fastened around his neck, like Zorro," Sanders remembers. "I liked him immediately. He had the same aura about him as the others." Maybe that's what bothered Paul the most. For now that the band was making progress, now that John had fallen back into the music, how could Paul and John truly focus on their musical partnership if Stuart was in the way? "I was always practical, thinking our band could be great," Paul said. "But with him on bass there was always something holding us back."

So Paul turned his critical eye on the Beatles' bassist, perpetually tracking his progress, or lack of same, and commenting loudly when Stu missed a cue or fluffed a note. The others snickered along with Paul's game—John always indulged a reflexive need to insult the people he loved—so no one looked askance when Paul's badgering followed the group onstage at the Top Ten one night. Paul had been relegated to the piano at the side of the stage, and as his frustration built, he started lobbing insults at the bass player standing a few feet away. Stu, smaller and more gentle-natured than the rest, at first ignored the abuse. But as Paul's commentary grew louder and more bitter, his face reddened. When Paul tossed Astrid's name into the mix, the blood drained from Stu's cheeks. He stripped off his bass, hurled his slim body at Paul, and smacked him so hard across the face that they both fell on the stage. They went at each other with shocking violence, a rolling windmill of punches and kicks that ended only when the song finally ended and John, George, and Pete could pull their bandmates apart.

Stu shrugged his bass back on and got back to playing. But the ugly fight, and John's unwillingness to rip into Paul for inciting it, proved useful: Stu realized then he had to leave the band. He broke the news a few days later, explaining that he had decided to move in with Astrid, now his fiancée, and to focus again on painting. Just to show there were no hard feelings, he handed his Höfner bass to Paul and told him to keep it as long as he needed. Not that Paul was eager to take on the bass. But George was the lead guitarist, and John had neither the interest nor patience to switch instruments. So Paul did what he had to do to keep the Beatles moving forward.

•   •   •

Back in Liverpool, the rock 'n' roll scene had erupted into a kind of regional youth movement. Riding the generational wave of postwar-babies-turned-teenagers, with an assist from Parliament's decision to end compulsory National Service for young men, the city and its suburbs swarmed with actively gigging rock 'n' roll bands—as many as 350, according to scene veterans. The influx of musicians and, more important, money-wielding fans, spurred a matching eruption of venues for the bands to play for young music fans. Town halls; union halls; pubs; nightclubs; even the once-strictly jazz Cavern Club—all now threw open their doors to the rock 'n' roll crowd. Record stores thrived. And Liverpool's city center now boasted two fully stocked music shops, their windows loaded with electric guitars, basses, amps, and drum sets.

One interesting fact: Liverpool's rock scene was literally an underground movement. This was because so many of the most important venues—from the Casbah to the Jacaranda's stage to the record department of the NEMS store on Whitechapel and so many other key rallying points—were located in basements. None of these others were nearly as subterranean-feeling as the Cavern, the cryptlike club located a few blocks away from NEMS at 10 Mathew Street. Set in the middle of a thin conduit that ran through a section of warehouses and produce-storage buildings, the club's door drew members up uneven cobblestones usually scattered with crumpled lettuce leaves and rotten fruit that had been tossed aside by the truckers and vendors. A naked lightbulb lit the eighteen stone steps that led down to a basement, whose three vaulted chambers, separated by stone pillars, had been built a century earlier as storage for casks of rum and molasses. Once imagined as a sophisticated jazz establishment à la Paris's Le Caveau, the Cavern had become a youth-oriented venue, its bar selling cups of lemonade and hot dogs to a young clientele whose numbers, and their frantic jiving in the club's side tunnels, created breathtaking heat and humidity. All but unventilated and often jammed to its six-hundred-strong capacity, the Cavern's ambient temperature would soar into the eighties and higher, and the ceiling and walls would run with sweat.

The Beatles played their first lunchtime session at the Cavern in early February of 1961, and once they returned from Hamburg in early July, they were a regular attraction at the club, with an increasingly large and enthusiastic following. "They were just in your face," recalls Mike Byrne, a club regular who worked in his dad's haberdashery around the corner on North John Street. He was in a band, too—Mike and the Thunderbirds—so Byrne was particularly impressed by the technical prowess the Beatles brought back from their months-long stands in Germany. "They still messed about onstage, but the music was so tight. The backing vocals so perfect. And those harmonies, with that hard-rock sound . . . it was just so great." The band had plenty of female fans, too, and Paul's angelic features and cheerful countenance always made him a favorite. No matter where you saw him—carrying his guitar case up Mathew Street, shopping for records at NEMS, or standing near the hot-dog stand at the rear of the Cavern, Paul always greeted admirers with a smile and a joke, particularly if they were adoring girls. "I think he was fancied by more girls than the rest of the Beatles," Byrne says. "But he was good-looking and cute, and he just loved performing for people. And he was always aware of his image."

So aware, in fact, that hardly anyone knew that he'd had a serious girlfriend for nearly two years. Her name was Dorothy Rhone, a teen-aged bank clerk he'd met at the Casbah during the Quarrymen's stand during the late summer of 1959. Rhone, whom everyone called Dot, was a diminutive blonde who, like John's girlfriend Cynthia Powell, bore a striking resemblance to Brigitte Bardot, the French starlet who featured in both of the young musicians' most lustful fantasies. The product of an unhappy home—her father was a drinker, her mother emotionally distant—Dot shared the wounded feelings Paul had carried since his mother's death. She also reveled in the warmth and stability she found on Forthlin Road. Jim McCartney welcomed her into the family's extended circle, and she spent many evenings in their sitting room, watching her boyfriend, along with his father and brother, enjoying one another's company. "They would sing 'Baby Face' and 'Peg of My Heart' and would play Dixie-style jazz," she recalled. Paul could also be remarkably affectionate and caring, particularly when Dot needed to talk about her troubled home. They became lovers after a few months, and as they came to know one another intimately, Paul began to speak of his mother's death, and how he'd been so shocked to hear the news he'd burst into uncontrollable laughter. Yet the intensity of his love for his mother was clear—flipping through a religious book with Dot one afternoon, he paused at a picture and pointed to a portrait of Jesus Christ. "Paul said it looked just like his mother."

Paul was also a uniquely willful boyfriend, with strong opinions about everything from the clothes Dot wore to how she did her hair and makeup. He expressly told her to stop seeing her friends and forbade her to smoke cigarettes, though he was an enthusiastic smoker at the time. Dot, by her own admission, was just young and vulnerable enough to put up with such directives. She grew even more vulnerable when, more than two years into their relationship, she realized she was pregnant. She gave the news to Paul, who confided in his father. What should he do? Jim all but insisted—his son would do the right thing. His grandson would not be put up for adoption. On the contrary, Paul would face up to his responsibility, marry Dot, and start his family like a man. Paul agreed and took Dot by the hand to suggest they have a simple wedding in the Liverpool registrar's office.

But fate intervened. Dot miscarried the baby, and all talk of marriage came to a speedy halt. Though their relationship—during which time she and Cynthia paid a visit to their boyfriends during one of their Hamburg sojourns—Paul clearly felt no obligation to remain faithful. On the contrary, he cavorted his way through the Reeperbahn ("It was a sexual awakening for us," he proclaimed to his friend and biographer Barry Miles in the early nineties) and in Liverpool began an on-again, off-again relationship with Iris Caldwell, a professional dancer who was also the younger sister of Rory Storm. Intriguingly, Iris had little patience for Paul's more controlling impulses. "I'm a bit of a free spirit," she says.

Iris had met Paul a few years earlier, when Rory was still putting on parties at the Morgue, the not-quite-legal venue he was running when John had finally agreed to allow the impossibly young George Harrison to join the Quarrymen. Iris and Paul got to know one another as friends, so when they started to date, she wasn't the least bit awed or starstruck. And while she was willing to put up with some of her boyfriend's authoritarian pronouncements ("Being a girl of that generation, you dressed for who you went out with"), Iris rarely sat still when he got on her nerves. "We had the most wonderful rows," she

recalls. At a coffee shop with friends one night, she grew so aggravated by Paul's noisy impersonation of Quasimodo (adopted from
John's reflexive lampooning of the disabled, no doubt), she poured an
entire bowl of sugar over his head. She bolted out the door to avoid
Paul's wrath and woke up the next morning more or less convinced
that their romance had just come to a sudden, if memorable, end. But
Paul showed up for their scheduled date the next night, which surprised Iris so much she had to sneak into the next room to telephone
the boy she'd already agreed to start dating as a replacement. Who
just happened to be another member of the Beatles: George Harrison.
He got back at his bandmate a bit later during one of the regular late-
night get-togethers the Liverpool musicians held at the Caldwells'
house. Someone pulled out the family's Ouija board, turned out the
lights, and gathered everyone to see if they could summon a spirit
from the other side. When the pointer began to spell out a message
from the late Mary McCartney, her son sat bolt upright in his chair.
Right until George suddenly burst into laughter. He'd secretly been
steering the pointer with his fingers. "Paul jumped on him," Iris says.
"He wasn't very happy about it."

Iris had long since realized the imprint his mother's death had left
on Paul. "It made him very self-contained. He never mentioned her at
all and kept a protective shell around himself all the time." Instead,
she continues, he preferred to talk about music—about the Beatles,
where they were headed and how he was going to get them there. "He
always had his eye on the next opportunity, the big chance, whatever
was going to come around. It was a game for my brother, but with the
Beatles it was something else."

It was, in fact, the only thing. Paul ended his relationship with Dot
not long after she miscarried their baby. He maintained his friendship
with Iris a bit longer, but eventually that fell away, too. She could see
it coming. "He knew music was his life, and that was what it was
going to be. He knew he was exceptionally talented. He knew what he
was doing, and he knew how to keep it together."

No matter what they were doing, the Beatles made a point of being
distinctive. They dressed differently from the other bands, setting off
their matching leathers with black polo sweaters that owed more to

German art students than they did to Marlon Brando. John had long since abandoned Art College, but he continued wearing his school scarf, so much that other musicians began to wear the scarf, too, even if they had never attended a single class or even knew where the Art College was. The four Beatles tended to travel together and stuck together when they got to where they were going. Tony Sanders, of Billy Kramer and the Coasters, recalls the two bands sharing a closet-size dressing room that was so eerily quiet it reminded him of a silent movie. "It was as if it was orchestrated, this aloofness, maybe to create this aura," he says.

The group's look took another leap in early October of 1961 when John and Paul hitchhiked to Paris to celebrate John's twenty-first birthday. They bumped into one of their German friends, Jurgen Vollmer, and took note of his hairstyle. A lot of European students had taken to washing the grease out of their hair and letting it fall naturally over their ears and foreheads. Long conditioned to slicking their hair back, the British musicians were leery about abandoning their tough image. But Stu had already experimented with the new style during his last days with the group, and the more they looked at Vollmer—from his Cuban-heeled boots to his collarless Pierre Cardin jacket to his floppy fringe of hair—the more his avant-garde style appealed to them. They rinsed their hair, drafted Vollmer to perform some light barbering, and came home a few days later with a Beatles look that was even more distinctive than before. George, perpetually the little brother, adopted the new style within days. Pete opted to keep his hair swept back and piled high, a gesture toward individuality that he would eventually come to regret.

John and Paul were also canny about using the media to create and perpetuate their group's image. The most reliable weapon in this offensive was *Mersey Beat,* Bill Harry's newly fledged music newspaper. Harry had befriended John back when they were students in Art College. Eager to promote his friends, and to fill space in his paper, Harry turned over a significant chunk of his first issue's front page to John's "Being a Short Diversion on the Dubious Origins of the Beatles," a bit of absurdist autobiography that included the revelation that the group's name had arrived courtesy of a man on a flaming pie. Subsequent issues featured regular doses of John's writings (published semi-anonymously under the pen name Beatcomber), along with Paul-provided band photos (many of which were taken by Astrid in Hamburg) and his hand-scripted press releases about the group's latest engagements and achievements. These pictures, along with a small but insistent parade of fans in search of the "My Bonnie" single the Beatles had recorded with Tony Sheridan in Hamburg, brought the group to the attention of a local record retailer named Brian Epstein.

He was the twenty-seven-year-old scion of the NEMS family, a sophisticated and exceptionally organized man whose interest in rock 'n' roll extended as far as his professional obligation as a manager in his family's business. After hours Brian preferred to listen to show tunes and the pop standards of his youth. But Brian was also a closeted gay man navigating an aggressively homophobic society, splayed perpetually between desire, fear, and self-loathing. Sensitive and mercurial, his internal life was what you might call complex. As an aesthete with a consuming attraction to rough-hewn men, Brian's eye must have been drawn to the pictures of the leather-clad Beatles he saw in *Mersey Beat*, for which he wrote a regular record-review column. Brian might also have recognized the group members from their appearances in his store's record department, where they often passed hours after their Cavern gigs, flipping through the imports and cadging free listens in the booths at the rear of the shop. Brian took a particular interest in tracking down the group's German record, which was much easier to locate when he realized that the label credited them as the Beat Brothers, thereby avoiding the confusion of the English *Beatles* with the German *Pidels* (pronounced *peedles*), which was a schoolyard synonym for "penis." Intrigued and, it seems, titillated by the sharp aroma of danger, the bored young executive summoned the courage to venture past the rotting fruit scattered on Matthew Street and take in one of the group's lunchtime performances at the Cavern.

What Brian saw there riveted him. Standing alone near the soft-drink bar at the back of the room, it wasn't just the heat and lack of fresh air raising a flush to his smooth cheeks. Brian had studied acting for a time at the Royal Academy of Dramatic Arts in London, and the experience had heightened his intuitive sense of stagecraft. The passion in the Beatles' voices, the intensity of their playing, struck him just as hard as the group's look. The combination, along with their wit and intelligence, which he discovered when he finally spoke to them, proved catalytic. He needed to make these boys a part of his life.

"He came and told me he was going to manage them," recalls Peter Brown, a close friend who worked for Brian managing one of the NEMS stores. Brown already knew Paul and John as part of the regular troupe of kids who loitered in the store's music department. They hadn't struck him in any particular way. "John was interesting," he recalls with a shrug. "Paul was cute. But so what?" News that his friend and boss was planning to go into business with that particular quartet made a much larger impact. "I thought, *you're crazy.*"

Most of Brian's friends and colleagues figured the same thing. "You see, I'd lived through Brian's enthusiasms," says Rex Makin, a prominent Liverpool attorney who often consulted on Epstein family business. "I figured it was another will-o'-the-wisp." Nevertheless Brian persisted, seeing more performances at the Cavern, and venturing through the crowd into the cramped band room behind the stage to visit with the group. They were skeptical at first, as they always were with outsiders. But they were also impressed by Brian, who presented himself with a kind of upper-class elegance they would never have imagined seeing within the subterranean-jungle murk of the Cavern. Asked if they might be interested in his "looking after" their affairs, the group agreed to consider the offer. They hadn't had anyone working for them since Allan Williams had arranged their first Hamburg bookings. Mona Best was still happy to organize their schedule, but she was hardly a real manager. Jim McCartney's warnings that Brian might somehow take advantage of the band made as little impact as the realization that he was gay. What did matter was that Brian was wealthy and well connected and said he wanted to help them get famous.

They set a time after one of their lunchtime sessions at the Cavern to come in and sign Brian's contract (actually a boilerplate document Makin had suggested Brian procure at the corner stationery store), and all showed up at the appointed time. Except for Paul, who for some reason failed to arrive. Minutes passed. Brian grew antsy, then his cheeks began to redden. Where *was* Paul? A telephone call revealed his whereabouts: he'd gone home to take a bath.

"He'll be terribly late!" Brian fussed.

George shrugged. "Yes, but terribly clean."

It seems strange that Paul would have gone all the way to Forthlin Road—a good dozen miles south—just to turn right around and make the twelve-mile journey back to the city center. Tony Barrow, who soon joined NEMS as the Beatles' chief publicist, figures Paul's tardiness for a deliberate ploy. "A bit of a drama-queen move, making a late entrance with a feather boa." The motivations for which Paul made clear in a whispered conversation Brian reported to Barrow not long afterward (and which he says Brian's assistant Alistair Taylor, also at the meeting, corroborated to him separately). "Paul took Brian aside and told him, 'Whether or not this band makes it, I'm going to be a big star,'" Barrow says. "He said, 'The band is fine, if we all make it that's fine. But if we don't, I'm going to be a star. Aren't I, Brian?' And he more or less got Brian to agree."

Brian got to work and, using his leverage as his region's largest record retailer, quickly booked an audition for the group with Decca Records, at the company's studios in London. The session was set for the morning of January 1, 1962, and the Beatles were overjoyed. But along with this breakthrough they also had to acquiesce to a litany of their new manager's directives. There would be no more smoking, drinking, eating, or gum-chewing onstage. No more showing up to play in unwashed leather suits and wrinkled black T-shirts. The time had come for the group to invest in matching suits and ties, just like a professional band. They had to write out their setlists before shows and stick to them. When they finished a song, they should acknowledge the audience's applause with a deep, choreographed bow. "And we'd do it," Paul recalled. "It was show business, we were just entering the whole magic realm."

Brian also helped them choose the songs they'd play for the Decca artist-and-repertoire executives, steering them away from their hard-rocking setlist and toward the show tunes and cabaret numbers that revealed the diversity in their act. "September in the Rain," "Till There Was You," and so on. They played three Lennon-McCartney originals, but the ones they chose ("Love of the Loved," "Hello, Little Girl," and "Like Dreamers Do") betrayed barely a hint of the verve or originality their compositions would soon contain.

It didn't go well. The group was hungover, for one thing, having chosen to explore London's New Year's Eve celebrations until well into that morning. They sounded sluggish, which only made their strange array of numbers ("The Sheik of Araby"?) seem all the more unsatisfying. Nevertheless, the presiding engineer, Mike Smith, ended the session with a smile and a double thumbs-up, proclaiming that he couldn't see any reason why they wouldn't soon be recording. Unfortunately, his boss, Dick Rowe, thought otherwise, and after much hemming and hawing, he told Brian the bad news. The Beatles would not be recording for Decca Records. Brian vowed to keep at it, and to show his faith in his band he eased their way to their next two-month stand in Hamburg by paying for them to travel to the Continent in style, in the luxurious, speedy confines of an airplane.

The band and their manager were booked on two separate flights out of Liverpool, with John, Paul, and Pete arriving slightly ahead of George and Brian. Once in Hamburg, the first arrivals stayed at the airport waiting for the next flight to hit the runway, and when it drew near, they wandered back to the gate. When they saw Astrid waiting for them there, they came running up to her, joyous to see their old friend. How did she know they were coming? Where was Stuart? Astrid didn't say anything at first. When she could finally speak, her words literally knocked them backward with shock.

"John was just laughing uncontrollably, in hysterics. Pete was crying, he couldn't stop. Paul was just sitting there with his face covered by his hands and didn't say a word." It's all still vivid to her, nearly fifty years later. "It's terrible for young people, when death is so far away, and suddenly one of your best friends isn't there anymore."

Stu, she told them, was dead.

In retrospect it all made sense. He had suffered from headaches for years, sudden fits of debilitating pain that sent him reeling for bed. The attacks had been growing worse in recent months, often accompanied by mood swings and bursts of violence. Still, neither doctors nor X-rays could isolate the source of Stu's problem. Try to relax, they told him. What they didn't see was the small but malignant tumor lodged in his brain. It continued tearing a terrible swath in his life until April 10, when Stu collapsed in the room he shared with Astrid in her mother's home. An ambulance arrived, but nothing could be done. The Beatles' first bassist died on the way to the hospital, just hours before his old bandmates arrived at the airport. Astrid had gone to the airport to meet Stu's grief-stricken mother, Millie Sutcliffe. Eventually the families returned to their homes and Astrid would wake up alone in the mornings and confront the new, emptier life that lay ahead. For the next few weeks she came to count on Stu's old friends to ease her through the hours. "They really cared about me, we talked a lot about Stuart and cried together," Astrid says. "It was very hard for all of them, especially for John. You could feel the anger in that boy."

The weeks in Hamburg passed in the usual high-decibel blur of alcohol and amphetamine, and the Beatles spun home just in time to travel to London for an audition with Parlophone Records, a low-end label in EMI's vast stable of properties. The label's chief A&R man, George Martin, left the group with engineer Ron Richards, who was impressed enough to summon his boss for a listen. Martin was generally impressed with the group's playing. But he especially liked the Beatles' personalities—at least those of the three of them who actually talked. Pete tended to sit quietly, nice enough, but more or less impassive. Which reminded Martin of his drumming, which didn't quite have the snap and drive he was after. Extending an offer to Brian on the phone a few days later, Martin made no bones of this. The guitar players were fine, but Parlophone would pay a journeyman drummer to play on the Beatles' recording session. It wasn't anything to worry about, he insisted. A lot of groups worked like that. Pete could surely continue playing shows with the Beatles.

Except that the other Beatles weren't so sure about that.

Was Paul jealous of Pete's appeal to the Beatles' female fans? Did John simply grow tired of the drummer's lack of style and wit? Had George simply had it with the turgid beat and the lack of swing in Pete's rhythm? Or maybe it was Brian—everyone could see how much he disliked Mona Best's aggressive opinions about his handling of her son's career. The whole thing begins to look like an Agatha Christie murder mystery. Everyone had a reason to want Pete Best fired from the Beatles. But even decades later, no one has ever quite nailed down the real reason. Possibly because the answer is more like: all of the above. Pete was fine. A sweet guy, a decent drummer, a good human being. He simply wasn't one of *them*. The Beatles had become some-thing, and he wasn't it.

Pete's three friends, the ones he'd played with, slept with, suffered with, triumphed with, gone further than any of them had ever dared to hope with, didn't lose sleep over it. They merely instructed Brian to break the news to Pete in his office when the rest of them were a long way away. None of them ever spoke to him again.

A few days later the Beatles played a show for local promoter Sam Leach at the Tower in New Brighton, just across the Mersey from Liv-erpool. The switch had gone relatively smoothly—some fans chanted their complaints (Pete forever!) between songs; one went so far as to jab George in the eye, giving him a shiner that lasted a week. But by the time they got to the Tower, Rory Storm's drummer, Ringo Starr, had already joined up with John, Paul, and George. Pete had made the switch to Lee Curtis and the All-Stars, and when Curtis's band was scheduled to play the Tower that night, too, Pete's presence became a point of worry for Paul. The Beatles, he realized, would take the stage right as Pete and company were leaving it—this meant they would nearly collide in the wings, and who knew what would transpire? The worried Paul went up to Leach and asked a favor. "He said, 'Will you walk John and me onstage when they do the change?' I asked why, and he said, 'Pete might give us a smack.'" Like any promoter with a profitable attraction on his hands, Leach did as he was asked and ush-ered the two main Beatles as they came within a foot of their just-fired drummer.

"I knew Pete wouldn't do anything, he's a gentle guy. And when they did pass in the hallway, Pete just put his head down. And I just felt rotten."

The Beatles simply kept moving. They were already traveling far too quickly to waste time on looking back, and their journey was just beginning.

6

It's tense before the show. It's always like that no matter how many concerts you've played, no matter how far you've come. The expectant buzz of the audience, the echoes of the announcements on the PA system. Time intensifies as showtime grows near, the weight of expectations feel like a physical burden. All the more so for the four Beatles in the early evening of September 3, 1962, in the dressing room they shared with Billy Kramer and the Coasters, and Sonny Kay & the Reds at the cavernous Queen's Hall in Widnes, just outside Liverpool. You could see it all in John Lennon's face, in the unyielding set to his mouth, the slitted eyes that regarded the musicians buzzing around him, buttoning their shirts, knotting ties, strumming unplugged guitars, scraping combs across glistening heads.

He was standing in the corner watching Paul fluffing his hair in the mirror.

The Beatles were on top of the bill, almost certainly the top band in all of Merseyside. Now that they had been signed to EMI's Parlophone label and were to record their debut single the next morning in London, they were poised to climb even higher. Yet John didn't seem happy. Maybe he felt the pressure of great expectations. Maybe he was still a little anxious about the group's new drummer, and the chances that Pete Best fans might be out there, readying some kind of protest. Or maybe he was anxious about the threshold the Beatles were about to cross, and how things might change once they got there.

He was standing on his own, shirtless and silent, watching Paul tending his dark locks. He'd just had a haircut so it was particularly tidy around the back and sides. So collegiate, so prim. Just the way Jim McCartney insisted he keep it. John was shaggier. Defiantly so. Wasn't that what the Beatles were all supposed to be?

"That's a terrible fucking haircut, that, Paul," John declared, loud enough for everyone in the room to hear.

Paul, meeting John's eye in the mirror, shrugged. "Oh, it'll be okay when it grows out."

John's face was impassive. "That's a terrible fucking haircut, that, Paul," he repeated, a bit more loudly this time.

Paul responded again, his tone deliberately even, "It'll grow out, John."

Now the room was completely silent. The other musicians were only pretending to be preoccupied with their own business. John's eyes flickered around the room as he repeated himself, louder still: "That's a terrible fucking haircut, that, Paul."

This time Paul simply pretended he hadn't heard. After a moment John turned to Ringo, sitting cross-legged with his sticks in his hands. He'd only joined the group two weeks earlier and still looked a bit awkward in his new haircut and freshly fitted Beatles suit. John caught the drummer's eye and spoke with the same chilly tone he'd just directed at Paul.

"Hey, Ringo. There are two sets of our maracas on the stage. Go get them."

The drummer glanced around uneasily as all the ears in the room turned in his direction, waiting to see what would happen next. Ringo seemed stymied. Was he really supposed to leap out of his chair and do John's bidding? Sitting just to John's side, Coasters drummer Tony Sanders saw the guitarist's eyes narrow to slits. "He looked slyly to see if Ringo would comply," Sanders says. A tense moment passed, then Ringo climbed casually to his feet. Oh, he was headed to the stage anyway, he said. "I'll just fetch the maracas on me way back." John nodded, a small glimmer of satisfaction playing across his face.

"That was Lennon showing them, and everyone else in the dressing room, who was boss," Sanders says. "Which he always had to be."

Some days it didn't matter. John was more than happy to sit back and let the Beatles' busy bassist run everyone through their paces and get all the musical loose ends tied up. Specifics like that didn't interest John—he played by feel, not precision. But that same intuitive sense must have told him that he was the one who had created the Beatles. He drew the original Quarrymen together, then overseen the addition of Paul and George. Both were unlikely choices, given their ages and distance from John's usual Woolton stomping ground, but John had recognized their value and worked happily with them as the Quarrymen evolved from skiffle to straight-up rock 'n' roll. Adding Stuart had been an even less likely move, given his relative disinterest in music. But John's Art College roommate had helped coin the band's name, then drew John, and the others, toward an artist's aesthetic, allowing them to see (or at least intuit) that pop music could be just as emotionally and intellectually engaged as any other form of art. "I depended on him to tell me the truth," John told Beatles biographer Hunter Davies in 1967. "Stu would tell me if something was good and I'd believe him." When John passed the word along to the others—about their clothes, about their hair, about which songs they should play, and the spirit animating their music—they believed him and followed his example.

But as the Beatles' ambition pushed them onward, things began to change. The new direction, embodied so neatly in the mohair suits the band now wore onstage, had been dictated by Brian. But such traditional theatricality came less naturally to John than it did to Paul. All those years of hearing Jim's stories about Jim Mac's Band, and all those backstage jokes ("It'll go better second house!") had left their mark. Paul liked making people happy. He wanted to see their faces light up when he stepped on the stage. If that required a little sparkle on his end, well, he'd let 'em have it.

Years later John would recall this moment as a crucial failure for the Beatles. "I knew that was where we started to sell out," he said in 1970. Clearly, Paul was to blame. He had not only helped Brian convince the others to abandon their leather for mohair, but had also taken it upon himself to police the more recalcitrant John, personally buttoning his partner's shirt and straightening his tie before they went onstage. Paul even badgered John to get his hair cut before photo sessions. "It was a constant fight between Brian and Paul on one hand and me and George on the other," John complained.

That's how he remembered it, anyway. But his words, filtered through a particularly bilious moment in the Beatles drama, may have been fanciful. Alistair Taylor, an assistant to Brian Epstein who worked closely with the Beatles from late 1961 until 1969, had no memory of John complaining, or even appearing to be annoyed, when Brian shepherded the group to be fitted for matching mohair suits by custom tailor Beno Dorn. "There wasn't even a murmur of dissent," Taylor wrote in his memoir. Instead, the Beatles were tickled by the genteel surroundings of Dorn's shop and delighted as he bustled around with his measuring tape and notebook, taking precise note of their measurements. "It was a great day out, as the boys enjoyed being the center of attention," Taylor wrote.

Indeed, the appearance of the custom-tailored suits, and the manager who had both the money and the faith to pay for them out of his own custom-fit pocket, represented a significant break for the still-aspiring band. Years later, it may have seemed like something else altogether. But first they had to walk up the stone steps toward EMI's surprisingly elegant recording studios on Abbey Road in St. John's Wood and record their debut single.

The distinctions between the two central Beatles had seemed evident to George Martin when he auditioned the group in June. No matter how scruffy the band looked, or how substandard their road-battered guitars and cheap amplifiers were, the innate musical ability of the group's bassist was impossible to miss. "Paul was the one most likely to be a professional musician, in the sense of learning the trade, learning about notation and harmony and counterpoint," Martin wrote in his memoir, *All You Need Is Ears*. "He's an excellent musical all-rounder."

Martin was intrigued by how each member of the Beatles added his own distinct facet to the group. On virtually every level—musically, physically, intellectually—they stood apart from one another, even as they came together in what appeared to be a perfect kind of unison.

Martin was even more impressed with the group's wit and intelligence. He had produced comedy records for the Goons—a particular favorite of John's, and he had passed along his enthusiasm to Paul and the others—and when they spent their time together cracking jokes and pumping Martin for information about Peter Sellers and Spike Milligan, the producer was both tickled and impressed. "When they left to go home, George and I just sat there saying, 'Phew! What do you think of that lot, then?'" EMI engineer Norman Smith, who also worked on the session, recalled. "I had tears running down my face."

Martin's connection to the group's offbeat sense of humor, and his intuition that it could be just as important to the band's success as any other factor, presaged a litany of wise choices he made in the next few years. The first batch of original songs they presented him with, including "Love Me Do," "Ask Me Why," and "P.S. I Love You," were fairly typical pop efforts, offering little hint of what was to come. He was, Martin wrote, "quite certain that their songwriting ability had no saleable future." Still, the band played well enough, and Paul certainly had the sweet voice and the puppy-dog eyes of a teen idol. A more ordinary producer would surely have followed industry standard and rebuilt the group with its bassist standing in the front, and the others reduced to a backup group. But Martin resisted this impulse, already having gleaned that it was the balance of Paul's ethereal romanticism and John's earthy intelligence that lay at the group's core. "I would be changing the nature of the group. Why do that?" Martin wrote. "Why not experiment in pop as I had done in comedy?"

Indeed, with the Beatles in the studio Martin tossed all common sense to the wind. He prefaced their first recording session by handing them Mitch Murray's "How Do You Do It?"—instructing them to work up their own arrangement to a tune he knew had the bounce and hooks of a surefire hit. They sketched out their own version, tossing in a bit of John-and-Paul harmony, along with a bluesy guitar break by George, designed to give the song at least a little Beatles topspin. But the sweet little tune still curdled on their tongues, and when they kicked off the session by complaining that the song really wasn't, you know, *them,* Martin pulled rank. *When you can write something this good, we'll release that!* They got to work, laying down a dutiful, if not inspired, recording of the song. At which point Martin indulged the group's desire and recorded the Lennon-McCartney original "Love Me Do." This time the bluesy harmonica riff stuck in his ear, and when the band returned to the studio the next week, the producer had decided they were right. The original songs were a far better fit for the group than "How Do You Do It?" They rerecorded "Love Me Do" on September 11, and three weeks later it was released as their first single, with Paul's romantic trifle "P.S. I Love You" on the flip side. The Beatles'"How Do You Do It?" went into EMI's vaults, though their arrangement was used as a model for Gerry and the Pacemakers' version of the song, which climbed, as Martin knew it would, to the top of the charts.

"Love Me Do" came out on October 5, to nearly no publicity push from EMI. "The people down south simply didn't have confidence in the record," Martin wrote. The legions of Beatle fans in the north (perhaps including one in particular who may have bought thousands of copies either to sell them in his NEMS music departments or else to give the band he managed a lift up the charts) pushed the record into the *New Musical Express*'s Top 20, which was good enough to leverage the band onto a few radio and TV shows. An ill-timed final stand in Hamburg set for the second half of December got in the way of any further publicity they might have done for "Love Me Do." But a distinct buzz was building, so much so that when they appeared on a live radio show in late November, the announcer's attempt to herald the band with individual introductions got drowned out by the studio audience before he got past "Their names are John, Paul, and—"

"The audience went wild," says Tony Barrow, who was watching the Beatles perform for the first time since Brian had wooed him away from a post at Decca to be the group's chief publicist. "This was after 'Love Me Do' had risen only as far as seventeen. But the kids had already figured out the names of these guys." And once they started playing, and the chiming energy of the guitars met the melodic throb of the bass and the crack and boom of the drums, and once John and Paul lowered their shaggy heads and knit their voices together—their eyes locking, faces igniting in smiles that reflected all the excitement the audience felt, and then some—they became unforgettable.

For George Martin the catalytic moment came in late November when the Beatles returned to Abbey Road to record "Please Please

Me" as a follow-up to their first single. Martin had already heard and rejected the song back in September when John played it slowly, with the theatrical melodrama of a Roy Orbison song. Told to sharpen it up a bit, he'd taken it to Paul, and between them they'd worked out an arrangement whose colliding hooks—the descending guitar (later switched to harmonica) riff that kicked it off; the harmonized lead vocal; the insistent *Come on, come on*s that led to the sudden, ringing leap into falsetto on the chorus—made Martin smile at the mixing console in EMI's Studio Two. "Congratulations, boys," he called down when they finished playing. "You've just made your first number one."

He didn't know the half of it. Exactly a month after "Please Please Me" ignited on the British charts, the Beatles were back on Abbey Road to record their first full-length album, instructed to work as quickly as possible to get the album out before record buyers could forget how much they liked the single. So on the morning of February 11, 1963, the Beatles set up their gear in Studio Two just before 10 a.m. and set to blasting through an even ten songs, most of them covers they'd been playing live for months or years. Less than thirteen hours later the final chord of "Twist and Shout" finished reverberating, and they were done: an entire album (including the front and flip sides of the two preceding singles) in just a hair more than half a day. The haste didn't matter. The Beatles had been pent up for so long the music fairly exploded out of them. What begins with Paul's taut count-in—*One-two-three-FAH!*—veers from hard rock to satirical ballad to soul weeper to Brill Building lament to sentimental show tune and right back to straight-ahead rock 'n' roll, with barely a breath between the tracks. And no matter what they were playing, the Beatles injected the songs with a conviction that made it sound like some kind of newfangled gospel music.

The excitement in their playing, the wide-eyed *belief* in their voices, electrified the grooves. Paul's gleeful horniness in "I Saw Her Standing There" is magnified both by John's brilliant revision to the original lyric ("She'd never been a beauty queen" traded out for the far more lascivious "You know what I mean") and the howl Paul unleashes to herald George's raunchy solo. Ringo's drums find the perfect groove on "Anna," a gently rocking rhythm that consoles John's vocal before a sharp snare fill goads him toward the full-throated angst that erupts in the bridge. Paul can't resist the urge to scream for joy during George's solo on "Boys," while John injects "Baby It's You," "Misery," and "Anna" with an unsettling current of paranoia, heartbreak, and humiliation. *You should hear what they say,* he wails. *Everybody knows.*

On the surface it might have seemed like any other rock 'n' roll album from the era. A hastily recorded collection of cover songs, with a few random originals tossed in as a bonus, created for the sole purpose of skimming more money from the fans who'd bought the band's first, and perhaps only #1 hit, for which it was named. But carried aloft on the band's skill, determination, and raw, unyielding desire, *Please Please Me* became something else entirely. "An intimidating standard," writes the critic Tim Riley. "An enactment of rock's implications and the thrills it can achieve."

For Paul the implications went in every direction. The Beatles played constantly, still doing multiple shows on many days. When they were between gigs, he'd still have a guitar in his hands, working out riffs or, better yet, sitting across from John as they felt their way through another song. The road was the perfect environment for collaborative songwriting since they had so many hours on buses or in hotel rooms or dressing rooms, with nothing to do but talk about chords and melodies and verses that might lead into choruses. "Nose to nose," was how they both described it later, both men evoking the same image of themselves as boys in shirtsleeves and loosened ties, reveling in their ability to pull perfectly constructed rock 'n' roll songs out of the air.

Paul didn't stop there. He filled sketchbooks with hand-drawn logos for the Beatles to use—one of his drawings, a cursive script with the capital *B* sprouting a pair of buglike antennae, ended up on Ringo's bass-drum head for a time. Paul sketched ideas for custom-built guitars and did preliminary drawings for the burgundy suits with velvet collars the Beatles would wear through the first months of 1963. Somewhere between signing with Parlophone and the release of "Please Please Me" he spent hours kicking around names for the group's first album. His favorite was *Off the Beatle Track,* which ended up in the sketchbook over a tentative cover design that incorporated the antennae-equipped "Beatle" logo and individual portraits of the four Beatles.

What couldn't he do? Even then, Paul didn't seem to have an answer to that question. He proved himself even more proficient at playing the role of an up-and-coming celebrity. "He had an intuitive understanding of publicity," says Tony Barrow. "He took control of situations and knew how to put people at ease and give them what they wanted."

All of which became evident to Barrow just after that radio show performance in London. Barrow and his wife watched the Beatles play on the show, then went with the group, Epstein, and equipment manager Neil Aspinall to have a drink at the Devonshire Arms pub, just around the corner from the studio. While the other Beatles chatted among themselves, Paul sought out the Barrows and introduced himself. "He very impressively asked everyone, including my wife, what we'd like to drink. And it was all 'You'll have a double, won't you? *Go on!* Have a double!' He did this to everyone in the group, not missing out on Neil, the roadie." Paul relayed the order, adding in two packs of cigarettes (his brand, of course), to the waiter he'd beckoned over. When the waiter totaled the cost, Paul turned immediately to the group's manager, standing across the room. "Brian! Two pounds, fifty-three!" he called. Brian reached for his billfold and strode over, bills in hand.

Paul was just twenty at the time, navigating London and the demands of national fame for the first time. But as Barrow notes, he already had an intuitive sense both of the publicist's craft, and also the limits of personal contact. "He wanted to be seen as being very generous and benevolent. The trick is to appear to be giving all, but in fact not giving that much at all."

John, by contrast, spoke his mind and rarely minded what he was saying, no matter who was listening. Paul tried to smooth down John's rough edges or at least flash his smile and charm to cushion the blow. But he also got a thrill from John's jagged sensibility, and when they faced each other with their guitars in hand and a pen nearby, the combination of their voices and ideas shot sparks between them. "The audience was always in my head," John said. But while Paul wanted to romance the crowd with melody, John wanted to jar them—to tell them exactly how he felt and force them to feel something. "But it could be the other way round, too," Paul has often noted. "John could be very soft, and I could do the hard stuff." Paul's not wrong, though his insistence on making that point reveals something important, but what mattered the most was how the things that made John and Paul distinct from one another also drew them together and made them better. John's literary aggression goaded Paul's musical daring, and vice versa. The sheer momentum of the band, ricocheting from gig to gig to gig, jacked up the pace all the more.

And the more songs they wrote, the more daring they became. "From Me to You" featured an abrupt key change in the bridge, stayed put for eight bars, then leaped back to the original key under cover of a bracing falsetto *Woooo!* "She Loves You" went even further by beginning with the chorus, then working in a multitude of tricky and/or off-kilter rhythmic shifts and a veritable pileup of clashing major and minor chords, all of which was in the service of a love story the narrator was observing, rather than experiencing directly. Would teenaged radio listeners be able, let alone willing, to make that leap? *Yeah, yeah, yeah!* And it didn't matter if Paul's dad thought they should rephrase the song's verbal hook (too many Americanisms, he counseled. Wouldn't the tune work better with "Yes, yes, yes"? Paul laughed it off with a quick no, no, no). Working together, John and Paul's confidence as a songwriting duo was immense and growing. "I'll get you in the end," they sang. And they meant it, whoa, yeah.

But John and Paul weren't the only showbiz professionals with an appetite for success. So while the musicians focused on the writing and performing, Brian Epstein turned his thoughts to how the material they generated might be published and owned. He'd sold publishing rights to "Love Me Do" and "P.S. I Love You" to a company called Ardmore & Beechwood, but when the single stalled on the charts, Brian figured the publishers hadn't promoted the song nearly well enough. With "Please Please Me" recorded and poised for release, Brian followed George Martin's advice and took an acetate of the new single to Dick James, a singer-turned-aspiring-music-publisher, who liked it so well he called a producer at the *Thank Your Lucky Stars* TV show, held the phone near his record-player speakers, and put the needle down. Less than a minute later the producer had heard enough. "That'll do. They're on the show," he said. "Please Please Me" took off like a rocket, so Brian figured the balding, fatherly Dick James was the right man to help John and Paul tend to the products of their inspiration. James, Brian said later, had "a small office and huge integrity."

The idea Brian and James hit on was revolutionary for its time. Rather than selling John and Paul's publishing to Dick James outright, Brian worked with the publisher to create a new company called Northern Songs, the ownership of which would be divided not quite evenly between James's company (which held an extra 1 percent, and thus control over the company) and Brian's NEMS. Of the NEMS half, John and Paul would each own 40 percent, while Brian kept 20 percent. John and Paul were thrilled. "John and I didn't know you *could* own songs," Paul said. "We thought they just existed in the air."

Paul may have been naive about the business of songwriting, but he had a well-honed sense for how credit might be apportioned. Even in their earliest days he had taken a moment to scrawl "Another Lennon-McCartney original" at the top of the notebook paper. Even then they figured they would always attribute authorship of their songs to themselves as a team, just like Rodgers and Hammerstein. Those were the people who wrote songs for a living, and so that's whom they'd model themselves after. But whose name went first? As you might expect, it depended on which songwriter you asked. According to Bill Harry, who recalls conversations from the months in late 1958 when the Quarrymen had all but broken up and John and Paul were contemplating songwriting as their only career, their initial agreement was to flip the credit to reflect which writer had actually composed most of the song. "They'd taken a vow to split the credits," Harry says. "And it was already clear that Paul was the more ambitious songwriter." But John had ambitions of his own, and when the time came to affix a standard credit to the songs published by Northern Songs, Brian convinced Paul to let John go first. *Lennon-McCartney* just sounded better than *McCartney-Lennon,* Brian argued. Besides, they'd both earn the same amount of money on each song, the order of the names wouldn't change that. Paul acquiesced, though he later had reason to regret it. For one thing, he felt played. "I think [John] fixed things with Brian before I got there. That was John's way," Paul said. And then there was the agreement they'd made to flip the credit when it seemed like the right thing to do.

By 1963 everything was going right for the Beatles. The *Please Please Me* album was released on March 22 and reached the top of the British charts on May 11, where it remained for an unbelievable thirty weeks. "From Me to You" and "She Loves You" each crowned the singles charts for weeks at a time, and when the group's next album, *With the Beatles,* came out at the end of November, it beelined straight to the top, displacing *Please Please Me* and holding the top spot for another twenty-one weeks.

Then the mania began. Even now it's hard to describe, let alone analyze for root causes and social implications. But what remains clear is the phenomenon's suddenness, and intensity. The girls who flocked to see the Beatles onstage started going berserk. Where once they danced to the music and cheered for songs, they now leaped and screamed. The sight of the four lads, their suits and moptops so different and yet so alike and so cuddly, inspired fits of hysteria so intense—just listen to the wails and see how their extremities go rigid—it looked as if an electrical current had infiltrated their nervous systems. For some girls the presence of the Beatles was powerful enough to prompt them to wet themselves. Others had orgasms. Either way, one wag noted, the Beatles rarely left a dry seat in the house.

The newspapers called it Beatlemania, and for once the tabloid language actually seemed to fit. How else could you describe hundreds of girls lurking outside a theater door for hours, all of them waiting for a momentary glimpse of their heroes in motion? What other term could describe a thousand teenagers stampeding after a single, speeding limousine? If it looked absurd from the outside, the four young Liverpudlians at the center of it all could only gape in wonder. Wasn't it just a year ago that they were playing Chuck Berry songs for their friends at the Cavern? How many weeks had passed since they landed that precious, long-denied record contract?

The moment of realization—this is actually happening!—came on April 18, when the Beatles performed at London's Royal Albert Hall. The show was actually a two-part concert that included a live BBC radio broadcast and sets by Del Shannon and an array of other smaller stars. But the throngs of wild, shrieking fans were all crying out for the Beatles. When the four Liverpudlians did finally scamper out into the footlights, the screams hit them with the approximate force and volume of a hurricane. "That was really the birth of Beatlemania," says Chris Hutchins, then working as the music editor for *Disc* magazine.

The group was thrilled during the show, but felt a bit more taken aback when the crowds lingering outside on the sidewalk—all of them chanting their names and goading one another into new fits of shrieks, screams, and other ululations—blocked them from leaving the hall. They stayed in the dressing room for quite some time, chatting with Hutchins, whom they had met a few months earlier when he was accompanying Little Richard through Hamburg, and a couple of girls who had been part of the show. Previously John, Paul, George, and Ringo had hoped to end their evening at the Ad Lib club, a celebrity hangout that had lately become a favorite late-night stop. But as the throngs of girls outside continued to wail, they realized they had better stay out of sight. Hutchins invited the entire group back to his apartment on King's Road in Chelsea, so off they went, with the two girls in tow.

Hutchins's flat—he was actually a boarder with a one-room bedsit, but the owners were out of town—didn't have much in the way of party supplies. Hutchins broke out the two bottles of rosé wine he had in the kitchen, while John sifted through the apartment's medicine cabinets in search of pills. Unfortunately Hutchins didn't have much speed to offer, so the party made do with the lukewarm wine, sitting on the floor in the front room and chatting. But John, who had been counting on his usual industrial-grade doses of pills and booze, became antsy, then surly. One of the girls caught his attention, and things went downhill quickly from there.

They had all heard of Jane Asher. She was a TV actress, a petite, flame-haired seventeen-year-old with porcelain skin and the precise manners of the highly educated, middle-class parents with whom she still lived. She had been working as an actress since she was six and was a regular on the *Juke Box Jury* TV show, which is where the Beatles had seen her. She had spent the evening working as a sort of youth-scene reporter, interviewing the band for *Radio Times* magazine.

Whether it was her cool confidence or her posh accent, something about Jane goaded John to direct his caustic eyes in her direction.

"Well. Let's all play a question-and-answer game!" he announced a bit too cheerily. Then he turned to Jane. "So tell us, luv, how *do* girls play with themselves?"

Silence. Jane's eyes widened. Paul, sitting close to her on the floor, put his hand in the air, as if he could wave John's words back into his mouth. "John! John!" he yelped. "Stop it. You can't do that."

John just smiled, peering intently through his glasses. "No, you can tell us. Come on. We all want to know, come on."

Paul, looking aghast, shook his head vehemently. "John. For chrissakes, *John.*"

By now Jane was climbing to her feet, muttering icily that it had grown quite late, clearly it was time to go. Paul stood, too, glaring at John while he helped Jane into her coat, saying he'd see her into a cab. The pair of them walked outside quickly, the door clicking behind them. It was late by then, already after midnight, and the dark London air was thick with fog.

The cultured, self-possessed Jane Asher may have intimidated John Lennon, but she was exactly what Paul had been looking for. When Hutchins looked out the window, he saw the Beatle holding the actress's arm, walking into the mist. "And then he never came back," Hutchins says. "I just saw both of them disappearing down King's Road."

7

It was, by all accounts, a lovely birthday party. A beautiful summer afternoon fading into a blossom-scented evening. Auntie Jin had agreed to host the event, given the number of fans who had taken to lurking near the Forthlin Road house Jim McCartney still shared with Mike and, on the occasional night when he wasn't living the life of a pop star somewhere on the road or in a London hotel, Paul. So the invitations directed everyone a few miles east of Allerton to 147 Dinas Lane in suburban Huyton, where elaborate preparations had been made for an event that came to seem as much like a coronation as a twenty-first birthday party for a working-class kid from Allerton.

The guests started arriving in the early afternoon, and by teatime the house was packed with more than one hundred friends, family members, and music-scene figures. All the Beatles were there, of course, along with Brian and throngs of friends from the Cavern and the Casbah. New friends were there, too. Jane Asher made her Liverpool debut as Paul's girlfriend. A few members of the Shadows—then the nation's hottest band—came to pay their respects. Mike's new band, not yet called the Scaffold, were set to perform some bits of their comedy/music hybrid in the living room. The Fourmost, old friends who had just signed on as Brian's latest NEMS acquisition, were poised to lead the dancing in the basement. The food and cake were out in the wedding-style tent that had been set up in the back garden, and Paul held court with typical charm, his jacket off and vest unbuttoned, his tie loosened as he accepted all the handshakes, hugs, and congratulations. This was how Paul liked it best, to be at the center of things, where everyone could see and no one could really touch him.

"Paul always had this aura about him," says Fourmost bassist Billy Hatton, who had shared stages and late-night meals with the Beatles since the early weeks of 1961. "He'd have a laugh with you, he was lovely. But he always had this protective screen, like there was something he didn't want to tell you. If you got too personal, too close, he'd shut down."

The empty bottles piled up near the bars, the conversations grew louder, the laughter more boisterous. Then Cavern Club DJ Bob Wooler, glass in hand, edged over to John and made a crack about the guitarist's recent trip to Spain with Brian. "Oh, it wasn't a joke," the lawyer Rex Makin says with a chuckle. "It was an overture. Bob was gay. It was definitely an overture." Maybe Wooler was drunk. He certainly didn't realize how drunk John was, or how violent he could be when he'd been drinking. John punched Wooler in the eye hard enough to knock him down, then set to kicking him, cracking his ribs with the sharp toes of his Beatle boots. The tall, solidly built Billy J. Kramer swooped in to pull the white-faced, screaming John off the prone and gasping disc jockey, then Brian Epstein joined in to help scrape Wooler off the ground and take him to the hospital. But John was still drunk and, it seemed, even more belligerent, so when he saw an attractive woman talking to some members of the Fourmost, he stalked over and grabbed her breast. She slapped him, and in a flash John had decked her, too, and was just rearing back to kick her when Hatton stepped in to pull him away. For a moment things seemed about to veer even more out of control. Hatton, a muscle-bound drummer who outclassed John in height and weight, pulled his fist back. "I was going to rearrange his face for him," he says. In a flash, he felt a hand on his shoulder and heard a voice in his ear. *If you hit him*, the voice said, *the Fourmost are finished. And you lads don't deserve that.*

"The party was a little subdued after that," Hatton recalls. "Not totally spoiled, but it did lose its edge."

Not for the guest of honor, though, who merely pretended not to notice that anything could possibly be amiss. "Paul just let it wash right over him," Hatton says. "He was totally unaffected by it all."

The Beatles swept across England during the summer, pausing every so often to spend a few hours in the EMI studios on Abbey Road, laying down tracks for their next album. With *Please Please Me* still lodged at the top of the charts, they had the confidence, and the authority with EMI, to decide which image of them should adorn the album's cover. Rather than accepting the standard joyous/boyish pop-star portrait, they asked photographer Robert Freeman to re-create a shot Astrid Kirchherr had taken in Hamburg. So when *With the Beatles* came out, the moptopped heads on the cover were partly cloaked in shadow. Their faces were still smooth, their eyes hopeful. But none of the Beatles were smiling. A melancholy lay beneath their harmony, an acknowledgment of darkness that only made the light in their music that much more powerful.

And if the *Please Please Me* album had been the sound of teenaged anticipation, *With the Beatles* was the longed-for explosion. While the previous opening track, "I Saw Her Standing There," had Paul's *One-two-three-fah!* as a warning shot, the first notes of *With the Beatles* come out of the darkness with all the subtlety of a freight train rocketing out of a tunnel. John screams *It won't be long!* and he's followed instantly by the band at full throttle, pounding their instruments with a wild, yet measured, vengeance. The song is all about expectation, but this time deliverance is just beyond John's fingertips and headed his way. Paul and George echo him in a *yeah-yeah, yeah-yeah!* chorus, and the tune climaxes with an ecstatic cry: *You're coming home!* John shouts. *You're coming home!*

It's a thrilling song, all the more so for the undercurrent of helplessness in the lyric. She's the one who walked out; he's the one waiting anxiously in the empty home. John projects the same vulnerability into the herky-jerky rhythm of "All I've Got to Do," in which love stops and starts according to the whims of both lovers. Paul's "All My Loving" gestures toward melancholy with its tale of separation and yearning. But the music tells a different story as chiming guitars race after Paul's tumbling bass line with a gleeful momentum that grows positively ecstatic during George's Chet Atkins–inspired fingerpicked solo. By the time Paul works in a Little Richard–style *woo!* near the end, it's clear that the pain of separation means little compared to the joy of playing music to the shrieking fans who greet him everywhere he goes. He hopes that his dream comes true? Clearly, it already has.

John's voice dominates the album, as he takes eight lead vocals and leaves Paul to split the remaining six with George (who covers "Roll Over Beethoven" and "Devil in Her Heart") and Ringo (who gets his spotlight turn on "I Wanna Be Your Man"). Still, the contrasts between the Beatles' two central members couldn't be more vivid. For while John injects life-affirming passion into Smokey Robinson's "You Really Got a Hold on Me" and life-ending heartbreak on the Marvelettes' "Please, Mr. Postman," Paul's cover of "Till There Was You" from Meredith Willson's Broadway musical *The Music Man* is all chirping birds and breeze-kissed flowers. John turns bitter on "Not a Second Time," just as Paul's "Hold Me Tight" fizzes with all the bubbly joy of an overflowing soda pop. *It's you!* he cries in the chorus. *You! You! You!* But John has other ideas, and the record ends with a blistering cover of Barrett Strong's "Money," in which all the original's swing gets stripped out in favor of a brutal, full-frontal attack. *I wanna be free!* he screams near the end, and with the guitars, bass, and drums thundering beneath him, and Paul's and George's crazed war cries above, his is the very voice of liberation.

Yet it was a curious kind of freedom, since it came attached to such a lunatic kind of adoration. As the Beatles rode their popularity through England, playing show after show after show in the nation's local theaters and cinemas (often the largest home for traveling shows in Britain's outlying villages), they were on the road for weeks at a time, living in a netherworld of hotel rooms, dressing rooms, light-and-scream-filled stages, then a frantic journey through the fans back to the hotel. As seen by American journalist Michael Braun, who accompanied the group for much of the fall and winter of 1963–64, the Beatles grappled with their newfound fame with varying degrees of astonishment, glee, and frustration. In Lincoln, a hamlet in the north of Britain, the police smuggled the group into their own headquarters to allow them to change out of their stage suits. As they left, the local police chief stopped John and Paul in their car to get their signatures for his daughters. Both complied, and after handing back the auto-graph books, Paul leaned out the window for a final smile and wave. "Ta!" he called to the police. "Thank you! Thank you very much!"

John stared stonily forward. "Dirty sods," he grumbled.

A few days later Braun sat backstage with John and Paul, musing on the intensity of the following they had suddenly attracted. John mentioned that they'd been told that girls had been seen masturbating at their shows, leading Paul to interrupt him. "We're still at the mas-turbating stage ourselves!" he chirped. "I'm joking, of course." From there, Paul launched into a rambling discourse about idolatry, and being the subject of it. "I don't feel like I imagine an idol is supposed to feel," he said. "Anybody who gets this amount of publicity is in ordinary people's eyes a fantastic being . . . it's like the royal family. You have to like them because you've read so much about them."

John gazed back blankly. "Why? I didn't like *them* even when I was little. I disliked having to stand, which sometimes I didn't."

Paul went on, talking about how excited he'd been to meet Cliff Richard for the first time, even though he didn't like his music all that much.

"We still hate his records," John threw in. "But he's very nice."

While Paul was still enamored of famous people, and more than will-ing to perform the tasks of politesse his audience seemed to expect from him, he also reveled in the authority and influence his newfound fame granted him. "We intrigue people," he declared to Braun. "Quite a few people mention the word *genuine*—"

"Which we're not," John put in, making a reflexive attempt to de-flate his partner's self-importance. Except that Paul kept right on going, describing the difference between successful and unsuccessful artists as being a product of their "awareness," and on and on. When a Catholic priest visited their dressing room in Sunderland, Paul lec-tured the cleric about the inequity of having such a wealthy church in so many impoverished countries. When the priest pointed out how humble his own salary was, Paul responded defensively, "Well, *we* get the going show-business rates!"

Paul's friends had long since come to understand how stubborn he could be. "Like a dog with a bone" was how the Fourmost's Billy

Hatton, who over the years shared many dressing rooms and late-night dinners and pints, put it. "And if you could actually prove him wrong, he shut down. He didn't *like* being wrong." And the magic of being famous was how people either assumed he never could be wrong or simply didn't dare challenge him.

With one notable exception being the young woman he had chosen as his steady girlfriend. For while Jane Asher might have been nearly four years younger than Paul (in 1963 she was all of seventeen years old), she had already been in the spotlight for years. What's more, she came into the relationship from a far more sophisticated background. So when she accompanied the Beatles to Paris for their concerts at the Olympia Theater in the first weeks of 1964, she wasn't the least bit cowed by his sharp suggestion that she join the group in their suite at the George V hotel, lest she be recognized while coming and going on the street.

"That's just typical Paul," she scoffed to Michael Braun. "It's just that he's so insecure . . . the trouble is, he wants the fans' adulation and mine, too. He's so selfish; it's his biggest fault. He can't see that my feelings for him are real and that the fans' are fantasy."

Paul may have felt this way because every creative artist must live with one foot firmly in reality and the other drifting off somewhere into the ether of his own dreamworld. By the beginning of 1964 so much of Paul's real life had come to exceed even the most far-fetched fantasy he might once have had, it's hard to blame him for displaying more than a bit of hubris. Astonishing things were happening, so many it was difficult to keep up with them. In Britain *With the Beatles* had rocketed to the top of the charts, where it would remain until early summer. Though EMI's American label, Capitol, had turned up its collective nose at the Beatles for the last year, the label had not only agreed to release the group's most recent single ("I Want to Hold Your Hand") and a repackaged version of their most recent album (retitled *Meet the Beatles*), it launched them with a promotional campaign powerful enough to install both at the top of the U.S. sales charts. The group got that last bit of news when they were still in Paris, where part of their postshow antics included, on at least one night, an orgy with a collection of call girls John had dialed out for from the group's suite in the George V. *Disc*-magazine music editor Chris Hutchins was with them that night and recalls Paul looking "disgusted" by the sight of John peeling off hundred-franc notes and hurling them at the girls, shouting to his bandmates, "It's on me! It's on me!"

Hutchins left for his own room at that point, and when he returned in the morning, he found Paul to be the only sentient Beatle, entertaining himself at the piano that had been installed in the living room of their suite. After a while their publisher, Dick James, walked in. He congratulated Paul for the success of "I Want to Hold Your Hand" and said he was sure there would be more coming, the trip to the United States in a few weeks was certainly going to be a huge success. By the way, he added hopefully, had they written anything recently? Paul nodded. "I think he saw his chance," Hutchins says. "This wasn't something he'd want to play in front of John."

Paul prefaced his performance by telling James how he'd dreamed this melody one morning at the Ashers' house in London, then climbed out of bed and found himself playing it, finding the chords that fit the tune, hearing it come together almost before he'd become fully awake. It had emerged so easily, so fluidly, he assumed he must have heard it somewhere else. But he'd been playing it to a few friends, and none of them said they recognized it. He didn't have real lyrics yet, but just listen to the melody . . .

He began to play. Hutchins was on the sofa listening in and still remembers how strikingly beautiful the song was. The placeholder words Paul had were nonsense, something to do with scrambled eggs and some girl's lovely legs, but the emotion in the piece, the stark sadness that would inform the ballad that came to be called "Yesterday" was already obvious. And it didn't impress Dick James at all.

"Dick's face fell," Hutchins says. "And he said, 'Have you got anything with *yeah, yeah, yeah* in it?' And Paul was shattered."

Then the other guys were up, crawling out of their rooms in search of tea and breakfast. Paul deposited "Yesterday" back into his creative fantasy world, and it would be nearly a year and a half before he found the courage to play it to anyone again.

Paul's biggest fear, it seemed, was that it would all go away. The girls would stop screaming, the records would fall short, the magic that had come to surround them would somehow fade away. "He keeps saying he's not interested in the future, but he must be because he says it so often," the always perceptive Jane Asher said. And if Paul wasn't fretting about the road ahead, he didn't have to travel far to collide with someone else who was. When the Beatles taped a guest shot for a TV variety show hosted by the comics Morecambe and Wise, a producer noting the weeks looming before the show's actual airdate spoke openly about the risk of committing the airtime that far in advance. "Let's hope they're still popular then," he sniffed.

In the first weeks of 1964 most of the anxiety revolved around the group's scheduled trip to the United States. Their first singles had been flops in the world's biggest pop marketplace, even as they ruled the charts in England. This was due largely to Capitol Records' refusal to release the Beatles' music, and the minimal promotion and distribution networks belonging to the small, independent labels that did agree to release "Please Please Me" and "She Loves You." The situation began to change in the last months of 1963. EMI's British chairman, Sir Joseph Lockwood, insisted his American label—whose reluctance was fueled in large part by the recalcitrance of one jazz-obsessed executive, Dave Dexter Jr.—at least give the Beatles a shot. When the influential CBS-television host Ed Sullivan happened upon a riotous airport welcome for the group in London, he decided instantly to book them on his show. Brian negotiated a three-show package deal and set up three concerts in the Northeast and a few days off in Florida to fill the rest of the group's time. The stars seemed to be aligning themselves for an auspicious American debut, but the group continued to worry. Cliff Richard, then a superstar in England, had failed miserably in the United States, John noted grimly a few weeks before the trip.

Years later Paul would describe it all as being very deliberate. They had always said they wouldn't go to America until they had a chart-topping single, and, lo, "I Want to Hold Your Hand" hit the apex of the American charts just a week before they arrived. But of course they had committed to making the trip weeks, even months, before that single had been released, let alone reached the pinnacle of *Billboard*'s sales charts. Even that triumph did nothing to assuage Paul's fears as their Pan Am jet soared westward over the Atlantic Ocean on the morning of February 7. "Why should we be over there making money?" he grumbled to Phil Spector, who wangled his way onto the

flight to assuage his own anxieties (the terminally afraid-to-fly producer figured a Beatles airplane could never crash because they were
obviously lucky). "They've got their own groups. What are we going
to give them that they don't already have?"

Plenty, as it turned out. From the moment the Beatles set foot on
the tarmac at the recently renamed John F. Kennedy Airport in
Queens, New York, it seemed obvious that the same mania that had
afflicted the British youth and media had taken root in the New
World. Greeted by a large contingent of screaming girls, the group
was shepherded into a conference room for a brief press conference.
The notoriously jaded New York press corps may have come expecting to grind the limey pop idols into powder, but they hadn't counted
on the Beatles' intelligence, let alone their Liverpudlian wit. How do
you account for your success, one reporter demanded. "We have a
press agent!" Do they hope to get haircuts? George: "I had one yesterday!" The reporters roared with laughter, a sound that also signaled
an abrupt 180-degree shift in how they planned to write up the
group's arrival. John, Paul, George, and Ringo were herded into some
waiting limousines, and the entire flotilla set off for Manhattan. Someone had handed each of them a transistor radio shaped, inexplicably,
like a Pepsi machine, and Paul flipped his on the moment the car took
off, spinning the dial until he found a Top 40 station spinning a Beatles song. This turned out to be WINS-AM, the home of the wildly
ambitious disc jockey Murray the K, who was spinning Beatles songs
more or less constantly and would ingratiate himself with the band so
thoroughly that he would soon be broadcasting live from their hotel
room, declaring himself, without embarrassment, the Fifth Beatle.

More screaming girls greeted the band at the Plaza Hotel in midtown Manhattan. The unofficial, but loudly chanting, welcoming
committee stayed in place through the afternoon and into the evening,
and the Beatles spent much of their time peering down at them
through the curtains of their suite's living-room windows. "They
didn't care much about what was going on with people there, or what
was said, because they were all so fascinated with the teenagers outside," says Geoffrey Ellis, a friend of Brian's from Liverpool who was
then working for an insurance company in New York. When they
weren't checking out their fans, they were either listening to their own

songs blaring on the radio or watching clips of their arrival on the TV news programs, often, Ellis recalls, with the sound off so they could continue listening to themselves on the radio. "I got the impression they were enjoying it all," he says.

Perhaps Paul more than anyone. He kept his Pepsi radio close at hand, spinning the dial from station to station, perpetually in search of the sound of his own voice. The entire visit was filmed by documentarians Albert and David Maysles, and the resulting film reveals Paul's wide-eyed glee as he discovered, moment by moment, how triumphant the group's trip was becoming. He's perpetually conscious of the camera, at one point wielding his Pepsi transistor at the lens with a cheerful "For the continuity of the film I'd like to reintroduce the radio!" Walking back to the suite after the first *Sullivan* performance, he looks at the camera and announces, "I *love* this place, America!" The group goes out for a late-night visit to the Peppermint Lounge, and when they return to the hotel, Paul is so fired up waiting for the elevator to arrive, he paces in fast circles, his face lit by excitement. He seems physically unable to stand still. He's less animated on the train to Washington, D.C., a few days later, but that may have been because George and Ringo had taken center stage, delivering drinks and cracking jokes for a delighted press corps. When the Maysles's camera finally finds Paul, sitting alone in an armchair, he looks lonely and glum. "I'm not in a laughing mood, even," he tells the camera.

He should have been ecstatic. The 73 million Americans who tuned into the Beatles' first appearance on *The Ed Sullivan Show* saw a band that seemed to be dominated by its bass player. Starting with a tight version of "All My Loving," the group segued quickly into Paul's doe-eyed cover of "Till There Was You." At which point the CBS cameramen were so convinced that Paul was the group's front man that they continued focusing on him as he mouthed along to John's solo lines in the third song, "She Loves You." Near the end of the hour the Beatles returned for Paul's "I Saw Her Standing There," and the jointly sung "I Want to Hold Your Hand." John got more of a spotlight during the group's second appearance, filmed in Miami Beach a week later. But if the appearances hadn't deliberately been constructed to showcase Paul as the central Beatle, they might as well have.

The overriding feeling the Beatles projected across America during those two chilly weeks in February was a renewed sense of joy. It was in everything about them. In the sheer exuberance of their driving, melodic rock 'n' roll songs; in their cheerfully insouciant wit; in their wildly shaggy heads and the glistening velvet patches on the lapels of their matching suits. It was in the way they harmonized so easily and constantly, and in the way John and Paul smiled at each other over the microphone when they sang "This Boy" on the second *Ed Sullivan Show.* And it was in the way John concluded that moment of bonding by improvising a falsetto *wheeeeee* just before the song's coda, prompting Paul to step back, laughing helplessly.

No matter where, no matter when, they almost always seemed to be having a terrific time. Even when they weren't—such as at the British-embassy reception in Washington, D.C., at which drunken British socialites ran amuck—the Beatles were always committed to one another, unified by mutual purpose, delight in their achievements, and a very evident feeling of love.

What the Beatles represented, in short, was a resumption of the life that had vanished the moment John F. Kennedy had been so publicly murdered in November 1963. Obviously, a president and a rock band are two very different entities. Yet the feelings they personify—youth; vigor; detachment from a fusty past; the endless possibilities of the future—can be quite similar. So it came to be that where a youthful, seemingly magical president once stood now emerged a youthful, seemingly magical foursome. None of whom worked harder at, or took as much joy from, his own Beatleness as their boyish, beaming, and eager-to-please bass player. "Run, girls, run!" he'd yell from the window as a flock of girls chased the group's car through the streets of Manhattan. Paul stayed shaking hands and posing for pictures even after his bandmates had stormed out of that contentious British-embassy party. In Miami a few days later Paul leaned over the balcony to flirt with the girls shouting up to their hotel-room windows. "Which one are *you*?" he called down. When the chief of police invited the group to spend an evening in the relative peace and quiet of his family's home, Paul spent part of the evening reading bedtime stories to the man's small children. Not that he was above getting to know the local women, too. But now that the world was offering him everything, he couldn't resist any of it. So he took it all and kept moving in search of even more.

•   •   •

More and more and more, and all of it looked so effortless. The Beatles spent a few weeks acting as themselves in a cheaply made rock 'n'
roll movie that came to be called *A Hard Day's Night*. Produced
largely as a quick way to extend the Beatle brand into the movie business and, (more than anything for United Artists, which would own
the sound-track rights) serve as a delivery system for an accompanying
album of original songs, the film instead became a cultural landmark.
Written by Liverpool playwright Alun Owen and directed by expat-
American Dick Lester (who, like George Martin, won the respect of
the Beatles by having worked with the Goons), *A Hard Day's Night*
was a lightly reimagined version of the group's actual existence as insanely popular pop stars. They ride on trains, they jump into limos,
they while away the hours in luxe hotel suites and dash off to dark,
drafty theaters to prepare for a TV show under the gaze of a bitterly
condescending, yet deeply insecure, director. Old men try to insult
them. Showbiz industrialists treat them as a valuable, yet entirely in-
terchangeable, resource. Photographers singe their corneas. Reporters
rapid-fire ridiculous questions. Matrons flirt. Young women make
eyes. The police hector them. Functionaries order them to behave. The
irony being that the Beatles are the only well-behaved people to be
found: it's the rest of the world that's gone batshit insane.

Yet nothing can touch the Beatles. They're so perfectly hip, so assured in their own groove, that reality bends in their presence. Tormented by a cranky old man on a train, they appear magically outside
his window, running down the tracks and yelling sarcastically, *Can we
have our ball back, mister?* Ordered to climb out of his bath, John
vanishes beneath the bubbles, only to emerge fully dried and dressed
from the other room. When the world threatens to collapse upon
them, the Beatles simply sprint into the pure whiteness of the stage to
belt out a new batch of brilliant songs to a theater full of ecstatic,
wailing, young fans.

The London-based production moved quickly—shooting took six
weeks from start to finish—and the central problem was trying to remember where the surrealist movie about the Beatles began and where
the surrealist reality they actually lived in left off. Street scenes involving shrieking girls were often disrupted by platoons of other shrieking

girls; frantic chase scenes on the set became frantic chases away from a set that had become overrun with real fans. When Paul tried to give a ride home to a young actress named Isla Blair at the end of a day, their stroll to his car went terribly awry. "As soon as we got outside, to my extreme horror, we were attacked by fans," Blair told an interviewer. "They all wanted a piece of Paul, but they all also had their fingernails out for me, and I got scratched and kicked." When he offered her another ride home after their second day of shooting (their scene together was eventually cut), Blair waved him off. "I said, 'Actually, Paul, I think I'll get back on the tube,'" she recalled.

Shot for about half a million dollars, which was next to nothing for a movie budget even in early 1964, *A Hard Day's Night* was an instant hit upon its release in July, attracting throngs of typically excitable fans, to be sure, but also atypical fans such as *New York Times* film critic Bosley Crowther, who noted how the "rollicking, madcap fun" had been laid across a visual and narrative structure "more sophisticated in theme and technique than its seemingly frivolous matter promises." True, Crowther felt obligated to insert fingers in waxy ears against the music itself ("the frequent and brazen 'yah, yah, yahing' of the fellows . . . has moronic monotony," he declared). Less fusty viewers, including a variety of other movie critics, heard the music with a bit more appreciation. And no wonder; the songs John and Paul had written for the film, often while "resting" between takes, or at home in the evenings, were even more wired with feeling than the tunes they had written for *With the Beatles* just a few months earlier. From the alarmingly unresolved chord that hangs over the start of the title track (and the movie itself) to the too-successful-to-care celebration of "Can't Buy Me Love," to the wounded finger-shaking harmonies of "Tell Me Why," to the perilously balanced vocal duet that so clearly limned the romantic anxiety at the heart of "If I Fell," the movie songs transformed the traditional sub-three-minute pop song into an emotional canvas as broad and vivid as any movie screen.

John's emotions, anyway. "I think a lot of these songs . . . may have been based on real experiences or affairs John was having, or arguments with Cynthia," Paul said. "But it never occurred to us until later to put that slant on it all."

8

Back in Liverpool that summer for the regional premiere of *A Hard Day's Night,* the Beatles were greeted like saviors, their drive from the Speke airport lined with thousands of waving, cheering citizens— including, Paul was delighted to discover, his old literature teacher Alan "Dusty" Durband, who lifted his child to see his former student slip past in all his splendor. Onetime Quarrymen drummer Colin Hanton saw them go past, too, a shiny black blur with smiles beaming from behind the glass. At first he thought it was the queen of England. Then he saw a familiar face flash past and realized that it was actually his old bandmates, back in Liverpool to greet the hometown crowd.

Downtown, the mayor ushered them into the city hall, just a few blocks from the Cavern, and took them up to a balcony to wave to the cheering throngs. Some held leaflets that had been handed about by a disgruntled man who claimed his niece, Anita Cochrane, had borne a boy named Phillip, who was, she believed, the product of a brief liaison with one Paul McCartney. The allegation had dogged Paul for months, and true or false, Brian Epstein didn't want to risk the bad press, so he had earlier struck a quiet settlement with the young woman, amounting to three thousand pounds and no official admission of paternity from the offending Beatle. If Paul was aware of the flyer contretemps that day, the glow on his face didn't betray it. "They were flying high," recalls Roy Corlett, a Liverpool Institute acquaintance who had started working as a journalist and interviewed the band at Speke airport at the end of the day. Thousands and thousands of people were cheering their every move, but Paul couldn't stop talking about his old lit teacher. "It meant a lot to Paul that Alan Durband had turned out with his kids."

They were gone by the end of the day, back to London and the thriving career that would soon make parades and city-hall openings familiar rituals, even though few carried the emotional significance of that drive through Liverpool. The mania had wrapped around the earth, the scream came in every accent, dialect, and language. "They were so cocooned at the center of it, they wouldn't know the half of what was going on," NEMS publicist Tony Barrow says. "It blew all around them, but didn't have an impact on them directly, they were still their own little clique, comfortable in this hotel suite, or wherever they were." Or maybe not entirely comfortable, according to Brian's then personal assistant, Peter Brown. "It was just madness," he says. "The whole point was that it wasn't wonderful. What it was, was stressful, tiring, you were always running out. And they always had to be bigger and better than they were before, no matter what they were doing. So really, there was nothing wonderful about any of it except the results."

Indeed, the results—the money, the intensifying of the mania wherever they went—were rarely short of incredible. In America that summer for a monthlong, twenty-five-show tour, the Beatles tore across the country like a portable riot; hysterical and loud, far beyond reason, perpetually on the verge of destruction. Previews of civic unrest's coming attractions, perhaps, but no one knew it at the time. From a distance it was just strange and silly: a tumult of running, screaming, cheering fans, mecca-like scenes in the concert halls, the fresh-faced acolytes massing to unleash screams with the approximate pitch and volume of a dozen jet airplanes. Crazy noise, crazy adulation, and crazy maneuvers from the local authorities, many of whom actively competed with the other municipalities to provide the tightest, most precise security for the visiting pashas. They had everything, didn't they? The world at their feet. Yet, perpetually at a distance. Twenty floors below double-glazed hotel windows, whizzing outside the walls of the Brink's armored truck (or laundry truck, if they were being even more stealthy), somewhere past the ten-thousand-watt lights and wall-of-scream in the night's basketball arena. Seattle, Phoenix, Kansas City, New York City . . . it was all the same: they could look, but never venture outside, let alone even think about really experiencing it for themselves.

Everything, yet nothing. Scotch and Coke, whiskey, TV, records, endless cartons of cigarettes, one lit from the smoldering butt of the last. Some promoters made sure to throw in a good selection of willing women, some professionally engaged. Everywhere, eager fans, proto-groupies, all of them wide-eyed and moist-lipped, so extremely eager to please in every way you can (and possibly can't) imagine. "Just think of *Satyricon* with four musicians running through it," John snorted in 1970, referring to Federico Fellini's adaptation of Petronius' ancient sex novel. He may have been overstating the case. Or possibly not.

"Paul was wild," recalls Chris Hutchins, by then at the *New Musical Express,* who both wrote about and partied with the Beatles throughout the tour. "He was lovesick for Jane, pining all across the country. But that didn't mean he wasn't going to get his rocks off wherever he could." Paul admitted as much in the early nineties, noting that the Beatles tours turned the musicians into "trawlers, trawling for sex, everywhere we went it was on our minds." Just like any other twenty-two- or twenty-three-year-old male, it seems. Except these particular males were the most popular band on earth, which made the seduction fairly instantaneous. The fun began at the tour's first stop in San Francisco, but when Hutchins foolishly mentioned this to an editor at his paper, and that guy turned it into a puckish brief on the gossip page (Hutchins recalls it as something like "Paul McCartney left his tart in San Francisco . . ."), the musician responded angrily, noting the potential hurt to his beloved at home in London. "He didn't speak to me for days afterwards," Hutchins says.

Eventually Paul forgave Hutchins, and life resumed as normal. Or abnormal, really, given the sonic screamscape and Technicolor blur. Days dragged together, time stopped, reality collapsed, imaginations raced. Unable to actually *do* anything, it was easy to feel capable of everything. For instance, Hutchins had not only met Elvis, but was still friendly with the Messiah's carny-style manager, Colonel Tom Parker. Paul's eyes lit up when he heard that: "Well, can you fix that for us, too? Without Elvis there'd be no Beatles!" Unfortunately, the King was terrified of his new competitors, and when the 1964 tour hit Los Angeles, Hutchins called Parker, only to learn that Elvis had just left town for Memphis. John was so insulted he refused to call the number Parker had passed on for a quick telephone greeting from their hero. Paul gladly did the honors, enjoying a brief, stilted dialogue that revolved largely around what Elvis was doing just then (watching a movie) and how Paul had been a fan forever. *I've got all your records!* Hutchins recalls hearing the British pop star chirp. "He was being the diplomat, as ever."

They kept moving. More screams, more flashbulbs, more acclaim. Paul reveled in it all, glowing in the spotlight as if it sustained him. To see him there, to hear him chatting up the crowd, was to recognize the features of a man completely at home in the current of adoration. John's smile, meanwhile, had taken on an acidic edge. To him the mania had grown toxic, the spotlight sizzled against his skin and made him angry. He confronted audiences with his legs spread wide, his weight balanced as if poised for a fight, then belted out his songs with fierce dedication. But no one was listening, really, so between tunes he'd stumble around the stage like a drunken cripple and speak to the audience in gibberish. What difference could it possibly make? When the hotel-suite door flew open in Las Vegas one afternoon, disgorging a chatty girl who explained her abrupt appearance in the Beatles' sanctum by proclaiming, "I'm Donald O'Connor's daughter!" John didn't skip a beat before extending his most sincere condolences. "I was just hearin' on the radio about your dad's being dead." Young Miss O'Connor collapsed into tears and had to be hustled out, reassured, apologized to, and steered back toward home and her distinctly *not* dead movie-star father, while Paul launched into his partner in no uncertain terms.

"John, fucking hell! You can't *do* that!"

But John was having none of it. "I'm fuckin' sick of everyone comin' in, I'm the lord mayor of this, I'm the daughter of that—I don't give a fuck! I'm John Lennon!"

What John didn't understand was that Paul did care. A lot. Because *he* was Paul McCartney. And P. McC knew all too well why that was important, and how quickly it might cease to matter altogether once the world's moist-eyed teenaged fans—including young Miss I'm Donald O'Connor's Daughter—lost interest. "We've *got* to behave," Paul shot back, gesturing urgently at the luxe room around them, the fans beyond, the adoration everywhere they went. "Or we're gonna lose all this!"

Nat Weiss, a lawyer friend of Brian Epstein's who handled the Beatles' legal work in the United States for many years, still remembers how eager Paul was to meet with local representatives from the Beatles' fan-club chapters, no matter where they happened to be: Detroit, Des Moines, wherever. "It was like his career depended on it, it was amazing how overboard he'd go," Weiss says. "Lennon was the exact opposite. He didn't want to see reporters, didn't want to see fans, used to go nose to nose with Brian arguing about it. He'd refer to them as 'fascists' and be very tough. When people used to give the Beatles presents—dolls and things—he'd actually throw it right back in that person's face. Didn't want to be bothered. But he felt he was just being honest."

Hutchins saw them in exactly the same light. "Lennon got looser and looser and more crazy and wild. He was great fun. Paul was the guarded one. A bit boring, really. Always trying to rein John in."

Not that Paul didn't enjoy letting himself go, on occasion. The fabled hotel-room summit with Bob Dylan during their visit to New York in August sparked an affection for marijuana that would soon become a life-altering passion. But while the other Beatles, and particularly John, seemed most eager to escape the pressures of fame and adulation, the drug only made Paul's eyes gleam more brightly. The freshly stoned twenty-two-year-old summoned group minder and Liverpool regular Mal Evans over and instructed him to bring a pen and paper. Wisdom! He'd found wisdom! "I discovered the Meaning of Life. And I suddenly felt like a reporter, on behalf of my local newspaper in Liverpool." Paul went on for hours, declaiming his insights. He then woke up the next morning and consulted his pad of Deep Thoughts, and the only thing he could make out was one curious assertion: *There are seven levels.* "We pissed ourselves laughing," he remembered. "I mean, what the fuck's that? What the fuck are the seven levels?" What, indeed? Though by the time he relayed that anecdote to Barry Miles, three decades of fame and 3 million joints (give or take) later, Paul felt obligated to point out the innate brilliance in his stoned reverie. "It's actually a pretty succinct comment; it ties in with a lot of major religions, but I didn't know that then." Your guess here is as good as mine.

When the group returned to America for a shorter, yet just as hysterical, run through basketball arenas and stadia during the late summer of 1965, Paul was once again in his element, dashing onto the stage, beaming happily into the spotlight, belting out his hits into the fathomless scream and riding the jet stream of the mania he had helped to create. He lived on it, yet it hardly seemed to affect him. "Paul was really the most normal of the four," Tony Barrow says. "Yes, he was very self-centered, a control freak, more than the others. But as a guy while John had these extraordinary eccentricities based on personal fears of inadequacies, Paul had no such fears. He was *extremely* adequate, as far as he could tell."

Which may have been why Paul was so enthusiastic about meeting Elvis in person on that 1965 tour, when the Messiah finally deigned to allow himself to be approached by his British-acolytes-turned-competitors. Hutchins brokered the meeting with all the shuttle diplomacy that goes into an official state visit. Hutchins's first step was arranging a lunch between Parker and Brian Epstein at the Beverly Hills Hotel. The conversation almost ended when they couldn't agree exactly *where* the summit should take place. The Beatles, Brian insisted, required too much security to move beyond the perimeter of the house they'd rented in Benedict Canyon. But Parker wouldn't budge: "No way. They come to Elvis. If we were in your country, we'd come to you!" Brian came to see the logic in that, and eventually the deal was struck for the group's final night in Los Angeles. The Beatles would go to Elvis. They could bring only Brian, Hutchins, Neil, Mal, and Tony Barrow. A pair of limousines showed up at the Beatles' house on time that night, but there was just one problem. John announced that he, for one, was staying in.

"He was dragging his heels, he really didn't want to go," Hutchins says. "But Paul couldn't wait to get into the car." John finally bowed to the inevitable, and they all shared a joint on the twisty hilltop roads

to Elvis's house in Bel Air. When they poured out of the car, they were
all happy and giggly, but the vibe grew far more stilted after they rang
the bell and were led into the living room, where they found Elvis sitting on the sofa, his dyed-black hair lovingly shellacked, his collar
turned up, surrounded by his usual Memphis crew and a bunch of
girls no one bothered to introduce. John greeted his onetime idol, for
some reason, with the same German accent Peter Sellers had used in
the title role of *Dr. Strangelove.*

"So, ziss is zee famous Elvizzz!"

Elvis nodded, but nothing in his expression seemed even remotely
tickled. Then John's eyes fell on a gaudy lamp sitting on the end table.
Shaped like a covered wagon, it had *All the Way with LBJ!* inscribed
on its side, a souvenir from the president's victorious 1964 campaign.
That's when John brought up the gruesome war in Vietnam. How,
John wondered, could Elvis support a president who was actively killing people in Southeast Asia? The air in the King's living room grew
suddenly icy. "Elvis had been in the army, he was having none of it.
And it began to get very heated," Hutchins recalls. The mood only got
sharper when Priscilla glided in, makeup just so; her hair piled high on
her head. John started rather obviously making eyes at her, turning on
his Liverpool Art College charm. "Anything to irritate Elvis,"
Hutchins continues. The evening, it seemed, was about to erupt into a
full-on ego firefight. But then, salvation, in the only terms they could
all understand. Hutchins again: "Finally, Paul said, 'Can we play some
music?'"

Happily, Elvis had thought to bring in some guitars. He apologized
to Ringo for not having drums, but the King picked up the Fender
bass he had next to him, and they started in on a few songs. The Beatles' most recent single, "I Feel Fine," was first, then some R & B favorites. With Elvis on (rudimentary) bass, Paul alternated between
guitar and piano. "Ringo beat out a backing rhythm on a coffee table
and a chair before packing that in to go play pool with the Memphis
mafia," recalls Tony Barrow. "They were harmonizing, they all knew
the songs," Hutchins says. Rock tunes. Country tunes. Elvis with
three-part Beatle backup vocals. "It was a bit stilted, mood-wise, but
John was enjoying it, the singing," Hutchins says. "When we were
leaving, Parker said to me, 'You tell the world they had a great time!'

But Elvis told me later that he blamed me for setting it up. And then he conducted a merciless campaign to get John thrown out of the country. Him and J. Edgar Hoover. And that famous meeting with Nixon? He was trashing the Beatles there, too."

Elvis had seen his doom, of course. Probably from the start, but the picture had to have been especially vivid during the summer of 1965, just after the Beatles had played their astonishing concert to a sold-out, all-but-levitating Shea Stadium in New York City. It was, to that point, the biggest, most spectacular show in the entire arc of American popular culture. To Geoffrey Ellis, recruited to NEMS by Brian, and just then watching from the packed stadium's infield as the Beatles descended from the night in a helicopter, the moment was nothing short of breathtaking. "The audience rose and screamed as the heli-copter came down, and I had this fantasy that they were gods de-scending to the earth," he says. "The same thing happened when they left. The kids screaming and waving, having paid their tribute to the gods, literally, in cash. And I remember at the end, walking away and talking to a friend, and these girls overheard me and were yelling, '*Ah! He's English!*' I denied knowing the Beatles because I had the impres-sion that if I did say I knew them, I would have been torn apart my-self. It was a very strange experience."

Yet it was the only life Paul McCartney knew or even wanted to imagine. He personified the Beatle image from the toes of his boots to the mop of shiny black hair that framed his sweet, boyish face. He was, Tony Barrow recalls, a publicist's dream client, with an encyclo-pedic knowledge of American fan magazines and a ready expertise on how to transform static photo setups into energetic displays of charac-ter and feeling. "He'd coerce the others to do one last photo or answer one last question. 'We really ought to do this one, lads, just because *you* haven't heard of that magazine doesn't mean it's not important!' The others wouldn't have a clue, but he knew *16 Magazine* sold con-cert tickets and records." No wonder Paul was so often the last Beatle to check his hair in the mirror before a shoot, and the first one to ask that the images be sent to him for his approval. Off-the-charts success had clearly done nothing to shrink his ego. But it had also come to define him. More than a job, being one of the four Beatles had become the dominant part of his identity. Certainly Paul knew he was a talented, even a brilliant, musician and songwriter. But without the band, without the image they had together and the success it brought him, it was hard to imagine where he might have ended up.

"Neil Aspinall used to explain that it was John's band," says Nat Weiss. "And at that point [in the midsixties] Paul was very conscious of wanting the approbation of John, in anything he did. I think Paul felt John was the cool one, the avant-garde one, the true artist. Paul is basically a very bourgeois, middle-class person. Extremely talented, for sure. But the rebel was John. He was the one who had created the Beatle image. Whatever they were, he created it."

The Beatles' London crash pad was on Green Street in Mayfair, a nice neighborhood near the edge of Hyde Park. Brian had leased the flat for them in 1963 when it became obvious that the band's suddenly thriving career would be keeping them in the city for days, sometimes weeks, on end. Which made for a better idea than an actual place for four men in their early twenties with barely any experience (let alone interest) in housekeeping to live. As if they might actually have the time to decorate the place. Almost completely unfurnished, the flat only had a kettle for tea. If they had teacups in the kitchen, the Beatles certainly didn't have a dining-room table upon which to rest them when they had their morning cuppa.

For Paul, a boy who had long since come to identify *hominess* with home, the Mayfair flat was a nonstarter. Instead, he made for London's West End and the home Jane Asher shared with her family. He'd come for a late-night meal prepared by the family matriarch, Margaret Asher, and sit holding hands with Jane in the living room. The hour would grow late and Mrs. Asher would tell Paul not to bother heading home, just stay the night in the guest room. Then he could wake up to a home-cooked breakfast, and a nice kitchen-table chat with the sweetly maternal Mrs. Asher. The routine became so standard that after a month or two she simply told Paul to move in. He didn't have to be asked twice. Here, in the Ashers' five-floor Georgian row house at 57 Wimpole Street, Paul set out to become the sophisticated, well-to-do adult he'd always imagined being.

Eventually the other Beatles would buy homes in the London suburbs, out in leafy, golf-course-centric developments where the city's stockbrokers and successful barristers raised their families and sipped their martinis. But Paul, for reasons that had as much to do with his intellectual aspirations as they did with his unending appetite for social stimulation, was having none of that. Though he has often been described as socially ambitious or simply bourgeois, nothing about the Asher house was stuffy. The family patriarch, Dr. Richard Asher, was a prominent psychiatrist whose best-known medical writings were about the dangers of going to bed and the deadly dullness of most medical writing. He kept his practice in the family home's ground floor (common for doctors in and around the Harley Street area), where he tended to his patients across from the music room where his wife, Margaret, a professional oboe instructor, tutored her students. A classically trained musician, Margaret Asher was also a registered member of the peerage and eminently patient with the ways of her husband, whose personal habits were often puzzling. He liked to wear a blue boiler suit around the house and would often undertake heavy household labors in the middle of the night. When he painted the stairwell, each floor got its own color—Dr. Asher had procured a box of remainders at a drastic savings. His sense of humor was notorious. He liked to give himself injections at the dinner table, in the back of the neck, when company was at the table. When a crack developed in the old house's stairwell wall, he pasted a piece of paper across it with a handwritten note: *When this paper tears, the house will fall down.*

Mrs. Asher had taught oboe and recorder for years; Beatles producer George Martin had studied with her during her days teaching at the Guildhall School. All of the fair-skinned, flame-haired Asher children attended topflight private schools, where they were educated alongside the children of London's other socially prominent families. But once school let out, the Asher kids usually had professional engagements in show business. Born in 1944, eldest child Peter first acted professionally at eight years old, with a role in a film called *The Planter's Wife*. A recurring role in the ITV television series *Adventures of Robin Hood* was the high point of his career, at which point his star was eclipsed by middle-child Jane (born in 1946), who earned her first credits at six years old and worked consistently in British films and TV from then on. Youngest-child Clare (born in 1948) took roles on radio dramas, and by the early sixties Peter had refocused his ambitions on music, performing as one-half of a folk duo with his schoolmate and chum Gordon Waller. "There was always something going on at the table," says Waller, who was a frequent guest. "They played word games and bickered about eccentric things."

In retrospect it seems like the setting for some kind of drawing-room comedy—this aristocratic family where the dad's a doctor, mum's an academic, and the school-aged kids double as famous actors and musicians. Then the front door opens and, *Hallo!*—it's the upstairs boarder: one-quarter of the most famous rock band on the face of the earth, just back from a day of filming the group's first movie! And he fit right in! "He was a well-informed, a very talented guy," Waller says. "We all became good friends." Jolly good, that.

In his role as the Ashers' bonus child, Paul had moved into a tiny chamber (a disused maid's room) in the attic, next to the much more spacious front room Peter had made his own with a hi-fi, an enormous stack of records, a few guitars, and enough Stolichnaya vodka to keep the late-night chat sessions going well past midnight. Paul's far more cozy room held a small, iron-framed bed, a bureau, his pair of Brenell tape recorders, and usually a guitar. When the fans tracked the cute Beatle down to his new address and took to lurking at the doorstep and baying for his attention at all hours, the ever-inventive Dr. Asher developed a secret escape route for his daughter's famous boyfriend, a vertiginous crawl out of his bedroom window, across a thin stone parapet into the window of the top-floor flat of a retired army officer next door. "Coming through, Colonel!" Paul would call through the window, and the elderly gent would let him in and show him to the elevator, which Paul rode to the bottom floor, where a young couple let him into their kitchen, then out through the garage door. When he noticed the couple didn't have a refrigerator in their kitchen, Paul had one delivered as a thank-you for their help. "It's quite funny to think now of some of the people I met doing that," he said.

As time passed, Paul's tiny room became a tumble of books, a few small prints for the wall, and a growing pile of unread, unanswered mail. His framed gold records were stacked under the bed, while his Höfner bass (in a black, hard case with BEATLES stenciled across its top) leaned against the wall in the corner, though Paul kept most of his instruments and records in Peter's room. When Paul had free time, he'd be in there, strumming his guitar or listening to records or, typically, both. He scratched away at songs, and when John came over to write, Paul would join him in Mrs. Asher's basement music room, where they could work in solitude. The first song they completed there was "I Want to Hold Your Hand," in late 1963. Years later John still recalled the moment Paul had discovered the unexpected minor shift (the part in the verse where the lyrics go *underSTAND*) that made the song come to life. "Paul hits this chord and I turn to him and say, 'That's *it!*'" John told *Playboy*'s David Sheff in 1980. "I said, '*Do that again!*'"

They wrote a lot of the *A Hard Day's Night* songs in the music room, and as their career picked up steam, and their frenetic work schedule grew all the more so in 1964, many of the songs that would end up on the group's next album, the somewhat ironically titled *Beatles for Sale*. The rapidly accruing exhaustion seems most apparent on that album, with its rich variety of cover songs, most taken directly from the old Hamburg-era setlists, and a scattering of originals that seemed inspired more by the demand for product than the artistic muse. Yet each song came with a distinctive twist—a seething lyric here, a surprising sonic texture there, chiming harmonies and soaring melodies virtually everywhere. *Beatles for Sale* is generally accepted as one of the group's least-impressive original albums. But just listen.

The opening set of John Lennon–dominated songs begins with a cinematic tale of romantic betrayal and public humiliation ("No Reply"), then segues into a piercing, Dylan-esque confession ("I'm a Loser"), before ending with "Baby's in Black," a darkly comic waltz about a man whose romantic intentions are stymied by his beloved's ongoing attachment to a recently departed, perhaps deceased, lover. John rips the stuffings out of Chuck Berry's "Rock 'n' Roll Music," clearing the air for Paul's "I'll Follow the Sun," a pretty bit of juvenilia with perhaps the most unappealingly passive-aggressive lyric he, or anyone else, would ever write. The singer is contemplating leaving, you see, but only because his beloved doesn't appreciate him enough. She'll realize her mistake eventually, he assures her. When, and if, he drifts away into the sunset. *And though I lose a friend,* he croons, *in the end you will know.* Or maybe she already figured out everything she needs to know, which is why she's pointing him toward the door.

It's all uphill for Paul from there, though, starting with his screaming run through another Little Richard tune, in this case the pompadoured master's arrangement of Leiber and Stoller's "Kansas City." The next tune, "Eight Days a Week," started life as an offhand comment from a limo driver Paul once engaged to drive him out to John's house in Kenwood. How hard had the man been working? More than humanly possible, the man said, employing a turn of phrase ("eight days a week, guvnor") that in turn inspired an impossibly bouncy pop song that transcends its giddiness with an innovative fade-in opening, unexpected chord changes, and vocal harmonies that ring with excitement. A feeling that emerges less from the singers' feelings for the (barely sketched) girl in the song than, one thinks, from the sheer pleasure of being able to write a song as good as this in less than three hours, then perform it with such energy and joy. For what began with a shared affection for the songs of Buddy Holly (whose "Words of Love" they cover as a duet in the next track) had somehow transformed John and Paul into achieving something beyond even their farthest imaginings. More than professional songwriters and musicians, they had, in extremely short order, become the leading songwriters and musicians of their generation.

They made it look so easy. John's "Every Little Thing," invested with Paul's soaring melodic line and thundering timpani, is equal parts joy and contemplation. Paul's deceptively cheerful kvetch "What You're Doing" starts with four bars of unadorned drums, then layers on jangling lead guitar, a shouting, humming chorus of backing harmonies beneath a melody that flirts with the blues, before diving headfirst into straight-ahead power pop. *Should you need a love that's true,* he declares, pausing for a moment as the instruments hold for a long, unaccompanied vocal glide down to the song's root note, *it's meeeeeeee.*

The cover of *Beatles for Sale,* shot in the early fall of 1964, describes the downside of fame in the musicians' bleary eyes and windblown hair. But photographs taken in EMI's Studio Two during the sessions (and published most visibly on the back cover of the album's

American counterpart release, *Beatles VI*) portray the group as the wildly innovative hitmakers they had become. John looking like an upmarket Dylan in impenetrably dark Ray•Bans and a sharp polka-dot shirt; Paul perched at the grand piano, beaming warmly at the camera; a more pensive George cradling an electric twelve-string guitar; while Ringo, still in his overcoat, hits his cue on the timpani. The four faces of effortless cool, making it all look not just easy, but incredibly *fun*. They were already on top of the world and nowhere close to their height. Everyone worth listening to, from Elvis to Bob Dylan, from British prime minister Harold Wilson to American proto-hippie novelist Ken Kesey, loved the Beatles. Could anyone be cooler? Would anyone even come close?

Everyone wanted in on the fun. In June of 1965, Prime Minister Harold Wilson tapped the Beatles for MBEs, introducing the outwardly cuddly, inwardly louche pop singers to the entry levels of the British aristocracy. In England, in the highest ether of newly swinging London, they rolled like gods from Olympus. "They were the kings. Absolutely the kings," recalls journalist Ray Connolly. "Everything went through them. The only other people who had Rolls-Royces were the royal family. They were that famous."

The cinematic follow-up to *A Hard Day's Night* grew into a high-budget romp that transformed the Beatles' real Mayfair flat (long since dispensed with by 1965) into an exceptionally groovy four-wide row house, furnished with all manner of strange and fun accoutrements, e.g., a kitchen equipped with Automat-style food dispensers; a pit-style bed for John; a cinema-style pipe organ for Paul; and a voiceless servant who "mowed" the green shag rug with chattering teeth toys. From there it spiraled into a multinational James Bond spoof, shot variously in a Swiss ski resort and the sunny, if not as warm as they would have liked, Bahamas. The Beatles wriggled and giggled through it all, partly because they knew they just needed to show up to make the thing a hit, but mostly because they were smoking so much pot so much of the time they couldn't do much else.

Though it was also directed by Richard Lester, the film that came to be called *Help!* offered little more than a comic-book version of the moptop image, with scant trace of the incisive cultural commentary that made the first film such a bracing document. Still, *Help!* boasted a killer title track (a real cry for assistance from a man being consumed by his own celebrity, John proclaimed later) and a handful of pop-art landmarks, from the stutter-rhythm "Ticket to Ride" to the call-and-response "You're Gonna Lose That Girl" and the acoustic confessional "You've Got to Hide Your Love Away." John was clearly in Dylan mode, aspiring to (and finding) lyrics that revealed his internal dissonance even as they cloaked the salient details in theatrical costumes and double meanings. But while Paul's movie songs ("Another Girl" and "The Night Before") were less remarkable this time around, the leftovers revealed as much about his own expanding musical horizons as John's songs did about his literary ambitions. "I've Just Seen a Face" is a double-time folk ballad, its acoustic guitars and brush-slapped drums careening after a tautly composed lyric whose subject—the heady thrill of falling in love—is underscored by the descending chord pattern and rolling, tumbling pace. The lyric is perfectly composed, each syllable timed and rhymed precisely to emphasize the song's meter. Consider how tightly constructed the song's third verse is; how its internal rhymes further the song's narrative while reinforcing each beat in the song's frenetic rhythm:

> *I have missed things and kept out of sight*
> *But other girls were never quite*
> *Like this*

Recorded on June 14, 1965, six weeks after filming for *Help!* was completed and six weeks before the film's sound track was due to be released, "I've Just Seen a Face," while one of Paul's most overlooked Beatles songs, also fits easily into the top rank. He would never write a more succinct lyric. At times it would be surprising to think that he once could. And that was just the first song Paul recorded in EMI's Studio Two that day. Next up was "I'm Down," the frantic screamer he'd composed specifically to replace "Long Tall Sally," nearly a decade after he'd started making Little Richard's kinky little backstreet anthem his most trusty party piece. "I'm Down" is the quintessential

garage-band rocker, a hard-edged complaint that is equal parts guitars, organ swoops, and pissed-off horniness. "Plastic soul, man, plastic soul," Paul muttered after one take. It would do for a B-side.

The band broke for dinner at five thirty, and when they returned at
7 p.m., Paul propped his acoustic guitar on his knee and played
through an elegiac acoustic ballad he was now calling "Yesterday."
John, George, and Ringo were in the studio, too, sitting on stools and
listening in as Paul sang the song for George Martin. The other Beatles had heard the tune before; this was the same song he'd aired for an
unimpressed Dick James in the George V suite eighteen months earlier.
Paul had been toying with the melody since the late fall of 1963, when
it had come to him in a dream. It was the strangest thing. Opening his
eyes in his attic room at the Ashers' house, he had all but rolled out of
the covers and down to the piano in Mrs. Asher's music room, his fingers finding the right keys, and the accompanying chords, even before
he was fully conscious. As he became awake, Paul could barely believe
what he was hearing himself play. The melody climbed and fell like a
feather riding a breeze, rising to create a tension that would hold for a
beat or two before tumbling down to resolve itself on the song's root.
Still in the thrall of creation, Paul composed a middle section that extended the theme a bit further in a melodic rise that was even more
jagged, and its resolution even more melancholy than the verse.

The melody was so beautiful, Paul's first assumption was that he
had subconsciously nicked it from some other song he couldn't quite
recall in his conscious mind. One of the music-hall standards Jim had
played in the family sitting room, perhaps. To avoid embarrassing himself, Paul took the song around to a variety of friends and professional
acquaintances, la-la-ing the melody over the chords. First to the saloon
singer Alma Cogan, then the theatrical composer Lionel Bart. Both
were familiar with the pop repertoire going back decades, both knew
their music backward and forward. Yet neither could recognize this
song as anything other than a Paul McCartney original. Bart told
Beatle biographer Bob Spitz that he never had any doubt that it was
Paul's song. Every accomplished songwriter puts a distinctive stamp on
his work, he explained, melodic imprints as unique as a person's DNA.
"In that respect, Paul's fingerprints were all over the score for 'Yesterday.' I told him that night that he was onto something important."

Yet the right words wouldn't come. The "scrambled eggs" lyrics he'd hum to himself—reputedly suggested by Alma Cogan's mother when she strolled out of the kitchen in midperformance and invited her daughter's friend to stay for breakfast—hung around for months. Nothing else came close to taking their place until late May of 1965, when Paul and Jane flew to Spain for a brief holiday. Riding in a car to the southern coast of Portugal, with his girlfriend snoozing at his side, a restless Paul thought back to the "scrambled eggs" song and began kicking around words to fit the three-beat opening riff. Then, somewhere in the hot, barren fields, the opening word arrived: *yesterday*. And that was it. Something about the word encapsulated the melody perfectly: reflective, melancholy. The rest came in a rush, the words of a man reflecting on his emotional isolation. Life and love had once seemed so easy, but then he'd blurted out something thoughtless, something stupid, and couldn't take it back. Everything had changed. "I said something wrong," he frets. "Now I long for yesterday."

Neither sentimental nor mawkish, "Yesterday" is a plainspoken description of heartbreak. The story of every shattered love affair. And also, in a subconscious way, the story of Mary McCartney's precipitous death. He'd said something wrong there, too, and had lived with the guilt ever since. Or is that an overinterpretation? Even Paul isn't sure—he's been musing on the ghostly presence of his mother in "Yesterday" for years. But when he unveiled the finished song to his producer and bandmates that June evening, the first question was how they should record it. Obviously, it wasn't a song that called for a full-band performance. Paul was at first leery of George Martin's suggestion that they work up a string arrangement; Paul didn't want to push toward a supper-club type of feeling. He even flirted with the idea of drafting the BBC Radiophonic Workshop to craft an electronic backdrop for his vocal. But Martin came up with a dignified, chamber-music-style string quartet to accompany Paul's acoustic guitar and vocal. This worked for everyone—John was particularly happy with the bluesy note Paul and Martin had crafted for the cello during the second iteration of the bridge. Paul sang the song with a dry stoicism that set off the ache in the strings, and when it was done, the only question was how the song should be released. "Yesterday" certainly had the sound of a single. But how could a song written and performed exclusively by Paul McCartney, with only a quartet of session string players behind him, be released under the Beatles name? Wouldn't it be more accurate to call it a *Paul McCartney* single?

The issue was too explosive to confront, so they simply dodged it altogether, tucking the song at the end of the *Help!* sound track, and leaving it at that (although EMI's American imprint, Capitol, released the song as a single, crediting it to the Beatles). The first live airing of the song came at the live taping of ABC TV's *Blackpool Night Out* concert on August 1. "We'd like to do something now which we've never done before," George told the shrieking fans in an introduction that turned into a brotherly gibe when he quoted the standard opening for a then popular TV talent show. "So, for Paul McCartney of Liverpool, opportunity knocks!" All but the most dedicated screamers in the crowd laughed. Paul emerged with his acoustic guitar, a quizzical expression on his face. "Thank you, George," he murmured. His performance, with live strings, was pitch-perfect—sweet, stoic, heartbroken. The theater was, for once, entirely silent except for the music. The screams recommenced the moment he was done, but the TV audience could see John sprinting out with a bouquet of flowers and hear his sarcastic punctuation to Paul's moment of solo glory: "Thank you, Ringo," he cracked. "That was *wonderful.*"

9

Seen together, Paul and Jane were, simply, beautiful. The silken-haired, stylishly dressed rock star; the sophisticated young actress. Like all the best celebrity couples, they seemed to bring one another into sharper focus, the presence of one magnifying the other's individual appeal. At a film opening with Paul, the aristocratic Miss Asher took on the electric zing of rock 'n' roll; sitting across from the refined Jane at a fashionable French bistro, or arm in arm with her at one of London's elite nightclubs, the cheerful, boyish rocker appeared deeper, more thoughtful.

The socially omnivorous Beatle profited from his Asher connection when the world wasn't watching, too. For now Paul had entrée into the cloistered world of old money: high tea with the duchess; weekends in the country, where the hosts left books at your bedside to give you something to muse on after a long day of exploring the countryside on horseback. So many secret rituals to learn, so many hands to shake and stories to hear. "It was stuff happening that I'd only ever read of in books," Paul said. "An overhang from Britain's genteel past."

Still, his Beatle-size reputation didn't hamper his social and cultural ascension, particularly when it came to cultivating the artists, writers, and musicians whose work and social lives defined England's place at the fore of world culture. Lionel Bart became a friend. So, too, the influential critic and writer Kenneth Tynan. When Paul wanted to learn more about Bertrand Russell and his work as a political philosopher and peace activist, he simply telephoned Russell out of the blue and asked if he could come round for a chat. Russell was in his nineties then, but the men "had a great little talk," Paul said. "He just clued me in to the fact that Vietnam was a very bad war. . . . I reported back to John, 'I met this Bertrand Russell guy, John,' and I did all the big rap about the Vietnam war and stuff, and John really came in on it all."

John, stuck out in his golf-course home with his wife and a toddler son whose emotional needs he could never quite fathom, envied his partner's more fast-paced urban life. Though the three suburban Beatles and their wives weren't exactly strangers to the London nightlife, Jane clearly set a very different standard. "Jane was a teenaged film star so she was part of the glitterati of London before the Beatles even appeared," NEMS employee and Beatle wingman Tony Bramwell recalls. "And she was incredibly well educated and sophisticated, while the other three wives weren't. Patti was a model, Maureen was a hairdresser, and Cynthia was John's wife. She'd gone to Art College, but Jane was different. She went to the theater and musicals and poetry readings." If the other Beatle couples bumped into Paul and Jane in London on a night off, Bramwell continues, it was usually at a nightclub such as the Ad Lib or the Scotch of St. James. "Paul and Jane would be there, probably with some strange people. So you'd have a drink, and that'd be it. They'd be off."

For his part, Paul loved to play the part of the autodidact. The world, he declared in one midsixties interview, was so full of wonderful new things: art, writing, music. He *had* to absorb it all. "I must know what people are doing," he said in 1966. "I vaguely mind people knowing anything I don't." Paul also took note of his three bandmates' lack of cerebral ambition. "I often felt the other guys were sort of partying whereas I was learning a lot," he said in the early nineties. Or maybe he didn't hit on that until years later, when the world had long since concluded that John Lennon had always been the intellectual, avant-garde Beatle. Paul finds such talk astonishing. "I had a very rich avant-garde period which was such a buzz," he wrote in the late 1980s. "I was living on my own in London, and all the other guys were married in the suburbs, they were very square in my mind."

Paul's introduction into the London avant-garde scene was another product of his residency on Wimpole Street, and the smoky, vodka-fueled salon Peter Asher ran out of his room in the late hours of the evening. Here, among the young musicians, artists, poets, and assorted other eccentrics Peter had come to know, Paul found his way into the crowd of artists, writers, and proto-freaks he would soon make his own. Beyond Peter, his point of entry was Barry Miles, an art-college graduate from a working-class family in Cirencester, a bit northwest of London. A sort of freak-of-all-trades, Miles (as he was universally known, no one ever called him Barry) came to London in 1963 and in short order established himself as a locus of hipster doings in the city. By the time Paul met him in mid-1965, Miles was an artist and a writer, a bookshop-slash-gallery-owner, and, more than anything else, a cultural provocateur and center of hipster life. Soon Paul was knocking on the door of Miles's own small apartment, where he found his friend's wife, Sue, in the kitchen with a fresh batch of Alice B. Toklas's favorite hash-laced brownies. Paul tucked in happily, and this was where Miles found them a bit later, deep in conversation.

"He seemed to know nothing about underground literature, music or radical politics, but he wanted to learn," Miles wrote of Paul in his memoir, *In the Sixties*. Paul dug into Miles's collection of avant-garde music, from Luciano Berio's electronic music to John Cage's minimalist modern classical to the abstract jazz of Sun Ra and Ornette Coleman. Paul bought books about drugs, spirituality, and philosophy and started collecting surrealist paintings by René Magritte, and others. He was particularly influenced by the plays of Alfred Jarry, the French absurdist playwright whose early-twentieth century works, particularly the play *Ubu Roi*, helped set the standard for the dadaists and surrealists who would follow.

It was all new and exciting to Paul, who returned the favor by turning Miles on to his favorite American R & B sides, telling stories about his experiences on stages around the world, and performing remarkably precise imitations of such famous friends as Little Richard and Mick Jagger. Thinking back on it all, Miles recalled an insight he'd gleaned from Derek Taylor, the Beatles' überhipster publicist.

"He was sure that no matter how Paul was standing or moving, he always knew just how the crease at the back of his trousers was falling or how his jacket was hanging at the waist," Miles wrote. "This was not a narcissistic thing . . . just an incredible level of show-business professionalism."

While Paul got a charge out of his new friends' creativity and their dedication to every conceivable form of artistic weirdness, he couldn't also help applying his own bottomless work ethic to their scene. Why just *talk* about cool poems they'd read and jam sessions they'd seen when they could record them and create a kind of sonic magazine— disposable records that would be inexpensive and easy to find, thanks to EMI's massive distribution system? When William Burroughs or Allen Ginsberg came to London, they wouldn't just hold a reading for the lucky freaks who would know enough to show up; they'd create a record of the visit and make it available for everyone. All they needed to do was buy some recording gear and a mixing setup, then lease a small apartment for a studio. How much would it cost? It didn't matter; Paul simply waved off the question and rattled off Brian Epstein's office number. Just send him the bill, everything would be taken care of.

When Miles teamed up with Peter Asher and gallery owner John Dunbar to open the Indica Gallery and Bookshop, a one-stop center for avant-garde writings and art they planned for the lower floors of an unimproved building in Mason's Yard in the swank Mayfair section of London, Paul pitched in with hours of physical labor, pounding together the shelves, spackling the holes in the walls, even hand-designing and printing up reams of wrapping paper. Who'd have thought a Beatle would be rolling up his sleeves and wielding a hammer and nails along with his beatnik buddies? Not the surprised passersby, who would, on occasion, gather in front of the windows to gawp at the world-famous pop star smiling and waving back at them. Eventually Miles and the others taped sheets of newspaper over the glass to keep the crowds at bay. Of course, Paul would be even more flirtatious with the young female fan-magazine reporters who showed up at the Indica to interview Peter in his role as one-half of Peter and Gordon. The writers, often inexperienced and tongue-tied in the presence of a moderately successful pop star, would nearly burst into tears when they realized that the young man winking from the sink with the spackling tool in his hand was—*Oh my God!*—Paul McCartney. Peter, already accustomed to being upstaged by his not-quite brother-in-law, just smiled until Paul left the room and the woman had regained the power of speech.

In the evenings Miles would escort Paul to the avant-garde event of the moment. Once they went to the Royal College of Art to see John Cage perform one of his random-sounds pieces; the audience was supposed to collaborate by making noises of their own, so Paul scraped a penny across the uneven surface of a radiator, not far from where the maestro himself banged the leg of the piano with a chunk of wood. An interesting evening, Paul decreed in a pub later, although a bit dull after the first hour or so. "It went on too long," Paul told the evening's organizer, Victor Schonfield. Still, he'd come away with a revelation or two about the uses of random sounds that might make their way into the next Beatles sessions. "You don't have to like something to be influenced by it."

Paul was less enthusiastic when the noise of Beatlemania encroached on his more sophisticated evenings in the artsy world. A pilgrimage to see Luciano Berio perform at the Italian Institute went completely awry when someone from the embassy alerted the newspapers, so they might capture the moment for the next morning's editions. Both musicians were aghast to discover the clutch of nattering reporters and photographers waiting to record their meeting after Berio's performance. When the photographers chased Paul and Miles down the street to their car, the Beatle grew irate and swore at them, albeit in the tongue of midsixties grooviness. "All you do is destroy things!" he snapped at his tormentors. "Why don't you *create* something?"

Paul used his Brenell tape recorders to tape random sounds—laughter, a car honking on the street, a guitar tuning, whatever—and turned them into small loops, which he could speed up, slow down, play backward or forward or inside out until the original sounds became unrecognizable, then mutated into something else altogether. He got an early home movie camera and made abstract films that employed the same techniques with visual images, saturating the film with double and triple images, reversing the action, following random lights until they seemed to become distant planets or descending gods.

Everything was within reach. When the groundbreaking Italian director Michelangelo Antonioni came round to meet Paul, his host sat him down and screened his own homemade films. "Dead cool, really," Paul recalled. Antonioni's estimation of the work has been lost to history.

All the Beatles bought their own houses by mid-1965, the other three settling into the suburbs (reputedly a direct result of their accountant's desire to have them close to his own house, which is just absurd enough to be true). Paul had no interest in being that far away from London's social whirl, so he found himself a house in St. John's Wood, near Regent's Park and—more to the point—just around the corner from EMI's studios on Abbey Road. The three-floor Regency home was on Cavendish Avenue, in a quiet block of similarly large and elegant houses, most of which rose from behind imposing brick walls and fences. Still, the upper floors of commercial buildings, with their aerials and industrial crowns, were clearly visible a few blocks away. When the windows were open, the sound of trucks and traffic on nearby Wellington Road rumbled over the sills. The house cost £40,000, and Paul spent half that much renovating its interior. But he wasn't after anything palatial—more like a combination of Liverpool working-class hominess and the Ashers' aristocratic clutter. Meeting with interior architects John and Marina Adams, a young couple whom he had met through the Ashers, Paul informed them that he wanted their work to evoke, as he put it, the smell of cabbages coming from the basement. "It was the strangest briefing I've ever had," John Adams said.

Paul made a point of furnishing the house himself, often with sofas and tables he and Jane found in thrift stores during afternoon-long shopping binges. When he finally moved in, during the early spring of 1966, the Cavendish house had few rock-star accoutrements. The extravagances were either artistic (a hand-painted door for his music room; paintings and sculptures he'd procured through art dealer Robert Fraser) or musical (a collection of exotic stringed instruments; an upper-floor studio outfitted with piano, guitars, his tape recorders, and some rudimentary electronic instruments). Paul also had an electronically lowered floor-to-ceiling movie screen, though it usually got stuck and had to be yanked into place before a film could be shown. As Paul recalled to Miles, the dual stereo systems were less an extravagance than a necessity: one or the other was usually broken. "There was controlled chaos in there," recalls Tony Barrow. "Chockablock with stuff, but he could pinpoint immediately where something was. It was elegant and comfortable as well." No matter how wealthy he had become, Paul made a point of outfitting his dinner table with a working-class lace cloth and plastic salt-and-pepper shakers, even when his shelves held at least one pair made from sterling silver.

The Cavendish house became a natural gathering spot for the other Beatles, particularly when they were preparing for, or unwinding from, sessions at EMI, which was about a five-minute stroll around one corner, down a small hill, then around another corner to Abbey Road. But Paul's decision to live in the city had also set him apart from the others, and particularly from John, who had assumed they would all end up living within a walk or an easy drive from one another. "He, at least, would never have dreamed of living more than a few minutes away from the other three," wrote John's boyhood friend Pete Shotton in his memoir, *John Lennon in My Life*. Paul's independence also alienated him from the others when he resisted joining their early experiments with LSD, despite George's and (especially) John's enthusiasm for the powerful hallucinogen, which they had first taken unknowingly at a dinner party in the early months of 1965. The initial experience had been terrifying, but also intriguing. They bought a few more doses of the drug at the start of the Beatles' 1965 American tour and talked Ringo into joining them for a trip during a day off in Los Angeles. Paul, however, was having none of it. He'd never indulged in the fistfuls of amphetamines John and the others had gobbled in Germany—he'd have one or two, when he took them at all—and John's promise that this new drug would alter his consciousness forever was far from appealing to Paul's relatively conservative mind-set. He liked to get weird, just not irredeemably fucked-up. "I was more ready for the drink or a little bit of pot or something," he said.

Other disagreements had crept into the Beatles' fold. The others had lost their patience with touring, exhausted as they were by the dehumanizing pressures of worldwide mania and the existential struggle they lost each night to the screamers, who overwhelmed any at-

tempt to play music. The final straw came during the dismal summer
tour of 1966, which first veered toward catastrophe when the group
blew off a state reception with the despotic (and downright strange)
government of Ferdinand Marcos in the Philippines. The Beatles had
been punched and kicked by irate soldiers at the airport, and for a
brief, scary moment it looked as if the situation might grow even more
dire. They'd escaped more or less unharmed, but within a few weeks
the dark side of the mania struck again, this time in the United States.
John gave an interview to British journalist Maureen Cleave, during
which he observed that his group had become more popular among
young people than Jesus Christ. He hadn't been celebrating the notion—John was in fact decrying it—but such subtleties were lost on
American zealots, whose own relationship with the sacred seemed to
hinge on their passion for rooting out apostasy in others. Some of the
faithful organized boycotts and holy bonfires of Beatles records and
other fan paraphernalia. The Ku Klux Klan made threatening noises;
the police in Memphis fielded death threats. The global tidal wave of
Beatlemania, it seemed, had developed a sinister undertow.

Paul, still playing the cheerful, smiling Beatle, tried to assuage hurt
feelings in both cases. In the Philippines he'd made a beeline to national TV cameras to lodge an official apology to the Marcoses and all
of their wounded subjects. When the group was greeted by the bigger-
than-Jesus firestorm in the United States a few weeks later, he helped
to shepherd John through his own apologetic press conference. At first
Paul, ever the musical extrovert, was determined to keep the show on
the road. But eventually the pressure of the mania, along with back-
to-back international controversies, brought him around. By the time
they got to the American tour's final stop, at Candlestick Park in San
Francisco, he confided to Tony Barrow that the Beatles had reached
the end of the road. He got Barrow to tape the final concert, the publicist holding the microphone of a portable cassette recorder up to the
public-address speakers on the field in front of the stage. Barrow made
a copy for Paul and kept the original locked in his desk at NEMS,
where it remained until he left the company two years later. He has
kept the tape in his own safe ever since, but no matter: bootleggers
somehow managed to get their hands on the recording (which runs

out partway through "Long Tall Sally," the final song) anyway. To
this day, Barrow has no idea how the tape might have leaked.

The one haven the group could always find, however, was the recording studio. Or, for John and Paul, wherever they could find a few
moments to unspool their latest compositions for one another. Most
often the songs would nearly be finished, but one collaborator could
always help the other by smoothing down the rough spots or identify-
ing previously unimagined directions for the lyrics or music to explore.
When Paul drove out to John's house with a funky song that had lame
words about a snotty girl who wouldn't give her boyfriend a golden
ring, he knew it wasn't working; he was on the verge of abandoning it
altogether. But John not only encouraged him to finish the song, but
soon transformed the lyric into the story of a woman determined to
diminish her boyfriend even though her actual success couldn't compete with her aspirations. *Baby, you can drive my car,* the chorus went.
And maybe I'll love you. Paul returned the favor to John, first by providing the sweeping melody to the verses of "In My Life," then by
helping him clarify his narrative in the romantic tangle of "Norwegian
Wood," capping it off with a wicked final verse in which the narrator
kisses off his not-quite girlfriend by setting her beloved apartment on
fire. *Isn't it good?* he gloats as he walks off, taking one final glance at
her expensive, and now blazing, Scandinavian paneling.

Most of the romantic songs Paul wrote for the album *Rubber Soul*
came with a Lennon-esque air of moral and intellectual indignation.
The deceptively cheery "You Won't See Me" is addressed to an apparently faithless lover whose refusal to see or even speak on the telephone with the narrator prompts him to scold her as if she were a
child. *I have had enough,* he finger-wags. *So act your age!* The target
of his frustration becomes far more apparent in "I'm Looking
Through You," which addresses a sophisticated woman who no longer intimidates the narrator the way she once did. *You were above me,
but not today,* he says. Certainly, both songs step back from being
out-and-out condemnations. It's love itself that has the nasty habit of
disappearing, he adds in "I'm Looking Through You," while "You
Won't See Me" notes that both lovers have lost the time for one another. But it's striking to note similarities in not just the mood and

tone, but also the imagery those songs share with "That Means a Lot" (recorded by the Beatles, but then found wanting and handed off to P. J. Proby) and, in collaboration with John, in "The Word" and "We Can Work It Out." Paul's voice has taken on the authority of a man who feels he knows an ultimate truth. He sees himself shining with the light of wisdom—all you have to do is open your eyes when he walks into the room. *Try to see it my way.* Can't you see? he urges. *I'm here to show everybody the light.* The girl who rejects him in "You Won't See Me" won't (or can't) open her eyes to him. When he considers his estranged lover in "I'm Looking Through You," the woman who had once been superior to him—*You were above me*—has not only descended in his eyes, but lost her form. When he looks at her, there's nothing to see: she has ceased to exist.

Clearly, Paul's relationship with Jane had grown tense. She had moved with him to the Cavendish house; anyone who cared knew they were a committed couple. But in the tumult of the times, and the heat of dueling spotlights, romantic commitment was tenuous. Paul had never lost his appetite for casual sex with groupies and other roadside acquaintances. What's more, he had a not-so-secret secondary relationship in London with Maggie McGivern, a young, dark-haired beauty he'd met when she was working as the nanny for John Dunbar and Marianne Faithfull's toddler son, Nicholas. The affair with McGivern was beneath the public's radar, but far more than a casual fling. They went out in public when Jane was out of town; they vacationed together; she came to Beatles recording sessions. The appeal seemed obvious: McGivern was beautiful, warm, and intelligent, but didn't challenge Paul or rival his authority in the way his independently wealthy and famous girlfriend did. Jane's dedication to her career, which kept her out of town and thus unavailable to his whims, was another problem. Worse, Jane was rumored to have had her own extracurricular romances and almost left Paul for an actor with whom she had supposedly been having an affair during her season with the Old Vic theater company in Bristol. The celebrity couple nevertheless held their relationship together, albeit tentatively, and with a cast of seconds in perpetual orbit around them. "I don't have easy relationships with women," Paul explained later. "I talk too much truth."

•   •   •

More fun, more craziness: Miles started an underground newspaper, the *International Times,* and Paul pitched in as an investor, as the subject of its first cover interview, and, under the pseudonym Ian Iachimoe, identified as a Polish "new wave" film director, as sponsor of a contest to provide the crucial but missing plot twist in a movie about a compulsively clean woman who ends up crawling through dustbins and becoming obsessed with dirt. "What is needed is the idea," Paul wrote. "What could cause her to have to become involved with filth?" Whoever provided the best idea would win a cash prize of twenty guineas. "This competition is for real," Paul's copy concluded. "It seems strange but is real."

Also real, if even more strange, was Paul's conversation with Miles that became the edition's centerpiece. They seemed incredibly stoned, rambling on about environments and where Paul felt most comfortable. "I don't know about the environment thing," Paul mused. "Because, you know, you just threw it out like a question and immediately there's a lot of things to think about. Because there I go saying everybody's the same and I know they're not. No, the only drag is that the words are pretty bad, you can't say much with words."

Which becomes even more true when you're ripped on the potent Moroccan hash they used to fling their consciousness to the furthest reaches of the inner ozone.

Paul seemed a bit more coherent talking to Hunter Davies, then serving as the Atticus columnist for the *Times,* about how his experiences listening to avant-garde classical composers such as Cage, Berlioz, and Stockhausen had altered his appreciation for music. "I can hear a whole song in one chord," he said. "I think you can hear a whole song in one note, if you listen hard enough. But nobody ever listens hard enough."

It was all coming together in 1966: the literary and the commercial; the hubris and the heartbreak; the pop savvy and avant-garde ambition. Pop songs could be art, rock albums should be conceived and executed as distinctive, extended statements. In California the Beach Boys' leader, Brian Wilson, heard *Rubber Soul* and compelled himself to produce *Pet Sounds,* a song cycle centered around love, loss, and the fraying of innocence. The songs were beautiful but the production— dense with strings, percussion, and exotic instruments that sounded even stranger when paired with rudimentary synthesizers—was even more stunning. John and Paul journeyed to the Waldorf Hotel for an insiders-only preview presented by substitute Beach Boy Bruce Johnston and came away both impressed and determined to go Brian one better. All bets were off, all boundaries officially nonexistent. Could people ever listen hard enough to hear a song in one note? Now the Beatles were going to make them do it.

They started in April with a song of John's he was calling "Mark 1." Inspired by Timothy Leary's LSD-refracted interpretation of the *Tibetan Book of the Dead,* the song was composed with a single, unchanging chord, the melody rising and falling in a chantlike pattern, like the voice of a monk echoing from a mountaintop, according to John. The first attempt to record the song focused mostly on an Arabic-cum-Indian droning sound. Then Paul strolled into the studio carrying a sack of his homemade tape loops, with the strange shrieks and yawps he'd been producing during his off-hours in the Ashers' attic. That guitar-tuning loop, run backward and at the wrong speed, sounded strangely like seagulls; the shrieks of electronic feedback became the laughter of the gods. Soon the song, retitled "Tomorrow Never Knows," grew into a collage of sound; the loops of noise and backward guitar playing over Paul's thrumming bass, the drone of a sitar (thanks to George), and John's electronically filtered, emotionally detached singing. "Listen to the color of your dreams," he intoned, describing the music with unintentional precision.

That was where they began, and the sessions that spring and summer ventured every which way. From Paul's Motown-fired love song to the mind-expanding possibilities of marijuana, "Got to Get You into My Life," to his baroque-inspired portrait of loneliness ("Eleanor Rigby") to John's floaty paeans to laziness ("I'm Only Sleeping") and the elements ("Rain") and rapier-cut portraits of Rat Pack arrogance ("And Your Bird Can Sing") and a drug-dealing quack ("Dr. Robert") to Paul's own incisive character study of literary ambition ("Paperback Writer") and alternately sweet and dark portraits of his up-and-down romance with Jane ("Here, There and Everywhere" and "For No One"). Both John and Paul were pushing their craft to new heights, finding new ways to incorporate disparate ideas, experiences, and influences into the three-minute pop-song format. But the months

Paul had spent steeping in London's avant-garde scene had obviously transformed his musical consciousness. Suddenly he was writing classically inspired songs as easily as dance-hall tunes, melding Beach Boys harmonies into songs that rocked as hard as the Who, and grafting punchy rhythm-and-blues horns onto trippy drug lyrics. If he had once tended to write romantic songs that opted for sentiment over the sort of human complexities John traced in his personal songs, now Paul had come up with the stark "For No One," whose description of a waning love affair had the clarity and chill of ice. *No sign of love behind the tears,* he sang. *Cried for no one.*

Listening to an advance tape of the *Revolver* sessions in their hotel room during a tour stop that summer, John, for a decade the most competitive of partners, made a stunning admission: "Your songs are better than mine."

Such moments warmed Paul's heart and fired his confidence even further. "I remember him, his amused smile, saying, 'Yes, that's it, that'll do,'" Paul said, recalling a songwriting session from the same era. "Quite a nice moment: 'Hmm, I've done right! I've done well!'"

John was, indeed, impressed with Paul. But also dismayed. For as he watched his boyhood friend and creative partner rising, John could only feel himself tumbling into an emotional abyss. "I was going through murder," he said later. Paul's burgeoning confidence was, in John's eyes, part of what was killing him.

IO

The way Paul described it to the *Sunday Times,* the four Beatles were well on the way to calling it quits. "We Beatles are ready to go our own ways," he proclaimed. "I'm no longer one of the four moptops." He pointed to the mustache that now bristled over his cupid's-bow lips. Such a mature, non-moptop feature, he said, was "part of breaking up the Beatles. I no longer believe in the image."

Not in the group's old image, perhaps. But Paul's hints about the end of the Beatles were actually intended to lay the groundwork for an entirely new and improved group identity: as pop artists and cultural oracles; psychedelic shape-shifters whose creative abilities could outstrip even the wildest imagination. When it came to the Beatles as a creative union, and particularly as the seat of Paul's partnership with John, anything was possible. Clearly Paul had no intention of letting that go. On the contrary, he was more determined than ever to keep it going.

He wasn't the only one. The months following the end of the American tour, and what they had resolved would be the conclusion of all Beatles touring, had been unsettling for all four of the Beatles. They'd certainly made gestures toward finding individual identities. George had been the most successful, following his new musical and spiritual interests to India to lose himself in his studies of the sitar and

Eastern religion. Ringo stayed home with his wife and their young children. John had taken a small role in a new Richard Lester film, a darkly comic jeremiad called *How I Won the War,* only to discover that movie acting was even more boring than touring with a rock band. Paul had turned his hand to film scoring, writing some quasi-symphonic theme music to go along with a Hayley Mills romance called *The Family Way.* When that was done, he traveled a bit, exploring France with the ever-faithful roadie Mal Evans, then taking an African safari with Jane.

It was the first extended break the Beatles had from one another since they were teenagers. Apart from George, who had long since lost patience with the limitations of the mania outside the studio and John and Paul's creative hegemony within it, the months of solitary exploration had seemed like a dead end. By the time the band reunited at the end of November, 1966, to start thinking about a new album, all four Beatles were ready to resume their four-way collaboration. Paul was especially eager to build on the creative momentum he had been riding since "Yesterday," an arc that had, in consort with John's retreat, elevated the Beatles' musical director to unrivaled leadership. If John wasn't happy to cede his control of the group, he also wasn't in any psychological or neurological condition to do much about it. The seething Beatle, the moptop with claws, had finally been overwhelmed by his circumstances. Dazed by fame and stunned by the premature senescene he'd fallen into in the London suburbs, he had as of late sunk into an emotional torpor. Unwilling to engage with Cynthia, unable to connect with his toddler son or to confront the disconnect between the life he needed and the one he was actually living, John lurked in the sitting room, curled uncomfortably onto a settee. He watched television for days on end, barely eating anything beyond the chemicals that allowed him to escape the reality he couldn't bear to face. "The more drugs he took, the more hurt and vulnerable he became," the journalist Chris Hutchins, still involved with the group nearly daily, recalls. "Paul was never vulnerable, he was always strong, he had that stiff upper lip. But John was getting lower and lower. At this stage he talked about topping himself. I sort of thought he would."

Instead, John merely did what was expected of him. Which, in late

November of 1966, meant reporting for work at EMI's studios on Abbey Road. Given his fractured psyche, and general unwillingness to confront anything in his life, he was delighted to hear Paul explain how the new album they were about to start making didn't even have to be by the Beatles, exactly.

Paul had been toying with the idea all fall: the Beatles had the freedom to become anyone they wanted to be. A brass band from Lancashire! Jim Mac's Band! And remember when his dad's band had fooled everyone by donning bandit masks and billing themselves as the Masked Melody Makers? *Now the Beatles could do that, too!* They could reinvent themselves in any of a thousand different ways. They could project themselves back in time, or into the future or some other alternate reality. They had already been actors, now they could work like movie writers and directors! Now that they wouldn't have to travel the world presenting themselves on stages, they were free to live out their fantasies in the recording studio, making whatever music they felt like making, no matter how elaborate or strange.

This would be their new album, a complete departure from *Revolver*, which was of course a complete departure from *Rubber Soul*, which you could barely compare to Help!—you get the idea. So how perfectly counterintuitive that they would begin with a triad of songs that look backward for inspiration, back to the sights, sounds, and feelings that animated the Liverpool of their youth. Only would anyone in that Liverpool recognize the version of Strawberry Field (the Salvation Army estate just behind Aunt Mimi's home in Woolton) that John described in his surreal tableau "Strawberry Fields Forever"? Neighbors from Menlove Avenue might recall John peering down at the world from a perch in the tree in Mimi's backyard. But as he sang in his bleary, floaty voice, none of them had the slightest idea what he'd been thinking up there. *You can't, you know, tune in, but it's all right,* he sang. "Strawberry Fields Forever" had started as a simple acoustic song, but followed the lyric through the looking glass, becoming a multipiece epic of jarring electronic sound.

Paul's bouncy musical-hall tribute "When I'm Sixty-four," lightly revised from the song he had originally penned as a teenager, would be familiar to anyone who knew the music of England's not-distant past. But his "Penny Lane," which celebrated the little business district where he and John used to meet up en route to Liverpool's city center and thus served as the companion piece to John's visions of Strawberry Field, bore more than a trace of its composer's new bohemianism. Why were the children laughing at the banker? Why did the barber keep pictures of people's heads in his window? And why did he keep calling this pleasant suburban world *very strange*?

All of these questions might have been answered by the slip of blotter paper Paul had recently been given by his friend Tara Browne (the wealthy Guinness heir, soon to die in a car accident), and the load of potent American LSD it held. Or maybe his long-delayed capitulation to the lysergic age was simply another step in what had already been a years-long journey through altered states of consciousness. Clearly, this new Beatles album would come filtered through a swirled haze of marijuana smoke and psychedelic hallucinations. This shift in group identity, Paul insisted, would allow them to be even more revealing and artistically daring than they had been during their fresh-faced-moptop era.

A concept album in only the loosest form, the songs that became *Sgt. Pepper's Lonely Hearts Club Band* are linked not by a story or theme but by a fundamental assumption: that, as John asserted in "Strawberry Fields Forever," the first song they recorded that fall, *nothing is real*. To John this notion came with an existential undercurrent: if nothing is real, then reality is nothing. Paul, of course, saw a far more affirming idea. That *anything* can be real, once you imagine it and then apply enough energy to make it so. Thus, the Penny Lane that mattered was the one that existed in his own ears and eyes, where all came with their own unique quirks and stories. The nurse selling poppies on the roundabout isn't really a character in a play—except that Paul still remembered himself as a teenager wandering that same street, looking at the faces going past and casting them all in an imaginary narrative. So obviously, the nurse could be more significant than even she could guess.

Swept up again in Paul's enthusiasm, John threw himself into the writing and recording, often leavening Paul's Technicolor visions with hints of the darkness that loomed beneath his own consciousness. The classic example came during a nighttime writing session when Paul suggested writing a song called "It's Getting Better." It had been a lovely spring afternoon and he'd been walking his sheepdog, Martha, in Regent's Park when he'd recalled how Jimmy Nicol, the session drummer who had briefly sat in for Ringo when he took ill in 1964, used to assure the other Beatles that he was adjusting to the rigors of Beatlemania. Tracing the concept at the piano in his music room in the Cavendish house, Paul sang the chorus to John, clutching a guitar a few feet away. "Did you say, 'You've got to admit it's getting better'?" John said, nodding his approval. A moment later he spat out the perfect answering line: "It couldn't get much worse."

Paul returned the favor when John emerged with "A Day in the Life," his abstract portrait of a society floating through time with no awareness of reality, let alone itself. The verses recounted a random array of events: a fatal car accident; the premiere of an unsuccessful movie; an official calculation of the number of holes riddling the roads of Blackburn, Lancashire. Each vignette had a literal meaning—the automotive death of Paul's friend Tara Browne; the release of *How I Won the War,* the movie in which John had a supporting role; an actual accounting of road damage by the Lancashire council—all taken from the morning newspaper John had propped on the piano while he was writing. But in his telling, all were devoid of meaning. No one's sure who the dead man was; the movie plays to an empty theater; the holes come to represent the spiritual emptiness of people in general. It was already a long way toward being a masterpiece, but "A Day in the Life" was still missing a few vital elements: a section and some way to transition out of the central verse; and a pair of musical transitions that would, in some way, suit the song's drift toward existential nothingness. Paul's answers to these quandaries revealed as much about the sweep of his creativity as they did about the uncanny symbiosis he and John had achieved.

Paul already had a scrap of a song that seemed to fit into the bridge section. He'd been toying with a brief vignette for ages, a marchlike verse describing a typical morning from back in his student days: waking up; having a cup of tea; running for the bus; climbing into the open-air section, where he could smoke. That's as far as it ever went, until this moment when they both realized how perfectly it fit the middle of John's song. For if "A Day in the Life" was, in essence, about the need to regain consciousness, Paul's bit described the *literal* act of waking up. Better still, he had another fragment—a floaty melody beneath the secret druggie invitation *I'd love to turn you on,* which in this case also reemphasized the song's core theme of regaining consciousness—that served as a perfect drift into the last missing element in the song: the musical punctuations to the ends of the two central verse sections. Which was where Paul offered his crowning contribution.

Thinking again of the avant-garde composers he'd been studying, and particularly the sort of experiments in formlessness and noise he'd observed John Cage performing that night he had pitched in with his penny-scratching-the-radiator sounds, Paul came up with an idea virtually unprecedented in music. They could hire a full orchestra and tell the musicians to play without any music. All they had to do was start on one low note, and over twenty-four bars, move up the scale to a climactic high note. The sound they made en route would be the sonic representation of chaos. An orchestrated big bang; a noise so pure and overwhelming it would erupt from the speakers like the creation, or perhaps the destruction, of an entire universe.

John approved immediately. "It just sort of happened beautifully," he said later, recalling how elegantly Paul's contributions fit into his original song. George Martin initially balked at the cost of hiring an entire orchestra to provide the musical climaxes, but he came up with a compromise, engaging a forty-musician ensemble and recording them four times, thereby actually doubling the effect a full orchestra would have achieved in one go. They booked the session for the evening of February 10, 1967, and, with an eye toward turning the recording into an Event, instructed the musicians to come in evening dress, as if playing in a concert hall. The Beatles showed up dressed in their own hippie finery, all brightly colored blazers, multicolored shirts, and wildly flared pants, and told the dozens of friends they had invited—including Mick Jagger and Keith Richards, Donovan, the Monkees' Mike Nesmith, Marianne Faithfull (then dating Jagger), various Beatle wives and entourage members—to do the same. Once the recording began, the guests sat at the musicians' feet, bouncing balloons, blowing bubbles, and wielding the various joke-shop novelties (clown noses; silly glasses; rubber cigars; bald wigs) the Beatles had brought in to lighten the mood. A camera crew circulated, capturing the entire event for posterity. While Paul fretted a bit about the audacity of the project ("The worst thing about doing something like this is that people are at first a bit suspicious," he said. "They're a bit like, 'You know, what are you up to?'"), he didn't let it slow him down. Paul's insistence on directing the orchestra himself, rather than letting George Martin do the honors, clearly grated on the producer's nerves. "Paul was upstaging him," staff engineer Geoff Emerick recalled. Perhaps because, as Emerick observed, Paul didn't have the training to know how ridiculous the session would seem to trained musicians. In fact, he flaunted his casual attitude by conducting the tux-clad orchestra in shirtsleeves, a psychedelic tie, and a kitchen apron.

The sessions continued through the winter and spring of 1967, producing songs whose diverse moods, subjects, and sounds were united by a common thread of untethered imagination and unhinged inventiveness. From the rooty-toot echoes of the music halls to incense-laced Indian temples; from a Victorian circus to the sixties generation gap; from string-led pop to hard rock; all the way to the furthest reaches of postmodern noise—*Sgt. Pepper's Lonely Hearts Club Band* grew into a work so far beyond precedent that even the Beatles themselves didn't quite know what to think. Except that George concluded early on that the overdub-intensive sessions did nothing to alleviate his boredom, to say nothing of his frustration at being treated like a second-class Beatle by Paul and John alike. As a result, he didn't always turn up, choosing instead to stay home with his sitar and mystical teachings. Ringo had less of a beef with John and Paul, but he didn't have much of a role, either, so while they spent hours fussing over the best way to mike a harpsichord, say, or which settings to use on the Mellotron track, the drummer perfected his chess game under the tutelage of Neil Aspinall.

Paul either didn't notice or simply didn't care and bowed to nothing but the whims of his muse. He alienated George even further by taking the guitar solo in his own "Sgt. Pepper's Lonely Hearts Club Band" title track, then another (blazing) turn playing lead on John's "Good Morning, Good Morning." Paul also aggravated the always impatient John by doing endless retakes on his own lead vocals, then kept the engineers occupied for hours as he labored painstakingly on his bass part for "Lovely Rita," playing so relentlessly for so long that his fingers bled. But if Paul didn't think twice about asking others to wait, he took immediate umbrage when George Martin asked for a few days before working out a string arrangement to Paul's freshly composed "She's Leaving Home." That Martin was busy producing a new record for Cilla Black made little impression on the Beatles' impatient bassist. "I thought, 'Fucking hell! . . . He ought to put himself out,'" Paul recalled. He stalked off to another arranger, Mike Leander, and gave him the job, much to George Martin's immediate and lasting unhappiness. "It obviously hadn't occurred to [Paul] that I would be upset," he wrote, with typical reserve, in his memoirs. Discussing the incident with Miles twenty-five years later, Paul admitted that he had only belatedly realized that throwing over his usual producer might actually hurt Martin's feelings. "But of course I was hurt that he didn't have time for me," Paul added. "And he did have time for Cilla."

Paul kept moving ahead, kept thinking of new twists the record could take, new ways to make it completely different from any other record that had ever existed. He came up with the original idea for the cover—the Beatles posing in front of a wall decorated with pictures of their heroes—then sketched out some more ideas with a scene from an old-fashioned park concert. He took them to his art-dealer friend Robert Fraser, who then introduced him to the pop artist Peter Blake, who created the final image for the front cover. The elaborate gatefold cover would also have a large portrait on its inner face, plus lyrics to the songs printed on the back. And more: a specially printed dustcover inside, and also a sheet of Sgt. Pepper cutouts to distribute to the kids.

And more. Why not turn the record into a movie? Certainly the songs they had composed offered more than enough opportunities for visuals—just consider the girl with kaleidoscope eyes in "Lucy in the Sky with Diamonds," or the sexy civil servant in "Lovely Rita." They had made a pair of intricately shot clips to accompany the release of the double-sided "Strawberry Fields Forever" and "Penny Lane" single and had already shot the entirety of the orchestral session for "A Day in the Life," so now all they had to do was keep rolling until they had a cinema-length film. "Nobody knew exactly how it was going to go, there was no such thing as videos yet," recalls Tony Bramwell, who had been charged with heading up film projects for NEMS. "The idea was to give each track to a different famous director. One to Visconti, one to Fellini, one to Antonioni, and say, 'Look, here's five grand, go and make a film for this song.' But the stingy people at EMI, bless them, the people in charge of the company at the time, actually didn't think *SP* was a very good album, as such. It had already cost them so much money in the studio, they weren't sure it was going to recoup anything, so they wouldn't come up with the budget for the film."

No matter, plenty of visions were to be found in the music they were making, particularly given the various pills, powders, and leafy substances they had to propel them to the furthest reaches of their imaginations. The Beatles had long since taken to smoking pot during recording sessions, even though they still felt obligated to keep their illicit activities hidden behind acoustic screens, and away from the trusting eyes of George Martin. Paul had also developed an appetite for cocaine, particularly when he needed a boost during late-night sessions. When a vocal session for "Getting Better" was interrupted by news that John had accidentally taken a hit of LSD (confusing it for one of the amphetamines he carried in the same pill packet), Paul decided the time had come for him to share a trip with his musical partner. He walked John back to the house on Cavendish, just the two of them, downed a hit of acid, and gradually felt the house lifting them into a whole new sphere.

They spent hours staring into one another's eyes. "You would want to look away," Paul said. "But you wouldn't, and then you could see yourself in the other person." After a while Paul felt compelled to walk into his garden, only once he got there, he felt just as urgent a need to go back inside. The effort of moving from one place to another exhausted him, so he sat down with John again and studied his face. "I had a big vision of him as a king, the absolute Emperor of Eternity," he recalled. "I could feel every inch of the house, and John seemed like some sort of emperor in control of it all."

On a trip to visit Jane (who was performing in a play) in America two weeks later, Paul paid a call to San Francisco, already well on its way toward the summer of love, to meet up with some of the hippie capital's local musicians, and to get a reading of where the American scene was headed. And, more important, to preview a few tracks from his band's latest album. Nat Weiss, who was traveling with Paul, made a call to local impresario Bill Graham, who arranged for the members of the Jefferson Airplane to visit the British musician in his hotel. After some small talk, Paul took out an acetate of *Sgt. Pepper's Lonely Hearts Club Band* and started playing the tracks to the assembled musicians. "You just have to imagine Paul playing the disc, like he's auditioning," Weiss says. "He was looking at each person, as if wondering what they were going to say about each song. He was *mesmerized,* wanting to hear how much they loved the new music. But there are only so many ways you can say, 'Oh, that's great!'"

The Jefferson Airplane, it seems, liked what they heard. Still, it's hard to imagine that their response could have prepared Paul for what was to come when the record was finally released at the beginning of June.

Never before, or since, has a rock 'n' roll record so perfectly distilled a moment in time. Released on June 1, 1967 (and twenty-four hours later in the United States), *Sgt. Pepper's Lonely Hearts Club Band* was an instant triumph, a "historic departure in the progress of music," according to *Time* magazine. The album sold phenomenally well, of course, and wasn't slowed a bit by the arrival of a new and completely unrelated single, John's "All You Need Is Love," part of which was recorded live in the midst of the global *Our World* broadcast on June 25. The single was en route to claiming the top of the charts. Sales for both projects were in no way wounded by the press brouhaha that Paul touched off by admitting, first in *Life* magazine and then on British television, that he had not only taken LSD, but actually enjoyed the experience. "It opened my eyes," he said, adding that he'd returned from the trips as "a better, more honest, more tolerant member of society."

The more conservative elements of British society turned out to be far less tolerant of Paul and the prospect of an acid-gobbling teen idol. His fellow Beatles were even less happy with him, not just because he'd more or less outed all of them—violating a long-held code of *omertà* regarding their drug use—but also, maddeningly enough, because he was the first to claim the hipster high ground even though he had been the last of them to try acid. "We'd been trying to get him to take it for eighteen months," George remembered. "And then one day he's on the television talking all about it!" John, for one, came to see a connection between Paul's headline-making revelations and his innate sense of how media attention could help move product through the shops: "He always times his big announcements right to the letter, doesn't he?"

Still, family is family, and as the Beatles contemplated their future as adults, their initial impulse was to move together, still the four-headed monster, even as they took on wives and children and interests all their own. Given more money and acclaim than even they could have imagined, propelled by the media to the fore not only of rock 'n' roll or showbiz, but of their entire generation, the group became expansive. Everything was within reach; they could start their own company; they could own shops, buildings, factories. And why stop there? They could set up their own Beatles society and live together in communal bliss; the four men, their families, their collaborators and employees, everything they would need to make music and art, to raise and educate their children. One of John's new acolytes, a self-proclaimed electronics wizard named Alex Mardas (call him Magic Alex, please), came from Greece and had connections with the government. So off they went, the four Beatles, wives, and friends, to take a sailing tour of Greek islands they could purchase and transform into Beatleland. They spent a charming few days in the Mediterranean sun and even arranged to buy an island to house their dreamiest dreams. But they never came close to moving and eventually sold the land to someone else at a nifty profit.

When George, in his ongoing pursuit to absorb Indian music and all manner of Eastern philosophies, became enamored of a guru named Maharishi Mahesh Yogi, who was visiting England to bring his message of peace, happiness, and regular tithing to Western society, George's first impulse was to tell the other three Beatles. Their reaction, just as naturally, was to nod their heads and follow their bandmate to the hotel where the sweet-faced guru was speaking. After an evening of mystical chat, they all agreed to journey all the way to Wales, to get a full three-day course in the mystical practice of what the Maharishi

called transcendental meditation. Still, he was far more than just another Eastern mystic, and once he had the Beatles attached to his venture, he made sure the newspapers knew all about it. The weekend
seminar in Bangor became a full-blown media event, and Paul, with
several days of meditation behind him, was eager to declaim on his
newfound faith. "You cannot keep on taking drugs forever," he said.
"We were looking for something more natural. This is it."

No one suspected that the weekend-long pursuit of enlightenment
would end with the group losing the center of gravity that had long
held them together. But the four Beatles, along with their spouses, assorted friends and staff, and the usual contingent of reporters were
only a day into their weekend of meditation training when a ringing
phone in the entry of the dormitory where the Beatles had been staying at Bangor's Normal College interrupted Paul's chat with a reporter
from the *Liverpool Echo*. They had been standing outside on the
grass, but Paul jogged inside to answer the phone, explaining to the
writer that no one else in the building was likely to hear the ring. A
moment later the reporter saw Paul, now ashen faced, dashing up the
stairs to the other Beatles' rooms.

Brian Epstein, he had just learned, was dead, the victim of an accidental overdose of prescription pills.

It was a shock, if not a surprise. As a gay person raised in a fiercely
homophobic society, Brian had spent the bulk of his life laboring
against a guilt, and a self-loathing, that often fed appetites that spun
pleasure and escape into self-destructiveness. Success had done little to
assuage his moods. He had grown increasingly mercurial in the midsixties, his moods magnified by the heavy diet of pills he took to rouse
himself in the mornings and ease himself into sleep at night. Brian had
also become a heavy drinker, and the toxic forces battling within his
nervous system only pushed him further into psychological dysfunction, and by 1967, to the brink of death. He'd tried to moderate his
habits, to find a way to ease his internal fires. But as with so many
brilliant people, Brian found it difficult to separate his brilliance from
his darkness. His passion for John had been fueled in part by a long-
standing desire to be humiliated by tough-talking young men. But he
also responded to John's sensitivity and a large part of what had

aroused Brian's fascination in the dank, noisy Cavern Club that after-noon long ago was his ability to intuit the artistic passion that fueled the band's rock 'n' roll.

So Brian had courted the band, even when its deceptively charming bass player had briefly hijacked the group's signing of their first mana-gerial contract in Liverpool, then taken the manager aside to assert, in only a half-joking way, that the McCartney star would rise with or without the help of the other Beatles. The group had soon eclipsed even Paul's ambitions, of course, and like the others his gratitude for their manager's role in their success came with no small amount of personal affection, even love.

Paul, with all his charm, knew how to bend people to his will. Tony Barrow, who saw Brian interact with all the Beatles in the London of-fices, recalls how John's attempts to bully Brian never worked as well as Paul's more subtle maneuvers. Brian may have found an erotic charge in John's bully-boy personality, but it was Paul, Barrow said, who knew how to seduce him. Platonically, but still. "He used the fact Brian was gay to get his own way," Barrow says. "He'd come in and put on his bedroom eyes. He'd use his own sex appeal to manipulate Brian into doing what he wanted the band to do."

It wasn't always a seamless performance, nor painless for Brian. As American lawyer Nat Weiss recalls, "Paul was a problem for Brian. He was late, and then he'd contest Brian's managerial decisions." Paul was particularly bitter when he'd learned that the Rolling Stones had secured a richer advance from their label than the Beatles had ever re-ceived from EMI. How was it possible, he fumed, that the most suc-cessful act in show business didn't have the best record deal? Maybe they needed someone else to manage them. Someone more like the Stones' manager, Allen Klein?

Such talk curdled Brian's blood, though it's unclear if Paul ever re-ally meant it as anything beyond the usual grumbling. In fact, the two men had seemed increasingly close in the final months of the manag-er's life. "Maybe Paul began to attach to Brian's very upper-middle-class ways," Weiss says. "But they were getting along well. Like, *really* well." Peter Brown, another longtime NEMS employee, remembers the same thing: "If you wanted something done, Paul was the one who'd say, yes, we should do that, let's do it. He realized the value in doing publicity, and taking care of business, and that's where Paul could be enormously helpful to Brian."

Ultimately, the four Beatles were centered by one force: the manager they all loved and trusted. "They believed he was a totally honest person, which he was," Brown continues. "Their area was performance and writing, and they didn't let him get involved in that. And the business side was his responsibility." And now that Brian was gone, that centering force had also ceased to exist. Paul, despite the sorrow of losing a friend and partner, tried to take it in stride. Not much would change, he figured. "We were almost managing ourselves, really." At the same moment John was having the opposite reaction: "I thought, we've fuckin' had it."

Once Brian's funeral was past and a few days had been given over to mourning, Paul got on the telephone and asked the other Beatles to come to his house. It was September 1; the summer of love, that watershed season the Beatles had defined so indelibly, was all but over. So now Paul was going to help guide them into everything that would happen next.

They would make a movie. Rather than turning to an outside writer to craft a script (Paul had already rejected Joe Orton's *Up Against It,* noting to the award-winning playwright, "All I've ever gotten from the theater is a sore arse"), this time they would work entirely from their own vision, based on the "Magical Mystery Tour" song Paul and John had worked on briefly during the *Sgt. Pepper's* writing sessions. The movie would expand the song's basic idea—an old-fashioned coach tour that became a magical trip, pun intended! They would star in it, of course, and provide the sound track. But this time they would also write the script and direct the cameras, while their own company would produce it. The Beatles would have complete control over every step, and every detail, of the project. The others nodded their approval, or at least didn't vocally disagree, so Paul sat in front of a typewriter to make notes of what they would need to go forward. A coach, for one thing. They would need a union face book so they could hire actors who had the right look for the various parts they would write. Not that they would be writing a traditional script, exactly—Paul had written out a vague story line months earlier in the form of a clock face divided into eight parts, with the "scenes" described within. *Commercial introduction. Get on the coach. Courier introduces* constituted the first piece. Numbers five and six read simply *Dreams*.

"You don't need scripts for that sort of film," Paul said later. All they needed were some interesting-looking people—a fat lady, a midget, a couple of hot blondes, and more—to steer themselves into the countryside, and wait for the Beatles magic to take hold. It had always worked before, right?

The Quarrymen play the Casbah Club in 1960. Paul sings to Cynthia Powell as her boyfriend focuses on his guitar.

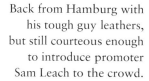

Back from Hamburg with his tough guy leathers, but still courteous enough to introduce promoter Sam Leach to the crowd.

Still at the Cavern in 1962, but armed with a new wardrobe and a recording contract, the Beatles were on their way.

Recording "Love Me Do" under the watchful gaze of producer George Martin, September, 1962.

Even as Beatlemania swept the group around the world, Paul made sure music was at hand.

Young, beautiful, and successful: Paul and Jane Asher (in 1964) were Swinging London's "it" couple.

Jim McCartney on one of his regular visits to Paul's house on Cavendish. As Paul always liked to point out, there was never a generation gap in the McCartney family.

"Sgt. Pepper's" band in 1967. A new look, a new sound and an entirely new horizon for popular culture.

They barely spoke at the "Sgt. Pepper's" release party, but after spending the evening at Paul's feet, American photographer Linda Eastman told friends she was destined to marry the last bachelor Beatle.

By the summer of 1969 Paul and John were both married and the bond between them had shattered.

With the Beatles in tatters, Paul fled to his farm in the rustic hills of Scotland.

February, 1972: With his new band in tow, Paul got back on the road, playing two weeks of surprise gigs at colleges around the UK.

Wings toured Europe during
the summer of 1972.
At a soundcheck in Tivoli,
Linda leaves her keyboards
to dance to Paul's music.

Like a band of minstrels,
Wings toured family-style,
with wives, kids, and dogs
along for the ride.

Here, there, and everywhere:
Paul and Linda (in Eric Stewart's
recording studio in 1974) were
usually within reach of one another.

Family business as usual: Mr. and Mrs. McCartney, circa 1974, take the kids to the circus.

By 1976, Wings (with Jimmy McCulloch and Joe English joining originals Linda, Paul, and Denny Laine) were ready to fly around the world.

By the mid-70s, Linda had become a comfortable, if not expert, onstage performer.

Say, say, say what?: After collaborating with Paul in the early '80s, Michael Jackson took his advice and invested in music publishing. Just not the songs Paul had in mind.

Paul's second attempt at filmmaking, *Give My Regards to Broad Street* was even more disastrous than *Magical Mystery Tour* had been.

Back on the road in 1989, Paul came with his Beatle bass and a setlist packed with the most beloved songs in popular music.

above: After mourning Linda for nearly two years, Paul found love again with Heather Mills.

right: Touring again in the twenty-first century but with his past never far away.

From out of the ruins to the top of the heap: Nearly fifty years later, the Beatles still stand as the world's most influential, and perpetually beloved, rock 'n' roll band.

11

Ray Connolly started calling Paul's house in the late morning of December 27. *Magical Mystery Tour* had aired on the BBC the night before, the reviews were in the morning papers, and the *Evening Standard* reporter was after a comment. But the only McCartney who was awake in the house was Jim, visiting from Liverpool. Paul was sleeping in, he'd had a late night. Could Ray call back in half an hour? Yes, he could. He called back three times before the elder McCartney decided his rock-star son needed to face the day and answer his phone.

"Tell you what, Ray," Jim said, ever the Northern gentleman. "God loves a trier. I'll go wake him."

Jim put the receiver down and padded up the stairs. Eventually, Paul came shuffling to the phone, and Connolly told him what he was after: the *Mystery Tour* reviews, had Paul seen them? What did he think? Paul hadn't seen them. His father handed him the stack of newspapers. Connolly could hear the rustling of newsprint. Then silence. Then . . .

"Bloody hell!"

Which was putting it mildly, given what he was reading. Here's the *Daily Mail:* "Appalling!" The *Daily Mirror:* "Rubbish! Piffle! Nonsense!" The *Daily Express:* "The bigger they are, the harder they fall." While the *Times* opted for a more measured approach, noting the "good-humoured anarchy" and the way "realities are annihilated by cinematic devices," the critic, Henry Raynor, still pointed out that the film's attempts to be avant-garde were a bit less than "particularly new." By the time the *Evening News*'s TV critic took stock of the reactions that afternoon, the conclusion seemed inescapable: "There was precious little magic and the only mystery was how the BBC came to buy it."

Actually, the real mystery was how the Beatles' psychedelic home movie, with its barely sketched plot, improvised dialogue, and surreal musical sequences, came to be shown on national TV on the day after Christmas (Boxing Day in Britain, traditionally a time for cozy family get-togethers and postholiday festivities) in a black-and-white broadcast that rendered its colorful abstract moments into little more than a murky blur. Certainly, the dream sequences—particularly John's vaguely sadistic set piece in which he played a sinister waiter serving a mountain of spaghetti to an increasingly upset obese woman—were puzzling, and the long scene that juxtaposed the four celestial magicians (the Beatles, of course) with a wild, if inexplicable, footrace made no sense whatsoever. Still, from the remove of the twenty-first century, *Magical Mystery Tour* may seem a bit less ridiculous. Its surreal humor anticipates the genre-bending antics of Monty Python's Flying Circus (albeit without that group's precise sense of narrative), just as its elaborately staged musical vignettes would endlessly be mimicked on MTV in the 1980s.

But after nearly five years of uninterrupted acclaim from the British media, the critical battering earned by *Magical Mystery Tour* seemed like a harbinger. Now that the Beatles had declared their independence, now that they weren't going to be anyone's lovely lads, they weren't going to be treated like anyone's national treasure. If this was a rude awakening (literally, thanks to Connolly's phone call) for Paul, he spent the rest of that day doing his best to take his punishment like a man. "Aren't we entitled to have a flop?" he asked in one interview. "The lesson is good for us, and we're not bitter about it." Still, he struck a note of defensiveness in the *Times:* "We thought we would not underestimate people and would do something new. It is better being controversial than being boring." Appearing on David Frost's live interview show that night, Paul took questions from the host and members of the audience. "There was no point and no aim," he said, attempting to explain the movie. When Frost invited the audience to indicate if they liked the film, Paul pointed to the scattering of raised hands and said, "There's a few, you know. I think it's all right. The next one will be a lot better."

There would be a next one, Paul was sure. "He really expected *Magical Mystery Tour* to open doors for him, to make him the film producer of the Beatles," says Tony Barrow, the NEMS publicist who had been at the September 1 meeting at Paul's house and had tracked Paul's filmic strategies through the succeeding months. Assuming the band wasn't going to play concerts, they had to connect with their audience in some other way. Movies, Paul felt, were the obvious answer. "He wanted them to start an entirely new phase in their career," Barrow continues. "But on his terms. He'd be the executive producer."

The failure of *Magical Mystery Tour* knocked the wind out of that strategy. The other Beatles didn't mind the film's critical failure—John took particular delight in having confused and infuriated so many people—and also didn't mind seeing Paul's estimation of himself knocked down a peg or two.

From the amazing highs of the summer of 1967, the last weeks of the year signaled an unexpected shift in Paul's fortunes. The *Magical Mystery Tour* disaster came just a day after he and Jane had made it official: after nearly four years of being the Beatles' most public couple, they had finally decided to get married. They didn't have a particular date in mind, but the news made their families happy, particularly given the tension that their dueling careers—and all the physical distance and emotional upheaval they caused—had put between them. Now, it seemed, they had found a new stability, and maturity, to guide them into adulthood.

The Beatles were looking for a new stability, too, and in the early weeks of 1968 it was George's deepening fascination with the Maharishi and transcendental meditation, along with John's curiosity for anything that promised to alter his perception, that became the group's central focus. So rather than move straight into recording a new album (which was Paul's inclination, unsurprisingly), they opted to take up the Maharishi's invitation to spend a few months at his remote meditation camp in the hills of Rishikesh, India. Ringo figured he'd go along for the ride, too, since he was always game to follow the others' lead. At which point Paul realized he had to go, too. He'd already risked alienating the other Beatles by resisting LSD for so long. So if the other Beatles were going to pursue this new form of enlightenment, he knew he needed to join the quest or else risk falling out of step. "Paul disliked the idea of them being together but so far away from him," Barrow says. "He wanted to keep his eyes and ears open and stay in touch with their moods." Of course they would all bring their guitars, so it could be a productive time for the group, too. Between meditation sessions they could write a whole new batch of songs. "I remember talking about the next album and [George] would say, 'We're not here to talk music—we're here to meditate!'" Paul said. "Oh yeah, all right, Georgie boy. Calm down, man."

They set out in mid-February, John, Cynthia, George, and Patti leaving three days before Paul and Jane left London with Ringo and his wife, Maureen. The Maharishi's hillside camp was dreamy, in its way, sunny and leafy and free of the many distractions and indulgences media-borne fame and wealth had brought into their lives. The other students were largely drawn from the ranks of the young, the moneyed, and the famous. Donovan knelt alongside the Beatles, as did the Beach Boys' singer Mike Love, Mia Farrow and her sister Prudence, and a variety of writers and photographers, some of whom (including *Harper's* magazine editor-to-be Lewis Lapham) would go on to document the adventure in print. The Beatles brought along Mal Evans, Neil Aspinall, and Alex Mardas, the somewhat shady Greek inventor, to round out their entourage. For a time they were all happy to meditate, take in the guru's spiritual tutelage, contemplate the jungle foliage, eat the camp's vegetarian curries, and, of course, strum their guitars.

The chittering jungle sounds animated hours that filled days, which slipped into weeks. The meditation was calming, while the Maharishi's high-pitched, giggly lectures revealed some glimmers of spiritual ease. The break from drugs and alcohol provided an additional dose of clarity, particularly for John. But no amount of group unity, let alone the shared appetite for transcendence, could assuage Ringo's gastronomic distress from spicy food, nor Maureen's hatred of flies, so they were gone after two weeks. Paul and Jane had their fill after five weeks, and George and John gathered up their spouses and returned to London on April 12 in something of a huff, acting on a tip from Mardas, who claimed to have seen the guru attempting a little transcendent bliss with one of the female campers. They'd gathered up their things and stormed out while the Maharishi trailed behind, wringing his hands and imploring them to at least tell him *why* they were going. "If you're so cosmic, you'll know!" John retorted. And off they went, John already composing the bitter verses of "Sexy Sadie," under its original title: "Maharishi."

That was only one of the three dozen new songs they had composed during the journey. Just as Paul had hoped, the jungle had proved a remarkably fruitful environment for their creative pursuits. But the larger purpose of the trip, the Beatles' quest for enlightenment, had not gone nearly as well. In a sense, the sputtering conclusion of the Beatles' Rishikesh sojourn also represented the end of all the journeys they had taken together since they'd set out for Hamburg in the late summer of 1960. Each trip had marked another step in their progress, from inexperienced teenagers seeking a group identity, to seasoned professionals seeking fame, then famous pop stars ascending to unprecedented acclaim, wealth, and cultural prestige. Having risen as far as mortal experience could carry them, they had followed one another into India's primordial mists, at least partially convinced that they had already amassed the power to catapult into yet another level of existence. They had already achieved everything else. Surely, there was nowhere else to go but up. But when they gazed toward eternity and saw only their own faces gazing back, even the Beatles could see they had come to the end of something. Now it was time to float back to earth. To confront the pop machinery, look into its grinding wheels and gears, and finally take control of their own destiny.

You'll get yours yet, however big you think you are.

The company began in late 1967 as a tax strategy. The Beatles were taking in so much money from their records and various other income streams they either had to invest it in something or else lose vast quantities of cash to Britain's steep personal income taxes. Far better to spend their own money their own way, particularly if it allowed them not only to have even more control over their work, but also to give other, less fortunate artists some control over theirs. So was born Apple Records. Only it was never going to be just a record company. "Paul wanted it to be just about everything," Peter Asher said. "Films, theater, television, records, and even spaceships." Only they'd do all those things their way, with the emphasis on inspiration and art, rather than on money. That's how they'd succeeded in music, after all. It made perfect sense that the approach would work everywhere else, too. "The idea is to have an 'underground' company aboveground," Paul told Miles in a 1967 interview. They'd share the profits evenly with everyone in the company, he continued, "so that everyone who needs a Rolls-Royce can have one, then, after that, we'll give them away to anyone who needs help."

They took the first step in December, opening the Apple Boutique, where they sold an array of custom-made clothes designed by the Fool, a nebulous group of Dutch hippie aesthetes who had somehow found their way into the Beatles' circle. The business model for the shop was nonexistent. The Fool were profligate spenders of the Beatles' money, insisting, for instance, on making the labels for their garments out of silk whose cost rivaled, or even eclipsed, the rest of the materials. They also created an elaborate psychedelic mural for the shop's exterior, which, while beautiful, was so far beyond the neighborhood's accepted standards they had to quickly recoat the walls in plain white or else face a lawsuit. Meanwhile, the four Beatle bosses weren't exactly helping matters, since their separate visits to the store often resulted in commands that contravened those of the previous Beatle. And which would promptly be contradicted by the orders issued by the next Beatle. Shoppers jammed the place when it opened, and it seemed like a huge success. Except that many of them were walking out without paying for the things they were taking. No one wanted to act like a heavy—that wasn't groovy—so the thieving went on uninterrupted. "It was a shoplifter's paradise," said longtime Beatle aide Alistair Taylor. The Apple Boutique lasted seven months and lost a bit less than £20,000. Shops, Paul explained, "just weren't our thingy."

Music and art, on the other hand, felt like a more natural fit. They were musicians after all, and if they didn't know some aspects of the business, they knew people who did and could hire the ones they trusted. Paul tapped Peter Asher to run the artistic side of the record label and hired Ron Kass, a canny American then living in Switzerland, to take care of the business side. A variety of longtime NEMS employees—many of whom were, such as Peter Brown, Alistair Taylor, Tony Bramwell, and trusted helpmates Neil Aspinall and Mal Evans, friends from Liverpool—moved into other key positions. Brian's original NEMS spokesman, Derek Taylor, returned from exile in Los Angeles to head up the Apple press office. They also insisted that Capitol appoint Ken Mansfield, a cool young executive they had all become fast friends with during the 1965 American tour, to represent Apple's interests in the United States. On May 11, John and Paul flew to New York to introduce their new company to America in a series of press conferences and smaller interviews. On the fourteenth they appeared together on NBC's *Tonight*, parrying awkwardly with substitute host Joe Garagiola and an apparently soused Tallulah Bankhead, who perched behind the host's desk with Garagiola, as if she were afraid to sit any closer to the longhairs.

Most of the interviews and photo opportunities had been performed in hotel suites, but John and Paul had actually camped out at the Upper East Side apartment of Nat Weiss, the NEMS attorney who still represented the Beatles' interests in the United States. It was easier to avoid the less appealing vestiges of the mania that way, though it also limited their prospects for meeting up with the sort of starstruck and perpetually willing women who tracked them to their hotels. As a result, the two Beatles had to compete to seduce the young woman Weiss had recently hired to be his maid. John eventually came out ahead, Weiss recalls. Nevertheless, Paul's visit wasn't a complete romantic bust. At a reception held in the Americana Hotel a few hours before the *Tonight* interview, his eyes fell on a familiar blond photographer. She was willowy and funky looking, with long, elegant fingers and heavily lidded, sleepy eyes. Hadn't he seen her in London a year or so ago? Indeed, he had; they had spent part of an evening in the same crowd at the Bag O'Nails Club. She'd turned up at the *Sgt. Pepper's* press-launch party Brian had thrown at his house a few days later, and she had perched at the foot of Paul's chair, snapping photographs from the floor as they chatted a bit. And now here she was again! Paul asked for her number, and Linda Eastman scrawled it across the back of one of her checks. He didn't get a chance to call until the next day, at which point he was already headed to the airport to fly home. Maybe she could come along for the ride and hang out a bit? Paul had the limo veer a few blocks uptown to pick her up, and when the car door opened at her door on East Eighty-third and Lexington, Weiss realized he already knew this woman. She was the daughter of Lee Eastman, the prominent music-industry lawyer. What's more, they had been seated together on the flight from London to New York a year earlier, after her first encounters with Paul in the spring of 1967. "She had never met Paul before," Weiss recalls. "But she was telling me all the way across the Atlantic that she was going to marry him."

While the Beatles' business may have been at the front of his mind, Paul's emotional terrain had started to shift in life-altering ways. He might not at first have imagined that John's decision to leave Cynthia for Yoko Ono, the Japanese-born, American-raised conceptual artist with the prankish aesthetic and ironclad will, would change his own creative and personal relationships. The partners certainly seemed in step during their trip to New York ("They were definitely close then," recalls Nat Weiss), still going everywhere together and completing one another's sentences when they got there. Talking to Ken Mansfield in Los Angeles a month later, Paul said he never minded giving John co-credit on songs he'd written essentially on his own because "even when John's not with me, I can hear him say if it's a good or bad idea. So we *are* writing together, even when we aren't." And this wasn't just Paul being fanciful—John said nearly the same thing when he spoke to Mansfield about their joint writing techniques. That same spring John reprised the "Fool on the Hill" melody in his omnibus Beatles reference song, "Glass Onion," noting that he and his partner were still "as close as can be." Later, John would describe the "Glass Onion" nods to Paul as a farewell gesture. But it's hard to imagine that being a conscious thought in the spring of 1968. After all, John and Paul were only ramping up the Beatles business right then, not just moving into the heat of production on a new album, but also diving headlong into the formation of their own multifronted entertainment industry.

By the spring of 1968 they were also both in the midst of domestic upheaval. Paul's engagement to Jane Asher had ultimately done little to repair the fractures in their bond. She had nearly left him for another man in December, though his abrupt proposal of marriage had drawn them together again. Only Paul had never been entirely dedicated to Jane. His relationship with Maggie McGivern, who now supplemented her modeling career by running an antiques stall, had continued over the years, and there had always been shorter-lived romances, too. So when Paul went to Los Angeles in June (accompanied by Tony Bramwell and old Liverpool pal Ivan Vaughan) to put in an appearance at a Capitol Records sales conference, he made as much time for pleasure as he did for business. And he did plenty of both.

Ken Mansfield, the Capitol executive the Beatles had hired to be Apple's face in the United States, served as Paul's guide and guard throughout his visit. Though Mansfield had known Paul in both official and unofficial capacities for nearly three years, Mansfield was impressed all over again with the Beatle's ability to tend to business with the same dedication and focus he put into his music. From the moment he made his surprise entrance at the back of the Century Plaza's ballroom (to a chorus of gasps and then wild applause from the label's army of sales reps), Paul projected nothing but eager enthusiasm. He shook hands, he schmoozed, he posed for snapshots with anyone who asked. "He wanted to do things the way they were supposed to be done," Mansfield says. "We had guys in from Des Moines, the guy from Arizona, everyone. And I was having him take pictures with everyone. I was pushing and pulling on him, making sure he wasn't spending too much time with anyone. But he did everything. He took the pictures with everyone, he came to the convention, he had dinner with all the low-level movers and shakers. That was way beneath his status as a rock star. But he had come over for the specific purpose of following the rules of being a company president."

At the bungalow they'd rented in the Beverly Hills Hotel, Paul took out his guitar and entertained Mansfield with the new songs he was still polishing for the album the Beatles were about to start recording. He sang songs he was making up on the spot, inspired by any and everything he saw around him. "He was like a fountain of music," Mansfield says. After a few drinks they went out to dinner, then off to the Sunset Strip to the Whisky a Go Go to take in B. B. King and the Chicago Transit Authority, whom they tried to sign for the then na-scent Apple Records. The group's manager, William Guercio, seemed intrigued, but said they had already been talking to Columbia Re-cords. Mansfield says he wasn't aware of any hanky-panky taking place at the Beverly Hills Hotel bungalow. But Bramwell provides a vivid account of Paul orbiting between two bedrooms, both of which contained models he was entertaining. Another female acquaintance, the actress Peggy Lipton (soon to become famous on the TV show *The Mod Squad*), paced the hotel grounds anxiously, hoping to renew her friendship with the visiting Beatle. But all of those antics came to an end when Linda Eastman knocked on the bungalow door.

Paul had telephoned a day or two earlier, dialing the number on the check she had handed him in New York, telling her he was in L.A. for a couple of days and inviting her to come out if she had the time and felt like it. She did and she did, so Paul got rid of the other girls and was still strumming his guitar with Mansfield in the bungalow's living room when Linda appeared at the door. The Capitol executive got up to answer her knock and gazed down at the mystery blonde with sea-soned wariness. "I had no idea who she was," he says. "I thought she was a groupie." He was about to tell her to get lost, but then the blonde rushed right past him and dashed into Paul's arms. The next thing Mansfield saw was the two of them vanishing into one of the bungalow's back bedrooms. The door clicked shut, and that was that. "I waited around for a while. Then I figured it was time for me to go. From then on she was always with us." Not quite, according to Linda, who recalled whiling away hours with Ivan and Tony at the hotel while Paul attended to the Capitol sales reps at the Century Plaza. But they did spend most of a day together in a group that had been invited by the director Mike Nichols to spend the afternoon cruising on his yacht.

When the idyll was over, Linda went back to New York, while Paul and his friends went back to London. Jane was off working on a play, as usual, but the sessions for the next Beatles album were beginning, and the Apple organization was just coming together in its temporary offices on Wigmore Street. One day a young American woman named Francie Schwartz turned up bearing a movie script she *knew* was a natural for Apple's film division, and what's more, Paul was the obvious guy to do the sound track. No one else was convinced, but when Paul glimpsed Schwartz in the waiting room, the attraction was immediate, if not particularly cerebral. Soon Schwartz moved her bags to Cavendish, and thus began a long, tempestuous summer of something other than love.

It all came out in "Helter Skelter," the end-of-the-world rocker Paul wrote specifically to be the loudest, raunchiest song in the history of recorded music. What he imagined, he said, was the sound of destruction: the collapse of the Roman empire; the musical equivalent of screaming chaos. "This was the fall, the demise, the going down." Or maybe "Helter Skelter" was the sound of his own life hurtling out of control. Screams and cackles. Come-ons verging on insults. *You may be a lover, but you ain't no dancer.* The band was up half the night doing that one, the four of them pulled close on the studio floor, the lights down and the amps turned all the way up, blasting into a haze of hashish smoke and red wine. Paul flails at the bass while Ringo pounds the drums and John and George go at their guitar strings with a fury to make them bend and snap. Paul screams himself hoarse, John and George wail like banshees behind him, then the whole thing collapses like a burning building falling into embers. *Comin' down fast,* Paul moans. He's not really chanting *Yeah, shit* as the thing flies apart in the end—it just sounds that way.

Coming down fast. An iciness with Jane, now so distant that even casual friends could see through their beautiful facade. Marianne Faithfull recalled a Cavendish evening when the lovely couple battled intently, if silently, over a living-room window. Paul tugged it open; moments later Jane walked over and gently slid it shut. Paul stood, sidled over, and wrenched the window wide. Jane, en route to the kitchen for another bottle of wine, slammed it closed. Open. Shut. Open. Shut. Not a word between them, though. Not even a sideways glance. "That really was like a Joe Orton play," Faithfull said. "It was fucking great." Paul loved Jane's intelligence and independence, but he was older now, more powerful and influential than anyone else he'd ever even heard of; why couldn't she see things his way? Possibly because he wasn't particularly good at talking about his feelings. He certainly couldn't find it in himself to tell her it was time for both of them to move on—he let Jane figure that out for herself when she came home unexpectedly one bright summer morning, only to discover her fiancé in their bed with a radiant Francie Schwartz. A comeuppance that was startlingly like John's ultimate dismissal of his wife, Cynthia, who had only weeks earlier come home to discover her personal bathrobe sitting across from her husband in the family kitchen, wrapped around an otherwise-naked Yoko Ono, who was in the midst of postcoital tea and toast. The Fabs were never good at saying goodbye, just ask Pete Best (or Eric Griffiths, for that matter). Jane ran off in tears and sent her mother back later that day to pick up her pots and pans.

Recording sessions for the new Beatles album began at the end of May, getting off to an awkward start when John trooped in with Yoko at his heels and made clear that she would be within arm's reach for the duration. True enough, Beatles sessions had in recent years become public performances of sorts, with select friends and acquaintances observing the *artistes* from folding chairs on the studio floor, or if perfect silence was required, from the control room at the top of the stairs. But while those guests were understood to keep their thoughts to themselves, John actually encouraged Yoko to offer comments, and even criticism. The first time this happened, in the midst of a vocal session for John's "Revolution," it proved so shocking that Paul, George, and Ringo could only gape at one another in stunned silence. Until, as Tony Barrow recalled, Paul finally found his most cutting, sarcastic voice.

"Fuck me!" he cracked. "Did somebody speak? Who the *fuck* was that?"

Of course he knew who it was; she was sitting right there in front of all of them. But the others joined in anyway, calling up to George Martin in the control room, asking in moronic tones if he had been the one who had talked. "Your lips didn't move! Have we got a new producer in?"

Not quite. But what they did have was a spiritually revived John Lennon, whose allegiance with Yoko had not only awakened his confidence, but inspired him to apply her anarchic aesthetic to the Beatles' new works. No longer willing to be cowed by Paul's unrelenting professionalism, John was now intent on driving the group toward a kind of rock 'n' roll nihilism that would detonate their pop image once and for all. You say you want a revolution? You want to talk about destruction? Count John in, and Yoko, too. And not just in "Revolution," but also with "Revolution No. 9," the eight-minute collage of chants, screams, mutterings, and other found sounds the happy couple had constructed, in consort with George, when Paul was either out of the room or, more thematically, when he was at the sales convention in Los Angeles. Once he heard the sonic montage, the pop-friendly Beatle was not, as they say, best pleased. Not that he hadn't been making these same tape-loop collages for years; he'd fucking well *taught John how to do it*. But when Paul brought the loops into the Beatles' studio, it was in the service of actual, recognizable songs. "Tomorrow Never Knows" had challenged the pop-music form, to be sure. But it had a melody and verses . . . it was music, not finger-in-the-eye provocation. When Paul got the other Beatles involved in making a nearly fourteen-minute tape-loop freak-out during the *Sgt. Pepper's* sessions, that was for a specific project (sonic accompaniment to the Carnival of Light event to be held at the Roundhouse), never intended to emerge on an actual Beatles record. Which was exactly what John insisted "Revolution No. 9," in all its endless chanting, screaming, sizzling, and car-crash noises, had to be. On the album, at least. And maybe even the next Beatles *single*! Paul was aghast. He was furious. He pulled John out into the EMI hallway to have it out, face-to-face. *You're trying to undermine the group!* he wailed. John just grinned back, gleefully cockeyed through his owlish glasses and lank, shoulder-length hair. *Spot-on! That's it, exactly.*

Paul took his revenge a few days later when he turned sessions for his bouncy, reggae-esque "Ob-La-Di, Ob-La-Da" into a grueling, days-long marathon, leading the group through dozens of renditions as he made minute adjustments to various rhythmic and melodic concerns. Paul's fussiness drove John to distraction, then beyond, as his mood veered wildly from enthusiasm to ennui to bitter antipathy. When Paul announced plans to re-re-record the song from the ground up, John finally stormed out, seething and spitting. As staff engineer Geoff Emerick recalled, John returned a few hours later, his eyes electric and pinwheeling. "I am fucking *stoned*!" he cried, reeling to the nearest piano. "And *this*," he cried, glaring wildly at Paul, "is how the fucking song should go!" He pounded out a double-quick intro that, amazingly, seemed to resolve the tune's rhythmic puzzle. Paul, Emerick wrote, seemed simultaneously furious and delighted. "Let's do it your way," he hissed. Which they did, quickly finding the groove that had been eluding them for so long.

Sometimes it was easier, and more fun, than that. When Paul played John and Yoko "Hey Jude" for the first time, the other Beatle was immediate and unstinting in his praise. "One of his masterpieces," he said. John was also convinced Paul had written the song for him, as subtle encouragement to leave the band, and his songwriting partner, and pursue his new life with Yoko. Paul explained that he'd actually written it with himself in mind (although he'd started it as encouragement to five-year-old Julian Lennon, whose family had just broken up), and John felt their bond anew: "Oh, check. We're going through the same bit." Still, "Hey Jude" also spurred more bitterness when Paul shook off George's attempt to echo his vocal with answering guitar lines in the song's final verse. Once the song was recorded, it revived John and Paul's ongoing struggle to claim the A-sides of the band's singles. John had assumed, or at least hoped, that his funky, snarling "Revolution" would win the spotlight. Instead, the other Beatles, along with George Martin, preferred Paul's song, even despite—or perhaps because of—the epic *na-na-na-na* chorus that drew the song's focus from personal relationships to the larger bonds of community and civilization.

Community is a beautiful thing, and also extraordinarily complex to maintain when visions and ideals come into conflict. When John needed a place to live with Yoko, Paul threw open the doors to Cavendish and invited them to move right in. It'd be just like old times, wouldn't it? Except it wasn't, now that John was so consumed by Yoko and they were both consuming the sort of hard drugs Paul preferred to keep at a distance. Francie Schwartz was living there, too, and recalled plenty of fine evenings watching TV with John and Yoko while Paul lurked elsewhere. One day the guests received a card, unsigned but with familiar handwriting. *You and your Jap tart*, it declared, *think you're hot shit*. John, who had known that handwriting since *Another Lennon/McCartney Original* was scrawled above their earliest lyrics in those Forthlin Road writing sessions, propped the card on the mantelpiece, and when Paul came home, he simply shrugged. He'd sent it, he explained, "for a lark." Message received, John and Yoko found their own apartment a few days later.

Friendship and rivalry, warmth and disdain, acceptance and dismissal, love and hate. The songs they recorded that summer were shot through with contradictions, and the chill of a darkening horizon. No tangerine trees and kaleidoscope eyes these days; now it was all smoking guns, rapacious pigs, and sexy rip-off artists. The songs flew in a dozen directions, but even the overarching theme of discord and disillusion could inspire harmonious efforts. When Chris Thomas, then a young engineer for George Martin, started work in September, he was impressed with the childlike sense of wonder the Beatles brought to recording. "They were very playful about how they approached their work," he says. "So they could discover new things simply by trying new things." When Paul came in with the riff for "Birthday" one afternoon in late September, they all joined in enthusiastically, working out parts and quickly knocking out a backing track. When 9 p.m. rolled around, they all agreed to run off to Paul's house, so young master Thomas could finally see their favorite rock 'n' roll movie, *The Girl Can't Help It,* on TV. Yoko came, too, of course, and they'd all had a fine time, smoking hash and remembering when Eddie Cochran had seemed too wild and revolutionary. Reinspired, they all skipped back to Abbey Road to finish off "Birthday," John sitting with Paul to polish the lyrics, then all of them arrayed around the microphones, with wives and girlfriends, to do the singing, family-style, until the session ended at 5 a.m. "They seemed like good friends to me," Thomas says. And they certainly were, that night.

But that wasn't the night Ringo stormed out, feeling lost and alone in the prevailing chill. He took a break for a few days—during which Paul doubled as the band's drummer—then returned to discover his drums covered with flowers. But most often the band went in two or three separate ways, each songwriter working on his own tunes, with only the most minimal input from the others. Ironically, John felt the most hurt when he realized Paul had cut him out, if only because he actually liked some of Paul's new tunes, particularly the minimalist horndog rocker "Why Don't We Do It in the Road" and wanted to be a part of them.

Paul was wild and free and desperately unhappy. He built a glassed-in meditation chamber in his back garden and put a mattress in so he could smoke hash and gaze up at the stars. Groupies moved in, often in pairs and threes, and wandered the halls half-naked, giggling and sifting through his possessions. He was alternately warm and icy and, according to Schwartz's account, engaging in wild sexual antics one day, then hectoring her about her clothes and locution the next. Visiting his father in Liverpool one weekend, he took her to a McCartney family party, then vanished. A cousin led her to a pub a few hours later, and she found Paul blubbering drunkenly about how far he'd come and how little it all meant. Money and success had turned him into a family patriarch, of sorts. He'd bought an elegant house on the Wirral for his father—now remarried to a younger woman, who came with her own daughter—and served as a musical godfather to Mike's band, the Scaffold. They were bright lads and had their own ideas and topped the charts with "Thank U Very Much," even after Paul had expressly told his brother it would never work. Big brother didn't like being contradicted and also didn't like being leaned on. "It's too fuckin' much!" he'd slurred to Schwartz that night in Liverpool. "Too fuckin' much!"

Back in the studio a few days later, waiting to record a take of "I Will," Paul sat with his guitar and played a taut fingerpicked pattern to himself, singing in a high, lonesome voice that had all the sad desolation of a man who felt truly and completely lost.

Can you take me back where I came from? Brother, can you take me back?

12

Groupies in the house, drugs everywhere, the toxic haze of everything, all the time. Yet what it amounted to, in the buzzless moments just before dawn, was nothing. Nothing that mattered, and this was when Paul's mind returned to the sloe-eyed blonde from New York. She was different: neither elegant nor high-end hipster; not cool; not sizzling hot. But that thing about her, that indefinable warmth, made him feel different, too. Closer to the ground. At ease and—could it be possible?—secure. Was he kidding himself? Paul could never be sure, so after their first intense weekend at the Beverly Hills Hotel in Los Angeles, he'd taken Nat Weiss aside and drilled him for information: Did Linda really own a horse in Arizona? Was her dad really a big entertainment lawyer? Did she really grow up with the de Kooning and Franz Kline paintings on the wall and famous songwriters dropping in for dinner? He didn't know what to believe anymore. "I don't blame him for not wanting to be taken advantage of," Weiss says. "He was used to these girls who were after his money or his fame."

He'd call her that summer, and they'd catch up, chat about the stars she was photographing that week, where she'd taken her young daughter, Heather, over the weekend. Paul wanted kids, too, but when and with whom? Ah, these were the questions. Was she coming to London anytime soon? No? He certainly couldn't come to New York anytime soon—the new album wasn't done yet, they had to have it out by Christmas, then he was trying to get Apple up and running, too. Maybe she could come visit? Well, he had to invite her first, didn't he? Yes, of course. But he couldn't seem to make up his mind. Paul had kept his quiet affair with Maggie McGivern going, and with Francie Schwartz out of the way by September, he spirited McGivern off to Sardinia for a week of carefree, romantic fun in the sun. They were lying together on the beach, she said, when he started talking about marriage. Had she ever thought it? McGivern shrugged. "I said, 'Yes, I suppose, someday.'" He never mentioned it again. "Looking back, it was obviously the wrong answer," she said.

Only Paul knows if he was actually contemplating asking McGivern to marry him. Either way, it wasn't long before he was on the telephone again with Linda and finally made the offer she'd been waiting to hear: *Come over*. Linda got a friend to look after Heather, bought herself a round-trip ticket, and took off. He was working in the studio when she arrived, so she explored the Cavendish house on her own. It was a terrible mess: broken furniture; dogshit everywhere you looked; nothing to eat in the fridge. How could a person live like this? Paul couldn't, was the thing. And she knew this already. She called down to EMI and got Tony Bramwell on the phone. "I'd love to see you," she said to him. "And can you bring over some milk, coffee, and dog food?"

So now they were together, though Linda had to share her man with the Beatles, who occupied most of his nights. During the day they did what young couples do when they're just falling in love: he showed her his city, they smoked hash, they listened to music, they made love, she made him dinner, then she did the dishes when it was done. Linda knew her way around a kitchen; she knew how to satisfy so many of his appetites, including the ones he rarely allowed himself to acknowledge. *Of course you can,* she'd say. *It's allowed.* Something about those words undid him. *It's allowed!* He could relax! He could be Paul and not always, you know, *Paul.* So they'd get into his car and drive aimlessly, steering up roads he'd never before seen, finding beautiful places he never knew existed. *It's allowed.* Linda was willing to follow his lead, in a way Jane never had, and showered a maternal warmth on Paul that the sophisticated young actress never did. Before long, he could feel himself falling for her.

But whom was he falling for, exactly? Francie Schwartz had already signed a deal to write a memoir about her Cavendish tenure for *Rolling Stone,* and a book would follow. So Paul kept his new girlfriend at a bit of a distance. He made a point of doing things on the cheap, or giving her the opportunity to pay for things every so often. And if Linda registered some surprise to her friends ("She used to write in to a colleague of mine and complain that Paul was being rough with her in terms of money," Weiss says), she made sure Paul knew she wasn't put out. She was used to having money, she didn't mind not having it, either. She wasn't looking to cash in on anyone.

She'd been there. Linda was born in 1941 and raised by Louise, a product of Cleveland's Jewish aristocracy, and by Lee, a self-made, Harvard-trained lawyer whose clientele of artists and musicians included heavyweights such as Tommy Dorsey, Hoagy Carmichael, and Willem de Kooning. Both socially and professionally ambitious, Lee had changed his name from the more Semitic *Epstein* (subsequent Beatles irony noted) and eventually moved his family from Manhattan's Upper East Side to the tree-shaded avenues of suburban Scarsdale. The eldest Eastman child, John, lived up to his parents' expectations, acing his schoolwork and eventually following his father to Harvard and law school, en route to becoming a partner in Lee's law firm. Linda, the second of the Eastmans' four children (younger sisters Laura and Louise followed), seemed to lack the family's ambition. She was indifferent to school, preferring to ride her horse or simply commune with the wildlife in the fields. As a teenager in the late fifties she honed tastes for rock 'n' roll, art, and boys. *A yen for men* is how they put it in the Scarsdale High School yearbook. Compelled to go to college, Linda chose the University of Arizona, thousands of miles from home, out in the desert where horses, and young women, could run forever. She didn't last long in college, unsurprisingly, and had already dropped out when her mother was killed in an airplane crash. It was a devastating loss for the family, particularly for Laura and Louise, the girls still at home. Still, Linda went back to Tucson and her boyfriend, a geology student named Melvin See. Soon she was pregnant, then married. Their daughter, Heather, was born at the end of December 1962. But the couple split up by end of 1964, then Linda was back in New York, a young single mother with more imagination than education, let alone actual prospects.

Nevertheless, Linda landed on her feet. She rented an apartment just a few blocks from the Metropolitan Museum of Art on Manhattan's Upper East Side, then leveraged her preppy charm and name into a job as a receptionist for the high-society-focused *Town & Country* magazine. She fit in with the media people and was at a party for Atlantic Records in 1965 when she introduced herself to a young photographer named David Dalton. She'd learned a bit about photography in Arizona and was eager to find out more. "I said, 'Yeah, babe! Come up to my studio tonight and we'll develop some film!'" Dalton remembers. Linda was at odds with herself then, he recalls. "Pretty, slightly overweight, and depressed, she slept a lot." But she was beguiling, too; smart and sensitive; and she had such a sweet relationship with her little girl, Heather, who slept in the apartment's one real bedroom and didn't miss a trick. "Linda and I would get high and Heather would say the most amazing things: 'My brain is talking but my mouth can't shape the words!'" Dalton says. "I'd think, 'This is André Breton at six years old!' That was this very charming aspect of Linda, her life with this wonderful child."

They became lovers, and Linda studied the way Dalton worked, how he set up shots, how he thought about composition and lighting. When she picked up a camera at a difficult session with Tommy James and the Shondells, Dalton was astonished at how she could maneuver unruly, uncooperative musicians into doing exactly what she told them. "They all wanted to fuck her!" Dalton recalls. "I mean, they *all* lit up. And I thought, 'This is good! You're gonna be good at this!'" Better still, Linda had a natural flair for the art, and when she talked her way onto an exclusive shipboard press conference with the Rolling Stones, she came away with a series of indelible portraits that became her first professional calling card. That was also the night Mick Jagger tried to seduce her. "She came up to me and said, 'Um, Mick just asked me for my number, what should I do?'" Dalton recalls. "I said, 'Give it to him!'" She did, he called, and they spent the night together. Soon Linda became a prominent figure in the New York scene, a particular favorite for the bohemian types who had gone to school before entering showbiz. "She was very upmarket to them," Dalton recalls. "She was kind of intellectual. You could mention things to her, like Thomas Mann or Nietzsche, and she'd know what you were talking about."

Linda liked the musicians, too. "She loved their energy, and insolent, wild behavior," Dalton says. When an appealing man beckoned— Jagger, Stephen Stills, the Grateful Dead's Bob Weir—she rarely hesitated. Don't call her a groupie, though. "You have to consider the times and the place," says longtime friend Danny Fields, who worked the rock scene as both a journalist and an industry insider. They were young and free, poised at the first glimmers of the hippie era. The possibilities seemed endless, the limitations nonexistent. So Linda fantasized openly about marrying everyone's favorite Beatle. When she actually met him and got to know him, then told her friends that he had actually asked her to come stay with him in London for a while, no one blinked. She fretted for a while, musing that he obviously had so many women around him, why would he need her? "What if I get there and I'm just part of a harem, or something?" she asked Fields. He told her she *had* to go. "Are you kidding? He's Paul McCartney! He's the most beautiful man on the planet! Get *out* of here!"

The Beatles had started Apple with the same utopian hubris they made real in their music. "A kind of Western communism" was how Paul described the company philosophy at first; a way to turn their unfathomable Beatles earnings into a fount of art and beauty. "They were very much into it," recalls Ken Mansfield, who attended many of the early Apple planning meetings in the spring of 1968. "They showed up on time, they were totally focused, and there was never any bickering." The good vibe at Apple continued through the summer, even as the recording sessions at EMI grew tense and chilly. "They each volunteered to do particular things, deciding on releases, on A-sides, and so on. They wanted to do things by the numbers." Once the Savile Row building was ready—its walls painted a sheer white; the apple-green carpet laid on the floor; the cordon bleu kitchen up and running; and Derek Taylor's pressroom stocked with vast quantities of Scotch, cigarettes, and hashish—Paul was a leader in everything from signing artists (his first success was with the teenaged Welsh singer Mary Hopkin, whose first single, a McCartney arrangement of the German folk song "Those Were the Days," dueled with "Hey Jude" for the top of the singles charts in the early fall) to overseeing the promotional campaign for *The Beatles*, which would soon come to be known, for its distinctively plain cover, *The White Album*.

The record was hailed as a triumph, yet another harbinger of cultural change, according to the critics, who noted how the four now-distinct voices wove into a pop-art collage that veered easily from sweet to dark, from love to contempt, from spiritual contemplation to drug-fired outrage. Singular works, individual voices, sometimes solo recordings. But arrayed together they informed and influenced one another. Paul's soft-shoe retread "Honey Pie" sounded different, an echo from the Weimar Republic, when heard as the preamble to John's cataclysmic "Revolution No. 9," just as George's whispered "Long, Long, Long" redeemed the smoldering wreckage of Paul's "Helter Skelter."

Paul's songs cover the gamut from rock 'n' roll revivalism ("Back in the USSR" and "Birthday") to folk ("Rocky Raccoon," "Blackbird," and "Mother Nature's Child") to playful pop ("Ob-La-Di, Ob-La-Da," "I Will," and "Martha My Dear") to chants and lo-fi digressions ("Wild Honey Pie") that are nearly as outré as John's flights of electronic weirdness. "Helter Skelter" is beyond menacing, while "Why Don't We Do It in the Road" struts and slinks with wicked glee. Even Paul's most mainstream tunes tend to include off-kilter elements that seem aimed straight at the icy stare behind John's owlish specs. "Rocky Raccoon" sneaks across the frontier into a netherworld town where everyone comes with at least two names and even more identities; the doctor's a drunk; the only thing close to wisdom is the Gideon Bible, sitting ignored in the hotel-room drawer. (Not quite Bob Dylan's mini-epic "Lily, Rosemary and the Jack of Hearts," but you can certainly draw a line from here to there.) "Ob-La-Di" evoked the then nascent reggae movement and ends on a gender-bending note as Molly works on the barrow and Desmond stays home "doing his pretty face." Even "I Will," the most straightforward love song in sight, pulls off an unexpected trick: Paul's typically fluid bass line is sung, not played, by the song's author.

Perhaps his greatest achievement on the double album is the beautifully understated "Blackbird." Inspired by a Bach piece, the fingerpicked bass and melody notes move in tandem, and sometimes in opposition, up and down the fretboard, jumping an octave before easing back down toward the root chord. The lyric, meanwhile, operates entirely in the metaphorical realm, projecting the plight of the repressed into the form of a wounded but resilient bird. Performing alone, accompanying himself on guitar and with the hard sole of his shoe (tapped to the beat), Paul sings in his most forthright voice. The final line of the chorus, and then the song, pushes the lyric toward the breaking point with "the light of the dark black night," but the elegance of the melody, and the simple beauty of the performance, overwhelms whatever literary weakness it contains. What remains is what shines through so much of the Beatles' best work: a glimmer of light in the darkness; a song to ease the pain.

As the four individual portraits seen on the album's inner cover implied, the Beatles had grown into four distinct personalities and voices. Yet, from a distance, with a perfect balance of opposing ideas, ideals, strengths, and flaws. Even when John and Yoko released their debut collaboration of electronic weirdness, *Two Virgins,* bedecked with a beyond-provocative cover shot of the happy creators standing together in all their uncircumcised and saggy glory, Paul not only provided a cover blurb (though the lines, "When two great Saints meet it is a humbling experience. The long battles to prove he was a saint," were chosen at random from the text of a nearby copy of the *Sunday Express,* an act Paul called "found object" artistry, but could also be interpreted as a trifle backhanded) but also defended the wrench-hurling nature of its cover, telling Ken Mansfield that John was simply too far ahead of the curve to be understood at first blush. "I'm not suggesting he was happy about it," Mansfield says. "But John was his friend and partner and so he wanted to show a united front." Paul, like most everyone else at Apple, was a bit less pleased than he let on. What a great time to get out of town.

So they left, Paul and Linda, heading to her unglamourous one-bedroom apartment on East Eighty-third and Lexington Avenue, to walk on her streets and live her life. Paul went incognito, growing a beard and wearing some surplus army fatigues and a baggy tweed overcoat he'd found in a used-clothing store. They traveled the city by subway and contemplated the smoked ducks in Chinatown and the lights of the Apollo Theater in Harlem. They walked in Central Park with Heather, who liked to pretend she was a tiger, stalking and roaring in the grass. They were a young family in the city, their days beginning with the clatter of the window grate being hoisted on the liquor store across the street, and ending to the echoes of taxicab horns on Lexington. Linda took him to meet her family, and when she escorted a real, live Beatle across the Eastman threshold, suddenly the under-motivated, black-sheep child no longer struck her father as being quite so disappointing.

When they saw a Buddhist temple advertising its wedding services, Paul proposed they walk right in and do the deed right there and then. But Linda shot him down—she'd just gotten divorced, remember?—and the most eligible bachelor in the Western world loved her even more for it. They went back to England, this time with Heather in tow, then off to vacation in Portugal. Musing over her birth-control pills one sunny morning, they decided to just leave them be and let fate take its course. They were definitely in love now, so their future had fallen into larger hands.

The Beatles, however, still seemed to require Paul's constructive ma-nipulation. Though only a few weeks had passed since the end of the generally strained sessions that produced *The White Album,* he was already scheming the group's next big step. A return to the concert stage struck him as the obvious thing; regaining contact with the audi-ence would not only freshen their bond with their fans, but also revive the group's sagging esprit de corps. They'd play music together again, see people get off on it, and remember why they got into a rock band in the first place. That was Paul's idea, anyway, but when he presented it to the other three at a meeting in their Apple headquarters that De-cember, John just stared back. He'd had one divorce that year, and that felt so good maybe it was time for another! The Beatles, he pro-posed, had run their course. It was time for them to move on. Paul went white, stammering angrily. Was John crazy? Hadn't they just started a joint business? How was Apple going to survive without the Beatles as its profit-generating center? Ringo, and even George, who had zero interest in reviving the Beatles' touring machine, didn't want to quit just yet, either. So a compromise emerged: they would gather just after the New Year to rehearse a new batch of songs they would record live, at a place to be determined. They'd film the rehearsals, then the concert, and get a new record out of it, too. With John more or less firmly on board, the momentum, if not quite enthusiasm, mounted. They hired Michael Lindsay-Hogg, fresh from the Rolling Stones' *Rock 'n' Roll Circus* project, to direct the footage for the TV show and/or movie they planned to make of the project, then booked the Roundhouse, a former train depot that had become one of the city's hipper performance venues, for January 18.

The rehearsals began, cameras rolling, on the morning of January 2. Even from the start everything seemed out of kilter. They had moved their instruments to the cavernous Twickenham movie studios, the better to accommodate the camera crews and their visual and audio needs. But whatever was gained in filmic convenience was lost in creative comfort. The building was cold; the film crew required the band to keep hours that began too early in the morning and followed a far too regimented clock. Paul came in early, Linda and Heather in tow, sporting a beard that gave him the appearance of a vaguely hip, and yet persistently uptight, grammar-school teacher. As with *Magical Mystery Tour* he stepped quickly into the role of executive producer, giving precise instructions to Lindsay-Hogg about how the cameras should move, just like this, while the sound should be captured just like that. When the others trooped in, they came in various shades of distracted and sullen, with John all but fogged over by his new fixation: heroin. Yoko was using the drug, too, of course. Her generally grim, expressionless face, billowing black hair, and constant placing within an arm's reach of John made her seem like a dark cloud hovering in his sky. Nevertheless, the group (and Yoko) perched on a circle of wooden chairs placed within a maze of amps, drums, baffles, rolling banks of lights, and other gear. A phalanx of helpers, minders, camera operators, and boom-wielding soundmen moved around them, filming and recording every moment from every conceivable angle, and not meaning to be anywhere near as distracting and vibe-killing as they were.

Not that the vibe was all that lively to begin with. Paul, as prim as a bearded longhair could possibly be, addressed his fellows as if he were standing at a blackboard, pointer in hand. "Okay, lads!" he'd proclaim, with efficient good cheer, when he figured it was time to focus. He led them through his new songs, barking out chord changes and directing the tempo and feel. John had a few new tunes of his own, and George a veritable embarrassment of lovely ones, including "All Things Must Pass." Paul took them all on eagerly, pitching in loud, high harmonies even before he'd been asked to do so. George Martin, who had been instructed to hang back and simply capture the sound of the group, mistakes and all, in their natural habitat, wasn't feeling all that cheery either, so Paul strolled into the producer's void, too, directing John to sing directly into the microphone ("I can't hear you!") and giving George precise instruction on the phrasing of his guitar breaks. George absorbed this for only a few days before snapping back to Paul, as well as the cameras and microphones, that he would play whatever Paul wanted or play nothing at all, if that's what he'd prefer. "I'm not trying to *get* you," Paul responded feebly. "I'm just saying, lads—the band—shall we do it like this?"

Shall they do another of Paul's songs? "The corny one!" he said with a wink one day, preparing to march his bandmates through the chords of "Maxwell's Silver Hammer," a song whose bouncy, music-hall-sound melody clearly made John and George more than a little queasy. Nevertheless, Paul drilled them through it, over and over, with Mal stationed over an anvil he'd been instructed to strike, clang-clang, at the key moments. Another day it was Paul's sprightly tale of a mis-understood child, "Teddy Boy," then the quasi-gospel "Let It Be," then his lush ballad "The Long and Winding Road." Patience began to wear thin. Halfway through another "Teddy Boy" run-through, John snapped completely, interrupting Paul's vocal with loud, sarcastic square-dance instructions. "When you've got it, let it go," he called out, and he meant it, too.

At times the others seemed ready to acquiesce to Paul's ambitions. They canceled the Roundhouse date since no one imagined they'd be ready by the eighteenth, but that only opened discussions about end-ing the project with an elaborate free show in a Tunisian amphitheater, or on the deck of an ocean liner. Thinking again of the stage put them in mind of the oldies they used to play, so they launched into ragged jams of the songs they had once performed with such blistering assurance in Hamburg and around Liverpool: "Slippin' and Slidin'," "Memphis, Tennessee," "You've Really Got a Hold on Me," "Don't Be Cruel." Dozens more, and newer songs, from Dylan, the Band, Canned Heat. They jammed on their own songs, too, including never-staged tunes including "Every Little Thing" (a particular favorite of George's), "Strawberry Fields Forever," with Paul on piano and lead vocal, and "I'm So Tired," with Paul sharing the lead with John. They all did a verse or two of "Love Me Do," flirting briefly with making the song a full-on blues shuffle. But the sparks failed to ignite, the guitar strings felt slack in their hands, and the tune broke down.

Linda's old boyfriend David Dalton had been tapped, along with Jonathan Cott, to craft the text of a book that would accompany the album's release, and given access to hundreds of hours of audiotapes from the sessions, they heard more than a few grim moments. "Paul and Linda trashing John and Yoko before they came in; and then vice versa. John's schizophrenia, which was brilliant and maddening. And then Paul's insane persistence, dragging them through thirty, forty, fifty run-throughs of 'The Long and Winding Road.' You could hear the dissolution on those tapes, how mournful and awful it all was."

It didn't take long for George to reach his breaking point. Tired of the struggle to get his songs heard, humiliated one time too often by Paul's persistent instructions, he unstrapped his guitar and leaped to his feet. That was it. He was leaving. "See you round the clubs," he called on his way out the door. Paul watched in horror and Ringo looked sad, but John merely shrugged. If he's not back by Tuesday, he averred coolly, they could simply anoint Eric Clapton and not miss a beat.

The *Evening Standard*'s Ray Connolly had become close to the band, particularly to John and Paul, and had thus become more than familiar with the currents and undercurrents that came to overwhelm the music in the Beatles' lives. What they had become, he says, was the very model of a dysfunctional family. "John was the ne'er-do-well father, Paul was the hardworking mother trying to keep everything together. George was a slightly surly teenager, and Ringo was this happy-go-lucky young kid with his model airplane. That's really how it was."

And, it seemed, how it would remain, at least for the foreseeable future. George agreed to rejoin the group as long as they dropped the idea of playing a concert for a live audience. The others welcomed him back, and with the tension-easing presence of the soft-spoken American keyboard player Billy Preston, soon a batch of new songs began to take shape. Climbing up to the roof of the Apple building to perform five new songs in a brief, unannounced lunchtime session on January 30, 1969, the love they shared for their music, and for one another, lit up their faces and electrified their bodies. Paul's "Get Back," the chugging rocker whose title served as the watchword for the entire back-to-the-roots project (and, John mused later, Paul's not-so-secret desire for Yoko to back off), kicked things off in high gear, with John pitching in with a prominent lead guitar. John stepped up next with his impassioned "Don't Let Me Down," a love song to Yoko that Paul had turned into an affectionate duet, the two singers falling again into the embrace of their harmony. "I've Got a Feeling," an actual, and seriously underrated, Lennon-McCartney collaboration, came next. Paul had come in with two-thirds of a song, a chiming anthem to the joys, frustrations, and confusions of a gathering revolution. As he describes them, the feelings animating the song are personal (deep inside) and social (everybody knows) and as unsettling as they are thrilling (how come nobody told me?). Still, the song lacked something, and miraculously, a fragment left over from John's batch of Rishikesh songs, "Everybody Had a Hard Year," provided just the right contrasting texture. Stepping up to the microphone, John answered Paul's verses with a litany of unifying comforts: *Everybody put their feet up,* he sang. *Everybody let their hair down.* When they reprised their parts together, Paul's voice jumped and twirled with his melody while John's luxuriated in his, an invitation to lie back, different words for another sentiment: let it be.

A few more songs. The revived "One After 909," from way back in the Forthlin Road sitting room, brought back to life with all its complaints and silly disconnections intact. John's "I Dig a Pony," lurching with the shambolic wisdom of a drunken oracle, again with Paul accentuating John's chorus with his flawless high harmony. Now they were in a groove, they looked as if they could go on all afternoon. But half an hour of high-decibel rock 'n' roll had attracted the local constables, and as the blue-hatted bobbies peered icily from just beyond the amps, the Beatles just had time for a spirited reprise of "Get Back." This one was sloppier, with John missing his first guitar break, the rhythm occasionally losing its focus. But the Beatles were in concert, in more ways than one, and with the disapproving glare of the authorities on their necks, they were in their element and couldn't have been happier. "You been playing on the roofs again, and that's no good, 'cause you know your mama don't like that," Paul improvised over a final vamp. "She gonna have you *arrested*! Aw, get *back*!"

The next morning they gathered in Apple's basement studios to perform the quieter songs—all of them Paul's compositions—for the cameras. Just a day later the good feelings had all but evaporated. Reduced to being supporting musicians, John and George hunched impassively over their instruments as far from the camera's eye as possible. They played "Let It Be" and "The Long and Winding Road," Paul sitting at the piano, the stark lighting making the best of his black blazer and buttoned-up white shirt. When he stood to play the acoustic guitar, he perched at center stage, peering directly into the camera. While John had once sung his part of "On the Way Home" (now rearranged into a folksy shuffle titled "Two of Us") standing eye to eye with Paul at the same microphone, he now lurked so far away he couldn't even be seen in the same camera shot. That the song had obviously been inspired by their friendship, even if its imagery came from Paul's jaunts with Linda (with whom he did not have "memories longer than the road that stretches out ahead"), either hadn't occurred to John or simply meant nothing to him.

Then it was all business, and then there was nothing but trouble. For all its artistic and chart success (and not just with the Beatles) Apple was hemorrhaging money. The group's other business interests had always been shaky; absent Brian Epstein they had grown even more dire. At the rate they were going, John had blurted to the papers, they'd be broke "in six months." He was, of course, overstating the situation. But clearly, something had to be done. And once he met the Rolling Stones' scarily effective manager, the gruff, bluff American Allen Klein, John knew exactly who should be doing it for them. This impulsive decision was fueled in large part by John's visceral sense that Klein was a rough-and-tumble loudmouth, just like him. Klein had also quickly realized that John's decision-making would flow through Yoko, so he charmed her most of all, soliciting her opinions and, according to Paul, promising to arrange a splashy solo exhibition of her art, to be funded by the Beatles.

George and Ringo were game, but Paul was so opposed as to be completely aghast. Klein was ill-dressed and ill-mannered, a screamer and finger-pointer, already notorious for wrapping his chubby fingers around money and copyrights a more ethical manager might not have tried to claim. Or so Paul heard, and so he came up with another candidate: a sophisticated American law firm with a long track record of representing brilliant artists and musicians. *Lads, I give you Lee and John Eastman!* And Paul was right—Eastman & Eastman was (and remains) a well-regarded law firm. Yet they were also, the lads had noticed, the father and brother of Paul's live-in girlfriend. Was he really proposing his veritable in-laws as the perfect, and perfectly objective, managers for the linked affairs of four very independent, and now extremely fractious, business partners? Yes, Paul was. Not just that, he was *insisting*. They worked out a Solomonic compromise, with Klein brought in to audit and reorganize the group's affairs, while the Eastmans served as legal counsel. But with John allied with Klein and Paul all but wedded to the Eastmans, and neither faction inclined to abide, let alone work with, the other, the arrangement was not designed for long-term success.

On the contrary, the "warm working relationship" between Klein and the Eastmans that Apple's press office described functioned mostly like a demolition derby. Teamed with Yoko, Klein personified John's most virulent anger, hurling insults and accusations with sneering contempt. Lee Eastman, on the other hand, reflected Paul at his most unctuous, ladling on the charm and modern-art chat to John, which only set the hypersensitive musician on edge and made him and Yoko that much more eager to accuse Lee of talking to John as if he were a rube. Things only got uglier when Dick James, the song publisher who had helped John, Paul, and Brian set up Northern Songs back in the early days, decided to sell his stake in the company. Northern Songs had been floated on the stock market in 1965 (largely as a way to turn highly taxed income into more sheltered capital gains), and though both songwriters had been issued an equal number of shares in the company, Paul had quietly instructed Apple executive Peter Brown to buy him additional shares when they became available on the market. He had neglected to tell John he was doing this—deliberately, it would appear. When Klein reported this discrepancy to his client, John, understandably, went berserk. "This is the first time any of us have gone behind the others' backs!" he shouted. Paul's response was beyond lame: "I felt like I had some beanies, and I wanted some more." This new wedge between John and Paul inspired even more infighting. And this, along with the bitter rivalry between the Klein and Eastman camps, demolished John and Paul's chance to gain control of Northern Songs. Virtually all the songs they had written in their careers would now be owned by strangers.

The company they had so cleverly dubbed Apple Corps (another Paul idea) was already, to borrow a bad pun, rotting to its core. Klein had moved into 3 Savile Row and set to dismissing any- and everyone who represented deadwood or, as often, a threat to his authority. Even Alistair Taylor, the NEMS functionary who had accompanied Brian Epstein to the Cavern Club on those first, chilly afternoons, later to become one of the group's closest and most able assistants, got the bullet. He couldn't believe it at first and dialed his four old friends to see if it was really true. True to form, none of them had the fortitude to take his call. Klein solidified his grasp on John and George, and once he had Ringo in the fold, he figured he didn't need to romance his stubborn, bass-playing adversary. When the intercom crackled in the midst of a meeting with a dozen or more Apple employees, Klein responded to his secretary's news that Paul was on the phone for him by barking that he was too busy to talk. "Call back Monday!" he snapped. Paul was both infuriated to be slighted like that and a little freaked out. It wasn't long before he was having nightmares in which Klein, dressed as a dentist, chased him with a sizzling drill.

To her friends in New York it was as if Linda Eastman had risen into another world. She knew a lot of people in the city, an entire community of professional contacts and personal friends, such as David Dalton, Danny Fields, and especially Lillian Roxon, an older, more experienced Australian-expatriate writer who had become something of a maternal figure to her. Linda and Lillian spoke every day, multiple times, about the most serious and the silliest things. Work and love, their diets. They were girlfriends in that intense way some women have with each other. It might have felt even more significant for Roxon, whose sexuality was amorphous. "I'm sure Lillian had a thing for Linda," Danny Fields says. No matter, when Linda left for England at the end of the fall, she went quickly and without an official farewell. Once she was gone, for weeks and then months, her only communications home were brief, cryptic postcards such as the ones she sent Fields, reading only *Wow!* and *You bet!* Between that and the London postmark, all they could imagine was that their friend had been drawn into the Beatles universe, from which real communication with the mortal world was not possible.

Or maybe it had more to do with the psychological dynamics of this intense, yet tentative new romance. For all his charisma and authority, the man of Cavendish Avenue was also, at least for the moment, excruciatingly insecure. To be in his life, his woman had to forswear the life she had left behind. All those friends; all those places; the vestiges of her pre-Paul life wouldn't and couldn't matter anymore. Linda, for her part, was happy to make the sacrifice. David Dalton bumped into his old girlfriend in Regent's Park one day, the first time he'd seen her since she had attended his wedding in New York the year before, and felt an immediate distance from the woman he had once taken under his wing. "She said, 'Oh, you must come to dinner one night!' But then she never asked for my phone number and certainly didn't give me theirs." Dalton had grown up in England, he knew the empty politeness of the British middle class when he heard it. "And that was the last time I saw her. Ever."

Then Linda was pregnant. The fates, it seemed, had no question that this relationship was meant to be. The two lovers were delighted, and somehow unsurprised. Now they obviously *had* to get married, it was the only proper thing for a Liverpool man to do. They wanted it to be low-key; a brief civil ceremony and then a luncheon for a few close friends. A lot like John's wedding to Cynthia, now that you mention it, though six years and several universes apart. Paul asked his brother to serve as best man and called on Mal Evans to be the witness. It was so very loose that Paul forgot all about buying his beloved a wedding ring; he had to sprint out to a jewelry store, arriving just at closing time, and leaving with a pair of simple gold bands costing less than £30 for both of them. Back at Cavendish, he and Linda got into an argument that nearly derailed everything. But they made up in time, and the next day, March 12, they took a car to the Marylebone Registry Office to make it official. Easier said than done, however, because word of the Last Great Beatle Wedding had leaked, and the street outside had become a late-era echo of Beatlemania, with teams of journalists and TV cameras shoving against a veritable wall of wailing, tear-moistened fans. When it was all over, Paul stood at the top of the stairs beaming into the throng, waving and smiling and throwing purple-wrapped candies at his keening fans. Later, he held an impromptu press conference at his front door. How does it feel to be married? he was asked. "It feels fine, thank you!" he proclaimed. Someone asked Linda if she was really a member of the Eastman Kodak family, and she denied it. "What?" Paul exclaimed in mock outrage. "I've been done! Where's the money!"

Paul was all smiles then, but less than forty-eight hours earlier he'd knocked on the door of Maggie McGivern's Chelsea apartment in a very different mood. His longtime secret girlfriend hadn't seen much of Paul since their trip to Sardinia the September before, but they'd been in touch, so she wasn't surprised when the bell rang and she found him standing at the door. It was after midnight, and he looked upset. "He was crying, and I knew he had been stressed," she said. "Suddenly he jumped up and said he had to go." She heard about his wedding two days later when she was walking down Kings Road and saw the headlines.

John saw the headlines, too, and once he got over clucking about Paul's cheerful glide through the screaming fans, he was on the telephone to Peter Brown, telling the Beatles' top factotum that he needed him to plan his wedding to Yoko. John wanted to do it as quickly as possible, preferably with no press at all. Not that they were interested in living in the shadows. Quite the opposite. They just wanted to save it for the honeymoon.

13

On the morning of April 14 the Cavendish phone rang, and Paul heard John's voice coming through the line. He was just back from his and Yoko's wedding in Gibraltar, and the weeklong "bed-in" they'd conducted in Amsterdam to promote their new international campaign for peace. Well on the way to leaving behind their individual identities for a new, unified profile (*Johnandyoko* was how John liked to describe them), John had written a new song to commemorate the union. This was "The Ballad of John and Yoko," and he wanted it to become the new Beatles single. George and Ringo weren't available—they were both out of town. But could Paul come down to EMI to record it this afternoon? Well, sure. Why not? Terrific! The bell rang a couple of hours later and there was John, a guitar case in hand and Yoko in tow, and then they were thumping upstairs to the music room so John could play the tune. *Christ, you know it ain't easy!* For all his behavioral transgression, this was rock 'n' roll in the straight-ahead Chuck Berry mold: three chords, a first-person story, and a lot of attitude. Paul got it and dug it instantly. So they gathered up Linda and Yoko and off they strolled, this awkward new foursome, down the street and around the corner toward Abbey Road.

Down to the floor of Studio Three, and with a new song between them everything was back to the way it was. John played guitar and called the shots; Paul played bass, drums, and maracas and pitched in a vocal harmony. The work went quickly, they were laughing and joking. "Quite a good vibe in there, actually," recalls Apple art director John Kosh, who popped into the control room on an errand. Kosh had his wife with him, and they hung around for a bit, watching the guys work until John had a moment to come up and look at the calendar Kosh was roughing out for him. Linda, still new to the scene but eager to shift into her new role as Paul's wife and protector, confused Marjorie Kosh for a random outsider. Maybe, Linda proposed icily, it was time for Marjorie to leave. Right now. "I didn't see or hear anything," Kosh says. "I just remember Marjorie saying, 'Fuck this!' and storming out." Word got around, and a little later John called the Kosh house to apologize. On the studio floor, however, nothing mattered that day except for the music. "Go a bit faster, Ringo!" John called to Paul on the drummer's stool. "Okay, George!" Paul called back. "It always surprised me how with just the two of us on it, it ended up sounding like the Beatles," Paul said. Except that it probably didn't surprise him at all.

The "Get Back" sessions had been disastrous, sort of. Once the most cohesive of units, the Beatles had grown fractured and fractious. They had depended on one another for so long—since they were children, for John, Paul, and George—and achieved so much that their individual thirsts for freedom were rivaled only by their resentments for the others' needs to be free of them. One week John was announcing that he wanted a divorce. George helped talk him down, but when George stormed out just a few weeks later, John was furious. "The point is, George leaves, and do we want to carry on the Beatles? I certainly do," he said, when arguing for the down-and-dirty move of replacing their childhood friend with *his* best friend, Eric Clapton. "We should go on as if nothing's happened."

Which is precisely what they did, with George back in the fold a few days later. And they kept on even after the "Get Back" sessions left them with the taste of ashes on their tongues. "Such a dreadful, dreadful feeling," John decreed a year later. "The shittiest load of badly recorded shit with a lousy feeling to it, ever." And yet. They'd aired out a lot of new material during that chilly month, and a lot of songs were still waiting to be recorded. Thus, only three weeks passed before they were back in the studio, working on John's "I Want You (She's So Heavy)." The group took March off, while Ringo filmed his part in *The Magic Christian* and Paul and John ran off with their respective girlfriends to be married. Then the good feelings that emerged during the session for "The Ballad of John and Yoko" in mid-April spurred another burst of recording, and by early May it seemed as if the Beatles were, once again, in the midst of making another album.

"'Get Back' just sort of morphed," recalls Chris Thomas, who engineered sessions when George Martin was around, and produced them when he wasn't. Martin wasn't quite committed to doing a new project—it was far too frustrating to be told, as he'd been during the "Get Back" sessions, to not actually produce anything. But at some point during the spring Paul called the producer to tell him that they definitely wanted to make the new album in the old way, a studio production they would work to polish, and everything. Martin agreed and the sessions continued through the summer. They all had songs, some left over from "Get Back," others dating as far back as *The White Album* and the trip to India. They were together again, as much out of habit as desire, and the mood was always tenuous at best. "Everything is true," recalls John Kurlander, who also engineered sessions that summer. "It was calm, it was relaxed, something explosive would happen. And it wouldn't take much . . . a business meeting or a friend coming in when the others wanted to work."

As the mood devolved on the studio floor, the producer and engineers in the control room would grimace and whisper among themselves. "You didn't want to see them like that," Kurlander continues. "And then we'd think, 'We should just leave, maybe.' But you couldn't, because then they'd suddenly say, 'Okay, play this.' And then they'd be going again."

Nothing had been resolved. In fact, the conflicts at Apple, and particularly the duel over whether the group should hire Klein to manage them, were only becoming more intractable. But the need to make music, and to do it in one another's company, was still overwhelming.

You could never predict how many Beatles would show up on any given day, or how they would divide themselves among the three studios at EMI's Abbey Road facility. But no matter what they were doing, it was always easier when they weren't all together. "It wouldn't happen with any two of them together, and not even with three," Kurlander says. "But when you had the four of them, when everyone was together, it was explosive."

They needed each other, they resented each other, they each wanted control, they each wanted to have their reliable partners around them, providing the same intuitive support they had offered for so long. When John presented "Come Together" to the group, it was an upbeat acoustic folk song, almost a talking blues, until Paul urged him to slow it down and put some funk into it. Paul came up with a swooping bass part and a swampy electric-piano riff that made John beam happily: *That's got it!* But when the time came to lay down the vocals, John double-tracked the harmony, rather than ask Paul to chime in. Paul had expected to do the high part, as he'd done so often, then when he saw John preparing to do it himself, he felt too awkward to step in. John, by contrast, made no secret of wanting to sing the lead to Paul's retro-rocking shouter "Oh! Darling"; he'd been edging into it ever since Paul first aired out the tune with the group in January. But Paul kept the song for himself anyway, singing and re-singing the lead once a day for a week to achieve the gritty edge John would have been able to summon instantly. Paul tormented John further with even more run-throughs of "Maxwell's Silver Hammer," then got his own back from George when the author of "Something" issued precise instructions on how he wanted the bass part to be played. Long-suffering producer George Martin watched it all unfold with a kind of stoic distance on his smooth, patrician features, usually shielding himself with one of the day's newspapers. "He'd be on his stool in the studio sort of half-listening," Kurlander remembers. But if they got stuck on some musical point, Martin engaged. "He'd look over the top of the paper and suddenly say, 'B-flat!' Then he'd go right back to reading."

Paul got Martin more involved when he proposed turning the second side of the album into a kind of suite, an uninterrupted span of music that would flow naturally from one song to the next. John resisted the idea at first, dismissing it as pretentious and silly. But once Paul asked him to contribute some songs, John tossed in a couple of *White Album*–era sketches, "Mean Mr. Mustard" and "Polythene Pam," and grew noticeably more enthusiastic about the entire enterprise. Certainly, the interconnected suite remained more a product of

Paul's musical sensibility than John's. But the intensity of his desire to pull John into the production, to weave their voices and musical personae into another collaboration, is underscored by the emotional fervor in the songs Paul had written for the piece. For while John darts madly from one outrageous character to another absurdist fantasy, Paul's songs address his partner directly, recalling the life they'd shared for more than a decade, mourning the ugliness of its end and contemplating the individual lives they were soon to confront.

"You Never Give Me Your Money" begins as a mournful, yet straightforward discussion of the state of the Beatles' relations. It's a portrait of disconnection—no generosity; no communication; no warmth. *And in the middle of negotiation, you break down.* Then the piano turns rollicking, the band kicks into gear, and the mood is transformed. Now Paul is looking back to the post-Hamburg end of 1960, working the cruddy job Jim made him take, a grammar school dropout with no real prospects, yet hot on the trail of a dream that would change everything. *Soon we'll be away from here / Pick up the bags and wipe those tears away.* Which leads to the final chant, a child's doggerel in which all good children go straight to heaven. A paradise revealed, more than a little ironically, in the languid tones of John's "Sun King," a typically outlandish portrait of mania-level fame, focused on a golden child so beloved no one cares that his wisdom consists of utter nonsense—exotic-sounding, yet meaningless scatterings of Spanish and Italian. The music is lush, but a quick drum break shoves the fantasy aside and hurls us into the harsh streets of London, where two of John's other creations, Mr. Mustard and Polythene Pam, engage in sordid antics: the former is bizarrely greedy; the latter is insanely generous with her favors. A series of descending notes, punctuated by John's cackle, then a sharp *Oh, look out!* leads into Paul's own character study, "She Came In Through the Bathroom Window," which describes a fervent admirer whose insistence on entering the narrator's life only accentuates her distance from him. She claims to be an artist (a dancer, at any rate), but sucks her thumb like a child. He refuses to help her or even give her the answer she's after, whatever it is. Was Paul modeling this woman after Yoko? She had just ordered up a pond to be installed at Tittenhurst, the country manor John had bought for them, just as the bathroom-window girl had her own la-

goon to contemplate. Yet, the bathroom girl, at least, could not dis-
rupt the harmony she'd intruded upon: *Sunday's on the phone to
Monday / Tuesday's on the phone to me.* Call it wishful thinking.

Which Paul recognizes all too clearly in the verses of his yearning
lullaby, "Golden Slumbers." There is no way home anymore, he sings,
all you can do is get some sleep and hope for the best in the morning.
"Carry That Weight" describes the chore that awaits in the dawn,
with a brief reprise of the "You Never Give Me Your Money" verse
(and Paul's acknowledgment of his own failure to understand his partner), which leads back to "Carry That Weight," then a kind of instrumental summation of the group's career: a brief drum solo leading
into a three-way guitar battle, the players trading phrases that revealed how distinctive their voices had become, with John using dis-
tortion to push his instrument's boundaries; Paul chasing a melody
high on the neck; and George floating somewhere between the two
extremes. In the end, the Beatles sign off with one final observation:
The love you take is equal to the love you make.

Such a beautiful and beautifully Beatlesque sentiment. A tribute to
universal equanimity, illustrated by the uncanny balance of four diver-
gent, yet definitively balanced musical voices. Just look at the cover of
the album. No name required anymore, not even a glance toward the
camera. The four figures are enough, bringing London traffic to a halt
as they march across Abbey Road. John's in the lead, a Christ-like figure all in white, his chestnut hair and beard flowing over his shoulders
and chest; Ringo next, in neo-Victorian black, with a hint of a psychedelic tie around his neck; then Paul, clean-shaven in a loose-fitting
blue suit, a cigarette in one hand and no shoes on his feet; George
comes last, a funky longhair in denim, detached and yet still in step.

The grown-up Beatles, striding confidently into the future on the
strength of yet another lovely, fully realized work of art. Released in
late September, the Beatles' *Abbey Road* soared from speakers like a
benediction to the extraordinary decade they had defined in so many
ways. It was a symbol of harmony and maturity; a signpost toward
the bright future that awaited them all. Maybe there was no way it
could be true.

John wanted out. Everything about his behavior in the last year made that clear, despite his occasional displays of ambivalence or even the enthusiasm he'd brought to the *Abbey Road* sessions. If Yoko seemed divisive—and it was hard to interpret her omnipresence, to say nothing of her eagerness to contribute ideas and criticism, as anything else—it was clearly at John's behest. Just as the Beatles had been unable to face Pete Best at his darkest moment; just as Paul couldn't pick up the phone to confirm to the longtime, loyal assistant Alistair Taylor that he had indeed been fired by Klein; just as John and Paul had both ended their longtime relationships (with Cynthia and Jane, respectively) by being "caught" with other women—John was saying goodbye the only way he knew how: via proxy.

Paul could surely sense it. But John had sent out the same signals after Julia's death a decade earlier, back when Stuart Sutcliffe had served as his human wedge. Patience had served Paul well then, along with the canny move of getting Stu into the band. John's moods were like London's weather in the spring. If you didn't like what you were seeing, just wait ten minutes, and it would change. So Paul kept up the same brave face this time around, too, making sure to include Yoko, just as he had once done with Stu. "The truth of it all is he loves Yoko," Paul told his Liverpool Institute schoolmate Roy Corlett, then a presenter for BBC-Merseyside in a radio interview conducted during a visit to Jim McCartney's home on the Wirral in the spring of 1969. "They may look like freaks. Even John says they do. But they're two great people, you know. And they're very much in love, so you can't say anything about it." When it came to the Beatles themselves, Paul had no doubts: "We're each other's mates. They're my three best friends. They're good lads, I'll tell you."

Still, even the productive, occasionally harmonious *Abbey Road* sessions hadn't changed anything, really. Once John found the courage to step onstage with his own band—responding to a last-second invitation to join a Toronto rock festival with an ad hoc Plastic Ono Band lineup that included Clapton, Klaus Voormann on bass, and Alan White on drums—he could finally see his way into a post-Beatles future. At the next Beatle's meeting, held at Apple on September 20, John could barely sit still while Paul pitched idea after idea for the group. How about playing small, unannounced shows in civic halls around the UK? "I think yer daft!" What about this new offer to do a

TV show? Absolutely not. Paul was particularly stuck on the TV special. If they weren't going to play live concerts, they had to give the fans something else. And obviously, TV was the easiest way to reach the largest possible audience—*No!*

Finally, John looked up, his face aglow, his eyes glittering madly. "The group is over! I'm leaving!"

Paul's face went "all sorts of colors," according to John's account of the meeting. "It's like he knew, really, that this was the final thing." Except that he knew no such thing. Even Klein, who was at the meeting, too, urged John to keep his decision under wraps. The group's not-quite manager had just finished negotiating the group's next deal with Capitol and didn't want the company's executives to figure out that there would be no more original records in the pipeline until after the paperwork for the group's new, elevated royalty rates were signed, sealed, and locked in stone. So they kept it hushed up, and Paul kept hoping for the best. "Nobody quite knew if it was just another one of John's little flings," he said. "I think John did kind of leave the door open. He'd said, 'I'm *pretty much* leaving the group, but . . .'"

But nothing. John had no intention of coming back. The more that became clear, the angrier Paul became. "I think he felt betrayed," says the *Evening Standard*'s Ray Connolly, who heard about the split from John (who swore him to secrecy) and spoke to both principals throughout the next weeks and months. "Go back to the family metaphor. He was the mother, and now the good-for-nothing but talented father had left him. They were divorced, and Paul didn't *want* to be divorced."

He also didn't want to hang around St. John's Wood, just around the corner from the converted home on Abbey Road he and John had made their own seven years earlier. Paul and Linda's daughter, Mary, had been born at the end of August, so now it was time to cocoon with the family. He and Linda gathered their things, packed up their baby daughter and seven-year-old Heather, and headed north, to the remote, stone-floor farm he kept ten miles outside Campbeltown in the windswept hills near the water on the Mull of Kintyre. There was nothing there, nobody to meet or greet or even wave to. They would vanish from the civilized world, was the idea. And they did such a good job of it that a small, but extremely vocal segment of the world began to imagine he'd left for good.

The whispering had actually been around for a few years. The Beatles had all been the subject of death rumors on occasion. It's a common, if macabre, phenomenon for celebrities, whose glamorous lives serve as projections for the hopes and fears of their most fervent followers. Still, when it came to the four Beatles, the rumors surrounding Paul were always the most intense. NEMS spokesman Tony Barrow's memoir describes one afternoon in the fall of 1966 when he received more than a dozen calls from reporters asking if Paul was still among the living. Finally, Barrow called the Cavendish house to check, though when Paul came to the phone sounding perfectly alive and even chipper, the publicist couldn't bring himself to explain why he was calling. That was strange, but it still had nothing on the ghoulish mania that swept across the media in the fall of 1969.

It started like any other rumor, with the random musings of a guy who either didn't have enough to keep him busy or had so much going on that he had lost his moorings. Either that, or someone was joking, and that joke spun out of control. All of which turns out to be what was going on. A college journalist at the University of Michigan named Fred LaBour was working on something in the newsroom when the telephone rang and he found himself speaking to a guy who kept insisting that Paul McCartney was dead. "It was really spooky," LaBour said, recalling how the voice pointed him toward the weird incantation that comes out of the murk at the end of "Strawberry Fields Forever"; doesn't it sound like someone saying *I buried Paul?* And why is Paul the only Beatle wearing a black carnation on *Magical Mystery Tour?* Why is his back turned to the camera on the rear cover of *Sgt. Pepper?* LaBour made a few notes, hung up, and shook his head. Ridiculous. But he had a bit of the prankster in him, so by the next morning he had an idea: "I talked it over with a friend of mine and said, 'I'm just gonna kill him. I'm gonna make the whole thing up.'" Which is exactly what LaBour did, stringing the caller's "clues" together with a wider variety of eerie-seeming observations he made up out of whole cloth.

LaBour's article, published in the *Michigan Daily,* ran beneath a portentous headline: "McCartney Dead: New Evidence Brought to Light." Only a significant percentage of the new evidence was complete nonsense. For instance, LaBour's assertion that the open hand held above Paul's head on the cover of *Sgt. Pepper's* is a Mafia sign of death was something he'd made up at the typewriter. Which is also how he came up with the revelation that word *walrus* was Greek for "corpse" (e.g., *the walrus was Paul*). The Greeks have no such word, let alone tusk-centric death imagery; they live in a warm climate, they don't know from walruses. On and on it went. See how Paul was barefoot on the cover of *Abbey Road*? Dead men wear no shoes! "I didn't research that one," Labour admitted. "But it sounded good." Note how the single-file march across the *Abbey Road* cover resembles a funeral march (John in white = Jesus; Ringo in black = a preacher; George in denim = the gravedigger), and it sounds even better. Good enough to attract the attention of a Detroit disc jockey named Russ Gibb, who read LaBour's story, including its outrageous theory describing a fatal car accident in the fall of 1966, and the subsequent top-secret campaign to replace Paul with a Scottish look-alike named William Campbell. Gibb played up the story on his WKNR-FM radio show, adding a few breathless revelations of his own, and promises of more to come, to keep listeners coming back.

So the work of a collegiate wiseass meets a ratings-hungry disc jockey. Nothing extraordinary about that. But as other radio stations, then professional news outlets, began to pick up the story, and as LaBour's satirical college-newspaper piece metastasized into a national, then an international, fixation, something else began to take place. In the weeks after the Manson family murders in Los Angeles (in which the titles of *White Album* songs, including "Helter Skelter," had been scrawled on the walls with the victims' blood); somewhere between Woodstock and Altamont; something in the collective subconscious picked up on the strands of darkness in the Beatles' music and wouldn't let go. Maybe that was because the years of war, assassination, and cultural discord had darkened the skies everywhere. Or perhaps something in the wind had made it clear that the world's most treasured rock 'n' roll group, the very sun in the pop-cultural solar system, couldn't survive the decade. Absent actual evidence of the split—even John had carried on speaking of the Beatles as an ongoing concern, and the others followed suit as they promoted *Abbey Road* in the press—the feeling took form in a fantasy: that the most Beatle-y Beatle of them all was dead.

Apple was besieged with calls from reporters, writers, and assorted ghouls from all around the world. Sales of *Abbey Road* and all the other Beatle albums shot skyward. The celebrity lawyer F. Lee Bailey mounted an entire TV special staged as a "trial" to prove or disprove Paul's corporeal existence. (Invited to participate, young Fred LaBour flew to Los Angeles and confessed to Bailey, moments before taping, that he'd made up the entire story. Bailey, far beyond the pale, let alone the constraints of the legal bar, thought this over for a long moment. "We have an hour of TV to fill," he finally decreed to LaBour. "You're going to have to play along.")

Paul, tucked away in his media-free hideout in the Scottish wilds, was quite alive, if not exactly well. His heart was thumping away, the blood swishing through his veins. But what was he, exactly? He'd only ever been a Beatle; he'd only worked with John on one side and George on the other, with Ringo laying down the foundation behind them. Through good times and bad, success and failure, they had always been his partners, his brothers. "My three best friends" as he'd told Roy Corlett. "I could write songs for them to sing, and for me to sing, and we could make records of them." But now that was gone, along with the friendship and creative partnership that had defined him for nearly half of his life, and for the entirety of his grown-up existence. After everything they'd achieved together, after all the time they'd spent nose to nose, their songs, souls, and imaginations torn open, John had tossed him aside. "I'd outlived my usefulness."

What he was feeling, Paul realized later, was the existential angst of the redundant man. Like anyone who gets laid off, he had lost his job, his identity, his friends. But unlike a factory worker, he'd lived his entire adult life with arguably the coolest job in the world, which had in turn given him the coolest friends and made *him* one of the coolest, most sought-after people on the planet. And now that was all gone. So what remained? Paul had no idea. He couldn't imagine anything. So he decided not to think about it. Tucked away in his rough, little farmhouse—with its stone floors, pumped water, and furniture he had

fashioned himself from castoff boards, potato boxes, and mattresses—
he slept through the mornings, and sometimes into the afternoons. He
stopped shaving, then gave up bathing. He sulked and smoked and
drank whiskey and went for days without even picking up his guitar.
"I remember lying awake at night shaking," he said. When he woke
up in the morning, he wouldn't know where to go, so he'd either stay
in bed, have a drink, or both.

Paul was still in bed late in the morning of Sunday, October 26,
when he was stirred by a sharp rapping on the farmhouse's front door.
It was death coming to call, in a sense. More specifically, it was a pair
of journalists from *Life* magazine's London bureau, a matronly corre-
spondent named Dorothy Bacon and the photographer Terence Spencer, who had spent weeks following the Beatles during the height of
the mania in early 1964. Fired up by the rampant Paul-is-dead rumor,
the editors in *Life*'s New York office had assigned them the task of flying to Scotland in search of proof that the cute Beatle was actually still
extant. Spencer, who had covered half a dozen wars during his career,
was a particularly shrewd newsman. Knowing that the road to Paul's
farm ran through the property of two other farmers, both of whom
had been instructed to keep invaders at bay, he waited until Sunday
morning, when the locals would more than likely be in church. Then
he and Bacon set off across the scrubby hills, crossing streams and
dodging sheep for nearly an hour before arriving at Paul's door. Bacon
knocked. Spencer, who had preloaded his cameras anticipating that
they might not be welcomed with open Beatle arms, poised to shoot.

There was movement inside. Then silence. Then the front door flew
open, revealing an unshaven and unkempt Paul McCartney, who was
definitely alive, and also extremely angry. And wielding a bucket of
kitchen slop in one hand.

"He was absolutely red in the face with fury," Spencer recalls. "He
had one look at me and hurled the slop bucket. The irony was that I
definitely got a shot of that. And he missed me, but then he stepped
forward and hit me across the shoulder. Now, I'd covered six wars
and never been hit by anything or anyone until Paul McCartney
punched me. So I told Dorothy, 'I think we've run out of our hospitality,' and we turned around and left."

Equipped with all the evidence they would need, Spencer and

Bacon set off back to town but had only walked about ten minutes when they heard a rumble and saw Paul's Land Rover headed straight for them. Spencer's first reaction was fear: "I told Dorothy, 'For God's sake, be careful, because that man is *mad*'"

But as Paul had stood on his porch, watching the reporters receding down the road, a glimmer from his not-so-distant past came back to him. Public and private, right and wrong, it all got tangled when you lived as a celebrity. If he wanted to find a new life beyond his existence as a Beatle, he was going to need these people on his side. *Fucking hell!* He called for Linda and ran for the Land Rover.

When he caught up to them, pulled over, and jumped out, Paul emerged smiling and extended his hand: "I'm really very sorry for what I've done, Terry, because there's no excuse." Spencer took his hand. Oh, it was perfectly fine; he would have done exactly the same thing! Paul was laughing, shaking his head, chums again. Better yet, he had an offer for *Life* magazine; he'd give Bacon an interview and give the magazine the right to use a packet of Linda's own family portraits. But only if Spencer agreed to hand over the roll of film with his red-faced tantrum on it. "It's not a very nice picture of me," Paul explained. "You've just got that bucket flying through the air."

They had a deal. And a cover story for *Life*, which was published under the title "Paul Is Still with Us" in the magazine's next edition. The rumor of his premature demise, Paul said for the record, "is all bloody stupid." It had started, he said, because he had withdrawn from the scene. "I don't have anything to say these days. The Beatle thing is over." He didn't explain what that meant, exactly. But he wasn't going to, either.

"What I have to say is all in the music. If I want to say anything, I write a song."

The only trouble was, Paul wasn't writing songs. A fragment or two, perhaps, but nothing more. He didn't have the focus, he didn't have the energy. He was lying in bed, he was drinking, he was watching the clouds scud across the darkening winter sky. Nothing made him feel better. He even tried heroin, snorting a bit some hipster friend had handed to him months, maybe years, earlier. "To escape. To be numb," he said. It didn't do anything for him, it didn't make anything better. "I was a zombie." Yet, no matter how hellish life had become for Paul, it was markedly worse for his new wife, whose charismatic rock-star husband had suddenly been reduced to a depressed, often drunk layabout. Already tasked with the care and feeding of a seven-year-old and a newborn baby, Linda could only marvel at the disparity between the life everyone else assumed she was leading with Paul McCartney, and what was actually taking place. "Here I am living on a stone floor, carrying water in buckets, and I'm married to a drunk who won't take a bath," she recalled to Danny Fields. Paul was lost. He only knew how to be a Beatle; he could never make music on his own. What point was there to a rock star without a band? As winter came, Fields says, Linda lost her patience. "She was yelling at him to get off his ass and be a man, already."

Eventually, Paul heard her. Or maybe it was the voice of Jim McCartney, from years gone by. *Soldier on. God loves a trier.* Finally, he took a bath. He helped Linda pack their things. They got into the car and drove down to London. Then he had a four-track tape machine installed in the Cavendish music room and scribbled down a few new tunes.

14

He started with "The Lovely Linda." That was one of the fragments he'd come up with in Scotland. Nothing to it, just a single line of lyrics about his wife and the pretty flowers in her hair. A few chords on the acoustic guitar, the simplest possible bass line, hand-on-guitar-case percussion, and a vocal that dissolved into a self-conscious giggle. That was the first track.

Then it was easier. Like an exercise in muscle memory. He'd come up with a bluesy riff, play it through a few times, and wait for a scattering of words to present themselves. *That would be something, it really would be something . . .* Overdub some more guitars, a drum bit, then "That Would Be Something" was another track. He was testing the Studer four-track he'd installed in the Cavendish music room, and testing himself, too. A rudimentary instrumental here ("Valentine's Day"); a tuning-up melody he remembered from years ago ("Hot as Sun"); then a couple of Beatles rejects ("Junk" and "Teddy Boy"). A multitracked version of the rubbing-the-rims-of-wineglasses dinner-party trick ("Glasses") came out of his avant-garde woodshed. It was all simple stuff, easily recorded by a one-man band working with an at-home setup.

But then he sat down at the piano and came up with "Maybe I'm Amazed," an impassionedly conceived, beautifully realized tribute to the woman who had just pulled him through his darkest moments. *You help me sing my song / You right me when I'm wrong . . .* Paul booked time at EMI to record that one, sneaking in as quietly as possible, then playing all the instruments himself. Another thoroughly composed song, "Every Night," came together in the studio, too. John Kurlander, who had engineered so many Beatles sessions in the last few years, was on the board for these first solo sessions, too. Linda was there, of course, so were the kids, drinking their grape juice and chasing their toys around the control-room floor. If the absence of the other Beatles consumed him, Paul could look up, see his family, and feel reassured. "Paul was relaxed, bearded, cheerful," Kurlander recalls. Linda didn't sing or perform, but she had opinions about what she was hearing, and Paul was obviously listening to what she said. "It was definitely a family business now."

Paul booked his EMI sessions under a phony name to avoid alerting the press to his new project. But when onetime Beatles engineer Chris Thomas happened upon a mixing session and sat in long enough to get a good listen to "Maybe I'm Amazed," he was astonished. "He'd played everything himself; wrote it, produced it. I was like, wow! *Amazing!*"

Mostly Paul wanted it all to be low-key. He wasn't competing with the Beatles, he wasn't trying to top *Abbey Road.* This would be his homemade album, a first step toward an independent future. Now, at least, he'd have control over every aspect of his career. Or so he assumed.

Oh, but wait: the Beatles had a little more work to do. The "Get Back" sessions, now retitled after Paul's "Let It Be," needed to be finished to accompany the release of the movie in the spring. George's "I, Me, Mine" and the title track needed a bit of polishing, so on January 3, 1970, Paul joined George and Ringo at EMI to start two days of overdubs. "You will have heard that Dave Dee is no longer with us," George announced into the microphone with mock seriousness before work began. "But Mickey, Tich, and I would just like to carry on the good work that's always gone down in number two." For two more days, at any rate. Would there be more? No one seemed to know for sure. George came off a few days of playing shows with Delaney &

Bonnie's expansive and flexible band and mused publicly about how he'd like to mount a similar tour with the Beatles. John talked about drafting the group to join the lineup for a peace festival in Canada he was helping plan for the next summer ("I'll try and hustle them!"), and when a reporter asked in January if the period of solo work amounted to the end of the group, John refused to describe it as the death of their collaboration. "It'll probably be a rebirth, you know, for all of us."

But John was too busy being reborn with Yoko to think all that much about the Beatles. Look at how they never went anywhere without the other; how they dressed alike, like twins or gang members or the long-ago Beatles. They even had the same haircut, now that husband and wife had shorn their hair to the nub to auction the locks off to support the peace movement. John released a statement on January 5 declaring that all future proceeds from his music would be dedicated to "promoting peace on earth." The first year of this new decade, they declared, was Year One. The end of all that and the beginning of all this.

Paul watched it all from afar, a trifle bemused, more than a little hurt, and increasingly angry. John had spurned him for Yoko, that was bad enough. But all the others, with Yoko on their side, of course, were so bedazzled by the huckster Allen Klein they couldn't see how ridiculous his demand for a 20 percent fee truly was. And if Paul knew anything, he knew how to keep track of what was his. "The way I saw it, I had to save the Beatles' fortune," he said. So he tried, and kept trying, to convince them. And they were having none of it. So Paul just sighed and got back to work on his solo album. *McCartney* was what he had decided to call it, and Paul took personal control over every aspect of its production. He oversaw the album's cover design, building it entirely from candid shots Linda had taken around the house or on their vacations. He pegged a release date in mid-April, and all was going smoothly until Ringo came around to Cavendish one afternoon bearing a handwritten note from John, George, and himself informing Paul that he would have to reconsider *McCartney*'s release date. The other three had just met with Klein at Apple and noticed a conflict: the *Let It Be* movie was scheduled to be released in mid-May; the album would precede it by a couple of weeks. Obviously, it made no sense for Apple to release a new Paul McCartney album only two weeks before a Beatles album. So he would have to delay *McCartney*'s release until early June.

According to the memo, this wasn't a suggestion as much as a decision made by three out of the four managing directors of Apple. Paul might not agree, but he didn't have the authority to do anything about it: they were simply forbidding him to release *McCartney* in mid-April. "Nothing personal," the letter concluded. Paul couldn't believe it. Were they serious? *He couldn't even control when his own album came out?* Ridiculous! No! This would not stand! "He went completely out of control," Ringo testified later. "Shouting at me, prodding his fingers toward my face, saying, 'I'll finish you all now!' and 'You'll pay!'"

Paul's face had gone crimson; his eyes were wild; he told Ringo to put his coat on and get the hell out of his house. He called George and got into it with him, snarling that if this was how things were going to be, he didn't want to be a part of Apple, after all. "You'll stay on the fucking label!" George barked back, adding a gruff "Hare Krishna!" before slamming the phone down. Paul called EMI's chairman, Sir Joseph Lockwood, to complain that he was being undermined. Finally, it fell to Ringo, who had taken it upon himself to give Paul the news in person, only to bear the brunt of his wrath, to derail the conflict by convincing John and George to let it go. "I felt that since he was our friend, and since the date was of such immense significance to him, we should let him have his own way."

So *McCartney* would be released in mid-April, as planned. But then Paul got an advance copy of *Let It Be* and the nightmare began all over again. Working at John's suggestion, Klein had handed the raw tapes of the "Get Back" sessions to American producer Phil Spector, so he could work his sonic magic and make them presentable for release. A strange call, given the contrast between Spector's glossy, multilayered production style and the much vaunted "warts and all," so-live-it-hurts concept that had governed the original recording. Indeed, Spector ran rampant over the "Get Back" tapes, adding echo and reverb here, piling on harps and strings there. Spector's hands were particularly heavy on "Let It Be" and "The Long and Winding Road," which had somehow been transformed from an understated piano ballad into a riot of violins, cellos, French horns, and what sounded like the entire Mormon Tabernacle Choir, swept up on a caffeine-and-sugar binge. Paul said he went instantly to Apple requesting—demanding!—changes, only to be told it was too late to do anything. At least, that's how he described things. John dismissed that version as ridiculous: they could have remixed a song in two hours; they could have remastered the entire album in two days. Paul had been delivered the record with far more than enough time. "If Paul had wanted to make any changes, he could have done so!"

Oh, but Paul didn't see it that way. Instead, he was infuriated by his lack of control; their complete absence of *respect*. "I couldn't believe it!" he cried to Ray Connolly. "No one asked me what I thought!" He was particularly wounded by the women's choir Spector had used. "I would never have female voices on a Beatles record," he sputtered, though that was patently not true: Linda had sung a high harmony on "Let It Be"; Yoko was all over *The White Album*, along with a chorus of other Beatles ladies (including, she says, Francie Schwartz) on "Birthday"; Paul himself had dragooned a pair of groupies off Abbey Road to help sing the chorus on the original "Across the Universe." But that wasn't the point, anyway. "It just goes to show that it's no good me sitting here and thinking I'm in control because obviously I'm not!"

So maybe that was it, maybe Paul was through with the Beatles now, too. He called John in early April to say he was leaving the group. "That means two of us have accepted it," John responded approvingly. But Paul must have reconsidered, because the q-and-a he crafted with Apple exec Peter Brown and press officer Derek Taylor to send out with the first copies of *McCartney* made abundantly clear that the most Beatle-y Beatle still wasn't ready to consider himself an ex-Beatle. Certainly, he took the opportunity to air his bitterness by pointing out that he had felt perfectly fine recording his music without the interference of the others. "I only had me to ask for a decision and I agreed with me," he said. Did he foresee himself writing with John again? "No." Why wasn't he working with the Beatles now, anyway? "Personal differences, business differences, musical differences, but most of all because I have a better time with my family."

So there was bile. But there was also hope, or at least ambivalence.

Was the start of a solo career also the end of the Beatles? "Time will tell. Being a solo album means it's 'the start of a solo career,' and not being done with the Beatles means it's a rest. So it's both."

No, it wasn't. Not according to Don Short at the *Daily Mirror,* who got an advance look at the statement early enough on April 9 to commandeer two-thirds of the tabloid's April 10 cover with the thirty-six-point, war-declared-caliber headline "PAUL IS QUITTING THE BEATLES." Short's reporting of the "shock news" was built entirely on the *McCartney* q-and-a, but only on the angriest parts. True enough, Short could draw on plenty of bitterness to fuel a Beatles-to-break-up story. But by overlooking the rest, he had not only taken Paul a bit out of context, but actually created an entirely new context that would quickly spread around the planet. For as the story rocketed around the world, the other Beatles were made even more furious at their stubborn partner. John was in an uproar: "He's fuckin' trying to get the credit!" he snapped to Ray Connolly, the journalist John had first told about his decision to leave the group the previous September. George said much the same thing, and as their anger grew more profound, the divide between the camps grew unbridgeable. Paul's more conciliatory words (e.g., "Time will tell") were lost. So thoroughly, in fact, that George continued to grouse about it a quarter century later during the *Anthology* interviews, when he noted how frequently Paul dropped PR bombs along with his new albums. "I think what he was trying to do was just grab a bit of the momentum of the time."

Paul tracked the damage for a few days, then called Connolly to meet him for lunch so he could set the record straight. He came dressed in a weathered blazer with an open-necked blue shirt. Paul was tense, but was intent on sitting in the restaurant's main room, where everyone could see them, Paul and Linda on one side of the table and the journalist on the other. It was all a misunderstanding, Paul insisted. "I just thought, 'Christ, what have I done?" He went on at length, through the appetizers, the fish course, then down to the end of the wine bottle, with Linda at his side, her hand resting over his. "He kept saying, 'It wasn't *like* that! I didn't leave the Beatles!'" Connolly recalls. "He said it over and over, 'Ringo left first, then George, then John. I was the *last* to leave! *It wasn't me!*'"

• • •

Then *McCartney* was out and loped easily to the top of the American album charts, if not quite to the apex of the British album-sales lists, where it peaked at either #2 or #3, depending on whose chart you were reading. Given the momentum of nearly eight years of Beatles fame, along with the world-ending news of the group's breakup, it might have been difficult to do much worse. It's actually a charming album, a folksy return-to-basics that serves the same purpose as those long-ago afternoons in the winter of 1957 when Paul's guitar voiced his grief at the death of his mother. Now the loss is the Beatles—his youth, his identity, his first and most passionate marriage—and the pain is every bit as profound. He's not challenging himself or dressing up for company; what you hear is what you get. "Man We Was Lonely" begins with a shimmering spray of chords that leads only to a campfire-style sing-along about the pleasures of home. "Oo You" rides a blazing guitar lick and funky rhythm to nowhere in particular. "Kreen-Akrore," for all its tropical sound effects and jungle drumming, sounds like sound-track music. Only "Junk," "Teddy Boy," "Every Night," and "Maybe I'm Amazed" seem to have required more than half an hour to compose, and the first two are Beatles retreads. For all its laid-back charm, *McCartney* is an act of defiance: he's sagging off school again and doesn't care who knows it.

In the shadow of the group's near-miraculous achievements, and in the immediate wake of the supremely accomplished *Abbey Road,* the rustic *McCartney* seemed curious, to say the least. Only "Maybe I'm Amazed" came close to recapturing the majesty of the most recent Beatles album, while the rest of *McCartney*'s rudimentary compositions and stripped-down productions struck most critics as somewhere south of disappointing. "Distinctly second-rate," according to *Rolling Stone*'s Langdon Winner; "sheer banality . . . one man sitting alone in a small recording studio noodling around with a few half-written songs," according to Richard Williams in the UK's *Melody Maker*. Williams's review proved so infuriating to Paul, particularly a line about Paul's increasingly obvious debt to George Martin's production skills, that he sent back a bitter response, published soon thereafter under his own sarcastic headline: "Who Does Paul McCartney Think He Is?"

By the spring of 1970 it was more significant to focus on *what* Paul was, which is to say, almost completely off-balance. For the first time in his career his expert blend of clever artiness, pop craftiness, and savvy media manipulation had failed him. Spurned by his mates; blamed for breaking up the group he had only wanted to hold together; tormented and ridiculed by the self-described asshole who had taken control of his band (and had the temerity to tell the *New York Times* that Paul's decision to leave the Beatles was due, in part, to his own "personal problems")—Paul was lost. He didn't want to come off like the sort of greedy, grasping jerk who would rip apart the world's most beloved rock band in the name of money or power. He made a point of sounding sweet and magnanimous when it came to the other Beatles. "I'll see him when I see him," he said of John in an interview with *Rolling Stone* editor Jann Wenner. "I love him just the same." Yet Paul couldn't get past the thought that someone was ripping off his money and diminishing his power. *Klein!* The problem was Klein! This man who had declared himself the Beatles' manager, despite never having received Paul's vote; who had somehow managed to put his company's logo on the back of Paul's own solo album. "I don't like him, and he's not the man for me," Paul insisted. "He's not good enough, and so I don't want him to represent me!"

When teddy boys had long ago jumped young Paul and Mike McCartney and relieved them of their spending money and wristwatch, Jim McCartney had marched them straight to the constables and then off to court in pursuit of justice. *Don't let anyone take what's yours,* he'd told his boys, and now those words were echoing in Paul's ears. Back in his Scottish exile again that summer, he spent hours, days, weeks, steaming and fretting. *Klein!* How could he be sucking up 20 percent of his Beatles money? How was his name smeared across the back of Paul's own album? How could anyone who claimed to be working for the Beatles not even take his calls? "Making me feel like I'm a junior with the record company, like Klein is the boss and I'm nothing," Paul fairly sputtered to Jann Wenner. "I'm a senior; I figure my opinion is as good as anyone's, especially when it's *my* thing."

But as long as the other Beatles refused to work with him, and as long as they persisted in employing Klein, he'd be locked in the worst of all possible worlds: without his partners' creative assistance and friendship; but with the perpetual annoyance of the manager he neither trusted nor liked. Worse yet, whatever money Paul made with his records would go into Apple's common pot, to be shared by the other three and, worst of all, *Klein*. Just the thought of it was infuriating. And he couldn't do anything about it. Except, his brother-in-law, John Eastman, reminded him, for one thing. He could sue to dissolve the partnership.

File a lawsuit against the Beatles? Drag his oldest friends and partners, the rest of the beloved moptops and the fabbest four of all time, into the maw of civil court? And not emerge from the court of public opinion as the nastiest Blue Meanie on earth? He couldn't imagine it.

"All summer long I was fighting with myself," he said. "It was murderous. I had a knot in my stomach all summer. . . . I first said no, we can't do that! We'll live with it. But all those little things kept happening." Eventually John Eastman came for a visit, and the brothers-in-law spent hours talking it through; walking the hills and going over the scenarios. How a filing would be made, how they would all have to give affidavits, how the group's most private dealings and most fetid, soiled laundry would get dragged out into the open. Too horrible to contemplate. But then Paul would think again of Klein, and the prospect of being under that vile man's chubby thumb. Standing on a hilltop one afternoon, peering down at the dark, wind-rippled surface of a loch, Paul finally realized he didn't really have a choice. Klein had taken his watch, now it was time to get it back. "Oh, we've got to do it," he said, and his brother-in-law nodded.

John Eastman had already been girding for a case, digging through Apple's accounting, searching for discrepancies and failures. He came away with a ream of complaints, more than enough to form the basis for a legal complaint. So on November 15, Paul filed his lawsuit, demanding in no uncertain terms that the Beatles be broken up in every way, shape, and form. News of *Paul McCartney vs. John Ono Lennon, George Harrison, Richard Starkey and Apple Corps., Ltd.* became public on December 31. As the New Year began, everything exploded to the surface.

John Lennon didn't require civil litigation to open the gates to his spleen. Interviewed by *Rolling Stone*'s Jann Wenner in early December, the musician-turned-peace-activist conducted a rambling tour of his darkest, angriest thoughts and suspicions. The Beatles, he declared, were "big bastards" who had roamed the world like Cossacks; they raped, they pillaged, they did the most vile things in the most egregious ways. Except John also felt victimized by the experience. He'd been fleeced by businessmen and manipulated by his employees. Still, the most brutal treatment had come from his so-called friends in the band, who had resisted his artistry, humiliated his wife, and were just generally "the most big-headed uptight people on earth." So there was that. And a lot more, when it came to Paul, whose first solo album he dismissed, succinctly, as "rubbish."

Published in two parts late that January and early February, John's thoughts struck many of his friends as just another product of his mercurial moods and pugilistic tongue. "I'd heard versions of that for years," Ray Connolly says. "It was always tongue-in-cheek, John exaggerated to make it funny. But in *Rolling Stone* Wenner missed that. He made it all sound awful, bitter, and mean."

Paul did his best to seem sanguine. "It was so far-out that I really enjoyed it," he told *Life* magazine. "This open hostility, that didn't hurt me. That's cool. That's John."

Secretly, though, it wasn't cool at all. Coming from John, the one person who had always seen Paul most clearly, the partner he had depended on to identify his strengths and sift his flaws, it was devastating. "I sat down and pored over every little paragraph, every little sentence," Paul recalled. "I thought, 'It's me. I am. That's just what I'm like. He's captured me so well. I'm a turd, you know.'"

It was only the beginning once Paul's lawsuit to dissolve the Beatles' partnership got rolling. All the Beatles filed affidavits in the case, and all provided deep, often unflattering insights into the group's inner workings, and Paul's role as self-appointed foreman on their shop floor. Ringo tried to be generous, noting that Paul was "the greatest bass player in the world." But then again, "he acted like a spoilt child . . . he goes on and on to see if he can get his way." George said much the same thing, minus the compliment for his ex-schoolmate's bass playing, and with particular emphasis on his "superior attitude." John doubled down on his *Rolling Stone* critique, adding that Paul had a weakness for limp, "pop-type" music and couldn't grok the hip sounds John and George preferred. "What is now called 'under-ground.'"

Oh, and all the other Beatles were eager to resolve their problems amicably, and perhaps even resume their collaboration. At least, that's how they had felt until Paul attacked them in the courts. "I still cannot understand why Paul acted as he did," George concluded.

In other words, if the world still wondered who exactly had broken up their most beloved rock group, the walrus was Paul.

Paul attended much of the trial, with Linda in tow, testifying in person as to the lack of pulse in the Beatles' collaborative corpus, and quoting John's own song "God" and its climactic assertion of "I don't believe in Beatles" as an ultimate proof. On and on, worse and worse. Klein, Paul said, tried to ingratiate himself to Paul by ripping John and especially Yoko when the happy couple weren't around. "You know why John's angry at you?" Paul recalled Klein whispering to him. "It's because you came off better in *Let It Be*." The evidence piled up. All the joy, magic, and love of the Beatles reduced to a bitter recitation of profits accrued, investments made and gone awry, deals blown, and insults lobbed. The judge, Mr. Justice Stamp, spent a few weeks sifting through the ruins and in mid-March announced that Klein had presented Paul with plenty of reasons for distrust and dissatisfaction. Stamp appointed a receiver to take control of the group's assets, and thus Paul was extricated from Klein's grasp. That's where the process began, at any rate, for it would drag on in various forms and legal forums through much of the decade. Many years later, after suits and countersuits and counter-countersuits, and let's don't even get into everything else, and Klein had been found guilty of financial high jinks serious enough to earn him a two-month sentence in jail, George offered Paul a measure of an apology. "[He] did say, 'Well, you know, thanks for getting us out of that,'" Paul recalled him saying. "Just one little sentence of recognition of the hell I'd been through. It was better than nothing."

Then it was time to make a real album. Paul had figured that out months ago, probably right around the time *McCartney* was getting drubbed for being so raw and stripped down. So, okay, fine. Paul knew how to make a fully realized album—he'd helped invent the form, after all. So off the McCartneys went to New York in January (zipping back to London for court dates) and set to finding some musicians. Not just any musicians, though. It wasn't enough to be super-accomplished on an instrument, either. As Paul had always known, the ability to make great rock 'n' roll had nothing to do with having technical chops: it was about playing your chops with the right attitude, and bringing the right vibe to the job. Linda still knew people in the city, got some recommendations, then made the calls for the auditions.

It was all a bit surreptitious. When Linda called Dave Spinozza, then a white-hot twenty-one-year-old guitar player best known for his jazz work, she introduced herself simply as "Mrs. McCartney" and added loftily, "My husband would like to meet you." The only problem was that Spinozza had no idea whom he was talking to, or who her husband might be. When the busy session player asked if he had worked with her husband before, Linda bristled. "Like," Spinozza said, "I was supposed to know Paul McCartney was calling my house?" Misunderstandings unraveled, they set a time for him to audition at an address near Times Square. Denny Seiwell, a young drummer just working his way into the top echelon of New York's session players, got the same call, although he was told that he would be recording demos with the folksinger Barry Kornfeld. Walking the down-at-the-heels streets of Hell's Kitchen, then following the directions down some ill-lit stairs to a funky-smelling basement, Seiwell worried that he was about to be mugged. Instead, he found a familiar-looking couple sitting in front of a battered drum kit that had been rented from the S.I.R. equipment shop. "Hey!" Seiwell recalls saying. "You're Paul McCartney!"

Indeed. Paul had three days of beard on his cheeks, and scruffy clothes on his back, but he was charming as ever, and quite direct: Can you sit down and play us something? So Seiwell did just that, setting up a rock groove with plenty of accents on the tom-toms, à la Ringo. Paul clearly liked what he heard, and Seiwell's blend of musical expertise and blue-collar directness felt like a good fit, too. He was in, then wonder boy Spinozza got tapped to handle the lead guitar, with occasional assists on rhythm guitar from Hugh McCracken, another pro from the Manhattan studios. The sessions began at a Midtown studio three days later and went on for six weeks, starting most mornings at 9 a.m. when Paul and Linda would breeze in, kids in hand. Linda set up Heather and Mary on the floor with their books and toys, then made tea as Paul bounced into the studio to get things going. He dressed casually, usually sweaters and tweedy trousers and shoes that didn't quite match anything else. But it was always stylish, somehow. "He always put himself together in an interesting way," Seiwell recalls. "He had that star vibe coming off of him."

Seiwell was far more interested in Paul's music. The first song he showed them was "Another Day," his sweetly melancholic portrait of a lonely office girl in the big city. "We just sort of looked at each other and said, 'This isn't just another tune!'" Seiwell says. "It was 'Eleanor Rigby' in New York City." This time Paul had constructed the songs with care, thought through the arrangements, and came to the studio with fairly precise ideas for the parts he wanted the guys to play. "We were told exactly what to play, he knew what he wanted," Spinozza said, recalling how Paul would sit down and sing what he wanted to hear each musician play. "He took some suggestions—two out of ten—but changed into a Paul McCartney thing." He did the same thing, more or less, to Seiwell, which didn't bother the drummer at all. "He had great ideas," Seiwell says with a shrug. Spinozza was less pleased to be held on such a short leash and got even more irked when Linda emerged from her maternal duties in the control room to weigh in with her thoughts. "It didn't make sense to me," he said a few months later. "But now she thinks she's a producer."

As Spinozza had figured out, Paul had elevated his wife into the collaborator position that had always been filled by John Lennon. It was precisely what John had done with Yoko, and no wonder: John and Paul had come into adulthood, and their world-bending success, by depending on one another for support and inspiration. The creative connection they had formed had turned into a love, trust, and dependence that had defined their lives for more than a decade. So once that had run its course, once they had found romantic partners with whom they were committed, it felt natural to extend the bond to creativity, too. "One day I just said to her, 'I'm going to teach you how to write if I have to just strap you to the piano bench,'" Paul said. "I'm going to teach you the way I write music." All she needed to realize was how easy it was. He did it by ear, almost like pulling the songs out of the sky. John did it the same way, no music involved, no actual writing, just kicking around ideas until something magical fell out of the air. "It's fun," Paul said, not comprehending the role genius-level talent might have in the process. Or maybe he just figured he was brilliant enough to carry the entire operation. Whatever, it was more fun to have someone else in the room, and Paul valued no one's company more than Linda's, so there it was: a batch of new songs written by Paul and Linda McCartney.

Now she was in the studio, too, keeping her ears open and tossing in ideas Paul was always eager to hear. Still, he called most of the shots and played keyboards, some of the guitar parts, then overdubbed the bass parts, usually at the end of the day after everyone else had left. "He never played bass with other people around," Spinozza said. "Which was weird."

For all his effortless musicality and style, no matter his chart-topping solo debut and the frantic anticipation that awaited this new album, Paul was still reeling from the collapse of the Beatles. It came out in the new songs, again and again, in shades of memory, frustration, and anger. "Too Many People" the stinging rocker that kicked off the first side, points fingers at a Lennon-like figure who was "preaching practices" while other people were starving, getting busted, not even coming close to living the dream the Beatles had thrown away. *That was your first mistake,* Paul scolds. *You took your lucky break and broke it in two.* The tuneful chorale "Dear Boy" addresses a clueless ex-partner who *never knew what* (he) *had found.* The bluesy "3 Legs" addresses various three-legged (and thus incomplete) creatures, before moving to a nameless antagonist who *let me down, put my heart around the bend.* Addressing himself, albeit cryptically, Paul sings to a person bearing his first (and only) Beatles stage name, Paul Ramon, in "Ram On." The anthemic "The Back Seat of My Car" describes two young lovers on the run, escaping the restrictions of the past—*honey, I want it my way*—en route to a climax that describes the point to the entire project, and to all the grim machinations that had grown to consume Paul in the last two years: *We believe that we can't be wrong.*

15

The band was family. That's how it had always been with the Beatles ("my three best friends," as of just a few months ago), and so once Paul started playing music with the New York guys, they became family, too. The recording sessions in New York drifted easily into dinners downtown and trips to the clubs. "He loved to hang out," Seiwell remembers. When they moved on to record overdubs in Los Angeles in March, the beachside house Paul and Linda rented from the Getty family became the social hub for the musicians. They swam in the pool, listened endlessly to the Jamaican reggae records Linda had turned Paul onto, then went out for dinner in Santa Monica. It was all carefree and fun, and no one ever once mentioned the Beatles, or the litigation that was still making headlines. "It wasn't like a big taboo or anything. But it was just uncool to bring it up," Seiwell says. So keep joking around and don't interrupt Paul when he picks up a guitar and gets that faraway look in his eyes. "He couldn't talk, he'd just nod his head," Seiwell recalls. "He was gone, dining at the astral cafeteria."

"Another Day" was released as a single at the end of the winter and quickly found its way toward the top of the sales charts, hitting the #2 spot in Britain and landing just below that mark in the United States, where it peaked at #5. The album, titled *Ram,* came out a few weeks later, hitting the top of the British charts and stalling at #2 in America, where the wondrously spaced-out single "Uncle Albert/Admiral Halsey" spent the late summer at the top of the sales charts. Nevertheless, reviews of the studio-honed *Ram* were every bit as sour as the ones that had greeted *McCartney*, albeit now for opposing reasons. "Suburban pap 'n' roll," according to one writer, succinctly summing up the critical disdain for an album whose credit (Paul and Linda McCartney), hand-drawn cover, and farm-based cover photo all seemed to describe a portrait of the artist as a middle-aged bore.

The other Beatles weren't impressed with their ex-mate's latest output either, and not just because of the no-explanation-necessary jacket photo of one beetle mounted upon the other. John Lennon had particular contempt for the non-album single "Another Day," citing its bourgeois office setting (though it seems strange that a self-described feminist would be so contemptuous of a song exploring the internal desolation of a single woman), and Ringo told *Melody Maker* that he thought Paul's new album revealed his old friend's enormous talent "going strange," almost as if Paul didn't want to admit he could write good tunes. "He seems to be wasting his time."

Or maybe he was just moving in a new direction. After all the heaviness of the Beatles—the wild ambition; the internal angst; the godly expectations—he could actually ditch it all and go back to the beginning, back when all were friends and all that mattered was having a good time. In early August, Paul called Denny Seiwell and *Ram* guitarist Hugh McCracken and invited them to bring their wives up to Scotland and hang out at the McCartney family farm for a while. The Mull of Kintyre is beautiful in August, it'd be laid-back and perfect. Only Paul wasn't really one for taking vacations, and the musicians had only been there for a day or two before he popped the question: *How about forming a band?* They'd had so much fun doing *Ram*, they could just keep it rolling. Make a new album, take it on the road. Paul had been itching to hit the stage for years, and now they could do it together. So how about it? Seiwell had no doubts and signed on instantly. McCracken asked to think about it for a day or two, then begged off; he was a creature of the studios, and his wife's acting career was in New York, he couldn't just join a British band and hit the road full-time. No problem, Paul called down to London and summoned an old friend he'd first bonded with in 1965, when the Moody Blues had been one of the Beatles' opening acts on a British tour. Denny Laine had been the group's lead singer then, but left just before they'd really broken through in the late sixties. He'd been on the verge of bigger things ever since and played with Ginger Baker's Air Force for a time, but was in between gigs (and living in a back room of his manager's office) when the telephone rang. "He just asked if I fancied putting a band together," Laine says. "He was looking for someone to be his second fiddle on the road. He knew we were both hardened veterans of the road."

Laine flew north a few days later, sitting next to Seiwell, who was returning from a few days back in New York. Paul and Linda didn't have any guest rooms in their house, so they booked the two Dennys rooms at the Argyle Arms Hotel in Campbeltown (though Laine recalls spending the first night on a mattress on the floor of the garage) and set up microphones, amps, keyboards, and other gear in the not-quite-swept-out barn, now dubbed Rude Studios. They started jamming, and Laine fit right in. "The band gelled on the first day, really," he remembers, and once they'd spent a few hours warming up on rock 'n' oldies, reggae tunes, and twelve-bar blues jams, Paul broke out the songs he and Linda had been writing. It was simple stuff. A couple of basic jams, some bluesy stuff, a couple of folky ballads, a reggae arrangement of Mickey and Sylvia's "Love Is Strange." Seiwell and Laine were both seasoned pros, they could master that sort of stuff while reading the newspaper. Now all they needed was a keyboard player who had the chops to keep up. During one break Seiwell brought up Paul Harris, a buddy of his who had been playing with Stephen Stills in Manassas. He wasn't a studio guy, but he knew the road and could play all kinds of stuff. Plus, he was just a great guy to have around, and . . . Paul shook him off.

"Actually, I'm gonna go with Linda," he said eagerly.

Seiwell gaped. Linda had played a little bit in the barn, but that was mostly fill-in stuff: one-finger melodies, a chord here or there. She'd never even tried to play rock 'n' roll before she married one of the Beatles.

"Um, why's that?"

"I can teach her anything she needs to know." Paul's eyes were gleaming. "But she's got a really good rock 'n' roll sense, and a good heart, and it's gonna be *fantastic*!"

Laine was listening, too, and didn't know quite what to think, let alone say. "I was used to going in with people who could do things really quickly," he says. Now they were going to record—and play concerts—with a keyboard player who was only just figuring out how to locate middle C? "It was kind of *weird* for me."

But what could they do about it? No one wanted to hurt Linda's feelings. She was a nice woman, a hoot to have around, and the boss's wife, to boot. And who wanted to doubt Paul McCartney's judgment? "When he told you any of his ideas, he did it with such exuberance, you got sucked right into it," Seiwell says. "He could do anything. He could take a bad player and make them play good."

If only because he'd done it before. John Lennon couldn't even play proper guitar chords when Paul met him. How many painstaking afternoons had he spent teaching him how to tune the strings, then sitting right across from John so he could twist his own fingers into the chords Paul was making on the neck of his guitar? He'd turned the Quarrymen into the Beatles, then pushed them from "Love Me Do" to *Sgt. Pepper's Lonely Hearts Club Band,* for God's sake. That's how he saw it, anyway, so Paul had no doubt he could get Linda up to speed, too. And even if she didn't quite reach the level of professionalism the other guys had reached, that might not be the worst thing: you never wanted rock 'n' roll to be perfect. The magic was in the rough edges.

So back to rehearsing and jamming and the serious business of applied goofing around. "Ninety percent of it was playing guitars, the other ten percent was laughing," Seiwell says. "Paul just loved to sing and play goofy old songs, make shit up." Paul was in charge, he was paying Seiwell and Laine £70 a week to keep them afloat while the band got itself together. It was a fraction of what Seiwell could earn playing sessions in New York, but no worries about that because, as Paul kept insisting, it was just the beginning. Once they got their act together they'd be playing shows, and those would pay even more. Then there would be records, and everyone would share the royalties from those. They were a band; that's how bands worked—even though they couldn't put anything on paper yet as much of Paul's money was still tied up in Apple, and the ongoing litigation made it impossible for him to enter into any serious business arrangements just now. But that wasn't going to last forever, so have faith and let's light another joint and get back to playing. "We were a family who lived together, smelled each other's sweat and blood, did all that stuff together," Seiwell says. "But the other dynamic was that they were Paul and Linda, and we were the band. They were paying for everything, fronting everything. So it was really strange."

Off they went to London, and the EMI studios on Abbey Road. A brand-new band with a brand-new attitude and absolutely no pretensions. They set up in the shadow of the Beatles and ripped through eight songs in a week; five were first takes; including "Mumbo," an improvised jam whose first words—"Take it, Tony!"—were actually Paul's shouted instruction to engineer Tony Clark to start taping the groove they had just found. Paul ended up overdubbing most of the keyboards himself, though Linda's parts come through clearly on "Wild Life," which became the title track. She's much more present on the microphone, sharing a lead vocal on "I Am Your Singer," and harmonizing with Paul on the reggae-fied cover of Mickey and Sylvia's "Love Is Strange" and the sweet, oddly defensive ballad "Some People Never Know," in which Paul wonders, *Who in the world can be right all the right time?* She wasn't in her element but she tried hard, and that was enough to earn the respect of the other guys. If only because it was so easy to see that rebranding herself as a keyboard player—no, the keyboard player for a recent Beatle—was not something she actually wanted to be doing.

Linda certainly felt the intoxicating allure of the spotlight. But she had also felt the dark tug of its undertow: the gossip columns that called her ugly; the rock critics who accused her of tearing the Beatles apart. To walk onstage with Paul now, to be introduced as the professional musician she knew she wasn't, was asking for abuse on an entirely new level. But she didn't really have a choice. "He wanted her to be with him all the time, onstage, recording the songs. It was a neediness on his part," says Linda's longtime friend Danny Fields. And maybe she needed Paul just as much. "They were always inseparable," Seiwell says. Looking back through all of the years they spent working together, the drummer can't remember perhaps a single afternoon he spent with Paul when Linda wasn't with them, or in the next room with the kids. "If Paul was there, Linda was there, too."

Paul wasn't necessarily wrong about Linda's instincts. She'd been a fervent rock 'n' roll fan since her teen years and had gravitated to the same obscure B-sides the young Beatles had always obsessed over. She'd been an early and enthusiastic supporter of reggae music in the 1960s, and her impulse toward the rough edges pushed Paul away from his safer, more pedestrian instincts. Still, Linda's insecurities could mount, and she'd gird herself with a distant tone that struck others as rudeness or arrogance. "She could be difficult," Seiwell says. "But really, she wasn't that way at all. She got the shitty end of the stick in a lot of ways. Getting blamed for breaking up the Beatles— just imagine having that on your plate. But she was so good for him and the kids."

Paul leaked news of his new band in early August, when they were still working out the kinks in his barn. They didn't have a name then, and he couldn't settle on one (top candidates included *Turpentine* and the *Dazzlers*) until mid-September, when Linda's delivery of their second child went briefly awry and the doctors rushed her off to deliver the child surgically. Left outside the operating room with nothing to do but fret, Paul found himself thinking of wings: airplane wings; the wings of a stage; angel's wings. That last thought seemed like a particularly good omen, and when the doctor emerged a bit later, the news was good: both Linda and Stella Nina McCartney were alive and well. So, too, was the brand-new rock 'n' roll band he had just decided to name Wings.

The official launch for the band came in early November, at a gala costume party held on a rainy Monday night at the Empire Ballroom on Leicester Square. Paul had handwritten the invitations to each guest (quite an undertaking given the eight hundred friends who turned up) and appeared in an oversize tartan suit, with a turtleneck sweater. In the midst of the fancy dress, the live bands, the dance-team performance, and star-packed room (Elton John; Jimmy Page; various members of the Who and the Stones; actors and writers and an avalanche of journalists), Paul and Linda did their best to seem like the least assuming country folks in the vicinity. "I sheared the sheep yesterday," he proclaimed to *Melody Maker*. Linda was next to him in a shapeless red-and-white farm dress. Why such a big send-off for the new band? "We thought it would be a nice idea to invite a whole lot of our friends to a big party where they could bring their wives," she said. *Melody Maker* was not impressed. "An ex-Beatle's odd happening," it sniffed. "A weird idea from the mind of someone recognized for being hip."

Released to a skeptical public a month later, *Wild Life* seemed like a pretty weird idea, too. Paul's name was nowhere to be found on the cover, the front of which featured a portrait of the group posed over and, in Paul's case, standing in a pond. The rear cover had the names of the band and the album in flowing type, then a list of songs and a biographical sketch credited to a previously unknown hepcat named Clint Harrigan (actually Paul, whose hand was also responsible for the line drawing of the group just beneath), who described the band's brief history in the grooviest terms, closing with "In this wrapper is the music they made. Can you dig it?"

Most people didn't. Reviews of the admittedly tossed-off album were harsh ("a discotheque album," "a futile exercise," etc.), and sales were so weak EMI backed off plans to release "Some People Never Know" as a single. Unperturbed, Paul steered Wings toward its next step: hitting the road as a performing band. In search of a lead guitarist, Laine suggested Henry McCullough, a hot-fingered, hard-drinking Irishman best known for his work with Joe Cocker's Grease Band. Invited down to London to jam for a while, McCullough fit right in and was duly invited to join up. He had grown up listening to the Beatles, like everyone, and before long his admiration for the band's leader turned into a protective impulse. "He'd been away from the rock 'n' roll circus for so long," McCullough says. "You felt a bit of a big brother to him . . . we all wanted to do the very best for Paul so he could come out rocking."

Paul's idea was for Wings to start in a low-key way, with an unadvertised, unbooked tour of British universities. It was essentially the tour he had first pitched to John and the other Beatles when he was selling them the "Get Back" concept in late 1968. When he tried again a year later, John had responded by leaving the group. But two years later, securely at the helm of his own band, Paul didn't have to worry

about getting anyone's approval. He simply rented an Avis truck for
the gear and a van for the band, hired a couple of roadies, and told
everyone to report for duty on February 8, 1972. Which is exactly
what they did, happily, heading north to Nottingham University,
where Wings played their first show the next evening. As with every
show on the two-week journey, there were no advance arrangements,
no nothing. They pulled in with no warning and sent one of the roadies into the administration building to see if they might be interested
in putting on a dance with Paul McCartney's band that night. Usually
they had to be convinced that the ex-Beatle was really outside. The
roadies, Ian and Trevor, would lead them outside and point toward
the van. "They'd step outside and Paul would lean out of the window
and wave and you'd see them go 'Ooh, shit!'" Seiwell says. They'd
strike a deal with the university—usually a fifty-fifty split of the door
receipts—and send the students off to spread the news. Then Ian and
Trevor would set up the gear in the gym or the student union, and the
band would go out to find a hotel or a bed-and-breakfast.

The first gig, a lunchtime session in Nottingham's student union,
which held only a few hundred kids, felt more like a dress rehearsal
than a major debut. They began with Paul's newest song, a political
rouser called "Give Ireland Back to the Irish," and played nearly an
hour of songs from *Wild Life,* one or two from *Ram,* an improvised
blues jam that featured McCullough, and a scattering of new originals, before ending with a couple of Little Richard tunes from Paul's
age-old party repertoire: "Lucille" and "Long Tall Sally." Paul never
mentioned doing Beatle songs, and no one else brought it up, either.
The band members already knew better, and the university kids were
just thrilled to be having such an unexpected and intimate performance from Paul.

When it was over, they'd sit down in the student union office with
the kid who had helped put the show together and split up the money.
"It was literally just 'one for you, one for me, one for you, one for
me,'" Seiwell says. Back at the hotel they'd gather in someone's room
and open a bottle of wine, light up a few joints, and have a grand
time. Paul and Denny Laine pulled out their guitars and sang old rock
songs and British tunes; when it got late, Paul and Linda tucked
Heather and Mary into their beds and pulled out a drawer in the bu-

reau to improvise a crib for Stella with a pillow and blanket. It was the very image of the minstrel life Paul had been yearning to live: a band on the road, living, eating, drinking, and making music together with no hype or expectations to get in the way. "I had returned to amateur status, trying to relearn the whole game," Paul said. "We thought we were in it for fun. This was music, not nuclear science."

Music and family, so they did everything together. Sleeping in neighborhood B and B's; eating in corner cafés and fish-and-chip take-aways. They rode everywhere in the van and fell asleep with their heads on one another's shoulders. "We've no managers or agents," Linda told *Melody Maker.* "Just we five and the roadies. We're just a gang of musicians touring around." To McCullough it was like living in *Magical Mystery Tour,* with kids and dogs and trips to the seaside for fresh air and ice cream on the wharf. "We just rolled off for a laugh, and you could tell that it was as big a thrill for Paul as the early days with the Beatles had been."

In March the group flew to Los Angeles to record some new material, then headed back to London in the spring to prepare for a proper summer tour, a real, booked-in-advance jaunt through Europe. This time there would be agents and promoters, real gigs, and all the accompanying media and criticism to deal with. Yet, the magical-mystery-tour vibe continued, thanks to the secondhand London Transit bus they reconditioned for the tour with psychedelic paint out-side, comfy seats, a functioning kitchen in the downstairs rear, and an open-air sun-and-fun area on the upper level, from which the roof had been removed.

The summer tour kicked off in France in early July, rolling into Germany and then through Scandinavia before heading down to the Netherlands and concluding in Germany in late August. "Quite a mad thing to do, to put a playpen on the top deck of the bus and put all the children in there," Paul recalled later. "It's not what you'd expect from a normal band. But we weren't a normal band."

Yet Wings' first real concert tour suffered some of the typical tra-vails of a band on the road. A show scheduled for Lyons, France, on July 14 was canceled at the last minute because they hadn't sold enough tickets. Then the tour ran afoul of the law in Sweden on Au-gust 10, when a package addressed to Paul, filled with almost half a pound of hashish, fell into the hands of police. The constabulary hands reached out to grab Paul at the end of the night's show at the Scandinavium hall in Gothenburg and took off with Linda and Denny Seiwell, too, dragging them back to the station house for questioning. An unpleasant few hours of interrogation led to confessions, then some steep fines. Which paid for themselves many times when Linda, in the midst of being searched and cuffed by the police, thought to tell the tour's official photographer, Joe Stevens, to get as many shots of the bust-in-progress as possible. "Cover of the *Daily Express* tomorrow morning!" the photographer recalled her shouting to him from beyond the phalanx of cops. She was right—Paul's drug bust made news all around the planet, a reminder that his unique kind of bohemian domesticity contained more than a trace amount of rock 'n' roll.

Indeed, Paul steered his new group on an eccentric musical and cultural course that veered from politics to nursery rhymes to the fringes of glitter-rock decadence. They started 1972 with "Give Ireland Back to the Irish," a gesture toward Lennon-style journalism rock made in response to the Bloody Sunday massacre in Northern Ireland. This tuneful broadside was led by McCullough's snarling slide guitar and a typically powerful vocal by Paul. But his lyrics are ham-fisted, at best, never quite acknowledging the horror of the slaughter. His heart's in the right place, but his impulse to disassociate from unpleasantness ("Great Britain, you are tremendous!" he feels compelled to acknowledge) undercut the power of his message. Nevertheless, the song was immediately banned by the BBC, giving it (and its author) a taste of counterculture street cred. Thus invested, Paul moved instantly in the opposite direction with his next single, a pop-lite rendition of a familiar nursery-school verse, "Mary Had a Little Lamb," for which Paul had composed a cheerful pop melody and a sing-along *la-la* chorus. Paul's fellow Wings-men could only shake their heads. "It wasn't my style," McCullough notes. "But it didn't bother me too much." The rest of the rock world, just then swept up in the dark majesty of the Rolling Stones' shambolic masterwork, *Exile on Main Street,* greeted the ex-Beatle's kindergarten-safe single with less aplomb. Paul did his best to shrug off the critical battering, noting the "heavy trip" in the song's final verse, "where [the lamb] gets chucked out." Plus didn't it land in the UK's Top 10? "It sold as many as 'Tumbling Dice,' so there!" he told *Melody Maker*.

The band ended the year on a much higher note, literally and figuratively, with "Hi, Hi, Hi," a flat-out rocker with blazing guitar leads by McCullough, and hot organ overdub from Paul, who belts out the tale of an evening full of sex, drugs, and illicit reggae records with a wild intensity he hadn't shown in years. The BBC banned that one, too, though at least partly by mistake. What the censors heard as Paul urging his beloved to prepare for his "body gun" was actually him singing less explosively, if nearly as suggestively, about his "polygon." Despite, or because of, the new controversy, the song hit the Top 5 in the UK and scraped into the American Top 10.

Paul kept Wings in constant motion, moving from tours to recording sessions to TV appearances to filming scenes in a largely improvised movie he had dreamed up called *The Bruce McMouse Show,* which Paul imagined would combine band performances with an animated story about a family of mice living beneath the stage. Paul wrote a variety of new songs for the project, including a screaming rocker called "Soily," which became part of the band's live set. He engaged a film crew to shoot concerts during the European tour, and during the afternoons they worked on staged sequences that involved sets (stages with mouse holes) and bits where the musicians leaned down and pretended to be talking to the mice. Song-and-dance scenes were included, too. "We went to a studio to learn how to do a particular dance step," McCullough says. "Old-time music-hall dancing, arms in the air and such. I don't think I ever quite made the grade."

The *McMouse* project lost steam after a while, too, which was probably just as well. Nevertheless, Paul's quirky blend of rock 'n' roll wildness, music-hall whimsicality, and bohemian domesticity continued to push Wings in unlikely directions. The group's next album, *Red Rose Speedway,* was a fairly undistinguished grab bag of hard rock, a love song or two, a Hollywood-style shuffle, and a long medley of apparently unfinished songs strung together in what seemed to be random order. The record's high point was its single "My Love," a languid ballad that was elevated on the strength of a searing guitar solo McCullough invented on the spot to replace the more melody-based break Paul had imagined for the song. But even as Paul continued to score hit singles, and even as his albums (including *Speedway,* which topped the charts in the United States) found legions of fans, it was increasingly difficult to reconcile the 1970s version of Paul with the Beatle he had once been.

And not just for his mullet and glitter-lite wardrobe, though they didn't help, either. Nor did his serene belief that the addition of his inexperienced wife as sole keyboardist might not hamper the artistic process of his new band. After so many years of helping to challenge the possibilities of popular music and popular culture, the seventies Paul seemed intent on emphasizing how laid-back and silly it all could be. Did John Lennon observe that "genius is pain"? Well, his former partner wanted nothing more than to prove to the world that his brand of genius was a breeze.

For a time that's how it seemed in the band, too. That feeling of possibility-mixed-with-ease animated the months of communal life up in Scotland: the hours of music they played in the barn; the laid-back afternoons sitting in the sun and sharing a bottle of wine and a joint or two. They were truly a family then, with Denny Laine crashing in the back of the trailer he parked on the edge of Paul's property ("I like being independent, and I'm not into hotels," he explains), while Seiwell and his wife, Monique, rented a house a few valleys over. The house had a grand view of the coast and the Mull of Kintyre beyond, and on clear afternoons Paul and Linda rode their horses over the hills to hang out, often sticking around for dinner as the long afternoon faded into the cool, liquid light of a Scottish evening. Back in London in November of 1972, Paul and Linda invited the whole gang to an elaborate Thanksgiving dinner at the Cavendish house. Like the nights they spent on the road, riding on the same bus and living out of the same hotels, that ended with even more music. "Paul and Denny breaking out their guitars and singing everything they knew," Seiwell says. "Rock tunes, British folk songs, old American tunes, you name it."

They were, as Paul had always hoped, a *band* in every sense of the word. Banded together, working and sleeping, sweating and bleeding and having fun. Paul and Linda certainly did open their homes to the musicians and their families; when it came to their personal lives, they were even more inclusive than the other Wings-men had expected. As

Paul had always promised, bands were supposed to do everything to-gether, including writing and producing and sharing in the fruits of their labors. "But on the other hand we had no rights whatsoever," Seiwell says. "This other dynamic would come out and it was just [Paul and Linda] and the rest of us didn't matter."

Not that the other Wings members expected to be promoted or written about in the same way as their famous leader. They also knew that Paul was paying their weekly salary, and fronting the money for all the band's expenses. But Seiwell, and probably the others, too, also knew they could be making far more than their £70 weekly salaries playing recording sessions in New York or London. So once the band got some momentum, selling records in quantity and playing larger halls on their tours, it seemed time for Paul's dreamy talk about royal-ties and profit sharing to become reality. "We'd hear stuff like 'We're gonna do this and you'll get that.' Which was grand, you know," Mc-Cullough says. "But when you work for a year and a half and you're on the same money you started with, and you're playing with the greatest rock 'n' roll icon in the world . . . it was a crack."

Still, no one wanted to mention it. "It was seen as uncool to bring it up," Seiwell remembers. Particularly when Linda was heard to mut-ter, more than once, that it was such a privilege to play with Paul that maybe the band ought to consider paying *him*. But eventually some-one did bring it up to Paul, and when the Eastmans next came to Lon-don, Paul set up a meeting between the musicians and his in-laws/managers. After which nothing changed. The £70-a-week retainer was a decent midlevel executive salary for the time, but it also bought a lot of commitment from the band members. "We were supposed to be on call twenty-four/seven for Paul, available whenever they wanted to work. But I was flying home to New York to make money," Seiwell remembers. "Charging things on my AmEx, just trying to live. And the checks from [Paul's] office were sometimes late, too."

Paul never really knew about any of it, it seemed. The promises he'd made in 1971 had been sealed with "a hippie handshake," as Seiwell says. Gestures of goodwill that carried nothing more than his good intentions. Beyond that he could only smile, shrug apologeti-cally, and say it would all even up in the end. Then it was back to work, back to the music, because that's what mattered, wasn't it?

But the music could be a problem, too. Not just the puzzling decisions Paul made from time to time (releasing "Mary Had a Little
Lamb" as a single on the eve of the band's first real concert tour, for
instance), but also his stubbornly autocratic way of working with his
bandmates. Paul usually marched into the studio with such strong
ideas about how things should be played, and how a line that comes
out one way on Monday pretty much has to be played precisely the
same way on Tuesday and Wednesday and every day from there on
out: improvising onstage, or anywhere, was not something he was accustomed to hearing. Some guys didn't care—Seiwell had been a session player long enough to be satisfied with the virtues of flexibility
and consistency. But McCullough was accustomed to expressing himself through his instrument. What he couldn't say in music, he
drenched in whiskey, and this combination of factors left him with
little patience for the sort of niggling critiques Paul felt compelled to
throw his way.

As far as Paul was concerned, he had his own way of doing things,
and it had been working out pretty well so far, hadn't it? Sure, he
wanted Wings to be a democracy. But anarchy was something else altogether: that's what had finished off the Beatles, in the end. Paul was
always interested in hearing other ideas—he'd stepped aside and let
Henry put his own solo on "My Love," after all. But he knew what
was right, and he knew what wasn't, and he couldn't think of a single
reason why he might want to change things around.

16

For a time they spoke only through the newspapers, or on their records. Paul's q-and-a from the *McCartney* release fueled John's bilious interview in *Rolling Stone,* which only underscored his assertion, in "God," that he didn't believe in the Beatles. Which, to his bandmates, meant he would no longer trust, or be defined by, the group of friends with whom he had lived, worked, and grown up.

Paul responded with *Ram*'s handful of angry, pointed songs. The songs on that album had infuriated John so deeply he posed for a photo lampooning the shot of Paul and his ram (John held the head of a pig) to include in the packaging of his second solo album, *Imagine.* Even more hurtful, though, was John's "How Do You Sleep?"—which took aim at his ex-partner and held nothing back. Set to a slow, swampy rhythm, ornamented with a wicked slide-guitar solo from George—*et tu George?*—the lyrics were as brutal as they were precise: *The sound you make is Muzak to my ears,* John snarled. *You must have learned something in all those years.*

John obviously knew how to hurt Paul's feelings, and before long he was firing back on his next record (*Wild Life*'s mournful "Dear Friend") and in the pages of *Melody Maker,* which described the other Wings sitting awkwardly as Paul steered a group interview into a point-by-point refutation of his former bandmates' complaints about him. George had asked him to play at his big Concert for Bangladesh that summer, possibly as a reunion of the Beatles, but Paul wouldn't give Klein the chance to claim the credit for such a "historical event." Then there was his ex-partner. "John and Yoko are not cool in what they're doing," Paul groused. And what did he think of "How Do You Sleep?" Paul sighed bitterly. "I think it's silly . . . he says the only thing I did was 'Yesterday,' and he knows that's wrong." Yet, Paul couldn't dismiss John entirely: "I like his *Imagine* album. He's all right, is John."

John felt the same ambivalence, almost instantly disowning the anger in "How Do You Sleep?"—then balancing the bitter letters he sent to newspapers (including his response to Paul's *Melody Maker* interview, published a week later) with a private missive he asked Ray Connolly to hand-deliver to Paul's house on Cavendish. "I think I might be able to solve this," John told the journalist. Connolly left the letter in Paul's letter box, but when he called back later to make sure it had arrived, Jim McCartney answered and said Paul had sent it on to his lawyers' office. "If I were you, son, I wouldn't get involved in all this," Jim said sadly. Still, the letter may have had some impact. Visiting New York a few weeks later, Paul and Linda met John and Yoko for dinner on two occasions, coming away from the evenings with an agreement to stop insulting one another in the press.

Yet it was impossible to escape the shadow of that other band. It didn't matter that Paul had formed a new group; no one really cared how many shows they played, or how many hit singles and albums they released. Eventually all anyone wanted to talk about was the Beatles. Were they ever going to make another record? Or just play a single reunion show together? And failing that, could Paul at least play a Beatles song, or maybe more than one, when he played with Wings? One of the promoters working on Wings' first tour of Europe had suggested, strongly, that Paul at least make a gesture toward his fans' ravenous appetite for the Beatles. *Just at the end of the show,* he argued. *Come up alone with your guitar and sing "Yesterday."* Paul shook his head, he just couldn't do it. "It was too painful," he told *Rolling Stone*'s Ben Fong-Torres in 1976. "Too much of a trauma, like reliving some kind of weird dream."

The dream wasn't over, no matter what John tried to tell people. All four Beatles kept up busy solo careers through 1972 and 1973, but two double-album Beatles' greatest-hits records (the so-called *Red* and *Blue* albums) rocketed quickly to the top of sales charts around the world, and these were followed by Paul's *James Paul McCartney* television special, an elaborate, hour-long presentation that included live performances by Wings, a big song-and-dance number featuring cross-dressing dancers, and an explosive performance of Paul's new James Bond theme, "Live and Let Die." Paul also played a medley of songs on his acoustic guitar and featured dozens of his McCartney relatives (including Jim, who was filmed handing over a wad of cash to help his millionaire son pay the tab at a bar) as they drank, smoked, and sang lusty versions of standards in a Liverpool pub. Yet the highlights, without a doubt, were the snippets of "Michelle" and "Blackbird" Paul sang during the medley, then the show-ending performance of "Yesterday," a selection made at the (staged) request of his fellow Wings-men, who sat at his feet as he sang on a dark and empty stage.

News that John, George, and Ringo had dismissed Klein from their service warmed relations all the more, and by the time Ringo's self-titled album came out at the end of 1973, it almost wasn't surprising to learn that *Ringo* contained songs from all three of the other Beatles and even featured John, George, and Ringo playing together on John's "I'm the Greatest," the first time a quorum of Beatles had played on anything since the "I, Me, Mine" overdub session nearly four years earlier. Where was it leading? No one could, or would, say for sure. Not conclusively, anyway. "I don't think that'll ever happen again," Paul told *Rolling Stone*'s Paul Gambaccini just after Ringo's album came out. Yet, he hastened to add, a reunion wasn't exactly impossible. "If things keep cool, I'd like to maybe do some work with them; I've got a lot of ideas in my head. . . . We couldn't be the Beatles-back-together-again, but . . . I wouldn't rule everything out, it's one of those questions I really have to hedge on. But, I mean, I'm ready." So, yes. Or possibly, no: "I don't see gettin' the Beatles back together."

Ambivalence—or at least the desire not to seem too eager to commit one way or another in public—could hardly seem more vivid.

But if the ex-Beatles were edging toward one another in 1973, the current members of Wings were moving apart. The *James Paul*

McCartney special aired in April, and the group mounted a thorough and well-received tour of Great Britain in May, with a few bonus dates thrown in during early July. They spent the time between tour swings at Paul's farm in Scotland rehearsing songs for a new album, then returned to the farm to continue the work in August. Wings was definitely a band now; two years of near-constant rehearsing and touring had tightened the rhythm section and created a unique blend between Denny Laine's rhythm guitar and McCullough's blues-fired leads. The band had a distinct vocal blend, too, with McCullough, Laine, and Linda weaving behind Paul's reliably strong singing. Meanwhile, Paul's new songs came with a renewed sense of purpose. The years of accrued post-Beatles warfare, along with the critical ignominy his recent work had earned, had finally pushed him away from his reflexively cheery, whimsical self, back to the urgent need that had always fueled his best work.

Still, the family atmosphere Paul had been so intent on creating among his bandmates was deteriorating, largely because the cooperative setup he had promised, the profit participation and the creative authority, had never become reality. Maybe it never really stood a chance, given Paul's role as Wings' chief financier and commercial draw, and the overwhelming confidence he had in his own musical judgment. Certainly, he intended to treat his musicians fairly, but someone had to decide what constituted fair. So maybe Wings wasn't a democracy as much as a benevolent dictatorship. And if Paul wasn't eager to come off as a heavy when it came to business—that would be uncool—the Eastmans were more than happy to enforce law and order within the commonwealth. If Paul noticed the frustration this was causing, he either wouldn't or couldn't acknowledge it. "Paul could never talk about how he was feeling," McCullough says. "Only about how the music would be affected." He could only smile, focus on his music, and assume everything else would work itself out.

Only it didn't. Seiwell was rapidly losing patience with the McCartney office's unwillingness to commit to anything beyond the £70 weekly salary he had been making since August of 1971; the issue became particularly grating in the wake of the group's sell-out UK tour that summer. Surely the band had been a fundamental part of that success and would be paid accordingly. But then they weren't, for whatever reasons, and Paul was already planning for the group to pull up stakes and zoom off to record their next album in Lagos. Another 24-7 assignment, in other words, for weeks, perhaps months, on end. And to what end—another million-selling album they wouldn't get paid anything for making? "He'd promised we'd participate in the rewards," Seiwell says. "It's reasonable to expect you might get something for your efforts. But then it never changed."

Another thing that hadn't changed was Paul's single-minded assurance that he knew exactly how the music should sound. This created problems, too, particularly for McCullough, who could rarely resist the impulse to change the guitar lines he played each time the band ran through a song. Blues players do that kind of improvising as a matter of course; that's how McCullough had been trained to play. But Paul had grown up in the rock and pop tradition, in which a band's performance is defined by its consistency from night to night. So as they honed the new songs, Paul wanted to hear the same lines played the same way. Earlier he'd allowed McCullough to follow his own path here and there, but Paul was determined to make these songs exactly right, and now the guitar player wouldn't stay in line. McCullough kept finding new variations, new riffs, to add to songs they had already played through dozens of times. The air between them grew chilly. Paul glared at the Irishman, who simply stared back. Then Paul interrupted a song and confronted him. "I just need you to play this!" he implored the guitarist. "You developed it; now just play it the way you played it before, so we get used to hearing it!" Everyone else could only stand and watch. "He backed Henry into a corner," Seiwell remembers. "And he'd just had it."

When the rehearsal ended, McCullough went with Denny Laine to a pub in Campbeltown, then after downing a few pints went roaring back to the farm. "I remember thinking, 'If I don't get out of this now, I'm gonna get sacked,'" he says. He found Paul in the barn and they started going at it again. Finally, McCullough threw up his hands. "Well, fuck you!" he yelled. "I'm gettin' out of here." He packed up his guitars, picked up his wife in Campbeltown, and was on the road for London that night.

Seiwell hung on for another couple of weeks, but his frustrations were getting the best of him, too. Why were they headed to Lagos without hiring a new guitarist and giving that guy a couple of weeks to get into the swing of things? Paul shook his head. They'd do this record just as they'd done *Ram,* he said. Denny Laine or Paul could double-track the lead guitar parts, no problem, and they'd worry about a new guitar player when they got home. But as the Lagos trip got closer, and Seiwell pondered the thought of all those painstaking overdubs, he realized he couldn't go through with it. To have gone through everything they'd done in the last two years, only to be back to the lineup that had made *Wild Life;* to have traveled this far with no realistic expectation that he'd ever be paid as much as he could earn as a studio musician in New York working banker's hours . . . suddenly Seiwell just couldn't see the point. He waited until the last minute—the car to the airport was literally honking outside his door— but then put his suitcase away and picked up the telephone. "I can't do this," he told Paul. "I'm done."

Paul was, by all accounts, speechless. But he wasn't going to beg or negotiate. He also wasn't going to ask what had pushed these members of his extended family to abandon him. "I don't think he ever knew why," McCullough says. "He certainly didn't ask. If it were my band, I'd at least want to pick up the phone and find out why they left, if only to keep my own head right. I'd worry I'd done something terribly wrong to make them want to go. But maybe that's not his way."

Instead, Paul turned the story into a central theme in the album's creation myth. The way he told it, McCullough and Seiwell quit the band together on the eve of the trip to Lagos. They'd abandoned him with no warning and no discernible reason. "I don't know quite why," he'd say, shrugging. Ultimately, though, Paul knew it was for the best. McCullough just wasn't adaptable enough. Seiwell was always replaceable. "I fancy playing the drums, anyway." Both of them, well, "they just didn't fit in." That version certainly elevates the drama, while also underscoring the triumph that was to come. "I was determined to do the best album we'd made." Maybe this double-barreled repudiation was exactly what Paul needed to focus his muse. He'd felt abandoned before; that's what had inspired him to pick up a guitar in the first place. So now he'd assuage his hurt and fill the empty space with the one thing that always worked for him best: music.

• • •

Paul's vision was that they should be recording in a lovely, exotic place. He pored over a list of the recording facilities EMI owned around the world, and when he realized the company had a studio in Nigeria, his imagination went into overdrive. They should record the new album in Africa! Guitars in the jungle; the sound of drums pounding over the veld! The music filigreed with the echoes of trumpeting elephants and roaring lions! *It would be magical!* Unfortunately, that vision didn't take into account a few crucial facts: Lagos was actually an enormous and not particularly appealing city; they were arriving at the height of the annual monsoon season; and EMI's studio was less a modern recording facility than a tin shed equipped with secondhand microphones and none of the acoustic screens they needed to keep separate sounds on separate tracks.

They ended up having to build the screens from scratch. "We all mucked in helping them so that we could start the sessions," former Beatle engineer Geoff Emerick, who Paul had imported from London to work on the sessions, recalled. "Even Paul picked up a saw and started sawing wood." Recording was delayed for only a few days, and they had rehearsed the songs in Scotland for so long they had a good idea of how everything would go. But it was, as Seiwell had anticipated, painstaking work to have three pairs of hands (actually two, since Linda could only play simple keyboard parts) recording arrangements that had been constructed for a five-piece band. Other intangibles made things even more stressful. One evening Paul and Linda were jumped by knife-wielding bandits who relieved them of their money, cameras, watches, and the bag of lyrics and demo tapes Paul was carrying. Fortunately, he had already memorized most of the new material, so the loss wasn't that devastating. Another day local musicians stomped into the studio and accused Paul of trying to steal their native sounds. He calmed them down by playing tapes of a few tracks, but the mounting anxiety was obviously taking its toll. Paul had been smoking even more heavily than usual in Africa, and the abuse took its toll. Waiting to record a vocal one afternoon, he suddenly fell to his knees, unable to breathe, and passed out onto the floor. Linda, Denny, and Emerick threw him into the back of the studio manager's car and rushed off to the hospital, more or less convinced that Paul was having a heart attack. Fortunately, it was just a bronchial spasm, the product of his substantial cigarette habit. He cut down on the smokes, and work resumed. After seven weeks they had an album.

Band on the Run was released in early December and zoomed almost instantly to the top of sales charts around the world. It went on to sell more than 6 million copies and spawned three hit singles, including the title track, which hit #1 on the U.S. charts. *Band on the Run* was also a critical triumph, earning ecstatic reviews everywhere from the *New York Times* to *Rolling Stone* in the United States, and in England's *New Musical Express,* whose critic concluded his review by asserting it was a "great album." It continued, "If anybody ever puts down McCartney in your presence, bust him in the snoot and play him this. He will thank you for it afterwards."

And no wonder: *Band on the Run* was the most consistent and musically adventurous album Paul had made since *Abbey Road.* The title track is constructed like a pocket symphony, moving from a pensive opening through a crunchy middle section to a triumphant climax built around the song's indelible chorus. Together, the sections describe Paul's relationship with music, the journey from feeling trapped—*Stuck inside these four walls*—to finding release and redemption in the simple joy of playing music with, and for, other people: *We never will be found* . . . Though the album launched Paul's reputation as a serious solo artist, the influence of the Beatles can be heard throughout the album. It's all over the title track, from the *If I ever get out of here* observation he recalled from George's mania-era observations of fan-blocked dressing rooms, to the tune's contrasting textures and sounds. The same feeling pervades the rest of the album. "Mrs. Vanderbilt" comes off like a more socialized "Mean Mr. Mustard," while "Mamunia" takes a more laid-back approach to the sentiment in "Rain." Most striking, perhaps, is how the contrasting sections and spoken-word backdrops to "Picasso's Last Words" evoke its subject's cubism by presenting him through so many sonic lenses and perspectives.

Other songs stuck to more traditional structures and sounds, but offered a fire of their own. "Jet" is propelled by blazing saxophones, a wicked synthesizer line, and Paul's elliptical yet fired-up vocals, while "Let Me Roll It" plays like a tribute to *Plastic Ono Band*–era Lennon, from its spare instrumentation to the raw snarl of its guitars and the primal scream that echoes over its final bars. John clearly didn't mind. "'Band on the Run' is a great song *and* a great album," he told *Rolling Stone* in 1975.

Band on the Run was an unalloyed triumph. Eager to ride the momentum forward, Paul hired drummer Geoff Britton, a burly blond who was also an expert at karate, and a twenty-year-old lead guitarist named Jimmy McCulloch, whose baby face contrasted with his hard-partying, hot-tempered Scots interior. In June the expanded band traveled to America, and the country-music capital of Nashville, Tennessee, to record some new songs, coming away with a mediocre country knockoff called "Sally G," a pulsing rocker in the "Jet" tradition called "Junior's Farm," and a fully orchestrated version of Jim McCartney's old composition "Walking in the Park with Eloise."

The band's new additions didn't fold in as easily as anyone would have liked. The brilliant but callow McCulloch reveled in playing the rock 'n' roll wild man. Meanwhile Britton, the competitive martial artist, was intensely disciplined and took a dim view of the green marijuana haze that tended to follow the McCartneys through the day. Wings was not unaffected by the habits and indulgences of its post-Woodstock era. Whatever pills, powders, and potions the other bands of the 1970s were indulging in were, almost certainly, part of their scene, too. They could be awfully cavalier about it, too, a factor in the Swedish pot bust of 1972, and a similar brush with the Campbeltown police (who discovered suspicious plants thriving in the McCartneys' greenhouse) a few months later. More, and worse, busts would yet occur. Britton was out within a few months, because either he couldn't stomach his fellow Wings' decadent ways (his version of events) or, in Paul's words, he'd caught the same disease that took out Denny Seiwell and Henry McCullough: "He didn't quite fit."

No amount of rock 'n' roll stonerism could derail Paul's musical ambition, so before long the band was in action again, shooting an hour-long TV show called *One Hand Clapping*, a part-performance, part-backstage feature piece that was never released. The band also performed on the solo album Paul produced for his brother, Mike, who was still performing under his Scaffold-era stage name, Mike McGear. The band took a few weeks off for the year-end holidays, then celebrated the start of 1975 by traveling to New Orleans to re-cord another new album in Allan Toussaint's Sea-Saint studio. Drawn to the city for its vibrant culture and particularly its storied jazz and rhythm-and-blues heritage, Paul and Linda sublet an apartment for their family and lived like residents for the weeks they were there, walking the streets and visiting the shops and restaurants. The couple dressed as clowns, complete with heavily painted faces, for Mardi Gras, and when they heard music blaring from a bar, they usually went in to check out the band.

They recorded one song inspired by their locale, an improvised jam called "My Carnival." But once again, the decision to record in an exotic locale wasn't intended as a way to draw from the local culture. Paul had written out all of his songs in advance—words, music, and arrangements—which he presented to engineer Alan O'Duffy on the eve of the sessions on four sheets of paper, all of which had been taped together into a poster-size sheet. When the group, now including American drummer Joe English, convened in the studio, Paul was clearly in control. "He was absolutely demanding and wanted some-thing specific and wonderful," O'Duffy remembers. "He still gave guys the freedom to play their instruments the way they wanted to play them. He just edited them psychologically and musically until he got what he wanted; end of story. They didn't even *know* they were being manipulated, but he always got exactly what he wanted."

In this case that was *Venus and Mars,* a highly polished, deeply as-sured album that took in styles and ideas ranging from hard rock to piano ballads to orchestrated forties pop; from comic books to science fiction; from the joys of young love to the ebbing light of senescence. Everything came with a purpose. The hard-hitting "Rock Show" tele-graphed the world tour to come; the light-as-a-feather "Listen to What the Man Said" was built for the American Top 40, the top of which it would quickly reach. The Fred-and-Ginger shuffle "You Gave Me the Answer" played like a prequel to "When I'm 64," minus the latter's undercurrent of dark humor, while the frantic rhythm-and-blues shouter "Call Me Back Again" renewed the soda-shop passion of "Oh! Darling." Not every song was a throwback, however: "Love in Song" and particularly "Letting Go" traced the thin line between love and obsession, the first time as a portrait of heartbreak, the second as passion in all its unhinged, dangerous glory. When Paul belted out the climactic *I wanna put her on the radio . . . ladies and gentlemen, a brand-new star,* Linda's harmony made clear that he meant every word.

The emotional heart of some of the other songs seemed less evident. "Magneto and Titanium Man" played like a comic book, only without any of the form's wit or pathos. "Spirits of Ancient Egypt" evoked shimmery kinds of mystery, but to no discernible end. The spirits get hung up on the telephone and we're left with someone making dinner with a pound of love.

Paul would not have submitted these kinds of songs to John Lennon, not without tasting his editorial wrath. Maybe Paul was hoping to get a dose of that when he invited his ex-partner down to New Orleans to sit in. "There was some thought that he was going to join us," O'Duffy says. "John was just up in New York, and they had been talking to each other." It never happened, but it wouldn't have been the first time they'd seen one another in a recording studio that year.

The possibility of a Beatles reunion had always been there, and by 1974 it seemed to be edging closer to reality. The nearly four-way *Ringo* collaboration brought it tantalizingly near, and even John seemed to wish it had really happened that time. "Yeah, the three of us were there," he told *New Musical Express* reporter Chris Charlesworth, talking about the session he'd played with George and Ringo in late 1973. "Paul would have most probably joined in if he was around, but he wasn't." Though Paul, like all the other Beatles, continued to deny the rumors that the group might reunite, he also couldn't resist musing on, even publicly yearning for, the possibility that they might. Maybe he was, in his quiet way, trying to make it happen. At least that's how it seemed the night he showed up unexpectedly at one of John's recording sessions in Los Angeles.

John was separated from Yoko then, living with the Lennons' one-time secretary May Pang and indulging in something of a renewed adolescence. But he was also working, juggling two of his own recording projects with an album he was producing for Harry Nilsson. He was leading sessions for Nilsson's record in March 1974 when Paul started hanging around the city. They saw each other first at the Academy Awards ceremony on March 9, meeting backstage to chat for a while. That public rendezvous inspired even more whispers about a Beatles reunion, and these would have grown even more feverish if any bystanders had seen Paul and Linda sneaking into Burbank Studios just past midnight on the night of March 28, headed for the studio where John was working with Nilsson, Ringo, and a rotating band of their famous friends. "We had no clue he was coming," May Pang says. "All of a sudden we turned around, and Paul was there."

John laughed as they hugged. "How'd you know we were here?" Paul shrugged and looked around at the studio. The Beatles' old assistant Mal Evans was there, standing with the few musicians still milling around, chatting and smoking joints, now watching this new scene unfold out of the corners of their eyes. But Paul had missed the recording session, and he couldn't keep the disappointment out of his eyes.

"So you're done for the day?"

Well, yes. But John had been staying late most nights, often he ended up jamming with whoever was around. Paul edged toward the drum kit—Ringo's drums—perched on the stool, took up a pair of sticks, and peered up hopefully. John shrugged. "Ah, okay," he said, looking around for his guitar. "Maybe we'll have a little jam."

Linda made for the organ; a musician from a session next door strapped on the bass. Stevie Wonder, recording down the hall, came in and sat at an electric piano. As the technicians scampered around setting up microphones, John improvised a jazzy tune, while Stevie and Paul played along. *It's so wonderful to beeee, waiting for my green card with yooouuuu,* John crooned, noting his ongoing struggle to stay in the United States. But that didn't lead to anything, so Stevie led the group into a gospel-style progression that became a slow, funked-up "Lucille," with Paul in full Cavern-style shriek, and John providing a low harmony. That faded out after a verse or two, and nothing much came together ("Someone give me an E," John said, attempting to tune his instrument, "or a snort"). "Stand by Me" came next, following some technical confusion. ("Turn the fuckin' vocal microphone up!" John commanded. "McCartney's doin' harmony on the *drooms!*") They kept playing, and then it was happening again. Briefly and a bit tentatively, but still: John on lead with Paul's voice slipping easily into the high harmony, as if no time had passed, as if they hadn't just spent four years wading through their own blood and anger. "It was like yesterday," Pang says. "They didn't skip a beat, just went right into it."

The jam continued, but so did the drinking and the coke snorting. The music wove in and out of focus, and John sounded edgy, growing quickly snappish when he lost volume in his monitors. Still, Pang remembers a particularly sharp version of the old spiritual-turned-skiffle standby "Midnight Special." When it broke up, somewhere in the wee hours, John invited his ex-partner to come by his house in Malibu the next morning. Paul nodded cheerfully and said, yeah, sure, he'd be there. Happily, in fact. He showed up with Linda and the kids at around noon, finding Ringo, the Who's Keith Moon, and a few other friends sitting around the pool. With nothing else to do, Paul sat at the piano and pounded out some old Beatles tunes, while the others laughed and sang along. When John finally roused himself, Paul sidled up to him and whispered that he had a message from Yoko.

She had been in London a few weeks earlier and called Paul out of the blue. Could she come over and say hi? Well, of course she could. He was staying in the Cavendish house that week, so it was easy. She showed up smiling, more quiet than usual. Obviously, Paul and Linda had heard that she and John had separated—she had sent him away, off to Los Angeles, to live with May Pang. "She was very nice and confided in us, but was being very strong about it," Paul told the writer Chris Salewicz a decade later. While she wasn't happy about the way John had been behaving, she wanted him to know she was open for a reconciliation. "But he's got to work his way back," she said.

"I said, 'Well, look, do you still love him?'" Paul said. "So I said, 'Well, would you think it was intrusion if I said to him, "Look, man, she loves you and there's a way to get back"?' She said she wouldn't mind."

Paul was bound for Los Angeles in a few weeks anyway, so when he found himself standing with John on his rented patio, the moment felt right to deliver his message. "I took him into the back room and said, 'This girl of yours, she really still loves you. . . . You're going to have to work your little ass off, man. You have to get back to NYC and you have to take a separate flat, you have to send her roses every fucking day, you have to work at it like a bitch!" John nodded, and that was that.

"It's like a Beatles song!" Paul told Salewicz, not quite realizing that the story he was telling was almost a straight-up dramatization of "She Loves You," minus the *yeah, yeah, yeah*.

The afternoon went on. Paul sat at the piano and started pounding out some standards, then edged into some more Beatles songs. Ringo sat next to him on the bench and sang along, laughing. John came into the room and watched for a few minutes, not looking happy, then walked back out to the patio. May and Linda took the kids to walk on the beach, then came back for a swim. When the light started to fade, the McCartneys gathered the kids and said their good-byes.

"Let's see each other again," Paul said.

John nodded. "Let's!"

Not long after that, Pang overheard John talking to Nilsson about the future. "Wouldn't it be fun to get the guys back together?" he said.

Nilsson nodded, knowing exactly which guys John was talking about. "I'd love to get in there with you guys."

"Oh, yeah!" John said even more enthusiastically. "We could do a show in the fall!"

Instead, John and Pang moved back to New York, taking an apartment on the Upper East Side, across Central Park from the apartment John had shared with Yoko in the Dakota on Central Park West. John started sending flowers to Yoko, and she came to see him perform with Elton John at Madison Square Garden. Then John moved back in with his wife, and that rekindled bond once again became his central preoccupation.

17

When the lights went down, the roar seemed to shake the Kingdome's concrete ceiling. The music started slowly, an acoustic guitar strumming, a bass, a synthesizer playing a simple, haunting melody. Then a voice. *Sitting in the stands of the sports arena, waiting for the show to begin* . . . and not just any voice, but that sincere, boyish croon. So familiar, yet so elusive; everyone knew him, but it had been so long since he'd performed in the United States that hardly anyone in the stadium had actually ever *seen* him in the flesh. Then a single spotlight shone down, and there he stood, a figure half shrouded in mist. The light was dim, his face only a blur on the projection screens. But you could still see him—the dark hair, the doelike eyes, the full cheeks—and that sudden recognition ignited another roof-shaking roar.

The "Venus and Mars" verse gave way to a brief instrumental passage, a circular chord pattern that picked up instruments as it rose toward a little electric-guitar riff sizzling toward the moment when everything explodes at once. The drums thundered, the bass boomed, the guitars snarled. Then the opening bars of "Rock Show," and that same voice at the top of its range, promising all kinds of wild antics to come. *If there's a rock show!* he screamed. *We'll be there—oh yehhhhhh!* The entire stage washed in light, you could see the entire band, five visions of spangled, feather-haired rock stardom. But the iconic figure at center stage held the eyes. More than seventy thousand pairs of them, all goggling, beaming, smiling, shining down on Paul McCartney.

Just remember that this is a band and it's called Wings. That had been the message for the entire American tour, and for the swings through England and Australia that preceded it. Paul's name didn't appear anywhere on the tickets, or on any of the ads. *Wings Over the World,* or in the United States, *Wings Over America,* was all anything said. And by the time they got to that climactic American leg, with the new album *Wings at the Speed of Sound* as their third #1 album in a row, that was all anyone needed to know. Or hear, for that matter. So after that explosive "Venus and Mars/Rock Show" opening, the band segued right into "Jet," then "Let Me Roll It" from *Band on the Run,* and kept the whole arena on its feet. A pair of newer songs, "Spirits of Ancient Egypt" and Jimmy McCulloch's "Medicine Jar," calmed things down a bit, but then Paul spun over to the piano to uncork "Maybe I'm Amazed," and the place erupted again. Song after song, hit after hit. He's on bass, then piano, then acoustic guitar. The spectacular James Bond theme "Live and Let Die," the achingly romantic "My Love," the summery "Listen to What the Man Said." Endless songs, all smashes. Then the brand-new chart-topper, "Silly Love Songs," and the just-released-and-already-rising "Let 'Em In." Then the climactic "Band on the Run," a full-throttle encore of "Hi, Hi, Hi," and, in a daring move, the previously unheard "Soily" as the show's closer.

An amazing rock show, by any standards. Yet that wasn't what people were talking about afterward.

"He played 'Yesterday'!"

And not just that, but also "The Long and Winding Road," "Lady Madonna," "I've Just Seen a Face," and "Blackbird," too. Five Beatles songs, played a bit tentatively, perhaps, but still—visions of rock 'n' roll nirvana, performed by one of the golden ones, right here, right now. When Paul sat alone with his acoustic guitar, singing the opening line to "Yesterday," the vast crowd went completely silent. Just one voice, a guitar, and nearly seventy thousand people hanging on every note.

The Seattle show, the biggest of Wings' 1976 tour, took place on

June 10, just a few days before the final show in Los Angeles. Every aspect of the tour, from the lasers and mirror balls to the schedule that allowed the McCartneys to avoid hotels in favor of a series of rented homes in hub cities, had been planned down to the microdetail. The McCartney kids were there, of course, tended by Rose, the nanny. But you didn't have to look hard to find the cannabis haze, the bottles of Scotch and overflowing buckets of beer, maybe even a generously cut line of Bolivia's finest. As ever with Paul, a bit of rock 'n' roll excess was always welcome, as long as it didn't compromise the show. "You just had to be sober enough to play," says Howie Casey, the Liverpool veteran Paul tapped to head up the four-man horn section. "We had a great time. Everything taken care of, no worries anywhere. Just a good feeling the whole time. Very relaxed, not uptight or stressed, but within limits." Maybe McCulloch didn't always know his limits. He was a youngster, all of twenty-three, a small man determined to do everything bigger, faster, and wilder than it had ever been done before. "He was a nice guy," Casey continues. "A rock and roller, right up in your face. I liked Jimmy a lot. But whiskey doesn't agree with some people, and when he drank, he changed." One night Jimmy walked off after "Band on the Run" and declared that he'd had enough and wasn't coming back for the encore. Paul sprinted after McCulloch, grabbed the little man by his lapels, and threw him up against the dressing-room wall. *Get on the fucking stage, you cunt!* he snarled. "And he did," Paul recalled cheerfully. "And played great!"

Linda needed no convincing to go onstage this time around, and once she was there, she perched happily behind a vast bank of keyboards she seemed to operate with ease. Her voice was a familiar facet of the Wings vocal blend, and she'd even taken a lead vocal on the new album, belting out the custom-written "Cook of the House" with something approaching confidence. If anyone didn't like it, or her, she offered a precise response: "Fuck off!" Music critics were just like schoolteachers, she said, and didn't we leave all their do-this, do-that hang-ups back in the classroom? "It's like having parents on your back," she told Fong-Torres in *Rolling Stone*. "This is a great band, and this is great fun. And that's all we care about."

Denny Laine was at his height, with four featured spots including his old Moody Blues hit "Go Now," and a fiery take on his contribution to the latest album, "Time to Hide," set among the barn burners toward the end of the show. "We were so tight by then, getting such a great reaction everywhere we went," Laine says. "No expenses were spared, and lots of experimental stuff was going on. They suspended the monitors above the stage, which was very revolutionary. And playing live brought the best out of everyone. That was really our high point, that tour."

No one flew higher than the man at the center of it all. Paul wore a black jacket with spangled shoulders and a chain with a Wings icon around his neck. His hair shaggy on his collar, his face full and glowing, his voice stronger and more flexible than it had ever been, once sweet then harsh, full of knowing grit. He could do anything, it seemed. Did his critics say he wrote too many silly love songs? Fine, here's a new tune *called* "Silly Love Songs," and now it's another #1 single, too. "And what's wrong with that?" Paul sang. "'Cause here I go again!"

Here he went again, and the world was bedazzled. "McCartney Comes Back," on the cover of *Time,* "McCartney: The Beatle with the Charm Is Back," in the *New York Times.* "Yesterday, Today and Paul" on the cover of *Rolling Stone,* Universal acclaim, and not by half measures. "A Beatle on the wing; A band on the run; But not quite the act you've known for all these years," *Rolling Stone* declared. This was his moment, all the magic restored, only this time entirely on his own terms. Well, nearly. Because you could never tell how he felt about those other stories that followed the tour from city to city.

Were the Beatles going to reunite on the tour?

The media almost seemed to insist it had to happen. After all, John was in New York. Ringo spent most of his time in Los Angeles, and George wasn't exactly a stranger to these shores. Everyone knew they had been seeing one another, playing on each other's records. How hard would it be for them all to scamper up and take a guest turn on Paul's stage? Particularly since Bill Sargent, an American promoter with Barnum-size aspirations, had only months earlier offered the Beatles $50 million for a single reunion show he would broadcast around the planet on closed-circuit TV. Would they even consider it? As ever, Paul was indecisive at best: "We might do it, and if we did, we'd try and make it good," he told a pretour press conference in London. "But then again, we might not do it. But then again . . . we might!"

Strangely, Sargent's outsize offer inspired a chain of events that very nearly led to a public reunion by John and Paul. The whim struck them late on April 24 during another of Paul's visits to his old friend and erstwhile partner. They had been hanging around for a few hours at John and Yoko's apartment in the Dakota, and at 11:30 p.m. John had switched on the then new comedy-variety show *Saturday Night Live,* which that night included a bit satirizing the $50 million Beatles reunion offer. The show's producer, Lorne Michaels, sat alone at a desk and declared earnestly that he needed to address all four ex-Beatles. He had, he continued, a serious offer for them to consider. If they agreed to reunite on *Saturday Night Live* and play the usual music guest spot of three songs, he could get NBC to pay them $3,000. "You know the words," Michaels said. "It'll be easy . . . and if you want to give Ringo less, that's up to you."

Michaels was kidding, of course. But he also knew how prankish the Beatles could be, and with John just uptown, well, anything was possible. Michaels posted network pages in the Rockefeller Center lobby, just in case. What he didn't know was that the band's two central members were watching the whole thing together, laughing, just twenty-two blocks north and two avenues west of where he was speaking. Then they started egging one another on. They should go downtown! It'd be easy. They could practically *walk* there! "We almost went down to the studio, just as a gag," John recalled. "We nearly got into the cab, but we were actually too tired."

Yet it had been a fun visit, and with comradeship and talk of reunions so thick in the air, Paul came back to the Dakota the next afternoon, guitar in hand. This time he'd come unannounced, bearing a guitar, and the welcome wasn't quite as warm. Tired by Paul's spontaneous visits, John gave his old friend a terse lecture about the importance of calling first. "It's not 1956, and turning up at the door isn't the same anymore," he said. Paul was visibly hurt and walked out quickly. "I didn't mean it badly," John said. But there was no time to set things straight—Paul left town that evening to join his band in Texas, where the *Wings Over America* tour was set to begin in a few days. Still, hurt feelings or no, Paul continued musing openly about the prospect that John would attend his concert when Wings got to New York at the end of May. They'd talked about it on the phone, Paul revealed. "I'm saying to him, 'Well, are you coming to the show at Madison Square Garden?' 'Well,' he says, 'everyone's kind of asking me, am I going? . . . ' and I'm saying, 'Oh, God, that's a drag, isn't it.'" The problem, Paul continued, was that no ex-Beatle could see him play without confronting the expectation that he would jump up and play, too. "Then if they get up, we've got to be good. Can't just get up and be crummy, 'cause then [the media] says, 'The Beatles really blew it on the Wings tour,' or something." With so much pressure, with so many reasons to stick with the killer Wings show and let sleeping Beatles lie, why would Paul want to risk it? Yet he couldn't let it go. "If John feels like coming out that evening, great, we'll try and get him in. Have it all cool, no big numbers. Just play it by ear."

Paul sent a pair of tickets to John, but if he expected to see his old friend at the Garden, he was disappointed. John gave them to his babysitter and spent the evening watching TV at home.

Then the *Wings Over the World* tour was over and Paul was home again, thinking about the future and wondering what would come next. The Beatles' faithful aide and sidekick Mal Evans had never quite recovered from his brush with, then separation from, the mania, falling victim increasingly to depression and drugs in the seventies. The outsize, yet gentle Mal somehow found his way into a drug-fueled standoff with Los Angeles police in the spring of 1976, which ended when the cops shot him to death. Closer to home, Jim McCartney had died in March, just seventy-three but weakened by arthritis and the years of toil. "I'll be with Mary soon," he'd murmured near the end. Jim remarried to a younger widow, Angela Williams, in the midsixties and inherited a new stepdaughter, Ruth. But while Paul could be sweet to his stepsister, he'd never quite got past feeling suspicious of his stepmother. Surely no woman could replace the sainted Mary, particularly once his father came with such an obvious fortune attached to his name. Though Angela recalled her tearful stepson hugging her during Jim's final days, thanking her for her vigilance and reassuring her that "you'll never want for anything," Paul apparently changed his mind once Jim passed away. The conflict between Paul and his father's widow would careen unhappily, if mostly quietly, through the years. "We don't exist—Paul's written us out of his life," Angela said. "We haven't had a penny from Paul since our father died," his stepsister, Ruth, noted.

Paul's own family continued down their placid, determinedly normal path. Eager to raise the children away from the pop-star pressures of London, he and Linda bought some property in Peasmarsh, a well-hidden corner of Sussex about ninety minutes south of the city, where they built a circular home whose intimate size and quirky, slices-of-pie layout emphasized family togetherness and intimacy. Heather, Mary, and Stella all attended the region's public schools and were well-known for their manners and modest wardrobes. Most of the neighborhood children came from well-to-do families, but the children of the resident pop legend contented themselves with hand-me-downs and scuffed sneakers.

Linda became pregnant again in early 1977, but that didn't slow down Wings' work schedule. They had barely taken a break after the end of the world tour, reconvening quickly to polish their live performances for a three-disc live set, *Wings Over America,* which was released just before Christmas 1976 and jumped quickly to the top of sales charts on both sides of the Atlantic. Sessions for a new studio album began in London a few weeks later, continued for a month, and took only a short break before resuming in the Virgin Islands, where the entire band, recording engineers, staffers, and families relocated to a small fleet of boats. The McCartneys lived on board one, the band and crew had another two, and a fourth was transformed into a floating recording studio. With the gear on the deck they recorded right there in the ocean breeze, with the cobalt sea at their feet and the Caribbean sun warming their necks.

Another McCartney notion made real! Still, the floating sessions were something less than a Caribbean dream. Denny Laine quickly got sunstroke; engineer Geoff Emerick received a nasty shock from some ill-grounded electronic gear; longtime McCartney staffer Alan Crowder fell down a ladder and broke a bone in his foot. The boats' owners took a remarkably dim view of the perpetual pot smoking taking place on their vessels and threatened to toss the whole lot overboard unless they could find a way to obey the nation's drug laws. Meanwhile, intraband relations were once again growing strained. Maybe with Jimmy McCulloch it had as much to do with his own mercurial temperament—magnified considerably by the effects of alcohol and drugs—as it did with Paul's autocratic ways. But the young Scot abandoned the band just as abruptly as his Irish and American predecessors had done, phoning one morning to announce he was forming a band with Small Faces/Humble Pie vet Steve Marriott. "I was a little put out at first, but, well, what can you say to that?" Paul said. Sadly, McCulloch died of a heroin overdose in 1979. "He was always a little dangerous," Paul continued. "He liked partying too much and was getting into too many things. In the end he was just too dangerous for his own good."

Joe English lasted another month or two, but he was gone by the middle of the fall, saying he was homesick for his stomping grounds in rural Georgia. His departure was relatively cordial, but his tone changed when he was interviewed by a reporter for *Beatlefan* magazine a few months later. Here, he unspooled a familiar litany of complaints about promised, but never quite paid, record royalties, arduous recording sessions (overdubs for the *Wings Over America* set had gone on endlessly), and the perpetual drag of Linda's not-quite-competent performances. "Linda is a nice chick, and I really like her," he said. "But let's face it—she can't play and she can't sing. Denny Laine can sing but he tends to sing off-key . . . most of the *Wings Over America* overdubs were necessary because of people singing out of tune, and I don't mean Paul."

As ever, Paul refused to engage the unpleasantness. "If someone didn't seem to fit, or we thought we could do better," he said, "then we had to go with it." Or, as he put it in "With a Little Luck," one of the gauziest songs they recorded in the Virgin Islands, willow trees survive happily by bending away from the bitter winds that blow in their direction. *And if he can do it, we can do it—just me and you!* A lovely idea for a suburban father of four (in September they added a long-hoped-for son, James). But for a thirty-five-year-old rocker with a legendary past, it only revealed how suddenly, and dramatically, his grasp on the leading edge of popular culture had slipped.

• • •

In England it was the year of the Sex Pistols, the year of the Clash. "White Riot" and "God Save the Queen" and skinny guys in torn clothing and leather jackets. Jagged hair, safety pins, spitting as political statement, and the kind of electric thrash that has nothing to do with polish and everything to do with feeling extremely pissed off about many, many things. Rightfully so, given the paucity of economic opportunity in Britain, the dead weight of the aristocratic past, and the decadent dregs of the sixties. "If I want to kill a hippie, I will," Johnny Rotten declared, and you didn't have to look hard to identify what might push him over the edge. "Mull of Kintyre" might have been a factor, if only because it was so inescapable that winter. The biggest hit in Paul's career; bigger than any of the Beatles' singles. Bigger than any other single in the history of British popular music. And it had *bagpipes*! A fucking army of bagpipes, along with acoustic guitars, a big campfire chorus, and lyrics so sentimental they compared the island near his Scottish getaway to smiles in the sunshine and tears in the rain. "Carry me back to the days I knew then," Paul sings. And the pipers blare and the guitars chime and the entire village sings along, and on a ratty stage somewhere Johnny Rotten gobbed up a big one.

Rotten would have hated the album that followed, *London Town*, even more. After having spent much of 1976 proving that Wings was a tough-minded band that could rock with fairly wild abandon, the album Paul wrote and produced as a follow-up was a distinctly reined-in affair, heavy on the keyboards and acoustic guitars, and almost completely absent of sharp edges, even when it aspired toward rock 'n' roll. While the title track achieves a pleasantly spaced-out perspective on city life, and "Café on the Left Bank" has some hot guitar, a striking melody, and intriguingly detached lyrics about a night in Paris, the vast majority of the songs are either ill-conceived, unfinished, or both. "Famous Groupies," for instance, strains for rock 'n' roll decadence and achieves only a high-handed misogyny. "I've Had Enough" has all the righteous outrage of a man who can't find his slippers. The overarching feeling is creative ennui: as "With a Little Luck" (yet another smash single) makes so clear, Paul's primary interest now was in avoiding difficult feelings, rather than confronting them and transforming them into art.

London Town was an unusually long album, more than fifty min-utes, which stretched the vinyl LP medium to the edge of its limits. So many new songs, the McCartney muse still bursting forth. But was it any good? After all these years Paul couldn't be sure. Even with the smash hit "Mull of Kintyre," he'd nearly released the single with its eventual B-side, "Girls School," as the featured song instead. Chris Thomas, once an engineer for the Beatles and by the midseventies a producer of albums for the Pretenders, the Sex Pistols, and other lead-ing acts, recalls the day Paul played him both songs, asking which should be the A-side. "I said, 'Are you *joking*?'" Thomas says. "It was so obvious 'Mull' was going to be enormous, but he had no idea." When Paul played *London Town* to Tony Bramwell, a Beatles intimate from all the way back to Liverpool, Bramwell's response—which fell quite short of a rave—triggered an immediate, and lasting, fury.

"I dunno," Bramwell said, and shrugged. "Doesn't sound finished to me."

Silence. Then: "What the *fuck* do you think you're talking about?" Paul leaned forward and started slapping the table between them. "I brought you out of Liverpool with the Beatles!" Whack! "You fucking work for *me*!" Slap!

Only by then Bramwell had long since started his own career, first as a publicist on a wide variety of music and movie projects, then as a director with Polydor Records, and he no longer felt compelled to serve as any Beatle's yes-man.

"There was a bit of a scene, I'm afraid," he says. "He didn't agree with what I said, and I didn't agree with him, so he got mad at me. And then we didn't speak at all for something like ten years."

Still, for every old friend exiled, and for every Wing who flew off on his own, there was always someone else to come in and fill the gap. Denny Laine pointed the way to a hot young session guitarist of his acquaintance named Laurence Juber and a young drummer who lived near him named Steve Holly, and they were duly invited to Paul's basement studio at his Soho Square offices for jam sessions, then swiftly anointed as the next pair of Wings. "Paul was reluctant to go through a drawn-out audition process," Holly recalls. "So we played for a couple of hours and Paul just said, 'Okay, sounds like a group to me!' and then he walked out."

Soon Juber and Holly were at work, first as stand-ins miming their predecessors' parts in the *London Town* promotional films, then up at the farm in Scotland, where they started to work out arrangements for the songs Paul had written for the next Wings album. Some things were different now. The musicians signed detailed contracts that spelled out every aspect of their responsibilities and privileges, and when they got up to the farm, they could bunk in the dormitory-style lodgings Paul had built above the rehearsal space in the old barn. Other things were exactly the same: the days began with long jams of Paul's favorite songs, everything from Chuck Berry to reggae to the perpetual "Twenty Flight Rock." When a new inspiration overcame him—*let's record a whole album of songs about Rupert the Bear!*—whatever else they were working on would be cast aside until that enthusiasm had run its course. "He just followed the creative flow," Juber says. And he'd do it pretty much every workday, week in and out, just as Jim McCartney had gone to his job at the cotton market every day, week in and out, when he was working. "The process was like breathing to him," continues Juber. "A very strong work ethic, just like the Beatles. He had this need, this hunger, to produce music. And it never went away."

So back into the studio, this time with Chris Thomas—riding high from his work with the Pretenders and the Sex Pistols, and so many other new-wave scene-makers—sharing producer's duties with Paul. As ever, they recorded in a variety of nontraditional settings, starting up in Scotland, then in a castle in the southwest of England, where they set up a remote recording system and moved the mics around to take advantage of the ambience of the ancient stone rooms, the stairwells, and even the fields outside. This time Paul wanted a more hard-edged sound, the record he should probably have recorded a year earlier, so he came in with a handful of rocking tunes they played at a blistering pace. "Spin It On" spun like a pinwheel, while "Old Siam, Sir" had the crunch of heavy metal, and "To You" set off a brittle melody and cryptic lyrics with a careening Juber guitar solo that Paul ran through a closetful of electronic effects to create a suitably distorted sound. Work went on for months, incorporating more songs, moods, and ideas. "The Broadcast" and "Reception" set instrumentals against found-object spoken-word segments (shades of "I Am the

Walrus"), while "Arrow Through Me" and "Baby's Request" could have come right out of the setlist Jim Mac's Band used to play in the 1920s. "Goodnight Tonight" was by-the-numbers late-seventies disco, then there were pop tunes, folk songs, and even a pair of songs performed by a vast all-star consortium Paul and Chris Thomas had drafted from England's leading bands (the Who, Led Zeppelin, and more) and termed, with suitably hubristic grandeur, the Rockestra.

An avalanche of songs, ultimately. "I think the album got overworked, eventually," Chris Thomas says. If another famous musician wandered past the studio, they would corral him into the control room and hit him up for advice. Paul Simon loved the keyboard sound in "Arrow Through Me," while David Bowie insisted that the weird spoken-word "The Broadcast" (two readings drawn from Ian Hay's *The Sport of Kings* and John Galsworthy's *The Little Man,* set to a lovely fragment of melody) *had* to be the single. Intrigued, Paul played Bowie every song the band had recorded over the months, from the burst of rockers they had done out of the gate and all that came after, and asked for a song-by-song critique. "He was saying, 'Like this, not that; this is good; keep this, not that one,'" Thomas recalls. "He chose all the original stuff we'd done!"

A stopgap single, "Goodnight Tonight," hit the Top 5 on both sides of the Atlantic during the spring of 1979, a particularly nice omen for CBS Records, which had just wooed Paul away from EMI by offering him the richest contract in the history of popular music. But the album, called *Back to the Egg,* thinking it represented a rebirth for the band, only just hit the Top 10 upon its release in June. Its singles ("Old Siam, Sir" in the UK and "Getting Closer" in the United States) were significantly less successful. Paul continued moving forward, holding regular recording sessions in London and booking a British concert tour for November and December, leading to a swing through Japan in January and then tours of Europe and America in the spring and summer. He later had cause to wonder if he was secretly yearning to finish the band off for good.

Not that the British shows weren't well received. Juber and Holly added new fire to Wings, while the mix of new songs ("Old Siam, Sir," "Goodnight Tonight," the as-yet-unrecorded "Coming Up"), Wings hits ("Band on the Run," "Mull of Kintyre"), and a few newly unearthed Beatles classics ("Let It Be," "Got to Get You into My Life") drove the crowds wild. The new guys were having a blast; the reviews were upbeat, to say the least. The only person who wasn't having fun, it seemed, was Paul. "I remember thinking the shows had been great, but when I asked Paul, he'd just shrug and say, 'Ah, it was okay,'" Holly says. "My sense was that he was less than thrilled."

The British tour ended in mid-December 1979, then the band broke for the holidays, apart from a one-off fund-raiser for UNICEF just before New Year's. They had another three weeks to rest before heading off to Japan to start a ten-day tour through Tokyo, Nagoya, and Osaka. Along the way Paul and Linda stopped in New York to visit family and friends. Though they didn't get to see John and Yoko during their visit to the city, Paul did hook up with a friend who supplied him with half a pound of high-quality marijuana. Paul had been warned against smuggling pot into Japan, but apparently this new shipment of weed was far too tasty to just give away. He zipped up his suitcase with the fat package of greenery ("a bloody great bag," he noted later) literally at the very top of his folded shirts, pants, sweaters, and socks. "Why didn't I even hide it in a pullover?" he wondered later. When they got to Tokyo and the customs agent opened the suitcase, the bag nearly fell in his lap. "It's like a pop-up book!" Paul said. "Here, check *this*!" The uniformed man was just another customs functionary; he hadn't come looking to get anyone in trouble or cause an international incident. For a moment Paul wondered if he was going to pretend he hadn't seen a thing and simply zip up the suitcase and wish them well in their visit to his country. But of course he couldn't do that.

Paul was busted. He spent ten days in near-solitary confinement, forced to sweep out his own cell, bathe with the other prisoners, and ponder that Japanese law basically required marijuana smugglers (e.g., the sort of person who brings half a pound of grass into their country) to pay for their crime with seven full years of rock-breaking labor. Paul was spared this fate, ultimately. But not before the tour had been canceled, at vast expense to the promoter, the band sent home, and his raised-thumb-and-wink reputation knocked down a few pegs. Back in England, Paul spent most of the spring alone in his home studio, recording a synthesizer-based album of riffs and sketches he called

McCartney II, after the homemade record he'd released ten years earlier. It wasn't much of an album, but it did feature a few catchy tunes,
particularly "Coming Up," a dance-friendly number with a distinctive
riff that like so many of Paul's better songs had a way of leaping from
the speakers and implanting itself in the brains of listeners.

One of whom turned out to be John Lennon, who first heard
"Coming Up" while riding in a car in a Long Island coastal town he
was visiting with his assistant Frederic Seaman. By the next morning
John was humming the song aloud, admitting to Seaman that the riff
was "driving me crackers!" John had spent five years on hiatus from
the music industry, but something about Paul's song, Seaman wrote,
had stirred his muse. "If Paul was writing decent music," Seaman
wrote in his memoir, "John felt compelled to take up [the] challenge."

Or maybe that was just one of the impulses pulling John back from
his self-imposed retirement. Whatever, John was soon spitting out
songs with a vengeance, a burst of productivity that spurred a tidal
wave of interest in the music industry, then the media, then in the
minds of followers. Almost all of whom wished him nothing but well.

18

The look on his face frightened her.

Linda had just driven the kids to school, she hadn't turned on the radio or listened to the news or heard anything beyond the happy chatter of another morning in the McCartney home. Then she came home and found her husband sitting on the steps in the December chill, his expression less sad than simply slack. Shock. Disbelief. Horror. That's what she saw, even from a distance.

His manager, Steve Shrimpton, had called from London with the awful news from New York. Linda was still out with the kids then, so Paul called his brother, Mike, at his home on the Wirral. Mike said his brother had been too upset to speak. Paul went out to wait for Linda to get home, and a bit later Yoko called. At about noon Paul decided to stick to the plan he'd already made for that December 9, to go to AIR studios in London and record some music.

Paul was working with George Martin again, hoping to refresh his muse by reaching back to one of the familiar faces from the Beatle years. They had started work only a few weeks earlier, excited to revive the spark, happy to get back where they had once belonged, as someone once said. This afternoon they greeted one another sadly and tried to find words to say something, anything, that made sense. Maybe they reminisced a bit, found a way to laugh. The work was fitful, at best. Mostly they listened to tracks they had already started, taking one or two halfhearted stabs at adding something here or there. John Eastman had called in a cordon of heavily armed security guards to watch over his brother-in-law, but even they couldn't hold the media back on a city street, so when Paul stepped out of the studio lobby that afternoon, he was surrounded instantly by a flock of reporters. He spoke briefly, trying to dodge the crowd and duck into his car. But one last camera was shoved into his face, one last reporter demanded to know how he felt, really *felt*, upon hearing that John Lennon had been murdered.

Paul flinched, his face grew even more ashen in the stark light of the city night. Were there words to describe what had been done? Could anyone describe what had been destroyed, what had been torn from him? On camera, on demand, off the top of his head, in twenty-five words or less? No reason, no logic, no words were big enough to trace the wound, let alone the exploded shards of love, anger, hate, beauty, guilt, rage, and yearning it created. How did he feel? How did he *feel*?

"It's a drag, innit."

Paul ducked into the car and slammed the door. The car moved away from the curb, and he was off, into the dark of the winter night and a future he never imagined would be awaiting him.

It wasn't supposed to end like that. Months, years, even decades later, it didn't make sense. They hadn't finished things yet. Hadn't found their way back to the harmony that had given their lives so much meaning; a sound that had risen from their mouths and become something else entirely, something powerful enough to launch them around the world. They had discovered the power together, and while Paul had gone out on his own and done just fine, thank you very much, it was never the same. No matter how good it got with Wings, no matter how much fun, no matter how much acclaim he won, it was just fine. Sometimes it was terrific. But it was never truly magical.

The dream is over. John had said it, and to most of the world he was talking about a pop band, a media obsession, a worldwide craze. But to Paul the dream was the friendship they had shared. The bond that had revived him after the death of his mother and carried him through adolescence to adulthood and then into a life with challenges and rewards beyond all previous human experience. So much of it was abstract to them; just a far-off roar and an astronomical figure on a balance sheet they hardly ever looked at. But John mattered. The gleam in his eye, the nod of approval. *That's done it,* he'd say, then Paul wouldn't have to question himself anymore. The one critic who truly mattered to him had granted his approval, and everything else was just everything else.

No one thought about that. No one else had been there with them on those afternoons in the sitting room at Forthlin Road, or with their guitar necks inches from one another on Mimi's front step, their voices chiming together, the blood pulsing through them in the same rhythm, their eyes locked on the same vision. *That* was the dream they had shared. *That* was what mattered. Maybe John had gone right on believing it, too. He never stopped caring about it, never stopped buying the bootlegs and all the old souvenirs. Then there was that day, deep in the depths of the bitterness in the early seventies, when John had strolled around Greenwich Village wearing one of those old I LOVE PAUL buttons. Some hippie had walked up and demanded to know why he was wearing that, was it a joke? John didn't even blink: "Because I love Paul!"

They all loved each other, deep down, and maybe that's why they still felt drawn to one another, pulled to the same beautiful idea the rest of the world yearned to see made real. The reunion rumors started up again in March of 1978, connected to a vast charity concert being planned by Friends of the Earth, whose publicists swore they had already signed Paul, George, and Ringo, with John the lone, and possibly temporary, holdout. Nothing came of that, but a little more than a year later Paul, George, and Ringo had actually ended up onstage together, jamming with a few other guests at an outdoor reception for the just married Eric Clapton and Patti Boyd. An "awful blues bash," according to one witness, had changed direction when Paul took charge (no surprise) and led the makeshift Beatles-minus-one-plus-a-few-others through a loose set of rock 'n' roll oldies, and even, according to the source, a raucous busk of "Sgt. Pepper's Lonely Hearts Club Band."

The reunion rumor erupted anew a few months later, this time in connection with a United Nations benefit for Vietnamese refugees in Cambodia, recently renamed Kampuchea. UN secretary general Kurt Waldheim called Paul, who spoke to the other three but succeeded only in getting George and Ringo to pledge to appearing in a larger group of musicians, à la the supergroup George had put together for the Concert for Bangladesh. John wasn't up for doing anything just then, and when word leaked to the press (blowing up into a September 21 New York *Daily News* cover whose massive type promised "THE BEATLES ARE BACK!"), George and Ringo backed out altogether. Paul showed up with Wings and hinted broadly that he'd welcome any ex-Beatles who showed up. None did, but when someone backstage sent a toy robot marching out into the spotlight during his set, Paul pointed to it and shouted, "No! It's not John Lennon!"

Edging into a new decade, suspecting that Wings had flown its course, Paul started mulling over the prospect of renewing his collaboration with his old partner. Tantalized by the news that John was getting back to work in the summer of 1980, Paul had even called him at the studio where he and Yoko were recording in New York, reportedly hoping to spur some kind of new collaboration. Write a few songs, maybe get John to contribute a bit to the album Paul was about to start with George Martin. Once they got those three into the same studio, who knew what could happen? Paul never did manage to speak with John, though, and if his messages got past Yoko, John never responded. Not directly, anyway.

He'd had plenty to say *about* Paul, however. An interview John gave to *Newsweek* in September promised great things in his renewed musical partnership with Yoko, but when the subject turned to his old Beatles collaborator, John was dismissive, recalling how Paul's last visit to the Dakota, more than four years ago, his spontaneous drop-by the morning after the *Saturday Night Live* they watched together, had ended with John tossing him out of the foyer. "It's ten years since I've really communicated with him," John said. "I know as much about him as he does about me, which is *zilch*." What if he and Paul tried to write together again? "It would be boring . . . I was never one for reunions. It's all over!" Asked to respond in a TV interview a few weeks later, Paul shrugged it off: "Anything I say he gets a bit resentful of. It's a weird one. I don't quite know why he thinks like that."

John was a bit more generous in his lengthy *Playboy* interview with David Sheff, which included his own song-by-song deconstruction of the Beatles catalog, noting who had written what and how John felt about it then and now. This time John was as generous with his praise as with his criticism, and as ever his words hit Paul in a tender spot nobody else could reach. Paul wanted, maybe even craved, that interplay, that connection to the one person he trusted more than anyone else to see into his soul and separate the brilliant from the stupid. Paul needed that, now more than ever.

And now it was gone, torn away so abruptly, so brutally, before they ever had a chance to talk it over, to set things straight. John was dead, and Paul was destroyed. "I feel shattered, angry, and very sad," he said in a statement released soon after his bungled sidewalk encounter with the press in London. What emerged this time was a paragraph that was as direct as it was tortured: "He was pretty rude about me sometimes, but I secretly admired him for it. There was no question that we weren't friends—I really loved the guy." Paul addressed his friend's place in history: "I think that what has happened will in years to come make people realize that John was an international statesman. He often looked a loony to many people. He made enemies, but he was fantastic. . . . He made a lot of sense."

So many people agreed with Paul that the public mourning took on the size and intensity usually reserved for a head of state or religious figure. Enormous gatherings in New York, Liverpool, and national capitals. John's face on every major newspaper and newsmagazine. The airwaves alive with his voice, his songs, his spirit. He was celebrated as a musical genius, a cultural visionary, a spiritual prophet. The Beatles, people wrote, could never have existed without him. Almost as if the others had all been John Lennon's puppets, following his lead, doing his bidding. As if Paul McCartney had never really mattered at all. At least, that's how it began to seem to Paul.

At first he didn't say anything about it. In early 1981 he had performed background vocals (with Linda and Denny Laine) on George's musical eulogy to John, "All Those Years Ago," singing along to a new lyric George had written for a bouncy tune he'd already recorded with Ringo on drums. The song was released just a few weeks after

Ringo's wedding in late April, at which the three ex-Beatles sang a few songs together and posed for a portrait gathered with their wives and children. The death of their old friend had eased the old hurts, had reminded the Beatles, of all people, that all they really needed was love. Ringo came to play the drums on Paul's new album, rumors flew that George would be there soon, too. Though the album wasn't quite the tribute to John some rumors purported it would be, the spirit of the fallen Beatle, and the troubled friendship he'd shared with Paul, shadowed the project even before John had died. If only because Paul's decision to seek George Martin as a producer was such a deliberate step back toward the work patterns they had all established back on Abbey Road. Paul had used Wings to sketch out some arrangements and cut the demos, but when Martin made it clear that he didn't want to produce a Wings album, Paul quickly agreed to dispatch the band. (So quickly, in fact, that he let slip news of the band's demise to the press before telling the other Wings-men.) When they started working, Martin didn't soft-pedal his opinions, responding to Paul's demo tape by telling him that only six of the fourteen songs were fit to be recorded. Of the others, he continued, "four need work, but we can do something with them. The other four you should just throw away." Paul, who hadn't heard such frank criticism from a colleague in more than a decade, blinked angrily. He didn't know he was supposed to audition, he shot back. Martin shrugged and reminded him, "That's what the producer's job is, Paul."

Even at the beginning Paul set out to do a serious record, and with Martin aboard the project took on a weight and narrative flow Paul hadn't aspired to since *Band on the Run*. John's death came just a few weeks into the project, and the mass of feelings that tragedy evoked swirled through the songs Paul had already written and came to inform the ones still bubbling out. All the conflicts they'd had, all the times they'd gone at each other with claws extended, only to tumble into that harmony that only they could make—it all came out in the music. "Tug of War," the wistful overture, heralded the album's theme that all human bonds are built as much of tension as by loving support. *We were trying to outdo each other,* he sings in what would become the title track. "Somebody Who Cares" wove Irish pipes and Spanish guitar into a testament to the warmth of the human spirit, while "Take It Away" evoked the transformative power music had always held for Paul, particularly in the darkest of times. Here he was the lonely driver on a dark road, the soul survivor, turning on the radio and hearing the same sound that had fueled his life's greatest moments. *You never know who may be listening to you,* he sings, and the background vocals return to shout the song's title, to remind him (and us) how a band can both start a song and deflect all the pain in the world with the same motion: *Take it away! Take it away!*

John, and the history they shared, were so much on his mind that Paul could spend a day in the studio singing to him and nearly forget what had happened. Then one afternoon, probably a few months into 1981, he looked up at Eric Stewart, the 10cc cofounder he'd called in to help with backing vocals, and was suddenly stricken with horror. "You know, John's dead," Paul said. "John's *dead*. It's just hit me. He's not around anymore." Stewart gazed back into Paul's eyes and tried to think of something reasonable to say in response. "I just nodded," he recalls. "He looked quite sad and shocked. I think it just came home to him that this guy he had done so much with just wasn't around anymore."

This realization fueled "Here Today," the one song that was explicitly addressed to the man whose friendship had always meant more to Paul than anyone who wasn't Linda. Singing to his own acoustic guitar, accompanied by the same sort of understated string arrangement Martin had once composed for "Yesterday," Paul reflects on the love that had sustained them in their youth, but also the distance and disdain that marked later years. Would John even admit that Paul had ever been his friend? Or merely scoff and dismiss him, as he had done in *Newsweek* just weeks before his death? Singing sweetly, yet with no trace of the sentiment that had filled his more recent love songs, Paul looked to the past to find a truth to guide him through the cruel present. *I really loved you and was glad you came along / and you were here today, for you were in my song.*

More than a beautiful song, "Here Today" was a revelation, a clear-eyed description of the most significant friendship in the history of popular music, from the perspective of its sole remaining partner. With *Tug of War*'s other high points, the song brought Paul right back to the heights he had once strolled so effortlessly for so long, back when John was walking beside him. But there were other songs, too, including the single "Ebony and Ivory," performed in collaboration with the great singer/songwriter Stevie Wonder. Intended as an anthem to further the causes of racial justice and understanding, the song instead plays like a stoned person's detached musings, stretching its central metaphor beyond the brink (black and white piano keys become more dissonant the closer they are together) as it offers pat reassurance in the place of an actual call to action. In a time when both singers' home nations continued to do business with institutionally racist South Africa, when even first-world nations somehow found a way to live with vast minority populations living beneath the poverty line, "Ebony and Ivory" grinned and winked and stuck its thumb in the air. Everyone's the same! They enthused. Ebony and ivory! Living in perfect harmony!

The critics who raved about *Tug of War* when it was released in the spring of 1982 either ignored or noted the good intentions behind "Ebony and Ivory," which rode its dual star power past all barriers of taste to dominate the top of the American singles charts for nearly two months. *Tug of War* also crowned the charts, due as much to lingering emotion from John's death as to the chorus of reviews that celebrated the album as "McCartney's masterpiece" (*Rolling Stone*), a "melancholy masterpiece" (*Newsweek*), and "exquisitely crafted, though lyrically flawed" (*New York Times*). It was Paul's greatest all-around triumph since *Band on the Run*. It couldn't have come at a better time, with a fortieth birthday right around the corner on June 18. But it still wasn't enough.

"People are printing *facts* about me and John," Paul fumed to Hunter Davies, the Beatles' first biographer and still a friend. "They're *not* facts . . . [but] it will come part of history. It will be there for always. People will believe it all."

At first it was a secret. In the months after John's murder, when his memory was still fresh and the shock of his loss still so raw, the world naturally wanted to romanticize his memory. Paul was in shock himself, still shot through with his own sorrow and guilt, still trying to tell himself that it had really happened, that one thing that had defined his life had truly ended for good. But then the unfairness of it all began to weigh on him. The way so many writers could only seem to celebrate John by dismissing Paul as a wanker. Just a few weeks after John's death a writer named Philip Norman published a bulky account of the Beatles he was calling the definitive account of their career, and the entire thing was thick with contempt for Paul. Norman titled his book *Shout!* Paul referred to it as *Shite*. Feeling stung, but without any socially acceptable way to argue his case for himself, Paul called Hunter Davies, whom he'd first befriended when the writer was researching his authorized account of the Beatles in 1967. They had kept in touch over the years, so Paul didn't hesitate to share his unvarnished feelings on the phone, not imagining that his old friend was taking notes.

Paul went on and on, for more than hour. How could Yoko say he had hurt John more than anyone else in his life? What about the times John dismissed Paul's songs as Muzak or compared him unfavorably to Engelbert Humperdinck? John, he continued, could be paranoid and jealous. John was hotly competitive and willing to do anything to get his way. "A maneuvering swine," Paul said in a memorable turn of phrase. "I idolized John," he said, but then he'd grown up and become an equal. And Yoko knew this, he swore. He had helped John. He had impressed him, too. "She told me she and John had just been playing one of my albums," he said. "And had *cried*."

Davies kept the conversation to himself, for a while. But the unfairness of it all continued to gnaw at Paul, and starting with the *Tug of War* media blitz in 1982, he made certain to argue his case, subtly, in interviews. He and John had spoken on the phone quite a bit in the late seventies, Paul told British journalist Richard Williams. "I've talked to Yoko since, and she's said to me, 'You know, he was really quite fond of you,'" Paul said. "I think we were pretty close."

But as John's reputation rose toward secular sainthood, Paul found himself being increasingly diminished by comparison. The growing distance from John's life served to smooth away all his flaws. Now he was becoming perfect: the working-class hero-turned-rocker-turned-brilliant artist-turned-peace-activist. As if he'd led the Beatles single-handedly, as if Paul were just his cute, shallow buddy. Writing in *Shout!* Norman even tried to snatch *Sgt. Pepper* for John, noting that Paul almost certainly knew that "John's *Sgt. Pepper* music was destined to outshine his." Only even John had said that album had been

Paul's baby, including the truly revolutionary aspects of "A Day in the Life." No wonder Paul's public line began to take on a more barbed tone. "I'm as intelligent as John was," he told the *Washington Post* in 1984, dismissing John's claims of working-class street cred ("He was the least working-class in the group!") and asserting plainly, that he was every bit as deep as the sainted Lennon. "I know where he was at, I know what he read, and I know what we talked about."

Paul moderated his observations in a long *Playboy* interview that same year, recalling how pleasant his final conversation with John had been. But now he was fielding attacks on the Wings front, too, most hurtfully in a series of tell-all articles written for the London tabloids by Denny Laine. Denny's pieces (since disowned by their putative author) denounced his former friend and bandmate for his greediness and bossiness, and for being patronizing to his own younger brother, who "resents him like mad." Jo Jo Laine had her own published go at Linda, slicing Mrs. McCartney for her chilliness, for not bathing or cleaning her house and for treating the resident sheep better than her human visitors. At least the guests, Jo Jo noted, did not relieve themselves on the living-room floor. It might all have been nonsense, but Linda responded with an attack on all of the former Wings musicians, asserting they had not measured up to Paul's standards ("We just picked the wrong people . . . they were good, not great"), and insisting, oddly, that no one had ever realized that Paul was actually a good musician. "I think they feel he's just a cute face," she said.

That seemed unlikely, but if it were true, it might have something to do with the work Paul was doing in the years after *Tug of War*. His 1983 follow-up/companion piece to the earlier work was another George Martin–produced album, called *Pipes of Peace,* and was largely built from the tunes that hadn't quite made it through the rigorous process that had created *Tug of War*. Only this time the songs were lightly written or fragmentary, with an emphasis on bloodless character studies and easy affirmations. Superstar assistance this time around came courtesy of Michael Jackson, by far the hottest star of the day, and his presence on the (undeniably catchy) single "Say, Say, Say" catapulted the song to the top of the singles charts, while its elaborately staged video (in which Paul, Linda, and Michael portray orphan-loving con artists in the Depression) became a fixture on MTV well into the winter of 1984.

None of this seemed to spring from the thoughtful, Beatlesque Paul whose reemergence had caused so much celebration. None of it warned the hearts of critics, but it also didn't prepare anyone for Paul's next, and arguably most ill-considered, solo undertaking. Because no matter what had happened to *Magical Mystery Tour,* that itch to move into moviemaking had never really left Paul behind. When the random musings he'd been having on the road between Sussex and London began to seem like a story, he made a point of writing it down. Once he had a page of notes, he told his manager to find someone he could talk to about turning his story into a TV show, or maybe even a movie.

So began a Hollywood-size story about the nearly real adventures of a fortyish pop star whose legendary past never quite keeps him from getting into career-threatening scrapes. Which was the plot Paul imagined, wrote, and starred in as the central character in *Give My Regards to Broad Street.* But the story that ended up on the screen still wasn't anywhere near as twisted, or darkly hilarious, as the story behind the making of *Give My Regards to Broad Street.* All they had in common was that they both starred Paul McCartney, and in both he was obviously out of his depth.

Once Paul told his manager, Steve Shrimpton, to help get his movie going, the McCartney Productions Ltd. executive spoke to famed British filmmaker David Puttnam, who had just won a Best Picture Academy Award for *Chariots of Fire.* The producer pointed to a director named Peter Webb, whose short "Butch Minds the Baby" had just won a BAFTA award. Webb's current project, an ambitious film about the Spanish civil war called *Comrades,* had run into difficulties, so he went happily to meet with Paul at EMI's studios on Abbey Road, where the musician fished a crumpled sheet of paper out of his pocket. "It begins with me in black tie, with my guitar at the Royal Albert Hall," Webb recalls Paul telling him. "Then the background will change into a medieval plain, with knights on horseback!"

"What he described was a cinematic version of the *Tug of War* album," Webb says. "The broad sweep of English history would then segue seamlessly into a downbeat scene in a contemporary Liverpool, where the hero, a young man in his late teens, was sweeping the floor as a lowly paid janitor. We would then discover he wanted to escape from this no-hope life into signing on as a mercenary in some foreign war."

Paul's role in the film was that of a singing Greek chorus, performing songs that would comment and expand upon the dramatic sequences. Webb suggested that Paul might want to find a writer to help flesh out his ideas, but the next time they met, Paul had continued writing on his own, ditching the serious *Tug of War* concept in favor of a light comedy he titled *Give My Regards to Broad Street*. "It's not *Com-Reds*," Paul said of his twenty-two-page script, pairing modesty with a subtle dig about the debt Webb's *Comrades* might owe to Warren Beatty's *Reds*. "He said he'd written it in the back of his car while driving to and from the studio in London," Webb says. "And he wanted to know what I thought."

Webb thought it wasn't bad. Paul's script had become an airy fantasy about a charming, deceptively deep pop star whose life careens out of control one day when the master tapes of his new album go missing and that puts his company in danger of being gobbled up by sinister financiers. Paul would play the main character, and the segments he'd denoted simply as "MUSIC" would be performances of his own songs, some new tunes and classics dating back to the Beatles.

Webb figured they were working on a TV special or perhaps a short feature for movie theaters, but Shrimpton encouraged the director to expand his thinking. Soon they were talking about sequences inspired by Manet paintings, Dickensian street scenes, and old-fashioned Hollywood musicals. The projected budget doubled, then tripled. The Australian actor Bryan Brown signed on to play Paul's manager, a bluff Australian not unlike the real-life Steve Shrimpton. Sir Ralph Richardson took a small, but crucial role as Paul's humble-yet-wise father, Jim. The up-and-coming British comedienne Tracy Ullman landed a supporting role, too.

As the production of *Give My Regards to Broad Street* lumbered into motion, Webb recalls that Paul was initially all charm and enthusiasm, serenading the director with songs on his guitar as they sketched out ideas on his patio in Sussex. But as the project went on,

Paul became short-tempered and autocratic. One day, just before film-ing was to start, Paul announced that Ringo, his wife (Barbara Bach), and Linda were now in the cast. "He didn't make any suggestions about what their dramatic function would be," Webb says. On the first day of shooting Paul grew irate when Webb proposed Paul wear his own jeans and Hawaiian shirt on camera. Why, Paul wondered, hadn't they thought to buy costumes? Webb assured him he was only trying to heighten the sense of reality, but Paul's fears continued until he arrived at a set that came with the usual complement of trailers, costume racks, lights, and cameras. "Look, Paul!" his assistant said cheerfully. "It's a proper movie!"

The filming went on for months, with Paul portraying himself as a charming celebrity who faced even the most outrageous events in moods ranging from mild bemusement to vague frustration. Paul's flat performance only emphasized how flawed Shrimpton's ever-increasing ambitions for *Broad Street* truly were. Absent fully drawn characters, a compelling story, or anything resembling dramatic stakes, the sketch-turned-movie drifts aimlessly, an attractive and occasionally tuneful wisp of amusement. Nevertheless, John Eastman managed to sell the American distribution rights to Fox for nearly $7 million, and the company was so excited by the prospect of a Beatle musical they penciled it in as their potential blockbuster for the summer of 1984, with instant wide release to thousands of theaters from coast to coast. All without seeing a page of the script, let alone a frame of exposed film.

Give My Regards to Broad Street was released in the fall of 1984, inspiring reviews that were nearly, if not entirely, brutal. "The kind of smothering tedium that leaves you screaming for air," declared the *Washington Post*. "Characterless, bloodless, pointless," said *Variety*. The audience at the London premiere in Leicester Square was more reserved, but just about as enthusiastic. "It was almost completely si-lent," recalls Eric Stewart, who had performed in some of the film's music scenes. "People were looking at each other saying, 'What was *that*?'"

So back to music. This is what came to Paul so naturally, what he could do without worrying that he had no idea which way was up. At least, that's how it had always been. Only now it was the mideighties, the time of Madonna, the Police, Duran Duran, Prince, Phil Collins, and Genesis. A new universe of booming drums and whirring, wailing synthesizers. And where did Paul McCartney fit into that world? He was well into his forties, more than fifteen years since the demise of the Beatles and nearly a decade since Wings' highest point. Now the only Beatles-connected records on the charts were by Julian Lennon. George was spending his time producing movies for his Handmade film company. Ringo was living like an international playboy, bouncing from Monaco to Los Angeles to London and everywhere else, underemployed and overserved at the bar.

Making records is what had always come most naturally, only now Paul didn't quite know where to begin. He called Eric Stewart, got him to bring his guitar to start writing songs for a new album. They met at Paul's house in Sussex one snowy winter day, and when they settled in with their guitars, Stewart asked Paul if he had anything started, anything he wanted to work on? Paul shrugged. Uh, no. He figured they'd start cold just as he used to do when it was time to write a new album with John. "So what do *you* think? Do you have any ideas?" Stewart plucked his guitar, looked out of the window at the trees and hills, just now cloaked in a fresh blanket of stark white. "Well, it's beautiful outside," he said. "Great!" Paul replied. "Let's start with that!" He hit a chord and then they had a song, "Footprints," about a detached old man wandering through a snowy country day. *His friends have flown away,* Paul sang. *He's left out in the cold . . .*

More songs followed: a rant about the media called "Angry," old-time rockers ("Stranglehold" and "Move Over Busker"), and a scattering of some psychedelic musings ("Talk More Talk" and "However Absurd") that evoked the Beatles' more abstract works. Gestures toward a whole array of styles and ideas. But did Paul mean a word of it? "We were both having a good time, but I think we began to realize it wasn't taking us anywhere exciting," Stewart says. "I just think, in retrospect, that he was a little tired."

Paul had asked Stewart to produce the new album, but then Hugh Padgham, a twenty-seven-year-old producer whose work with the Police, Genesis, Phil Collins, and others had dominated the charts in recent years, came to Paul's attention. Padgham had been sitting with an acquaintance when "Ebony and Ivory" came on the radio. "What a piece of shit *that* is," Padgham averred, not knowing that the man he was addressing was married to the artist's personal assistant. Word of the musical phenom's unvarnished opinion found its way to MPL, if not quite to Paul. Nevertheless, the faltering superstar did hear that Padgham had some strong opinions about his work, so the young producer was invited in to talk, and he soon signed on to produce the new album. Paul never mentioned that he had also asked Eric Stewart to fill the same position (and never mentioned to Stewart that he had tapped Padgham to do the job he'd already asked his fellow songwriter to fill), but Padgham wouldn't have minded if he had: he loved 10cc, too. So much, in fact, that when Paul handed him a cassette of the new songs the two had written together, Padgham could only assume that the innate brilliance of the songs was lost somewhere in the murk of the homemade tape the two icons had made. "I didn't think it was possible that they *couldn't* have written something amazing," he says.

Paul, on the other hand, seemed splayed between the overwhelming confidence of a Beatle and a more mortal kind of crippling insecurity. On the one hand he would brook no criticism whatsoever. When Padgham, in his role as producer, pointed out that a song they were about to record might benefit from a stronger chorus, Paul's eyes shot bullets at him. "How many number one hits have *you* written?" he snapped, cutting off the conversation. But on the other hand, Padgham had to talk Paul into not hiring a session pro to play the bass parts on the songs. "He asked me who we should get to play bass, and I said, 'Are you joking? You're the best bass player on the planet!'" Padgham remembers. But then Paul spent hours fussing with his bass overdubs, obsessed with capturing just the right performance. "That would go on forever because he'd be all in a dither about it."

They worked in the studio Paul had built in a disused windmill near the coast in Sussex, and the pattern they established became as familiar as it was stultifying. Paul arrived sometime in the late morning and talked at length about the TV shows he'd watched the night before. "It was like he'd seen everything that had been on telly," Padgham says. "He was like a walking *TV Guide*." Then he'd get into telling Beatles stories, and after an hour or so they'd finally get to work. They'd take a lunch break after a couple of hours, at which point Paul vanished upstairs to his private office. "He'd go have a spliff, pretending we didn't know, and then he'd come down and try to do a bass overdub or something," Padgham says. Never eager to hear criticism or contrasting ideas, Paul also doubted himself so much he tossed a blistering take of "Angry" he'd recorded live in the studio with Stewart, the drummer Jerry Marotta, and another guitarist in order to make room for a new version with Phil Collins and Pete Townshend. "If it's got Phil and Pete on it, people will like it," Paul told Stewart.

Paul could be remarkably warm and down-to-earth, inviting Padgham to dinner at his house one night and sitting with him and Linda at the kitchen table for hours, drinking wine and chatting about music right up until 10 p.m., when Linda suddenly realized she had forgotten all about making anything to eat. Paul opened another bottle of wine, she produced a few plates of beans on toast, the good old Liverpool standby, and the evening went on. Stewart had similar experiences at the McCartney house, marveling at how laid-back they were, how open and generous. When Stewart made an offhand comment one day about a guitar he liked, that very guitar was waiting for him in the studio a few days later. When a session went particularly well, Paul took the time to call Stewart's wife, Gloria, at home. "Give that man of yours a kiss and tell him he's a fucking genius," Paul said. But he could just as quickly turn cold and sulky. When Padgham gave Paul the pop-music version of the game Trivial Pursuit as a birthday present, the musician was at first delighted, but later became enraged. "He was all pissed off because one of the questions was about the year Paul McCartney's mother had died," Padgham says. "Like it was my fault that question was there, or I should have known."

Sensing the dire direction the sessions had taken, and increasingly frustrated by having Padgham in the producer's chair he'd expected to fill, Stewart walked out one afternoon and never came back. Padgham remained, and he and Paul did manage to bend the new technology toward creating some compelling sonic textures. But nothing could hide that the songs they were working on were uninspired. Titled *Press to Play,* the album came packaged with a gauzy black-and-white cover shot of Paul and Linda, cheek to cheek, eyes shut in an attitude of romantic rapture. "I looked at it and thought, 'Oh, *that*'s crap, too,'" Padgham says.

Released in the fall of 1986, *Press to Play* sold a scant six hundred thousand copies around the world, barely cracking the American Top 30. It was the worst-selling pop album Paul McCartney had ever made. Coming so soon on the heels of *Broad Street,* and so long since the real glories of the Beatles, even Paul didn't know what to make of himself. Was he a genius or a loser? Was it possible for him to be both at the same time? The strangeness of his situation had burst into particularly vivid flower a year earlier at the enormous Live Aid concert at Wembley Stadium on July 13, 1985. When Paul was called upon to close the show with a solo piano performance of "Let It Be," his appearance at the keyboard raised a ground-trembling roar among the hundred thousand concert attendees. He barely looked up as he played the brief instrumental intro, but he allowed himself a glance as he began to sing the first verse. He saw, then heard, the audience booing.

His eyes widened. He looked back to the keyboard and kept going, his playing a bit robotic, his tongue spitting out the familiar words while he tried to figure out what was going on. Were they really booing him? Had it really come to this?

What Paul didn't know was that they couldn't hear him. An electronic bug had come between his microphone and the vast sound system, rendering his performance of one of his most beloved songs into an accidental instrumental. The connection was restored in time for the start of the third verse, spurring an even greater roar in the stadium, but Paul was by then surrounded by all the other stars, who had come out for the show's grand finale. For a moment he was at the center of it all again, still the jewel of the crown, even as he helped hoist Bob Geldof up for a congratulatory shoulder ride.

But the glory of "Let It Be," and all it represented, was nothing new. Yesterday's news, in fact. But that moment of terror . . . the dismal feeling that comes with the hiss of a hundred thousand vipers . . . that was new. And maybe it was his future.

19

So then he went back to the beginning. A warm July afternoon in the windmill studio in Sussex, a bit of a get-together with some guys who were into music, too. Just like the old days, no real rehearsal or expectations beyond having as much fun as possible. Just the four of them: Paul on bass, a Cavern veteran named Mick Green on guitar, Ian Dury/Clash keyboardist Mick Gallagher on piano, and a fresh-from-music-school drummer named Chris Whitten. Set up the amps, plug in the guitars, tell the engineer to roll the tape, and *A-one! Two! Three! Four! Well, I gotta girl with a record machine / When it comes to rockin' she's a queen* . . . Just as you'd hear at a church fete, say, in a Liverpool suburb in the summer of 1957. Only now it was thirty years later and it all meant that much more to Paul.

Just keep on rocking. One take, maybe two, then off to the next song. "Lucille," "Lawdy Miss Clawdy," "Midnight Special," "That's All Right, Mama." Close your eyes and you could be at the Casbah. *We're the Quarrymen and we're here to play you some rock 'n' roll!* The songs were the same, so was the freewheeling joy. The session ended after a few hours, then they did it again the next day, with one or two alternate players sitting in, and got down a few other tunes. Remember how they used to fill time in Hamburg by running standards through the Merseybeat rock 'n' roll machine? Here's another,

"Don't Get Around Much Anymore," only now it's a stomper with a wild guitar solo in the break.

They weren't supposed to be official recording sessions, Paul wasn't working on anything in particular, just trying to get the blood flowing and remember why he had started making music in the first place. But then he took a listen and began to change his mind. Christ, it was all so fresh and raw! Just a few guys rocking and rolling, and wasn't that what it was all supposed to be about? This gave Paul an idea: *Let's bootleg it!* Knock out a few copies, put 'em in mimeographed sleeves, and make them look like some shitty Russian knockoff! New manager Richard Ogden had his doubts, but he dutifully took the notion to EMI, whose higher-ups did exactly what he expected and nipped the quirky auto-bootleg idea in the bud. "Oh, we're boring these days, aren't we!" Paul grumbled. "Too elevated to have *that* kind of fun!" Ogden made it up to his client by pressing a few albums as a gift, packaged in mocked-up covers with Cyrillic writing, as if they had been smuggled in from the hard-eyed Eastern capitalists of Paul's dreams. Very funny, and merry Christmas.

Only then Paul's mind was spinning again, what with the warming breezes of perestroika blowing across the continents. Why not actually *release* the album in the USSR as a goodwill gesture? He sent Ogden on a mission to the offices of Melodiya, the USSR's official state record company in Moscow, and in the spirit of peace they talked EMI into releasing four hundred thousand copies of a twelve-song album titled *Choba B CCCP,* which in English translated, inevitably, to *Back in the USSR.* Just as inevitable, of course, came the blossoming of a new international market in album smuggling and retail sales. What sold for less than the equivalent of US$7 in the Soviet shops could fetch as much as $250 in the United States, and a jaw-dropping £500 (nearly $900) in England. Paul didn't see a dime of that, of course, but he got his bootleg, anyway. And once copies of the bootleg found their way to critics, the rareness of the thing, and the playfulness of the original sessions, spun their heads in a way his original albums hadn't done in more than a decade.

Maybe it was silly for Paul to worry about selling loads of records and being the world's most popular middle-aged rock star. God knows he already had enough money, and an intensely loving marriage with

Linda, still the most supportive, gently challenging, perfect mate after all these years. They had four healthy, happy, and well-adjusted kids, all of them products of, or still working their way through, Sussex's neighborhood schools. Certainly, the McCartneys had the challenges and problems of every growing family. But whatever high jinks Heather, Mary, Stella, and James got up to, it was never beyond the pale of normal suburban youth. No one told stories about the McCartney kids lording it over the other kids. When they became adolescents, they resisted the urge to vomit from limousine windows and hurl champagne bottles at photographers. Say what you will about Paul in any other arena, even his harshest critics had to concede that he was not raising a house full of tabloid stories. For a star of his wattage, in a time of 24-7 celebrity coverage, this was no small achievement.

Credit his insistence on living as normally as possible. Certainly the wealth and opportunity Paul's family enjoyed changed their circumstances just a bit. No one from Forthlin Road was jetting off to Jamaica for their holidays, for instance. But just as Jim McCartney had raised Paul to be a hardworking, unpretentious, family-loving fellow, Paul tried to raise his own kids with the same basic philosophy. So while other rockers of similar or even lesser means bought themselves castles and kept them staffed with cooks, maids, nannies, and footmen, Paul and Linda had one domestic helper, a sweet older woman named Rose, and kept their family in that charmingly weird pie-shaped home until 1982, when he drew up plans for a slightly larger and more traditionally wrought farmhouse. Designed by Paul after his memories of the Forthlin Road home, the new house was a simple two-floor, five-bedroom family home constructed to pull the family together. Everything revolved around the airy, multiwindowed kitchen, where Linda held court at the counters or from the table where the family took most of their meals. From there, family and guests could easily flow from one room to the next, walking past artworks whose casual placement in no way indicated that they were priceless works by Matisse and Magritte. The kids' artworks and family photos were displayed just as proudly. Notable for its absence, however, were gold records or any trace of glittering showbiz hardware: Paul kept that stuff in the London office.

In Sussex, where life was defined by kids, school, and family concerns, the pop world rarely intruded. Outside, the nonsculpted grounds had plenty of room for grazing horses, meandering dogs, geese, chickens, and cats. Fans and obsessives rarely turned up, thanks to the six-foot security wall, the guards that could occasionally be seen keeping watch, and most important, the protective eyes of Peasmarsh, whose residents phoned in warnings whenever a curious outsider wandered through the village.

Like many men in their forties, Paul made concessions to advancing age. He gave up cigarettes, took up jogging (a hedge against the belly that had been pressing against his belt line), and didn't panic when silver strands threaded their way into his famous dark locks. The wildness of youth receded, making way for a more reassuring stability. Still, some habits of youth never quite went away. He and Linda remained enthusiastic pot smokers, but even that habit was part of their settled, domesticated life. When they lit joints in the house, they did so with lighters hanging from the drapes, a working-class smoker's habit now adapted for herbal purposes.

Mostly, Paul liked the settled-in feeling that went along with being a middle-aged, working-class husband and dad, the comforting rhythms of family life, the thump of the kids' feet on the stairs, the echo of young voices shouting from one room to the next. Then there was Linda, the golden light reflecting on her hair in the kitchen, the wicked gleam in her eyes when she had something funny to say, the steaminess in her eyes when the kids weren't around. Oh, it wasn't always easy between them. He'd been too famous for too long to be perfectly reasonable about everything, and she was nobody's pushover. At times, she'd admit later, she'd storm off thinking that this time she'd really had enough of him; now it was time to go. But that's just the downside of passion, and Paul and Linda were an especially passionate couple.

They rarely found a reason to spend much time apart. Once the kids were up and launched into their morning, the senior McCartneys usually headed off for their own gambol, either on horseback or on foot through the emerald countryside. In the evenings they orbited quietly through a small, but close, social circle. The couple's close friends included Twiggy, the famous sixties model now living a much quieter existence; the screenwriter and animal rights activist (and Liverpool native, though Paul hadn't known her then) Carla Lane; and Pretenders leader Chrissie Hynde, another animal rights campaigner. Paul usually spent the most time with whomever he was working with in the studio—music remained the central bridge between his emotions and the outside world. Still, his most constant male companion was John Hammel, the all-purpose assistant (he served as driver, guitar tech, bodyguard, errand-runner, and confidant) who had been at Paul's side since the midseventies.

Paul's business was thriving, too. MPL Communications, the corporate presence he'd started to keep his own accounts away from Apple in 1970, had grown over the years, gradually becoming a powerhouse in the music-publishing industry. Paul might not own his own Beatles songs, but he had long since snapped up the rights to Buddy Holly's catalog, along with classic works by Harold Arlen and Meredith Willson. The six-floor brick building Paul had bought on Soho Square to serve as the company's offices had been renovated with a glass facade on its ground floor and art deco woodwork and fixtures in its sleek lobby and public areas. Paul employed a variety of managers over the years, some lasting longer than others. Other employees dealt with the press or tended to other personal and organizational matters. Yet hardly anyone had a proper job title: no matter what their daily duties, they all followed the same job description: keep Paul happy. It wasn't an easy task. For behind that cheery smile and elevated thumb beat the heart of a man who had long since grown accustomed to having things work out his way. When they didn't, being near him wasn't always a happy place to be.

All that success, all that beauty, all those years of unrestrained adoration. Maybe it was inevitable that such a surfeit of feeling would create an emotional undertow. Maybe the darkness the Beatles were trying to escape through the music wasn't ever going to give up that easily.

So the Beatles hostilities continued, and once again the others were blaming Paul for causing their troubles. This time the conflict was prompted by a deal Paul signed with EMI at the height of his post-Beatle career in the seventies. One of the stipulations in the six-album deal was a royalty hike retroactive to Paul's earlier works, including his share of the Beatles' records. Thus, he was now receiving a higher rate of payment than his fellow Fabs. This made perfect sense to Paul—if he was successful enough on his own to squeeze a bit more juice out of his work from EMI, that was his business. He wasn't taking anything away from the other guys. Except George, Ringo, and Yoko didn't see it quite like that, so they filed a lawsuit against him. Paul paid them back a year or two later by refusing to pitch in to a Beatles lawsuit against EMI and its American label, Capitol, filed when an accountant going over the company's records realized the company had been underpaying Beatles royalties to the tune of something like $80 million. Not that Paul wouldn't claim his 25 percent share of whatever the Beatles won in the suit, because he certainly would. But he just wasn't going to help fight for it. A spokesman explained it like this: *Paul dislikes giving depositions.* Well, of course he does. And he's not crazy about getting sued, either.

Then there was the Northern Songs catalog. The Lennon-McCartney copyrights had been up for sale a few times over the years, and something always stood between Paul and those precious songs from his youth. When ATV put the catalog on the market in 1985, Paul had an inside line on buying Northern Songs for a reported £20 million. But then Paul had decided to bring Yoko into the deal, either because he thought it was the right thing to do for his ex-partner's widow and sons, or because he couldn't simply imagine having to drop that much cash on songs he had once grabbed out of thin air. "I wrote 'em for nothing!" he told Bill Flanagan in *Musician* magazine. "Twenty million. Great, terrific, here we go." Either way, Paul called Yoko and proposed she join as halfsies on the deal. Yoko agreed, but took over the negotiation herself, assuring Paul that she could get the catalog for a fraction of the £20 million asking price. Naturally, Paul was all for getting a better deal, but what he didn't see coming was that his old friend and collaborator Michael Jackson was getting into the game, too. When the dust had cleared, all of Paul's most beloved songs belonged to the guy who lived in his own amusement park, with a chimp for a companion. "I woke up," Paul told Flanagan, "and said, 'What the fuck is going on?'"

What, indeed. Only the closer you looked, the more convoluted it all became. Consider how sanguine Yoko was about losing out to Michael. "I feel like a friend has [the songs]," she was quoted as saying. Consider further that young Sean Lennon had spent part of his previous summer vacationing with, yes, that's right, Michael Jackson. And also appeared in one of the aspiring tycoon's videos. Then there was the wrinkle in U.S. copyright law that saw to it that the heirs of a songwriter who died during the first twenty-eight years of his copyright were automatically granted ownership for the second twenty-eight-year term, no matter what. In other words, *Yoko was going to get control of John's 50 percent of the songs without dropping a dime.* So the only person who got screwed as a result of the botched negotiation? Paul McCartney.

Now Yoko, and George and Ringo, were suing him for getting a better deal out of EMI than they had been able to negotiate? None of this was making Paul happy with his fellow ex-Beatles. Not in the least. Then news came, late in 1987, that the Beatles were going to be inducted into the Rock 'n' Roll Hall of Fame. They were all going to be there, George and Ringo and Yoko. Of course, Paul was supposed to be there, too. Waving and smiling and then picking up his bass to play with them. That's what always happened at these ceremonies— the legendary artists got onstage, even the ones with long-standing, angry grudges, and put the bad vibes aside for one night. A testament to harmony, a moment of peace, love, and understanding. And Paul had no intention of doing it.

Public anticipation mounted in the first weeks of 1988, heading toward the ceremony on January 20. So many crucial artists were being inducted to the Hall this time around: the Beach Boys and the Supremes, Bob Dylan, the Drifters, Motown founder Berry Gordy Jr., as if the very essence of the sixties rock generation was coming together for one last go-round. The supporting cast wouldn't be bad, either: Mick Jagger, Bruce Springsteen, Elton John, Little Richard, Ben E. King, Paul Simon. Yet all of them resided in the shadow of something else: a potential Beatles reunion. A three-way version, anyway, but something—a gesture toward the beautiful idea they had once personified, back when so many things seemed possible and the Beatles served as the sound track to youthful dreams everywhere.

But when the night arrived, Paul McCartney was nowhere in sight. In his stead was a brief statement, distributed to journalists by his

American press representatives. The Beatles, he wrote, still had business differences, even after twenty years. "I would feel like a complete hypocrite waving and smiling with them at a fake reunion," he concluded. So the night went on without him. Once Jagger finished his funny, loving introduction, and once George and Ringo took the stage, joined by Yoko, Sean, and Julian, Paul's absence sounded a sour note. Particularly when George, poised between a #1 album (1987's *Cloud Nine*) and an unexpected, hotly acclaimed supergrouping with Dylan, Roy Orbison, Tom Petty, and Jeff Lynne in the Traveling Wilburys (whose first album would reach the Top 3 a bit later in 1988), provided all the Beatlesque, if bittersweet, jokes anyone would have expected. "It's too bad Paul's not here because he's the one who had the speech in his pocket," he said. "We all know why John's not here; we know he'd be here. . . . We all loved John very much, and we love Paul very much." Given her moment to speak, Yoko expanded on George's implicit critique of Paul: "[John] would have been here, you know. He would have come."

Listening to a tape of the ceremony on the telephone the next morning, courtesy of Linda's old friend Danny Fields, Paul responded to Yoko's gibe in no uncertain terms. "Fucking *cunt*," he sputtered into the receiver. "Makes me want to *puke*!"

Shocking words, but Fields wasn't surprised. All the nastiest insults, he notes, get hurled between family members.

The idea came from Richard Ogden, the music executive Paul hired to help restore some momentum to his career. If Paul was looking for a collaborator who could serve in the John Lennon role of sparking his competitive fires and goading him beyond his creative comfort zone, why not turn to the songwriter critics compared most readily to the original? That Elvis Costello hailed from Liverpool only made it seem that much more perfect. They called Costello, and when he proved to be quite enthusiastic (being, like virtually every musician of his age, a big Beatles fan), they got together, had a cup of tea, then pulled out their guitars. At first Paul played Costello a not-quite-finished song he called "Back on My Feet Again." It was already a good tune, melodic and propulsive, with a bridge that leaped unexpectedly into another key. But then Costello saw it from a slightly different angle, and by the time they were done, the song had grown and changed. What had started as a thoroughly McCartneyesque recitation about a downtrodden man swearing his resilience now zoomed into a whole other orbit, with a new layer of lyric that circled back on the song's main narrative, ridiculing the man's confidence as a ridiculous act. *We tried hard to know him,* the lyric concluded as the man's shouts continue to echo. *He's a case where there's clearly no hope.*

Whether we're supposed to identify more with the song's subject or its narrator is left to the listener to decide. But the tension between the voices offered precisely that sort of narrative complexity that Paul's songs had lacked in recent years. So the two songwriters kept at it, gradually developing a rich variety of new and vibrant songs. All were clearly the product of a fruitful collaboration, with Costello's long lines of verse strung across Paul's arching melodies, while Paul's reflexive good cheer was leavened by Costello's interest in misanthropic characters and dark, unsettled emotions. Thus came "That Day Is Done," a New Orleans–style funeral song sung from the perspective of the corpse; "Pads, Paws and Claws," an off-kilter rocker about a couple on the rocks; "Veronica," the tale of a senile woman's life of love and tragedy set to a surprisingly upbeat tumble of chords and bass notes; and "Tommy's Coming Home," an intricately harmonized duet about a faithless war widow. More and more. "My Brave Face" contrasted major and minor chords to look behind the devil-may-care facade of a jilted lover. "Mistress and Maid" offered another portrait of domestic dysfunction, while "The Lovers That Never Were" tacked in the opposite direction, describing an unrequited romance that verges on obsession.

Then they got to "You Want Her Too," a careening argument between sweet and sour voices that come either from one woman's dueling lovers or from the contrasting facets within one man's psyche. Another brilliant song, according to everyone who heard them sing it. But so many things about it seemed familiar to Paul—the way the harmonies slid together; the way he took the sweet lines while Elvis bit off the bitter ones—he felt himself edging away. "I said, 'We can't do this, man, this is me and John,'" he told the *Rolling Stone*'s James Henke. But Costello had reassured him ("It's your style . . . there's nothing wrong with it!"), and as 1987 turned to 1988, they began to think about extending their collaboration into a new album, a coproduction with Costello an equal partner in the recording studio. And this was where things got sticky.

It didn't happen immediately. Running through the arrangements, Costello encouraged Paul to get back to the musical vocabulary he had created for the Beatles, pushing him toward a more melodic bass sound and harmony parts that drew obviously from the blend he'd once had with John. Paul had to admit it sounded good. But such a deliberate evocation of the Beatles' sound, complete with the most Lennonesque character currently working in rock 'n' roll as cowriter and cosinger, did squeamish things to Paul's imagination. "I thought the critics would say, 'Oh, they're getting Elvis to prop up his ailing career,' you know?" To make things even more awkward, the two collaborators had very different ideas about how the songs should sound. Costello's idea was to make the album like the bare-bones Merseybeat of Paul's youth, with a couple of guitars, bass, drums, and a few piano accents here and there. "He didn't want to use any technology, he just wanted it to be rootsy," recalls Hamish Stuart, the former Average White Band guitarist Paul had called in to play on the project. And while Paul always liked getting tracks in the can without endless fussing, none of it sounded quite finished to his ears.

Nor did he enjoy having to argue his points with another stubborn northerner. It had been nearly twenty years since he'd gone into the studio with anything other than complete control, and if he'd ceded some authority to George Martin in the early eighties, the producer came to the studio toting his own Beatles legacy, along with years of shared history. Was Paul really supposed to let the younger artist take him over, the way John Lennon used to do? If he simply bowed to Elvis's raw sensibility, the record might be a terrible failure with a mainstream audience. Or worse yet, it might be a huge success . . . in which case all those stories about his being John's lesser partner would be revived, only this time his superior would be this knock-kneed kid who had been retracing his steps for the last ten or twelve years.

Sometimes the sessions grew tense. Still, nothing ever seemed to get explicitly ugly between the cowriters and coproducers. They liked and respected one another, and better yet, they both loved the songs they had written. As ever, Paul preferred to joke his way through the disagreements, which Costello both appreciated and resented. "Paul has a clever way of sidestepping confrontation by making jokes like 'Well, you can never trust anything he says 'cause he hates effects!" he told Bill Flanagan. "So rather than disagreeing with you, your argument's devalued before it's started." There was never a blowup, exactly. But as Hamish Stuart recalls, in no uncertain terms, "Obviously it just wasn't working."

Still, "Back on My Feet" came out as a B-side to another single, "Once Upon a Long Ago," in late 1987. They finished an album's worth of tracks in early 1988, and Costello went back to his own projects, leaving Paul to do whatever he wanted with the songs they had finished. But Paul couldn't imagine releasing the songs as they were and for a time considered shelving them all, at least for the foreseeable future. But he still needed a new album out sooner than later, so he brought in a chain of new producers, tasking each to take on a few songs in their particular way. Mitchell Froom and Neil Dorfsman worked on a few. Trevor Horn and Steve Lipson worked on a few others. There was a load of stuff to choose from; the remnants of short-lived collaborations with superstar producers David Foster and Phil Ramone, and a couple new songs he'd just written on his own. The recording went on for months, on and off, and gradually Paul amassed both an album's worth of new material and a band he could take on the road. The album, titled *Flowers in the Dirt,* came out in the early summer of 1989, earning his strongest reviews in years, due largely to the strength of the songs he'd written with Elvis Costello. Whatever, he was mostly delighted to have finally released an album the reviewers didn't savage on sight. Particularly now that he was ready to hit the road.

More than anything, Paul loves having a band. He loves to have the guys around, loves to have loud music blasting, the bass-drum pattern thumping against his chest. So once he figured out that Hamish Stuart could play and sing as well as advertised and was also such a sweet and fun guy, he was in. Chrissie Hynde, the head Pretender, pointed to her just-resigned lead guitar player, Robbie McIntosh, who had hot fingers and a cool harmony voice and just the sort of even temperament Paul could live with for months or years. Paul went back to Chris Whitten, the drummer he'd used on the rock sessions in 1987, then sifted through a variety of keyboard players (including the Stones' old piano player Nicky Hopkins) before hitting on Paul "Wix"

Wickens, who was every bit as sweet as the other guys, while also being conversant in a variety of keyboard techniques that allowed him, with the flick of a synthesizer, to reproduce horn parts as easily as he could re-create stately string arrangements. This was Paul McCartney's new band.

Or it would be once they made room for Linda, because obviously she was in the band, too. Maybe this still wasn't what she would have preferred to do with her time. Linda knew her limitations, she knew she wasn't a great musician or singer. But as ever, she knew what Paul needed, and if he needed her to be onstage with him, that's exactly where she was going to be. With Wix there to take on the complicated parts, and to come up with parts she could handle easily, while adding her vocal parts or even hitting a tambourine, it all worked out wonderfully. "You could always hear the character of what she did on the records," Stuart says. "And when she wasn't there, the chemistry changed."

They had new songs to play, and ten years' worth of Wings hits to play, too. But what about the Beatles' songs? Paul's first impulse was to edge away from his most golden repertoire, perhaps playing the small handful of older songs he'd taken on during his 1970s tours. Just enough to give the night a little gilding, you know. But, as Richard Ogden knew, that was back when Wings could send new albums soaring to the top of the charts. By 1989 the market had obviously changed. So maybe it was time to take on a few more of the classics. Particularly if Paul expected to fill basketball arenas and the odd stadium. "So he came in one day and said he wanted to do 'Can't Buy Me Love,' and we were like *yeeeeeaaah!*" Stuart says. After nearly thirty years Paul had written so many hit songs, everything from cheery pop tunes to screaming rockers to disposable disco to front-porch folk to high-sixties avant-pop to works that came with all the historical weight of Western-civ liturgy, the only problem was figuring out which ones *not* to play. Take all that and season with computerized lights and digitized sound, prop the whole operation up with a boatload of corporate-sponsorship money from the Visa credit-card people, and you've got yourself a truly modern rock 'n' roll show.

20

The first glimpse of the new old Paul came in the video for "My Brave Face," the all-important first single from *Flowers in the Dirt*. Music videos were at their height in 1989, still the most important part of establishing the tone and image that a pop artist wanted to project with his new work, the very foundation of the next stage of his career. As Paul set out to reestablish himself for yet another decade, the new image he crafted to go along with his new Beatlesque song, the new album it previewed, and the world tour that would follow came girded with his most powerful talisman from the past.

He was playing the Höfner bass. The Beatles bass, unseen in Paul's hands (apart from a self-mocking appearance in the "Coming Up" video) since he stood on the rooftop on that fabled afternoon in January 1969, back when giants still strode the earth. Just in case you thought this violin-shaped vision from the past was a stand-in, look again and note the yellowed setlist from the Beatles' 1966 tour, still taped near the base of the neck. It was the real thing, in other words. Him, too.

The band's performance (lipsync, actually) shots were set off by a silly drama involving an obsessive Japanese collector of Paul McCartney memorabilia, whose ill-gotten collection contained more than a few key Beatles artifacts. As the music played, the man showed off his idol's blue *Sgt. Pepper's* suit and unspooled homemade videos of the beautiful young Beatles in their most private moments, playing cards, goofing in hotel rooms, dancing to their own secret songs. Every precious glance designed to connect the older (if still amazingly boyish, at nearly forty-seven years old) Paul to his beloved younger self.

The video's message: This Paul is *that* Paul. And now he's back to being the most Beatle-y of the Beatles, the act you've known for all these years!

That was just the beginning. At every stop of the 1989–90 world tour, official staffers issued each and every attendee a free, hundred-page, full-color program, a high-dollar production intended to introduce Paul to a new generation of fans. A series of essays written by London music journalist Paul Du Noyer (himself a Liverpool boy, then the editor of *Q*, founding editor of *Mojo*, and author of reams of exceedingly smart articles and books) retold the star's story from Forthlin Road through the Beatles years and right through to the modern era, complete with detailed digressions on how Paul introduced the group to avant-garde music, and how he and John had always been creative equals in the band. "The great thing about me and John," Paul McC said via Paul Du N's pen, "is that it was me and John. End of story." A bit cryptic, that. But the point was that anyone who pretended to know more about the mysterious chemistry behind the Beatles was, clearly, pretending. Particularly when it came to assigning credit. "There are certain people who are starting to think [John] was the Beatles. [That] there was nobody else. . . . Now that is not true."

Then the arena lights flickered out and the vast video screens above the stage exploded with images of the Beatles. There they were again, romping and beaming their way around the world in strobe-cut shots set against newsreel shots of the Kennedys and King and peace marches and seemingly every greatest hit from a generation that wanted the world and wanted it *now*. This sizzler reel was from the sanctified hands of Richard *A Hard Day's Night* Lester, virtually every moment set to the electric cry of yeah-yeah-yeah. This earned cheers and probably tears, too, and only added to the hysteria as the arena went dark again. Then—lights! color! magic!—there he stood. Beaming down into the tidal wave of cheers and applause, a full-grown man with modish clothes, a silver-flecked mane of hair, and that age-less grin you'd just seen on the video screen, conquering the world all over again.

And now it was happening right before your eyes and ears: the Beatles! (At least one of the ones who truly mattered.) Alive and in concert!

Wait for it, though, because when the band kicked into gear, the first tune was "Figure of Eight," not quite the second single from the new album. Next came a flash of ecstatic recognition for the night's first Wings standard ("Jet"), but then one more unfamiliar tune (the slinky funk of "Rough Ride," not the least bit Beatle-y) before the aces would start to drop. "Here's a little song Robbie [or Hamish or Wix, depending on the night] just wrote in the car on the way here," Paul teased. "You probably haven't heard this before." But then came that familiar blast of horns (an alarmingly precise synth-ulation from Wix), and ecstasy *I was alone, I took a ride, I didn't know what I would find* theeeeeere! That was just where it started! From here on out the night became Christmas morning for aging Beatlemaniacs. Song after song after song, louder and liver than you'd ever dreamed. It's "Birthday"! It's "Can't Buy Me Love"! Holy shit, it's even "Eleanor Rigby," in all its lovely Victorian melancholy!

Then more. Paul led off "The Fool on the Hill" by calling out to "three mates of mine, John, George, and Ringo, without whom—" Whatever he said next would be lost in the tidal rush of raw, leather-lunged emotion. For a while Paul considered doing a full tribute to John, projecting his visage on a black-bordered screen while singing one of his fallen comrade's best-loved songs. "Then I thought, 'Fucking hell, Diana Ross does "Imagine,"'" he said. He changed his policy when the tour made it to the Liverpool docks on June 28, 1990, working up a medley of "Strawberry Fields Forever," "Help," and the chorus of "Give Peace a Chance." Observant concertgoers noticed that while those three songs are all associated with John, even the concluding bit, from his Plastic Ono Band days, bears the Lennon-McCartney authorship credit, thanks to John's last-minute decision to extend the partnership bridge one last time.

Still, Paul didn't require nearly as much convincing to reclaim his own Beatles monuments. "Let It Be." "Hey Jude." "Yesterday." "Get

Back." More Beatles songs, ultimately, than the Beatles played during any of their thirty-minute shows. By the time Paul kicked off the big "Golden Slumbers/Carry That Weight/The End" finale, holding another vast arena spellbound as he sang about the way to get back home, it was easy to assume that this once-and-future Beatle, standing alone in the spotlight, his beautiful, loving wife within arm's reach and his crack band coiled and waiting for his cue, was there already. He had finally found his way back to where he once belonged.

He wasn't the only Beatle in a mood to reclaim the wonders of the past. The last great courtroom battle—George, Ringo, and Yoko's lawsuit against Paul for his escalated Beatles royalties from EMI—ended when the company agreed to give the others the same rate as a way to resolve other litigation. This development cleared the skies of Beatle-land for what proved to be a long and fruitful season of cooperation. For soon they were talking again, and visiting and laughing. Seen having dinner in London! Visiting one another at home, just to hang around and nose through the garden! Goofing and giggling and remembering why they had loved each other in the first place. "The first thing we talked about," Paul said, "was maybe we could do something together, maybe we don't have to live our lives completely separately from here on in."

The amazing thing was that it took so long. How could anyone who had ever been that beautiful resist the temptation to reach back through the years and become the treasured one all over again? No matter how toxic the mania had become, no matter how it had twisted their lives and turned them against one another, its magic still called to them. The Beatles was home, in a weird way: where they had grown up, where they had been defined, the place anyone would yearn to reclaim, the calendar and Thomas Wolfe be damned.

So it began. First with a two-CD release of vintage performances from their BBC radio shows. Then, more significant, came the long-delayed Beatle autobiography project. They'd talked about it as far back as 1970, before the band had even officially broken up. It kept coming up over the years, usually described as a feature documentary called *The Long and Winding Road*. But the idea, along with the possibilities offered by new technology, had grown with the passing years.

By the time it really got going again in the early nineties, it was many things: a multimedia extravaganza incorporating a six-hour TV series, multiple albums of rare and unreleased music, an expanded version of the TV series to be sold in home-video formats, and also an elaborately illustrated book. Imagine the possibilities for revenue, for increasing the Beatles' grasp on sales charts in virtually every form of entertainment media.

So now the long and winding road would include a whole new array of twists and turns and even a gift shop or two. But, um, did this massive new campaign really have to be named after one of *Paul's* songs? George wondered. Cheerfully, but still. So, in the new spirit of comradeship, Paul saw it George's way. Understood completely and agreed on a new title that bore no relation to anyone's song, let alone the literal meaning of the word itself: *Anthology.*

Nearing the start of his sixth decade, still bright-eyed and floppy-haired, and only a bit battered by the storms of his past, the middle-aged Paul McCartney rode higher than ever before. In front of the cameras he was stubbornly upbeat and unflappable, the public visage easily imagined as a perfect reflection of his actual mood. Two decades after the Beatles, he had grown into the very model of the grown-up pop star: the owner of otherworldly wealth, a blissful marriage, and a thriving career. Indeed, the way Paul and Linda (and everyone else) described it, daily life in the McCartney home was a dreamy pastiche of peaceful country mornings and amazingly productive afternoons, rehearsing or recording music at the Mill, or in the sleek art deco chambers of MPL's Soho Square offices in London, taking meetings or charming the wide-eyed reporters. And they weren't tending just Paul's career, either. He was just as likely to accompany Linda to the photo shoots she still did for friends or special clients, and to whatever engagements that went along with her new, already thriving empire as a vegetarian-food icon, with her bestselling cookbooks and a frozen-food empire that had sold nearly as many helpings of butternut-squash ravioli and mushroom-and-spinach pizza as her husband had sold records.

All the McCartney kids were nearly grown now, yet still close to their parents and devoted to one another in the sweetest way. Heather was nearly thirty and living mostly out of the spotlight as a potter and housewares designer. Dark-haired, dark-eyed Mary was in her twenties and keen to follow her mom into photography. She shared Linda's eye for composition and emotion, but like any aspiring artist she made sure she had a day job, first in a publishing house in London, then in the family business at MPL Communications, where she supervised the vast photography archive. James, still a teenager, was more rambunctious. An enthusiastic surfer whose taste for adventure led to the occasional mishap (turned-over Jeeps, oceanic misadventures, subsequent need for rescue, visits to the emergency room, etc.), he was still a soft-spoken lad who went out of his way not to mention his own famous surname when he was out in the world.

The crackerjack among them was always Stella, a wide-eyed, beguiling blonde who made up for her shaky academics with her talent for design and fashion. She had earned an internship at the Christian Lacroix design house in Paris when she was fifteen, then went on to the St. Martins College of Art & Design, where she prepared to make her own name in a hotly competitive industry that had nearly nothing to do with pop music or photography. Yet the McCartney family traits were clearly visible: the determination; the work ethic; the charm; the clear-eyed confidence in her own judgment. Paul and Linda had raised all their kids to be vegetarians, but Stella had become a vocal activist for animal rights, particularly when it came to the wide use of fur and leather in fashion. She was also funny and down-to-earth. "You could tell she was going to do something, you could see it in her," says Hamish Stuart, who got to know all the kids during his years as their father's musical coconspirator. He recalls Stella's revelation during the band's tour of stadiums in South America, when so many of their concert venues shared the same dark history of being transfer stations for political dissidents being "disappeared" by government agents. Now times had changed, but ghosts remained. So Stella gazed out at the faces shining up and singing along with her father's music and declared that the concerts were performing a spiritual service. "She decided the concerts were cleansing rituals," Stuart says. "We were helping to heal the spirit of the stadium."

It was a sweet idea, and Paul's South American shows were particularly spirited affairs, drawing unbelievable crowds. One 1990 show in

Rio de Janeiro drew 184,000 paying customers, a new global mark, according to the Guinness book of records. Nearly four times as many as the Beatles had once played to at their Shea Stadium height.

It's hard to imagine how cheers of that magnitude, on top of so many years of uninterrupted idolatry, echo in the ears of the man who receives them. How does his own face appear to his own eyes in the mornings when he stands at the sink running the razor across his cheeks? Surely, Paul McCartney could find reasons to feel satisfied. He could listen for the voices of his children and anticipate another day of companionship with the woman who had shared nearly every moment of his life for twenty-five years. Yet Paul still felt the same drive that had always pushed at him. The restless sense that there was more to do. More ways to express himself, to prove himself, to leave an even bigger and better mark on the world. If only because he found it so irresistible to prove that there was nothing he *couldn't* do.

So he kept right on thinking, right on moving, right on doing. In 1991 Paul unveiled his first major classical composition, a sweeping, semiautobiographical work called *The Liverpool Oratorio*. Cowritten with Carl Davis, a symphonic conductor and prolific composer of film scores, the oratorio veered through a variety of classical styles and compositional ideas, telling the tale of a McCartney-like character named Shanty, from his birth in the war-shadowed year of 1942 through his growth, education, marriage (to a woman named Mary), and a variety of challenges leading back to his eventual reclaiming of hope and innocence. "Our love survives!" Shanty sings with Mary at the oratorio's climax. The piece was ecstatically received at its debut at the Liverpool Cathedral (where young J. P. McCartney had once been rejected for a position in the choir, as the CD sleeve noted), though the critics were a bit more reserved, if generally respectful. No matter, the recorded version of the oratorio leaped instantly to the top of the classical music charts, much to its author's delight. Don't mention the power of mass-market name ID, and the relative intimacy of the classical-music-buying public: the point is, he'd triumphed again.

But there was so much more to do. Here he is burnishing his dance-club street cred with an album of trance electronica cocreated with the whiz-kid producer Martin Glover, better known as Youth, released in 1993 under the semisecret joint pseudonym the Fireman. And there, producing animated children's films, including his favorite, *Rupert the Bear*. These needed original songs, too, so he set aside some time for the next "Mary Had a Little Lamb." Once that was achieved, Paul could stride into his home painting studio to devote some time to work on his latest abstract canvas. Remember those art awards Paul had won at the Liverpool Institute? Now he was back at it, as something more than a hobby, given how he had honed his skills with the personal help of the great abstract expressionist Willem de Kooning, who just happened to be the McCartney's summerhouse neighbor on Long Island. Thus all of Paul's original canvases (hundreds of them, over the years) were cataloged and stored carefully in case he ever felt like exhibiting his work. When he hung up his brushes, Paul also found the time to compose poems, all of which he kept on hand waiting to be gathered for publication.

Meanwhile, Paul pursued roles in a variety of causes, some below the radar (cash donations; unexpected calls to lend support), while others were as high-profile as possible. Paul and Linda were eager environmentalists as well as frontline warriors in the animal rights movement, speaking out aggressively against laboratory testing, hunting, fishing, and virtually every activity that might lead to the death or suffering of a sentient creature. They had lived that way for years, but the couple's deepening commitment came from Linda. "She wanted to be more noisy about it," says Carla Lane, who had met Linda at a strategy meeting held at Chrissie Hynde's home in London in the eighties. "He's a faithful animal lover, but didn't want to push it too much, to put people off." But if Linda was going to make like a rock star to keep him happy, he could join her in her activism.

Whatever he imagined, Paul made real, and made really successful. Or felt capable of doing it, anyway, and when he was in Liverpool and noticed how his alma mater, the once treasured Liverpool Institute, had been shuttered and was falling to pieces, Paul took up its cause. His ambitions were soon linked with those of Mark Featherstone-Witty, an educator who had started a performing-arts college in London and now hoped to open a similar, music-centric institution in Liverpool. They merged their causes in the early nineties, though Paul maintained his well-worn skepticism about formal education, particularly when it came to popular music. "The fact that I had a double-barreled name and was clearly middle-class didn't go down well either," Featherstone-Witty recalls. Still, Paul donated millions of pounds and served as the nascent Liverpool Institute for Performing Arts' public face at fund-raisers held all around Europe. He was a generous, but occasionally difficult, patron, upbraiding Featherstone-Witty when Paul didn't like (or understand) points of curriculum, and, worse, commanding the actor-turned-administrator to perform Shakespeare. When Featherstone-Witty demurred, his financier turned chilly. "Then get up and get me a bevvie!" Paul snapped.

Featherstone-Witty recalls stumbling out of the room, feeling simultaneously humiliated, infuriated ("It's wrong to scream at people who can't scream back," he notes), and terrified that his chief funder was about to desert him. Paul rarely apologized. Most often reassurance would come from Linda, who had long since grown accustomed to dialing whomever her husband had just unloaded upon to urge them not to take it personally, that sometimes he just does that, and we still think you're great, so don't sweat it. (Though, Featherstone-Witty hastens to add, Paul did send him an apologetic note when he saw his tantrum recounted in the administrator's 2000 memoir. "He just wrote, 'I can be a right bastard sometimes, can't I?' So he does have some self-awareness.")

There was always more rock 'n' roll music to make. Once Paul and the band finished their first world tour, they took the shortest of breaks before reconvening to work up a (nearly) all-acoustic show for MTV's *Unplugged* series, playing a variety of rock 'n' roll oldies, solo gems, and Beatles favorites (including never-before-performed selections such as "And I Love Her," "Here, There and Everywhere," and "We Can Work It Out") for an intimate show that was televised, then released as a limited-edition "official bootleg," with only 1 million copies available. The record sold better than expected, selling out quickly and becoming the first in a line of successful *Unplugged* albums. A good development, you'd think, though it also became a point of rancor between Paul and his manager, Richard Ogden, when Paul saw how many millions of copies Eric Clapton and Mariah Carey would sell with their *Unplugged* albums. Why, Paul wondered, had Ogden decided to make *his Unplugged* a limited edition?

A brief, attention-getting tour of relatively tiny European clubs came next, with a new drummer (Blair Cunningham, formerly of Echo & the Bunnymen) taking over for Chris Whitten. Next they reconvened at the Mill to record another album of original songs. Paul was eager to capture the band's unique chemistry in the studio, hopefully resulting in an album that sounded more unified than *Flowers in the Dirt*.

The band was red-hot and raring to go. Trouble was, Paul didn't have much in the way of songs to offer. Maybe he'd spread himself too thin, maybe his muse simply couldn't keep pace with his need to keep the product flowing. Whatever, the album that came to be known as *Off the Ground* was filled with songs that seemed composed either by rote or without anything resembling inspiration. A few tunes work—most notably the pair of leftover Elvis Costello collaborations and the deliciously melodic single "Hope of Deliverance." Beyond that, the album turns increasingly detached and/or cranky, particularly when Paul reaches for social and political currency. "Looking for Changes" focuses Lennon-like indignation toward laboratory testing on animals, but overplays its hand by turning scientists into psychopaths who actually *enjoy* torturing their subjects. "Long Leather Coat" (released as a bonus track with the "Hope of Deliverance" single) is a revenge fantasy in which a seductress locks her swain in a back room and defaces his jacket (*nothing but a handful of skin!*). Then "C'mon People" works hard to drum up a movement of some sort, but offers no guidance beyond loopy instructions to gather minstrels, form a party, and do *what never has been done before*. Which could mean anything, and thus nothing at all.

Paul achieved the same dubious distinction with "Big Boys Bickering," an antigovernment song he performed on MTV, then released as a bonus track, largely for the shock value that comes from dismissing politicians as greedy, war-hungry despots who are, the chorus repeated, *fucking it up for everyone*. Eagerly describing the song as "Lennonesque," Paul was particularly proud of his unrestrained vocabulary. "I'm not a teenybopper," he proclaimed. "I'm an artist." Which was true, but it still didn't mean he was capable of writing coherent political songs.

But never mind that when there's so much more to get done. Another world tour in 1993, documented by yet another live album, which included even more unearthed Beatles gems, a scattering of new songs, and two improvised jams from the band's lengthy preshow performances, so-called sound checks that often stretched to two hours of rock 'n' roll oldies, reggae favorites, and abstract musical improvs they made up on the spot. Long days, but that was the point. "Paul wanted togetherness in every aspect of the tour, to keep the integrity of the thing, the band thing," Hamish Stuart says. "No matter where we were, he wanted us to move as a unit."

That was what the Beatles did, after all, marching around the world in lockstep rhythm made necessary because the worldwide mania they caused made it all but impossible for them to ever travel outside their protective bubble. So even if the world had changed over the decades, even if virtually every member of this new band could stroll off the stage and into the crowd without raising a fuss, Paul insisted they all move at the frantic pace of the Beatles at their peak. So even as the night's final notes still hung in the air, they sprinted off the stage and onto the tour bus, which careened out of the venue and headed full bore for the airport or the hotel, if they were staying in town. Even if they were in London, all with family and friends waiting to greet them in the postshow hospitality rooms, the band members were herded onto the bus to accompany Paul and Linda to the golf course where a helicopter waited to zip them back to their suburban family home in Sussex. "Then we'd get back in the bus and go back to the gig," Stuart says. "Which I guess was a bit weird."

The McCartneys couldn't control every facet of their regal hippie world. On *Saturday Night Live* Dana Carvey made a recurring character of his Paul impression, performing the musician as a sparkle-eyed space cadet, beaming and winking and speaking what amounted to a secret language of utter nonsense. Worse, someone with access to the band's sound-board mix leaked a tape that isolated Linda's vocal track on a performance of "Hey Jude" at the 1990 Knebworth festival. She drifts out of tune, she loses the meter of the climactic *na-na-na-na-na-na* chorus. Was it possible she could have been that detached from music, after all those years? It was easy to smirk, but music industry insiders blanched when they contemplated the cruelty of whoever had leaked the tape. Who knew what quality of sound mix she was, or wasn't, getting in her monitors that night? "Anyone can be made to sound shit onstage if their mix isn't right," the producer Hugh Padgham says hotly. "She wasn't a lead vocalist, but she wasn't bad." Caught between his own hardwired perfectionism and the loving spouse's protectiveness, Paul was beyond rationality, pointing instead toward how Linda had been waving and clapping. "She was the big cheerleader. But you don't see the visual. You just hear the out-of-tune voice."

Paul preferred to portray himself walking in light, bathed in the devotion of the fans who paid premium rates to see his face, to hear his voice, to feel the spirit of the music that had defined or even changed their lives. This is what Paul felt as he traveled the world, and the performance films he had shot along the way were cut to emphasize the communion between performer and audience, focusing as much on the glistening eyes and gaping mouths of the faithful as on the golden man who held them enraptured.

The next Beatles legend began in Liverpool, New Year's morning 1994. Paul described it in typical whimsical fashion: he woke up in a good mood after the annual McCartney family celebration, then picked up the phone to extend his best wishes to a family member to whom he hadn't spoken in a while. "She was a little surprised to get a call from me because we've often been a bit adversarial because of the biz stuff," he said. "But we got chatting. I rang her a few more times after that, we got quite friendly, and this idea came up." Maybe it didn't happen exactly like that. Yoko has been quoted as saying that the first time she heard about any of this was weeks earlier, when she got a call from Neil Aspinall and George Harrison. They were wondering if she would let the surviving Beatles have a go at one of John's unreleased songs, adding their own parts to create a postmortem, digital, modern collaboration. "If only we could pull off the impossible," Paul continued. "I talked to Yoko about that and she said she had these three tracks, including 'Free as a Bird.'"

Paul went to New York a few weeks later for John's induction into the Rock 'n' Roll Hall of Fame as a solo artist and shared a very public hug with the honored man's widow, now his own no-longer-quite-as-estranged bandmate-in-law. Soon Yoko had Paul over for an evening listening session of John's leftover demo tapes. "I went over to the place, the Dakota, sat up late just jawing and drinking tea and just having fun and stuff. And she said, 'I should play you the tapes!' And she played us three songs: 'Grow Old with Me,' 'Free as a Bird,' and 'Real Love.' And I liked 'Free as a Bird' immediately. I just thought, 'Shit, that is really—I would have loved to have worked with John on that.' . . . If John had played me those three, I would have said, 'Let's just work on that middle one first.'"

Ultimately Paul went home with tapes for something like a half dozen songs, including "Real Love," "Grow Old with Me," "Girls and Boys," "Now and Then," and "I Don't Want to Lose You." Some of these titles may have been different versions of the same song, but what's certain is that Paul kept coming back to "Free as a Bird." He took the song to George and Ringo and, as he told the story later, was careful to tell Ringo to "have his hanky ready." Then Paul punched the play button and they all heard their old friend captured at his living-room piano sometime in 1977, singing a bittersweet, yearning melody about how freedom is really just the next best thing to the comforts of home. That John had left the bridge unfinished (with a few lines of la-la'd words and an awkward modulation back to the verse) only made Paul happier—it was so much closer to their original process, back when they had both been in the habit of taking their nearly finished songs to one another for last-minute tinkering. This time George and Ringo would share the duties, too, to make it that much more inclusive. They gathered at the Mill on February 11, 1994, with George's friend and Traveling Wilbury's bandmate Jeff Lynne in the producer's chair (Lynne being digitally savvy and Martin being retired from frontline recording due to hearing problems) and set to work.

More interviews, more myth, more legend: Before they started work, Paul eased the tension by telling the other guys to imagine John had merely gone on holiday, leaving them to finish up his tune. For these hours, at least, they would pretend that everything was right with the world. "So it was great," Paul concluded. "And then we did it again a year later."

Only it wasn't that simple, of course. George didn't like the words Paul had sketched out for the bridge of "Free as a Bird" and told him so in no uncertain terms. "And you know when you've been writing a long time, you hope people will like your lyrics," Paul said. "He was right, but it was a little tense for a moment." Then Paul got irked when he began to suspect that George and his fellow Traveling Wilbury would inevitably team up to marginalize Paul's impact on the song. "I felt at one period early on like I wish I had a few people on *my* side in this!" Particularly when he suspected that Lynne's idea that George play his leads with a slide guitar would make the record seem more like one of his own solo songs than a true Beatles track. "I thought, 'It's "My Sweet Lord" again.' It's George's trademark. John might have vetoed that," Paul said. But then he waited to hear how it actually sounded, and when he did, Paul changed his mind. "I thought he played an absolute blinder."

The "Bird" session ended up going more or less swimmingly, so they reconvened at the Mill on June 22 to have a go at "Now and Then." But this time technical problems—a recurring buzz and rhythmic shifts on John's original tape—and the many missing words made it impossible to contemplate filling in without knowing John's actual intent. The session broke down early, and George suggested they shift to the recording studio he kept in Friar Park, his beloved Gothic mansion in Henley-on-Thames. The original plan was for the three Beatles to be filmed recording a new version of "Let It Be" to use as the *Anthology*'s climactic scene. Who knows whose idea that had been, but when the sun came up and they all gathered to do the filming, George, and possibly Ringo, decided that this was far too Paul-centric a way to end what was supposed to be the story of the entire group. Their resistance sent things skittering sideways, and the three Beatles marched off together into the arboreous fringes of George's garden, leaving the cameras and microphones behind, for a lengthy (perhaps as long as three hours) argument/air-clearing session. Whatever they said to one another was left among the brambles. Nevertheless, it cheered them up enough to stroll back to the studio and take up their instruments (George and Paul on acoustic guitars; Ringo on drums) and entertain the cameras with a few Casbah-era oldies, then with some warm, three-way banter, occasionally to (George's, and sometimes Paul's) ukulele accompaniment while reclining on George's sun-dappled grass.

Perhaps no amount of time, nor joyous reunions, nor shared history, could resolve all of the tension crackling in the air between the Beatles. It seems less evident when they're chatting, far more so when they're actually playing music together, when it all seems to be on the surface. On one level they're perfectly in sync—they can whip out their old arrangements of "Roll Over Beethoven" and "Raunchy" as easily as pedaling a bicycle built for three, it's all muscle memory and reflex. Deeper still, George can still recall the guitar intro to "Thinking of Linking," and that song of Paul's never even moved past the intro and first-verse stage. But then Paul begins to do his showman thing, and George seems to retreat into himself. He doesn't sing with anything like Paul's enthusiasm; his sideways glances seem to underscore how Paul is seated closer to the camera than he is. Was he thinking of John just then and feeling his absence? Or was George intuiting again what Paul would later confess: that no matter how old they all got, he could never quite get past seeing George as his kid brother. Only eight months Paul's junior, a man of musical and movie-industry achievement, of evolved spirituality and astonishing life experience. Yet, in Paul's eyes, never quite as sophisticated, never quite as accomplished. Did Paul ever wonder if George might have picked up on this attitude and resented it just a bit? It's hard to know, but George had already jumped up from his stool when Paul called out to play "Blue Moon of Kentucky," and when George sat down again to honor his bandmate's request, he made clear how limited his energy had become: "Just a shortened version." Paul's eyes were sparkling, he was thoroughly in control of the music and the moment, just where he liked to be. George played along, dutifully adding the low harmony to the chorus. But his smile was gone, and his eyes were already creeping toward the door.

The work continued. The group had a more fruitful two-day session with Jeff Lynne the next February, adding their instruments and voices to John's demo of his all-but-finished song "Real Love." They also did more fiddling with "Now and Then," but this didn't lead anywhere. Then they spent a few afternoons back at EMI's Abbey Road studios that winter and spring, listening to old session tapes. They seemed to enjoy the experience, and one another's company, immensely. One afternoon the three Beatles all but brought business to a stop by wandering down the hall to the studio canteen, where they helped themselves to salads and cups of tea. History's most popular and influential rock group's one additional request was for an extra-large bowl of chips so they could all split them. Then they sat together eating and giggling, just as they might have done between "Love Me Do" takes in 1962. "Older and slightly different maybe, but neverthe-less it was still three of the Beatles sitting there," Paul said. "And with who? *George Martin!* And what boxes were we looking at? *The actual boxes from the sessions.* And although it sounds silly, I swear to God, as we played the tapes, I was praying that I wouldn't make a mis-take."

The original idea was that they would finish three of John's songs, tucking one on each of the three *Anthology* CD sets. But they ran out of gas after "Real Love," so that ended up on the second set, while the third would have to make do without any new Beatles product. Every-one agreed that "Free as a Bird" had to be the *Anthology*'s opening shot: the opening track on the first *Anthology* CD and the climax to the first televised episode of the *Anthology* TV series. After all, it was the first four-way collaboration they had attempted since *Abbey Road*. More important, it was the first time the Beatles had ever spoken as one about their breakup: what they had meant to one another; what they had lost; what they had always yearned to reclaim, even at the depths of the bitterness. But just as it seemed impossible that the Beat-les could ever have existed, let alone reunited as a foursome twenty-five years after they had shattered, and nearly fifteen since the mania they had created had turned murderous, they found a way to do it one more time. For just a few ticks less than four and a half minutes, it was once again truly them.

It begins with Ringo establishing the downbeat, then George's gui-tar bending a single note above John's piano, Paul's bass, and Ringo's simple snare, bass drum, and hi-hat. The four of them, in unison, and then John's vocal begins. *Freeeeee* . . . his original lo-fi tape emphasizes his distance, as if he's beaming in from another realm. Which is ex-actly right. But he thought to leave this message, and somehow, magi-cally, John's thoughts crystallize everyone else's feelings. Paul waits only four beats before joining in to harmonize with the rest of John's initial thought—*as a birrrd.* Then finally it's happened. They're back together again, those two perfectly matched voices, singing not just with one another, but *to* one another; to George and Ringo, too; to the Beatles. And it's all there, in the layers of concept and execution, in John's bittersweet voice, in Paul's restless bass pattern, in George's understated guitar and Ringo's straightforward percussion. Diverse elements in near-perfect balance. Together they're singing about the end of the group, the need to escape one another, to find the creative and personal freedom such close bonds could never allow. And that's exactly what they'd found, but to what end? It is only, John admits, the second-best thing in the world. Right after being home and dry. And this is where he imagines going, a bird in an empty sky, now a homing bird swooping determinedly back to where he'd come from.

In the newly written bridge, Paul, and George, the second time through, call back to John in their own words. *What happened to us? How did we lose one another?* Then they all realize the same thing together: the creative and spiritual unity they'd once had was as liberating as anything they had ever experienced in life.

A sentimental interpretation, perhaps. But then they got to the last moments of the song, a false ending that segued into a psychedelic-era tag incorporating a one-chord vamp that faded into a music-hall-style ukulele bit, which faded along to a familiar voice muttering something that was supposed to be backward gobbledygook. They had taken a snippet of tape that had a posttake John saying, "That came out nice," reversed it, and patched it onto the end. Only once they played it through the speakers, they heard something else, as clear as day: "Made by John Lennon!" The other Beatles were flabbergasted. "None of us had heard it when we compiled it, but when I spoke to the others and said, "You'll never guess. . . ." they said, "We know, we've just heard it, too!'" Paul said. "And I swear to God, he definitely says it! We could not in a million years have known what that phrase would be backwards. It's impossible. So there is real magic going on. Hare Krishna!"

21

Her diagnosis came the same week "Free as a Bird" was released. Strangely, it was also the fifteenth anniversary of John's death. Stranger still, it was the same disease that had taken his mother all those years ago. It was December 8, 1995, and the news couldn't have been worse: Linda had breast cancer.

It began with a routine scan. A small lump, then a quick operation to have it removed a few days later. Paul was with her in the hospital in London, and by terrible coincidence that was the same night a bunch of thieves broke in and ransacked the Cavendish house. What had started as a search for valuables had turned into some kind of psycho melee: drawers dumped out, shelves cleared onto the floor, televisions hurled across the room. The thieves didn't get away with much, a camera and maybe some CDs. But the violation stung, and also, Paul admitted, the fact that this wasn't the first time this had happened at his Cavendish house. "We are improving security. But obviously this incident doesn't help at a time like this."

Yet, they hastened to add, Linda's medical news was nothing but encouraging: the lumpectomy had been 100 percent successful, the shadow the doctors had seen on her liver was nothing to worry about, her prognosis was entirely favorable. "The doctors have told her now just to get some rest," Paul told the *Daily Mirror* the morning after the operation. "We're very optimistic about the future, and for the moment everything goes on as normal."

That was the public version. In truth, Linda's prognosis was always a bit more cloudy than that. The disease had already progressed past its early stages, so she would require an immediate course of chemotherapy. The next year would be harrowing, at best. So they girded themselves for battle in the quiet way the McCartneys always faced their most stern tasks—with family wagons circled and mouths all but sealed. Even their closest friends were kept in the dark once they had the basic facts. "Linda sat me down in her kitchen and said, 'I just want to tell you something. And I don't want to talk about it ever after I've told you,'" Carla Lane recalls. "She just looked me in the face and said, 'I have cancer.' I didn't say anything because I knew that's what she wanted. I said, 'Oh, Linda!' And she said, 'Okay, that's it. You know and I know, so let's forget it and go write a song!' And so that was it. We went into the other room and tried to write a song. And I never said anything about it again, even as I knew she was getting worse."

For Paul, it was like living a nightmare beyond all other nightmares. Decades later his actual life had merged with his darkest memories: the terrible, not-quite-secret suffering of his mother's final weeks; the bloodstained sheets he glimpsed during their final visit in her hospital room. She had kissed him and baby brother Mike, assuring both boys everything would be fine again, soon. Then she was gone, with nothing to replace her. And now it was all happening again, only more vividly. The ravages of chemotherapy, the loss of weight and hair and energy, a vital person whittled down to bone, shadow, and misery. Yet Linda refused to surrender her smile, or her spirit. When Lane came over to visit, Linda might look pallid, but she acted as energetic and silly as always, pulling her friend out into the garden to pick melons and pose them for photographs on the lawn. Paul would come out and beam at the women—"that look like 'Oh, they're daft, but aren't they nice?'" Lane says. Then he'd shake his head and go back inside. If Linda was feeling strong, he'd saddle up their Appaloosa horses and help her up, and they'd trot gently down the wooded lane toward the farthest reaches of their property, and off somewhere into the verdant landscape.

But beyond those bright moments, he was terrified. He walked softly, he didn't erupt into rooms the way he used to do, all smiles and enthusiastic energy. "He became very quiet when she was ill," Lane says. "He was so sad, but he never spoke about it."

Whom could he speak to? Linda had been his most consistent, maybe his *only*, confidant over the last quarter century, and she was obviously not in a position to be much comfort to him now. He had no religion to turn to, no overarching philosophy beyond his belief in hard work and keeping busy. A friend sent some coping advice from Alcoholics Anonymous, and this proved helpful. "When everything is on top of you and you've really got nowhere to turn," he said, describing the lesson he'd learned, "'hand it over, give it all up, and say this is too much for me.' You know, I'm crazy, I'm crying, I'm weeping, I am frightened. *Hand it over*."

Nevertheless, they maintained their upbeat public facade. By September Paul was back out on the town, declaring victory. "All the doctors are amazingly pleased with her," he proclaimed. Asked to clarify Paul's statements, MPL spokesman Geoff Baker said, "You can take Paul's words to mean Linda has beaten the cancer." All this talk of Linda being seriously ill? "A lot of rubbish!"

Yet Linda stayed out of the public eye for virtually all of 1996, so much so that in mid-December a forty-two-second acceptance speech she had videotaped with Paul to accept a lifetime-achievement award from the People for the Ethical Treatment of Animals proved to be big news. Particularly given her close-cropped hair and a wan complexion that no amount of makeup could enliven. Clearly, Linda was still in the midst of a terrible crisis.

Paul kept working. It was an escape, at least, to head down to the studio and lose himself in music for a few hours. He was already most of the way through a new rock album and was working on a new classical work, a Celtic-themed piece called *Standing Stone*. The pop songs, some of which had been written or even partially recorded years earlier, were now linked together by the darkness falling around them. The singer's voice has a coating of rust, and a distinct sadness beneath the sweetness. His reflexive cheeriness has lost its authority. No wonder—the chill seems to be encroaching from all directions. The elegiac guitar ballad "Little Willow" came to Paul in the hours after Ringo's first wife, Maureen, died of cancer, coincidentally just a few weeks before Linda learned she had contracted the same disease. He sings to her children, but no amount of reassurance can diminish his foreboding: *Now and forever / Always came too soon.* The same feeling mottles "Calico Skies," an autumnal love song for Linda, pledging to hold her forever, even in a life tangled by war and *the innermost secrets we hide.* Another love song, "Heaven on a Sunday," describes a placid summer day as a brief respite in the midst of an onerous campaign to learn what he describes, cryptically, as a new song: *a long and lonely blues.*

In the wake of *Anthology,* memories return of those Forthlin Road afternoons with John ("The Song We Were Singing"), along with an echo of John's famous Beatles creation myth written for the first issue of Bill Harry's *Mersey Beat* newspaper, in which the name for the group arrived to him via a man on a flaming pie. Only this time Paul puts himself at the center of the story: I'm *the man on the flaming pie!* As he would later admit, this defiant revisionism was intended to tweak Yoko for recent comments that attempted to elevate John's absurdist tale into something akin to a spiritual vision. "Yoko insisted that John had to have full credit for the name," he grumbled. That song became the album's title track.

Produced by Jeff Lynne, the *Flaming Pie* album is only partially successful, its moments of emotional honesty rivaled by substance-free blues jams (one with Steve Miller on guitar, the other with Ringo on drums) that spin clichéd words and stock riffs into nearly nothing at all. But the closing two tracks, a decade-old ballad called "Beautiful Night" and the simple acoustic "Great Day," end things on a high note by evoking Paul and Linda's dreamy life together at both of its extremes: the former in all the royal splendor of outrageous wealth and fame; the latter in the suburban bliss of their lovingly scuffed kitchen table. Indeed, "Great Day" was a family song, sung by Paul and Linda to rouse their sleepy children and get them up and excited about what the morning had to offer. *Get up and grab a chair,* they sang. *It's gonna be a great day!* It was a promise they'd kept to one another every day for nearly thirty years. As the breeze around them grew chill and the light dimmed, the shared memory of those mornings came to mean even more.

•　　•　　•

So many things were going awry. Now George was cranky at Paul, not returning his calls or answering his letters, for reasons Paul didn't quite comprehend. Yoko was at it again, too, ridiculing his classical compositions, then adding insult to injury by comparing John and Paul's relationship to the real-life characters at the center of *Amadeus*. "[John] was the visionary and that is why the Beatles happened," she proclaimed. "Paul is in the position of being a Salieri to a Mozart."

Obviously, Yoko had to know that wasn't quite true. But she also knew how to push Paul's buttons, so they were going at it again, the Itchy and Scratchy of Pepperland, off on another great adventure in celebrity enmity. Meanwhile, Paul both applauded and was reportedly a bit put out when Queen Elizabeth II made George Martin the first Beatles-related knight, while the actual *author* of all the music Sir George had become so famous producing still had to make do with his lowly MBE. And don't even get Paul started on the Rock 'n' Roll Hall of Fame, which persisted in not recognizing him for his post-Beatles achievements, despite having recognized John's solo career in 1994. Linda's old friend Danny Fields was on the hall's nominating committee in those days and thus grew accustomed to getting a call from Sussex every time a new list was released and Paul's name still wasn't on it. "It was always Linda, saying, 'Daaaaaannnnnny, I see Paul wasn't nominated . . .'" Fields tried to remind her of the role sentiment and sympathy played in such awards. John, after all, was a martyr to the cause. "I said, 'Linda, when Paul gets into the Hall of Fame, you might well be the widow McCartney!'"

No one wanted to hear that, but Fields had made his point. Then came even more trouble on the Beatles front—George found a lump on his throat, and now he had cancer, too. His prognosis was less gloomy and his treatment less debilitating than Linda's—he got away with a lumpectomy and a few weeks of radiation. But somehow it seemed as if the darkness were only coming close.

Yet life wasn't completely devoid of bright moments. The queen did finally tap Paul for his knighthood in 1997, elevating the former council-house boy to a level of aristocratic authority that would surely have stolen his father's breath. The once-and-still hippie made a point of shrugging it all off. "No, you don't! No, you don't!" he scolded one reporter who tried to refer to him by his proper title. Though he couldn't also help betraying his delight at the prospect, smiling cheerfully as he continued, "Well, you can if you want—but you don't have to."

Linda didn't make it to Buckingham Palace for Paul's investiture in March 1997, but they chalked that up to the limited number of tickets the family had been granted, and her desire to have the kids see their father kneel before the queen. And she did venture out in public a few times in the second half of the year. When she attended the New York premiere of *Standing Stone* at Carnegie Hall in November, her hair was shorter than usual, but she moved easily through the crowd, and when Paul walked onstage for his curtain call at the end of the evening, he dedicated the performance to his wife—"My favorite New Yorker!" She beamed down from the balcony and looked close to radiant. "We've had a couple of scary years there," Paul said a few weeks later. "Touch wood, now she is very well."

Only she wasn't. The cancer had spread. Though her doctors and her husband tried to spare her the darkest of the details, Linda was aware of what was happening to her. "One day she said to me, 'I haven't got long, you know,'" Carla Lane says. "And I said, 'Oh, don't say that!'"

But Linda could only shrug. "Well, I've got to live with it."

The early weeks of 1998 followed the same pattern. In public Paul and Linda persisted living as if she were recovering at a steady, if slow, pace. She ventured out in public a bit more frequently, traveling to Paris on March 11 to attend the unveiling of Stella's latest line of designs for Chloé. Sitting between Paul and their son, James, Linda held her husband's hand and told reporters she was "feeling great!" A month later Linda, Paul, and all of their children but Heather flew to America. They told friends they were headed to Santa Barbara, the breezy village northwest of Los Angeles on the California coast. But the people who really knew recognized that as code. The family's actual destination in the American Southwest had always been the ranch they kept in the Arizona desert. This was one of Linda's favorite places, with its sweeping vistas and endless skies full of clear, liquid light. They kept horses there, too, and she loved to ride across the mesas, feeling the sun on her shoulders and tasting the dry desert breeze on her tongue. It was nothing new for them to visit Arizona.

But what only they knew was that this time Linda was almost certainly not coming home.

"She called me the day she left and said, 'I'm going away,' which wasn't unusual," Carla Lane says. Then her friend started quizzing her about chickens, insisting that when she got back from America, she'd need seven or eight new birds to join the flock she kept in Sussex. Meanwhile, Lane could hear Paul calling out to his wife, saying it was time to go. "Then she said, 'I love you, Carla,' and that was extraordinary. I thought, 'What on earth does that mean?' But I said, 'I love you, too,' and off she went."

A few days later Lane found a package from Linda in her mailbox. She'd sent a few glass beads Lane had once admired. There was no note beyond a simple greeting, but even then Lane could sense the gift's deeper significance. Linda, in her quiet, loving way, was saying good-bye.

In Arizona the scene played out smoothly, albeit with unexpected speed. At first Linda felt sort of okay; energetic enough to climb onto her horse and ride off with Paul, trotting across the desert for a sweet, if brief, look at the arid landscape she had been yearning to see again. She didn't quite feel up to that level of exertion the next morning, but was still upbeat, spending most of the day up and about, chatting and laughing with her husband and kids. Linda felt a bit less hearty the next morning so she stayed in bed, watching the sun's progress across the sky from her pillows. Her energy faded with the sunset, and as the spark in her eyes dimmed, it seemed as if Linda was drifting toward the end. The kids gathered around, then Paul climbed into bed so he could cradle her in his arms. He stayed that way until midnight, then beyond, holding her close and talking her through the night. As the new morning approached, Linda's breathing became more faint, and by 5 a.m. it seemed clear that she was entering her final moments. The children came close to give their mother one last hug and kiss, then Paul held her even closer, whispering gently in her ear, *You're up on your beautiful Appaloosa stallion. It's a fine spring day, we're riding through the woods.* Her breaths were shallower now. He kept whispering. *The bluebells are all out and the sky is clear blue . . .*

Linda closed her eyes. She took one last breath, then she was gone.

Paul released a statement a few days later: "This is a total heart-break for my family and I. Linda was, and still is, the love of my life and the past two years we spent battling her disease have been a night-mare."

This raw, emotional testimonial to the woman he loved recalled her dedication to her causes, her kindness, her toughness, and her inno-cence. And more: her talent as a photographer, her success with her vegetarian-food business, the love she had for her children, the close-ness of their family. "Her passing has left a huge hole in our lives. We will never get over it, but I think we will come to accept it."

The world was a better place because of her, he wrote. He closed by addressing her directly: "I love you Linda. Paul xxx xxx."

Paul was, by all accounts, beside himself. On the phone with Carla Lane a day or two later, he spoke for nearly an hour, doing as much to console her as she could do for him. When Danny Fields called, both he and Paul burst into tears. Paul first regained the ability to speak, urging Fields to think of her life, not her death: "He kept saying, 'Wasn't she great? Wasn't she beautiful? Wasn't she smart and together and wonderful and loving?'"

Back in Sussex a few days later, Paul called a few friends and asked them to come over for a drink. Now he needed consoling. "He looked totally bewildered," Lane says. "So stricken. He just wanted to talk to us, about how shocked he was. He had that look like he'd been up for a week without being to bed. There was definitely no laughter or cel-ebrating her life. You didn't know what to say."

At first Paul could focus on the work that needed to be done. The necessities that come with death, which in this case included dispelling rumors that Linda's death had been an assisted suicide (this due to its abruptness and media confusion arising from the McCartneys' asser-tions that her death had taken place in California, rather than in Ari-zona). Then there were memorial services to plan, one in London and the other in New York. All that kept Paul busy for a few weeks. But when those were finished, all that loomed ahead was the rest of his life. And Paul was lost.

In Peasmarsh his neighbors had to look twice to recognize the stooped, gray-haired man who now walked in Paul's shoes. At times he seemed astonished to be surviving on his own. "How am I still here?" he said to the *Daily Mail*. "How am I talking, eating? I just am." Paul's kids took charge, making certain that at least one of them was with him at all times. Unable to stop crying, he started grief therapy with a psychologist. He spent hours in his painting studio, working on canvases for an exhibition he'd planned for the next year. He couldn't imagine making new music of his own, so when he went to the Mill, he occupied himself by tinkering with Linda's last musical project, a set of songs she had been preparing for a long-delayed solo album she had already titled *Wide Prairie*. Mostly he tried to feel his grief, to surrender to its power and let it carry him wherever he had to go. "I just let it all out, talked to a lot of people, just let any emotion come in," he said. "I cried more than I cried in my whole life, 'cause guys don't cry." When he spoke in public, the things he said were often sad beyond belief. He couldn't imagine playing live again, he said, because so many of his songs were written for Linda. How could he ever sing about the joy of being with her when fate had turned so cruel as to deny him that possibility forever?

In the absence of music came only months of psychic misery. A recurring pattern of endless nights and frigid mornings. No matter where he went, no matter whom he was with, Paul was always alone. Abandoned. Bereft. Beyond the reach, even, of music.

Then a melody came back to him. A shuffling rhythm that began in his memory and then tumbled across his tongue and down to his toes. A story he remembered about a girl with a record machine, an elevator that had stopped working, a boy who marched up the stairs to spend the evening dancing, or maybe just holding hands. *Get to the top, I'm too tired to rock!* Maybe this was what carried him back to his guitar. One way or another, Paul's mind had flown back thirty-two years, back to the winter of 1957, when the shadows of that first devastating death had eventually given way to the sparkle and flash of rock 'n' roll. Those simple little songs, three chords, drums, and an endless belief in fun. It sustained him then, maybe he could give it a try this time. Paul called Chris Thomas, the young Beatles engineer who had gone on to build a reputation among the punk revolutionaries of the late seventies before working on that last Wings album, *Back to the Egg*. An old friend, an old hand at rock music, he was always eager to spend a few days in the studio with Paul and knew now exactly what spirit Paul needed to get going again. "He wasn't think-ing it was going to be the next big record," Thomas says. "He was just free to enjoy himself."

Paul dialed a few musician friends, enough to form a basic rock 'n' roll band, and booked time in studio two at Abbey Road, the ances-tral homeland of his work as a recording artist. When Paul showed up, carrying his old Höfner bass, the faces were friendly and familiar. Pink Floyd's Dave Gilmour on one guitar, while another Liverpool veteran, Mick Green, held down the other guitar. Ian Paice from Deep Purple sat at the drums some days, Dave Mattacks played on others. Keyboard duties were divided between Pete Wingfield and Geraint Watkins. As Paul had already told Chris Thomas, the point was for them to just play and have fun. Nothing should be fussed over; no time could be spent on applying spit and polish. They had a week to record as many songs as they felt like playing, and whatever happened was exactly what should happen. "We were just going to do the songs, and that was it," Thomas says. "No postproduction, all very quick." Paul had a list of songs he wanted to play. Mostly the titles of the re-cords he had brought home to play during that first rock 'n' roll year in 1957. Elvis and Little Richard, Eddie Cochran and Gene Vincent. He had a couple of originals he could throw in, too, tunes he'd writ-ten with the same three-chords-and-a-howl attitude. So he stepped to the mike and counted down the first song, and they were off.

"These were just incredible performances," Thomas says. "The wild abandon came back, and his smile came back." Paul's fingers were flying up and down the Höfner's thin neck, the great surging bass runs that not only sustained the rhythm but also created a whole new layer of melody and harmony. That was great, yet still not as awesome as his singing, which had renewed strength and vitality, plus also an unhinged wildness he hadn't displayed in decades. "When I asked him to do that for 'Oh! Darling' in 1969, he shrugged and said, 'Well, I'm too old,'" Thomas says. "But now, thirty years later, he could do it again."

Yes, he could. And then some. Paul released the sessions a few months later under the title *Run Devil Run,* and you don't have to listen long to hear the voice of a man only just brushing past the hellhound that had been tailing him through the last few years. All but three of the songs are old rock 'n' roll songs, products of other pens and most often traced from other singers' interpretations. Yet it is, in its way, the most deeply autobiographical album of Paul's career. For once, he holds nothing back. Instead, he crafts a map to the headwaters of his musical imagination; a musical description of the link between his most overwhelming emotions and the artistry they fueled.

The album begins with "Blue Jean Bop," a Gene Vincent tune from 1956, the same year Mary died. What we hear is Paul alone, singing gently to himself. *Blue Jean baby, with your big blue eyes . . .* he plucks notes on his bass as his voice floats dreamily, drifting toward the moment when his vision takes root on the earth.

Can't keep still, so baby let's dance!

The snare drum cracks, and he's off, just another heartbroken boy pulling redemption out of three chords, a simple melody, and a need that flows deeper than even he can understand. So just dive in and feel the familiar waters on your skin. Crunching takes on Larry Williams's "She Said Yeah" and Elvis Presley's "All Shook Up." A loping Cajun arrangement of Chuck Berry's "Brown Eyed Handsome Man," a country shuffle through Carl Perkins's "Movie Magg." These were Forthlin Road songs, echoes from those long afternoons with the sitting-room record player. Other musical memories evoke more recent pain. Ricky Nelson's "Lonesome Town" describes the world Paul had been inhabiting with a clarity he makes even more vivid with the ferocity of his singing. He put even more into a new arrangement of "No Other Baby," a fairly obscure 1958 single by a group called the Vipers. He'd never bought the record, but it made enough of an impression that he could summon it from his memory thirty years on and realize how closely it described his feelings for the woman he had always liked to call his girlfriend, even after they had been married for more than two decades. He performs the song with a brooding intensity, a kind of understated desperation. *I don't want no other baby but you,* he sings to the one woman he knows he'll never hold in his arms again. *'Cause no other baby can thrill me like you do.*

The title track is an original. So, too, are "What It Is," a frantic, period-style rocker written to Linda during her final months, and "Try Not to Cry," a hard-rocking litany of a widower's sorrows, confusions, and regrets. The album climaxes with "Party," an old Elvis number Paul and friends perform with a speed and intensity you'd associate with the MC5 or the Ramones. The last verse ends after two minutes, but he keeps going as the band trails off. *I'm not givin' it back, I'm gonna have a party!* he cries, inciting the other musicians to flail noisily at their instruments. *I'm not goin' home yet, send 'im to the store, let's buy some more!* Even as the track fades, Paul's voice still echoes, as it always has in his best music. A distant scream against the growing silence.

Danny Fields's Rock 'n' Roll Hall of Fame prediction turned out to be right, albeit in reverse. Now that Paul had suffered such a terrible tragedy, the nominating committee, from *Rolling Stone* publisher Jann Wenner on down, could suddenly see the extent of his contributions to the form, even in the years after 1970. Paul came to the ceremony at the Waldorf-Astoria with Stella, who accompanied him to the stage wearing a sleeveless T-shirt of her own design, its chest bearing the simple, if pointed message ABOUT FUCKING TIME.

Then life went on. Paul's daughter Mary had been married a few months after Linda's death to Alistair Donald, a filmmaker, and in April of 1999 gave birth to a son named Arthur. Always a doting father, Paul was just as charmed by and taken with his first grandson. Paul spent time at Abbey Road in May to record more songs for the album that would be *Run Devil Run* and found his way back into the whirl of openings, concerts, and charity events. At one of these London events, he first glimpsed Heather Mills. A former model, she had lost part of a leg after being hit by a motorcycle. She had refocused her career on helping other disabled people and was presenting an award at a dinner in April to an audience that included the prime minister, Tony Blair. Paul was sitting at the PM's side, and the sight of the graceful woman with the flowing blond hair and limpid blue eyes clearly made a deep impression. They didn't speak that night, and she left for a vacation the next morning. But when she got home, he had left several messages on her answering machine. When he finally reached her, he said he had been calling to see if he could help with a charity she had set up for the victims of land mines. Which is exactly the cover a guy will use when he's sussing out a woman's availability.

But she was intrigued, as many women would be, and soon they began to see one another.

First came the rumors, then the denials. Then the confirmations that they were indeed friends, and quite fond of one another, but still not lovers. It had only been a year and a half since Linda's death, after all. Still, the British newspapers were intrigued by Macca's New Luv, as they put it, and given the media's fervent curiosity and the multitude of reporters teeming in London, the couple eventually had to own up. "We are an item," he confirmed to reporters in mid-March 2000. The world swooned—who doesn't love a happy coda to a tragic story?—then wanted to know more. Who was this woman the British tabloids liked to call Brave Heather?

Here the story took several turns. At thirty-one, Mills described her life in striking shades of childhood abuse, hunger, forced thievery, and teenaged homelessness. Her father, a former paratrooper, spent some time in jail, which was when fifteen-year-old Heather had run off to join the circus (!), ending up living in a cardboard box (!!) beneath a platform at London's Waterloo train station. Then things get a bit hazy, with one serious boyfriend in London in the mid-to-late eighties, then some time in Europe, during which Mills allegedly was a mistress to a wealthy Lebanese businessman, while also modeling for photographs, some of which were what you might call soft-core pornography.

Mills was just getting started. She returned to London and married the first boyfriend, Alfie Karmal. This didn't last long, but Mills found work as a model and also pursued a new interest in the civilian victims of the Croatian war, personally helping to transport refugees. Then in 1993 she had her accident, suffering wounds that resulted in the amputation of the lower part of her left leg. This misfortune led Mills to write a memoir (strikingly titled *Out on a Limb*) and to become involved in the antiminefield cause. There were other relationships and even an engagement, but this got called off. Then Mills met Paul McCartney and her life became even more interesting.

Later, friends and observers would debate the chain of events that took place behind the artfully presented facade of newfound romantic bliss that had fallen across Paul's no longer quite so distraught visage. Did he really take pains to gain his children's' acceptance of the blossoming romance? Had they granted their blessing, as he said they had, and beamed happily as Paul's bond to Heather deepened and led to their engagement in the summer of 2001? Certainly, other stories weren't anywhere near as pleasant. The most persistent of them revolved around Stella and what seemed to be her visceral dislike for her stepmother-to-be.

All of this would eventually emerge. But as the twentieth century concluded, the world the Beatles had changed continued to sweep the aging musicians up in its wildest extremes. In early December, Paul took his *Run Devil Run* band to Liverpool and the rebuilt Cavern Club (just a couple of doors up Mathew Street from the demolished original) for a night of old-time rock 'n' roll, broadcast over the Internet to an estimated audience of 150 million. A spectacular night, complete with old friends, family, and all the devotion he remembered from those lunchtime sessions in the early sixties. The reborn mania made another appearance at George's house in the wee hours of December 30, when he awoke to discover a mentally disturbed man lurking in his front hall. The man had come armed with a knife, crazed misreadings of Beatles songs, and murderous intent. George danced around the intruder, chanting "Hare Krishna" in attempts to calm, or at least confuse, his wild-eyed antagonist. This strategy didn't work at all, and the intruder lunged and plunged his blade into George's chest. In moments he was sitting on the musician's chest rearing up to strike again. George might have died were it not for the intervention of his wife, Olivia, who sprinted onto the scene wielding the business end of a heavy ornamental lamp.

By luck alone the blade had missed piercing George's heart. He recovered from his wounds with relative speed and customary grace. But fate didn't leave him much time to contemplate his good fortune. His throat cancer returned, then spread to his brain and lungs. Various treatments provided no help, and George went to America to seek treatment in the fall of 2001. He continued to wane. Paul took the Concorde from London to pay a final visit. George was reportedly in a famous mood throughout, laughing and joking, not just resigned to but, after years of spiritual questing, actually welcoming his fate.

Paul had long since put his faith elsewhere—in the music he made, in the love the music evoked and inspired, in the friends he made along the way. They had created so much together, yet lost so much of themselves along the way. Later, Paul marveled at the physical affection he'd been able to show his friend during their last hour together. He reached for his friend's hand and wove their fingers together, sitting just like that for the entire time. Feeling the warmth, the rhythm of George's heart, the electric pulse of life. The echoes of the music they had made, the existence that had come with it, all it had offered, all it had cost. It brought them together and ultimately repelled them from one another. Who knew why, you never knew why. In the end you can only reach out and hold on for as long as you can, wait for the light to fade, and say your good-byes.

When Paul left with Heather, onlookers saw the ex-Beatle sobbing inconsolably.

George died at a friend's home in Los Angeles on November 29, 2001. Paul got the news at home, and later the next day he addressed the press gathered outside the gates of his home with downcast eyes and an articulate recitation of both his personal sorrow and professional admiration for the friend he had just lost. "To me he's just my little baby brother," Paul said. "I loved him dearly."

22

On the morning of September 11, 2001, Paul was in New York City, sitting on a jet that was waiting to fly to London. He watched the horrific attack on the World Trade Center from the runway, then after the plane was sent back to the terminal, he returned to the smoky, shattered city and, like everyone else, watched the tragedy unfold on television. Waking up the next day feeling frightened and angry, he picked up his guitar and began playing the chords of "Freedom," a song that projected the global spirit of "All You Need Is Love" into a more bellicose age. Now he came at the world as a two-fisted defender of life and liberty. *I will fight for the right to live in freedom,* he proclaimed, the words strung to a simple, yet stirring melody.

Called to perform at a benefit concert for the families of the victims, Paul headlined the star-packed night at New York's Madison Square Garden, ending the show with a trio of Beatles classics selected to channel all the tangled skeins of outrage ("I'm Down," oddly enough), sorrow ("Yesterday," in a stark, near a cappella rendition), and spiritual yearning ("Let It Be") unleashed by the cataclysm. He also debuted "Freedom," proclaiming it to be about something "these people," meaning the terrorists, didn't understand. "It's worth fightin' for!" he said, raising a fist in the air. Eric Clapton contributed guitar to the song's first performance, and as the rest of the night's stars gathered onstage for the show's conclusion, they all sang it together, as the studio full of friends and rivals had once harmonized to the chorus of "All You Need Is Love." Only now Paul, and the rest of the world, seemed a long way from the days of love, love, love.

Yet, he was still here. Closing in on sixty, with loosening jowls and increasingly craggy eyes, the stubbornly boyish pop star had achieved the stage of life in which he was beloved simply for being himself, for remaining on his feet. He'd been around for so long that his mere presence evoked the way things used to be when we were all that much younger and stronger and full of possibility. As he'd said himself on *Flaming Pie, I go back so far, I'm in front of me!*

This compelling statement offered a piercing insight into the artist's actual circumstances. For to stand in Paul McCartney's shoes now was to live perpetually with one eye in the mirror, aware not just of the man he knew he was (aging, successful, scarred by tragedy and yet getting on with life), but also of the man he knew the world expected and perhaps needed him to be. Ageless, cheerful, endlessly creative, effortlessly beautiful. In the absence of the Beatles he had become, simply, The Beatle. The last Fab standing, assuming you didn't count Ringo, which hardly anyone did.

Then there was another new album, and another world tour. Another chance to feel that magnetic rush, the jet-engine roar in the darkness, the eruption of light in the eyes of the faces stretching away from his feet. To be at the center of it all and glimpse himself as the world would always see him: young and beautiful; the definitive artist of his time.

The shows in 2002 and 2003, his first tour in nearly a decade and the first time he'd ever played a solo tour without Linda at his side, began with costumed performers in the crowd, silently emulating characters and poses from famous artworks as they edged toward the front of the hall. The live-action surrealism drifted onto the stage, then faded to black when the houselights clicked off. The blackness filled with cheers, and these intensified as a large electric wall on the stage flashed to life, clicking through abstract patterns that eventually resolved into a sheer white screen that contained one larger-than-life black image: the trim, yet feminine profile of the Höfner bass. This incited another roar, then the real Höfner came into view, slung around the shoulders of another icon, now in shadow but just visible as he turned to check on his band, a quartet of younger, largely unknown musicians just settling into their places on the stage. Then the spotlights fired up, and there he stood beaming cheerily, his sixty-year-old cheeks smooth and flushed, his hair a glossy shade of chestnut. A quick count-off, then, that quickly, the place erupted in color and joy, drenched in a note-for-note re-creation of the sweet, tuneful psychedelia of "Hello, Goodbye," the air alive again with the eternally youthful puzzle of yes and no, high and low, stop and go, go, go.

And he sounded great! His voice somehow stronger and more clear than it had been in 1993. Go, go, going from Beatles standards to Wings hits to a handful of tracks from the brand-new album, then to impassioned tributes to fallen comrades George (a ukulele-laced take on "Something") and John (Paul's own musical eulogy, "Here Today"). The crowds paid homage on their feet, children and grandchildren hoisted on their shoulders, arms wrapped around childhood friends, newfound lovers, and longtime spouses, all singing, wiping away tears, thoroughly enraptured by the music and the moment, and all the memories of where they were and what they were doing back then. His music was their lives. Such was its staying power, such was the cultural, nearly spiritual, authority Paul McCartney could now claim.

Somehow, the engagement ring flew out the window. It was mid-May of 2002, less than a month before their scheduled-but-as-yet-top-secret wedding in Ireland. They were in Miami, vacationing at the Turnberry Isle Resort & Club in what the tabloids described as a "GBP 1,000-a-night" suite on the hotel's fifth floor. In just a few weeks Paul would turn sixty. His fiancée was thirty-four, several years younger than his stepdaughter, also named Heather, and just a bit older than Mary.

Other guests in the hotel heard shouting. It was late, sometime after midnight. Another guest apparently called for the hotel security guards, one of whom reported hearing the unmistakable voice of Sir Paul McCartney railing angrily, apparently about the couple's upcoming wedding. "He kept yelling that he wanted to call it off," the guard reported to England's *Daily Mail*.

Maybe the anonymous hotel employee was actually telling the

truth and not just dishing celebrity scandal for a quick payday. The reports noted a bit more screaming, then a sudden quiet. A few minutes later Sir Paul called down to the hotel's front desk asking for help. His fiancée's wedding ring, a sparkling diamond-and-sapphire bauble valued around $40,000, had accidentally fallen from the balcony and into the night.

Or maybe someone hurled it out of the window. The report in London's *News of the World* tabloid indicated that Paul's hand had done the honors, at or near the same time he had been heard to shout, "I don't want to marry you! The wedding's off!"

Or maybe they were just having fun. Mills, a few months later, dismissed the event as nothing but a silly game of toss-the-ring, in which the happy couple unwound in the predawn hours by chucking the diamond from hand to hand. As couples will do, just for laughs. "Having a joke, doing catch with the ring!" she said. This didn't explain the dismayed calls to security from the hotel guests awakened by the sound of a lovers' quarrel. The good news was that the ring was eventually located outside beneath a bush. The sharp-eyed hotel staffer who found the piece was handsomely rewarded, and the McCartney-Mills nuptials took place as scheduled. While Paul's wedding to Linda had been a simple registry-office procedure, a brief dash through wailing fans, then a quick luncheon with friends, McCartney Marriage version 2.0 resembled something closer to a coronation: a $3 million–plus affair held at a lakefront Irish castle, with family and friends in attendance alongside stars from music, film, and sport. And at a distance, a teeming horde of news reporters. In the United States, *People* magazine made the wedding a cover story, complete with photos of the castle, a reproduction of the official invitation, a bloom-by-bloom description of the flower arrangements, and a shot of the motorboat that served as their wedding-night boudoir.

Only the British tabloids were tacky enough to describe how Mary and Stella had only hours before begged their father not to go through with it. "It's still not too late to change your mind!" one so-called insider recounted hearing Stella insist.

Except that it obviously was too late, since his mind was made up, and that was all he needed to know. He had shrugged off the widower's cloak and come back to life. His then current album, *Driving*

Rain, overflows with testaments to his new love, described in the terms of loving flames, glittering sunbeams, and, in a tip of the imaginary bowler hat to nonsense poet Edward Lear, a "runcible tune" meant for the "queen of my heart." It's heartening to hear his enthusiasm, particularly in the wake of the emotional holocaust Linda's death had been. Meanwhile, the vibrant sonic textures Paul created with the help of producer David Kahne did a lot to make up for the songwriter's tendency to drape his happiness in layers of gauze and sentiment.

The upbeat songs also become more compelling when heard alongside the album's less settled tracks, from the cry of desperation in "Lonely Road" to the allusive study of post-traumatic life "She's Given Up Talking." Paul returns to cheerful trippiness with "Spinning on an Axis," but even here his optimism comes with an existential caveat: just because the sun rose yesterday morning is no guarantee that it will do the same thing tomorrow. *Certainly there's no guarantee / But I gotta believe it will be.*

At his age, Paul knew he had to gird his beliefs with a certain amount of action. He'd been around long enough to think in terms of the long view, and at the dawn of a new century he took store of his own legacy and set to refurbishing the parts that didn't quite satisfy him.

First came *Wingspan,* an *Anthology*-like look back at the first decade (or so) of his post-1970 career, from the ashes of the Beatles to the bust in Japan and then into *Tug of War* and thereabouts. "The great thing is [*Wingspan*] vindicates Linda," he told Paul Du Noyer, who was writing about the project for England's sophisticated pop-music magazine *Mojo.* "With all the slagging off she got . . . she always wanted the record put straight. And this does. You see her playing, you hear her singing beautifully. And you see what she was to the group. You see why she had to be in the group—she becomes the ballsiest member of it." Which seems particularly true when you see the footage of the group in its earliest incarnation, with Linda perched so tremulously behind her Fender Rhodes, her fingers stabbing away at chords she had only just learned and had yet to feel as anything other than numerical variations arrayed on the keys before her.

That's how it looks, at any rate. She seems far more comfortable in later tours, and it's easy to see (and hear) her influence on the band as the other musicians began to pick up on the loose-limbed charm that defined her husband's life so thoroughly. Still, *Wingspan* is a Paul production, so much so that his on-camera interviews are conducted by his daughter Mary, whose poise and professionalism are no match for her father's cheerful revisionism. Everything happens for a reason; no story has a sad ending; disputes are either glossed over or ignored completely. Of the six surviving Wings members, exactly zero are asked to speak, which is a bit odd. Was Paul afraid of what they might say, or simply unwilling to surrender the spotlight, even for a moment? It's hard to imagine it was strictly a financial decision—when Denny Seiwell, who gave Paul access to home movies he'd shot on the group's first tours, took the opportunity of their renewed correspondence to remind his old boss of the profit-sharing promises that had never materialized, his phone rang days later. "He called back in tears and said he was gonna make it right, and that's exactly what he did," Seiwell says. "Look, he's a great guy. He just got so insulated from his own life and problems . . . and as an artist you almost have to be."

Yet, certain problems were too troubling to escape his attention. For years Paul had been stewing about the way the songs he'd written for the Beatles had been credited. His secondary status in the traditional Lennon-McCartney composing credit had always bugged him a little, particularly given its ad hoc nature, and the way he'd been pushed to accept it by Brian when Paul was all of twenty years old. That stamp continued to define his career, which didn't trouble him when it came to the songs he and John had actually written together. But John had barely touched or not troubled himself at all with so many songs. They had, Paul insisted, always left room for the names to be shifted around, particularly if one partner had written the bulk of a song. But then everything had happened so quickly, then Brian had died abruptly, then the band was consumed by so much bitterness it was hard to imagine tossing the writing credits issue into the mix, too. Paul let it rest until late 1976, when he'd released the *Wings Over America* album and credited the five Beatles songs he'd played—all of them composed entirely or predominantly by himself—as McCartney-Lennon. Yoko complained a bit about that then, but John hadn't uttered a word, and so the issue faded.

Years passed. Then John was gone, and how could Paul even begin to raise the issue after that tragedy? So he didn't, for nearly twenty years. But it continued to bother him. Boy, did it bother him. Particularly when it came to the landmark songs he had written. Consider "Yesterday," a song he'd not only written alone, but also had to shield from John's teasing and, at times, vocal contempt. Now it was one of the most played songs in the history of recorded music. *His* song. *Entirely* his song. Yet when you looked at a songbook, whose name came first? Late in 1995 Linda finally picked up the telephone to ask Yoko if she would be willing to let Paul have primary credit for "Yesterday." Just that one song, that was all they were asking. "[She] had just been diagnosed with cancer," Paul recalled in 2003. "And Linda, God bless her, spent quite a bit of time on the phone with Yoko. Who said no."

It didn't matter anymore, Paul kept saying. "Now I must be resigned," he said with a shrug. "I don't think anyone gives a shit. It's an unfairness I'm willing to live with. I don't give a shit."

Though obviously he did care, quite deeply, which might explain why he had thought to throw in the detail about Linda being made to suffer simultaneously from the ravages of breast cancer and Yoko's intransigence. He continued to care when he came across a poetry anthology, just like the ones Dusty Durband used to show him back at the Liverpool Institute. Only now Paul's words, the lyrics to "Blackbird," were *in* the book. Which meant kids were studying his work, just as he'd once studied Chaucer, Shakespeare, Whitman, and all the rest. All of these impressionable children would stroll into the future certain that the primary author of this "Blackbird" poem was a fellow named John Lennon. "Now, John had nothing to do with those words which are extracted and put in a poetry book," Paul grumbled. "I think it's fair enough to put it in a poetry book by Paul McCartney."

Once again, Yoko didn't agree, and as the executor of John's estate, she held veto power over any move Paul wanted to make regarding Northern Songs credits. Unless, of course, he just went ahead and did it himself, which is precisely what Paul did for the nineteen Beatles songs he included on *Back in the U.S.,* the 2002 live album documenting his *Driving Rain* tour. Yoko threatened to sue, then backed off, perhaps because the issue had quickly blown into a media ruckus, most of which painted Paul in distinctly villainous terms. He was coming off so badly, in fact, that even Paul had to admit defeat. He was getting letters, he told one reporter, from fans accusing him of trying to do in his martyred old friend. "People saying, 'The fuck's he playing with! What the fuck!' I got a letter from a guy saying, 'Paul, you're doing yourself no favors. I've been a big fan of yours for years, but this terrible thing of your trying to ruin John's reputation . . .'" Paul practically wailed in frustration. "*Get the fuck out of here*! I'm not trying to ruin John's reputation at all!"

Of course not. He just wanted the record to reflect the truth as he knew it. Which was also the impulse behind *Let It Be . . . Naked,* the revised version of the Beatles' final, if not quite climactic, album. Paul still despised Phil Spector's heavy-handed mix of the album they had once envisioned as being completely raw and unprocessed. Spector's everything-plus-the–Mormon Tabernacle Choir approach to "The Long and Winding Road" had always seemed particularly egregious to Paul (though the "wall of sound" producer had been just as merciless in his ornamentation of John's "Across the Universe"), and Paul had spent the ensuing decades cursing the misbegotten "Let It Be," particularly in light of Glyn John's original, warts-and-all mix. "It was bare," he said many years later. "Kind of scary bare. But I loved it like that—no gloss at all." And guess who didn't allow it to be released that way? "Allen Klein decided it wasn't commercial enough, so we ought to gloss it up a bit and add some stuff."

Then in 2001 Paul bumped into Michael Lindsay-Hogg, who had directed the original *Let It Be* movie, and the two men commiserated about the sorry state of their multimedia project. The home-video release had gone out of print; the album was still a mess. But now they could change that! They could enhance and rerelease the movie; they could go through the original reels of audiotape and dig out the great, unprocessed album that still existed there! George approved of the idea before he died, but any Beatles fan who stayed up late fantasizing about finally having the "scary bare" version of "Get Back," perhaps loaded up with even more of the many, many hours of jam sessions and outtakes that had yet to be plucked from the tapes, would be disappointed. The 2003 *Let It Be . . . Naked* may have lost the strings and choirs of Spector's wildest imaginings, but it was every bit as tweaked and polished as his album. Some of the "live" songs are constructed from the best bits of separate performances; many of Spector's original edits and overdubs remain; others are added. The bawdy Liverpool drinking song "Maggie Mae" has been cut out entirely, along with John's improvised "Dig It." Also missing: the bits of John's witheringly sarcastic commentary that had once been inserted between the songs. Meanwhile, the release's bonus disc, teasingly called "Fly on the Wall," is little more than a trifle, a conglomeration of cheery on-set chat and slivers of unreleased music, none of which lasts longer than thirty seconds.

Not quite naked, as much as clad in a suit of Paul's design. As the last standing Beatle visionary, this was his privilege. It was his burden, too, though no one ever seemed to see it quite like that.

Forty years into his life as a world-altering celebrity; a working-class boy turned billionaire; a council-house resident turned landed aristocrat—there wasn't much anyone could tell Paul about anything. When he woke up in the morning, he'd take the time to cut up elaborate fruit salads, and he'd be damned if even the most fruit-resistant house guest didn't come to realize how wonderful it was. "People say, 'I never bothered to have fruit!' but once you cut it up and it's on a plate, you go, 'Yeah!'" he said. "People *love* it." Once he'd had his morning meal, he walked where he wanted to walk, took the tube to the office when it suited him, strolled with his dog in the park, and took his lunch in the pubs he had always frequented. The constraints of fame weren't for him. A stubborn mix of ordinary guy and other-worldly monarch, Paul had grown accustomed to following his own star, wherever it led, no matter what anyone else said.

So he'd married Heather Mills. So he laughed and rolled his eyes when she would hear him play his most famous works and not be able to place them. Then she had become pregnant and given birth to his daughter Beatrice in 2003. He had given up marijuana at his young wife's behest (or so he said) and taken up her anti-land-mine cause with all the enthusiasm he had once shown to Linda's animal rights activism. The couple became regular habitués of the world's tabloid newspapers and celebrity magazines, the timeless pop star and his golden-tressed model perpetually on the town, strolling the red carpet, bathed in the piercing light of media fixation. *Step out in front of me, baby,* Paul sang to his wife in a song written in the bloom of love, *they want you in the front line.* In interviews Paul chatted up his new life with joyous enthusiasm. "I've got a wonderful woman," he said repeatedly. Yet the marriage struck his friends and colleagues as something other than a perfect union.

Heather was reportedly uncomfortable in Paul's Sussex house—the home he'd shared with Linda for all those years—so they bought another, far more expensive home in the English countryside, then also a Beverly Hills manse located, happily enough, on Heather Road. They took to living and traveling at a pace far more plutocratic than the generally laid-back one he had long shared with Linda. Paul's longtime friends found themselves splayed between relief that he had found a new life and a growing dismay at where that life seemed to be headed. A wave of employees washed out of MPL, some after many years of reliable, valued service. Some were let go, others left of their own accord. While no one wanted to say anything in public, if only to avoid seeming bitter or mean, the talk in private had become overwhelming. "I never really got to know her," one longtime friend of Paul's says, only after being assured his name would never be associated with his words. "But I just never met anyone who ever had anything nice to say about her. And that tells you something."

Every relationship has its secret core, it's impossible for any outsider to truly know why one couple stays together while another falls apart. None of Paul's friends ever claimed to know exactly what was going on between Paul and his younger, seemingly mercurial spouse. But they saw what they saw. And the anecdotes they came away with were often unsettling.

At a Liverpool Institute for Performing Arts event, Mark Featherstone-Witty presented Paul with a copy of his memoir, *Optimistic, Even Then,* published as a part of the school's tenth anniversary celebration. Though Heather had never betrayed any interest in the school, he says, she snatched the book away from her husband and rifled quickly through its pages as the men chatted. "After a while we heard a voice saying, 'But I'm not in it! It's all *Linda*!'" Paul said nothing. Featherstone-Witty stammered something about Heather being in the next edition, and the conversation between the men resumed.

In London in 2004 the couple made a surprise appearance at a party celebrating the fortieth anniversary of *A Hard Day's Night*. A screening of the film's digitally enhanced print was followed by a reception for all the cast and crew members who had turned up. Old friends Paul hadn't seen in years were there, including the actor Victor Spinetti, the Apple executive Denis O'Dell, fellow Liverpudlian turned NEMS and Apple staffer Tony Bramwell, and others. They were all having a fine old time, drinking and laughing and carrying on together, right until Heather marched up to Paul and, with nary a nod to the faces around him, announced that she'd had enough. "There's nobody interesting here!" she snapped. "I'm going shopping!" Bramwell, who was standing with Paul just then, saw his friend gape. "His face was like 'What? *What!*'" But off she went, never to return. "He just stayed and got drunk. Maybe not drunk, but he stayed till the end, having the time of his life chatting with his old chums. Though he was obviously astonished she'd say something like that. It was unbelievable."

She wasn't the only one testing the limits of believable behavior. Paul made headlines one day for getting into a "foulmouthed fracas" with a photographer and bystanders who noticed the star taking a late-night gander at illusionist/publicity seeker David Blaine during his campaign to hang in a plastic box near London's Tower Bridge for some absurd period of time. The conflict began when a newspaper photographer, with a few camera-phone-wielding pedestrians in his wake, sidled up to take a snap of the ex-Beatle as he peered at the spectacle. This didn't suit Paul, who started shouting at the photographer and the camera-wielding bystanders. "Fuck off!" he yelled, gesturing at the Plexiglas box that held the inert form of David Blaine. "I've come to see *this* stupid cunt!" Whatever points Paul might have earned for his spot-on analysis of Blaine were sacrificed a few moments later when the star learned that his companion and longtime publicist, Geoff Baker, had actually pointed out his boss to the newsman and *suggested* he take the pictures. "I was drunk and stoned and no one seemed to be paying attention to us," Baker explained later.

Now Paul turned his ire on Baker, loudly firing him on the spot, then storming off into the night. Paul reconsidered and rehired Baker the next morning, but soon Paul was off on another misadventure, this time an ill-considered public argument with the London traffic warden who ticketed his Mercedes for being parked illegally near Stella's apartment in West London. True enough, Paul didn't have the correct tag to park in a residents-only space. But when the warden refused to accept that the disabled tag Paul did have on his car (due to Mills's artificial leg) might be an appropriate alternative, the star went ballistic. Much to the amusement of bystanders and then the city's tabloids, which noted the disparity between the price of the ticket (£50) and the billion-pound fortune Paul could draw on to pay it.

Other stories simmered in the media. When Baker did finally part ways with MPL in September 2004, word in the papers was that his exiling had been Heather's doing. Baker had worked for Paul for fifteen years and had been particularly close to Linda. None of this appealed to the new Mrs. McCartney, whose hand had already, the stories said, been placed on the whip leading the purge around MPL. Paul denied it all, heatedly, along with the ongoing rumors about the rift between his daughters and their young stepmother. But all this, along with a general suspicion about her role in his now heavily dyed hair and "groovy granddad outfits" (according to the *Mirror*), seemed to indicate that this ambitious young woman had led her national institution of a husband astray.

Something was going wrong in his life. Loath as Paul was to ever admit that in public, he couldn't help revealing himself in his music. His next album, *Chaos and Creation in the Backyard,* gestured toward the traditional McCartney palette of sweet romance, ebullient pop, and eccentric musings on life's quirks. But everywhere, even when it doesn't seem intentional, the songs slip toward darker, less settled terrain. Coproducer Nigel Godrich (best known for his work with Radiohead) encourages the drift by dropping in tape loops and other unsettling textures. Paul's melodies float in unexpected directions, often in the service of lyrics that portray love in terms of desperation and surrender. Another song, "Riding to Vanity Fair," is an icy farewell to a friend who hasn't lived up to the narrator's standards. *I'll use the time to think about myself,* Paul sings, without even a hint of sorrow, let alone empathy. The target of "Vanity Fair" remains a mystery, but it's easier to connect the dots in "Friends to Go," sung from the perspective of a husband hiding away from his wife as she entertains friends downstairs. *I've spent a lot of time on my own,* he says, then muses about a passing domestic storm and the future of the relationship, *if we're gonna carry on.*

That's a compelling *if.* But as the leadoff track (and album title) made clear, it's often impossible to distinguish between courage and recklessness, to say nothing of creative tumult and full-on chaos. Both Paul and Heather continued to deny their marriage was troubled. But the rumors continued in the papers, and when the couple announced their split in May 2006, the stories about Mills grew more dark. Aspects of her biography, particularly those that involved child abuse and other traumas, were called into question. More than one old acquaintance referred to her as a compulsive liar. Which seemed comforting when the split veered toward divorce, and Mills filed papers that made the darkest possible allegations about her husband. That he was a problem drinker and serious dope fiend. That he was physically abusive and had even stabbed her with the shards from a broken glass.

Then it all got even worse. In the fall of 2006 Mills and her associates started leaking accusations about Paul that were so shocking and unbelievable that they felt compelled to point out that they had all been captured on tape. Paul, she asserted, had not only beaten Mills, but confessed that he had physically abused Linda, too, during their supposedly idyllic marriage. Mills had even mocked Stella on this account, accusing her husband's daughter of being full of bitterness. "Is it because you can't forgive your father for what he did to your mother?"

It all seemed to say more about the accuser than the accused. If Mills had counted on the media's skepticism toward her estranged husband to help her cause, she had miscalculated. No matter his well-established flaws, the man the papers referred to as Macca was still a beloved figure in the United Kingdom, a pop-culture institution and a knight of the realm. Mills quickly devolved into a villainous figure known as Mucca—a grasping harridan attempting to tear down a national monument. When she announced plans to sue the London tabloid the *Sun* for libeling her during its (heatedly pro-Paul) coverage of the divorce, the newspaper not only stood by its original reporting, but went on to taunt her by printing a graphic that reasserted six central accusations (you're a hooker; liar; porn star; fantasist; trouble maker; shoplifter) and instructed her to tell them which ones she found inaccurate: "Tick the appropriate boxes."

Mucca. Lady Mucca. Liar Mucca. Every newspaper seemed to have its own variation, and Mills did her best to live up to all of them. She ran through lawyers and publicists at an epic rate, then launched a public relations campaign that divided between criticism of Paul and tearful talk of her own inner torment and suicidal impulses. Her ex-husband, ex-boyfriends, and a litany of ex-friends took turns ripping into her, often noting their own recollections of her lying and cheating her way through life. While such talk seemed to underscore her lack of trustworthiness, it also diminished Paul. He had not only fallen for her, but had done so with such ill-placed trust he had married her without a prenuptial agreement that might have protected the bulk of his fortune.

What was he thinking now that things had turned so ugly? After all, Paul could almost certainly have bought his way out of the mess with a small fraction of his accrued wealth, but parting with money had never been his strong suit. He knew he was right; he knew it was really his money. What had Jim McCartney taught him about fighting for what was his all those years ago when marching his son off to testify against the boys who had stolen his watch? So, publicity be damned, Paul rode the roller coaster all the way into court, where his estranged spouse served as her own lawyer. Perhaps her most striking achievement as such came at the end of the trial, when Mills dumped a glass of water over the head of her ex-husband's attorney, Fiona Shackleton. Mills left court with slightly more than £24 million (more than £100 million less than she had asked for) and even more sour words for her ex-husband. The judge's ruling dismissed Mills as "erratic, out of control and vengeful."

Even Ringo, who in nearly fifty years of public life had never seemed to have a bad word for anyone, couldn't bear it. Asked his opinion on Mills just after the breakup, his words described the feelings of the empire, and perhaps the rest of the world, too: "She's just awful."

More chaos, even more creation. Now he was sixty-four, sixty-five, sixty-six years old, and moving just as quickly as ever. In 2007 he bailed on EMI for the second time in forty-five years, moving to Hear

Music, a boutique label run by the Seattle-based Starbucks coffee monolith. He'd had it with old-fashioned record companies, Paul explained. They moved too slowly, required too much machinery, and generally did things in a way that had nothing to do with the twenty first century. Certainly, Starbucks made a point of heralding *Memory Almost Full* as if it had been retrieved from Mt. Sinai itself. The wave of publicity swept the album into Billboard's Top 3, and it sold far better than his last two studio albums.

No coincidence, perhaps, that it was also his most tuneful, emotionally striking work in some time. Recorded with the production assistance again of David Kahne, the album moves through a mostly appealing litany of ballads, rockers, and one or two art songs on the way to an *Abbey Road*–style medley of tunes that serve as a kind of musical autobiography. Beginning with "Vintage Clothes," a joyous paean to the circular nature of life and fashion, the cycle continues with "That Was Me," a bass-driven series of glancing memories of childhood games, early shows at the Cavern, the *Royal Iris* party boat, the EMI studios on Abbey Road, and beyond. *It's pretty hard to take it in,* he wails. *But that was me!* On and on, through languid memories of adolescent torpor ("Head in the Clouds"), then the awesome/hideous world of celebrity ("House of Wax"). This vision ends in flames and ash, then a moment of silence introduces the unadorned piano of "The End of the End," in which the most boyish of celebrities projects himself into his dying breath, then beyond. Singing with the piano and a simple string arrangement, his voice traces a melodic line that rises like a departed spirit, slow and meandering, but ever upward as he wishes for his survivors to greet his death with nothing but continuing life: stories and jokes, the sound of bells and songs to sing. *Hung out like blankets that lovers have played on / And laid on, while listening to songs that were sung.*

It's a gently majestic song, as direct as it is unsentimental. For even as the sky around him darkens, Paul continues to reach for the light on the horizon. Once again, he sounds the theme that has always animated his music. In the darkest of times—when the night is cloudy; when there's nothing but a sad song to sing; when he's feeling lost and alone with a hundred miles to go—he does what he's always done. He turns on the radio and keeps right on moving.

• • •

He's still moving. Now with a whole new reason to smile, given a new girlfriend, this one closer to his own age and experience. A much more natural fit, according to the friends who speak of such things in public. Nancy Shevell now accompanies him on his meanderings on the earth; seen one day sailing in the Bahamas, then on another day buying gas and snacks to fuel a weeklong journey west through the American Southwest on what's left of Route 66, then on his arm strolling through the throngs of gallery visitors and pub crawlers on the streets near his offices on the edge of Soho Square.

When Liverpool was declared Europe's cultural capital for 2008, a year of activity extended to arts of all disciplines, but it climaxed in June as the city's favorite surviving son played a vast open-air concert at the Anfield soccer stadium. That was the night he opened with "Hippy Hippy Shake" (for the first time in, what, forty-eight years?) and included yet another stirring tribute to John, this time a medley connecting "A Day in the Life" to "Give Peace a Chance." He played to a reported 350,000 fans at a special show in Kiev a few weeks later, then traveled to Quebec to help celebrate the city's four hundredth anniversary with 275,000 fans in attendance. From there he traveled to Tel Aviv, Israel, to perform a peace-themed concert for a relatively intimate crowd of forty thousand.

Everywhere, Paul's appearances were greeted with the publicity and gravity of an official state visit. In Israel he was denounced by pro-Palestinian activists and threatened with death by radical Syrian Islamists. "My message is a global one," he said. "And . . . a peaceful one."

Increasingly peaceful. Paul's on-again, off-again feud with Yoko Ono has simmered down in recent years, thanks in part to their joint sponsorship of Cirque du Soleil's successful staging of Beatles music in Las Vegas' Mirage Casino beginning in 2006. The show combined some compelling (if a bit conservative) mash-ups of Beatles music, co-produced by George Martin and his son, Giles, with the troupe's gymnastic choreography into an abstract narrative. The piece is often quite moving, in unexpected ways, though the effect diminishes a bit when you stroll onto the casino floor and notice the bars and shops rebranded with Beatles iconography. Paul, Ringo, and their partners' widows appeared together at *Love*'s first-anniversary performance in June 2007, at which Paul helped dedicate a monument to John. Yoko accepted the honor for her late husband, referring to Paul as "a magnificent man," and all the surviving Beatles and their kin as "family," with all the breakups and arguments such bonds entail. "The Beatles family," she concluded, "is a very, very strong family."

They have to be, given the toll Beatledom seems determined to extract. Brian Epstein's abrupt death in 1967, then Mal Evans gunned down in strange circumstances by the Los Angeles police in 1976, then John in 1980, then George nearly done in by his own lunatic in 1999, only to die of cancer in 2001. Ringo's first wife, Maureen, died of leukemia in 1994, then Linda passed away in 1998. Neil Aspinall had parted ways with Apple in 2007, after more than forty-five years of nonstop service to the Beatles and their various iterations. But he remained the insider's insider, one of the few mortals who had seen it all—from the Liverpool Institute to the Cavern to *Ed Sullivan* to the roof of 3 Savile Row, all the way to the *Anthology* and beyond—from the inside looking out. This only made his death, to cancer in March 2008, all the more shocking.

Less news-making, yet no less devastating, was the 1993 death of Ivan Vaughan, the schoolmate who had thought to introduce Paul to his neighbor and occasional bandmate John Lennon back in the early summer of 1957. Ivan, who shared Paul's June 18, 1942, birthday, had ended up living the life Paul might have had, had he never become a Beatle, the version that ran through college and then into a career as a classics scholar and teacher, the hardworking middle-class father and husband. Ivan had been stricken with Parkinson's disease in the late seventies, but he had cheerfully endured and remained close to his famous friend. They saw one another regularly, if not often, and traded silly notes and postcards. Ivan's death inspired Paul to turn his hand to poetry, something he hadn't done since they were both students at the Liverpool Institute. The first poem was called "Ivan," and soon there were others, some just scraps of verse, others longer and more thought through. Many were published, alongside an array of song lyrics, in the volume *Blackbird Singing* in 2001.

Created in solitude, away from his own sense of his audience's presence and expectations, the poems are intensely emotional, sometimes bracingly intimate explorations of Paul's feelings. So many years of cheerful pop tunes and lush ballads make it all the more surprising to confront such erotically charged love poems, then the starkly composed descriptions of the grief that followed Linda's death. As he'd done after the death of his mother, Paul called out again to God to explain the meaning behind this latest unthinkable tragedy. Was there something they had done wrong? Something they should have known? How could a rational, loving God take so much away from him, for no clear reason?

Lying alone in his bedroom on Forthlin Road in 1956, Paul heard only the wind in the street and felt only emptiness. But four decades later even his darkest moment contained a glimmer of light, enough to imagine the voice of God calling back to him. "I am here," he wrote, contemplating the sound of the creator's words in his ears. "I am here in every song you sing."

23

Paul has visited the house at 20 Forthlin Road in the Liverpool suburb of Allerton at least twice in the last decade. Unfortunately, he didn't think to call ahead to the house's live-in caretaker, so John Halliday was out both times, leaving his door locked. Thus, Paul got only as far as his old front stoop. He contented himself to peering in the window and charming bystanders with tales of neighborhood days gone by. He seemed like such a regular guy, they all said later. Just another neighbor, come and gone.

Except he's so much more than that. Consider that Britain's National Trust bought the deed to 20 Forthlin Road in 1995. The Trust spent a few years restoring the furnishings to the tastes of the home's 1950s residents, then in 1998 opened its doors to the public. Now anyone who books a visit with the Trust can walk past the neat hedge and through the stamp-size yard, then step into the house that once was Paul McCartney's boyhood home. Walk up the stairs and take the first door to your left, you'll find yourself in Paul's small, thin room. A single bed stands against one wall, a bedside table is beneath the window, a green wicker chair against the other wall. Look out the window to your left and off in the distance you'll see a line of trees on a hill. That's Woolton, the much nicer neighborhood where John Lennon's old house has also been restored and opened for viewing. "Pop music . . . has helped to transform British popular culture," notes a National Trust booklet about Paul's house. "From this ordinary council house emerged a sound that touched the lives of millions."

The tourists come in specially painted vans, wave after wave of them during the season, and walk in Paul's footsteps with a kind of ecstatic detachment. By standing on these floors, by breathing this air and peering through these windows, they're trying to forge a deeper connection to the music. To dip their toes in the Beatles' headwaters and feel the spiritual current that animated everything that would come. Maybe some of them succeed. It's not always easy to find, let alone gain access to, as Paul would surely attest. But the feeling is still there, somewhere. Paul has spent a lot of the last forty years trying to, too. Sometimes he can't even make it through the door.

It's been nearly thirty years since John's murder, but memories of him continue to inspire Paul and haunt him a little bit, too. At times you can feel him straining to live up to his old partner's example: his rapier wit; his searing insights into people and the world around him. Other times Paul seems to thumb his nose in the old boy's direction, stomping on his spectral toes, daring him to reappear and make himself known. *Go ahead, have a vision,* he snarls. *I'm the man on the flaming pie!* Paul has taken to playing that song, "Flaming Pie," in concert, and it's always a curious moment in shows so dominated by the Beatles, by the harmonious ideal they embodied, both in person and in song.

At times Paul seems a captive of that ideal. A prisoner of his own past, doomed to spend the rest of his life as an increasingly faded version of himself in more glorious times; singing the same old songs the same old way, straining to hear the same otherworldly roar his labors have always attracted. This is when he seems most detached from his real brilliance, when he seems to be enacting a modern version of the legend of Narcissus, too in love with his own youthful reflection to recognize how unappealing his mature face has become.

Paul doesn't make all the decisions at Apple Corps., the Beatles once-and-ongoing corporate seat, but the company's tightfisted grasp on the group's legacy has led to some surprisingly self-defeating gestures. Consider the group's years-long trademark battle against Apple Computer, and the resulting absence of all Beatles product from the increasingly important iTunes online sales center. Similarly, the Beatles for years refused, somewhat inexplicably, to allow the vast majority of their catalog to be remixed with the precise tools of the digital era—an intransigence that grew all the more infuriating when you heard the few songs (the *Yellow Submarine* song track; the remixed songs on the sound track to the Cirque du Soleil's *Love* production) that have been granted the clarity and power of a digital remix. They bowed to the remix demands, quite belatedly in 2009.

Yet Paul works overtime to maintain his own currency in the post-millennial age. He provided a live vocal to a verse or two of "Yester-day" in a rap/rock/pop performance led by Jay-Z and members of the group Linkin Park. He grants interviews to bloggers and alternative weeklies, even as he turns away some major magazines (and biogra-phers). He keeps his hair darkened and his skin strangely smooth, cruis-ing toward seventy with all the casual ease of a man half his age. Sometimes he gets away with it. Other times it just seems . . . awkward.

Right until he falls under the spell of the music again. As ever, it's his most intuitive and truest language. *Take a sad song and make it better,* he sang once, and that has, more or less, been the mission that has guided his work. Music is his balm, particularly in times of trou-ble. The dual shocks of Linda's death and his calamitous second mar-riage sent him reeling, but as long as he could find his way to the studio, he could project his troubles into sound, organize them into music, and find a way to resolve them. *Take it away,* he sang, and that's exactly what happens when he starts to play. The music takes him away, it eases the pain, it takes the sad song and makes it better.

In 2008 Paul spent time in the studio with Martin Glover, the pro-ducer better known as Youth, with whom he formed a duo they called the Fireman. They had worked together on and off during the 1990s, creating two albums of trance-style electronica, most of it pleasant, if unspectacular, dance music. But as they started a new album in 2008, Paul and Youth decided to apply the Fireman ethic of spontaneous creation to some traditional song structures, complete with vocals. The unmistakable tone of Paul's voice would obviously keep the work from being truly anonymous, but even the pretense of working under-cover helped free his muse, Paul said. It was, he said, the same impulse that had guided the Beatles when they pretended to be Sgt. Pepper's band. "It gives you the feeling that anything is possible." Or, as he put it more whimsically on his own Web site, "The Fireman takes your hand and leads you through the blaze to places you didn't know you wanted to go."

Which in this case turned out to be the deepest recesses of his own psyche. After thirteen days of work, during which they recorded thirteen songs, each imagined, written, arranged, performed, and produced in a single day, the duo had slightly more than an hour of music. They called the album *Electric Arguments,* a phrase Paul found in an Allen Ginsberg poem, "Kansas City to St. Louis," that had mentioned hearing "Michelle" on the radio. "The music soars above," Ginsberg wrote, and so, too, does *Electric Arguments.*

Once again, it's Paul's life set to music. It's the gut-wrenching outrage over his ruined marriage, now played out as an electric blues, complete with wailing harmonica, sneering slide guitar, a dive-bombing bass, and the full-throated screams of a man done wrong. It's childhood memories of magpies paired off on a tree limb (*one for sorrow / two for joy*), projected into a cryptic reminder to *face down fear,* particularly when following one's heart. It's renewed promise and love, projected into anthems to innocence ("Sing the Changes") and the simplest rituals of courtship ("Dance 'til We're High"). It's the mysteries of far-off lands and the slinky pulse of people on the move through the night ("Highway," in which *everybody's wonderin', What's that sound!*). It's the spiritual fervor of the weird old America, and the affirmation that comes with each day's sunrise. All these things and more, woven into layers of instruments, voices, and electronic noise. Bird noises and Indian melodies; ringing guitars and wheezing harmonicas; the thump of a guitar case; the light jangle of a mandolin; a bass line leaping up from the floor, doing a quick melodic pirouette, then settling down again, making way for another line of melody, another thread of harmony.

It might stand the test of the ages, or it might not. But for now it's a joy to hear, if only because it's so easy to feel the joy that went into its creation.

Listen to me . . . can you hear me . . . This is the essential question, it's the deepest, most important question he can ask. *Feel the choir, feel the thunder,* he sings, and the skies open again. The music plays and the light pours down. *Everywhere a sense of childlike wonder!*

NOTES

CHAPTER 1

6 *"more than a place where"*: Paul Du Noyer; *Liverpool: Wondrous Place* (London: Virgin Books, 2002), p. 1.

10 *"uncomplicated"*: Bob Spitz, *The Beatles* (New York: Little, Brown, 2005), p. 73.

10 *"He looked like"*: Hunter Davies, *The Beatles* (New York/London: W. W. Norton, 1968), p. 23.

10 *"He turned out"*: Ibid., p. 23.

12 *"The McCartney boys"*: Spitz, *Beatles*, p. 80.

12 *"He was a charmer"*: Author interview with Tony Bramwell, 3/08.

12 *"He could charm"*: Spitz, *Beatles*, p. 80.

12 *"like a superspy"*: Barry Miles, *Paul McCartney: Many Years from Now* (New York: Henry Holt, 1997), p. 10.

13 *"Dear me, my first"*: Miles, *Paul McCartney*, p. 9.

13 *"Lots and lots of pictures"*: Ibid., p. 7–8.

CHAPTER 2

15 *"eminently likable"*: Chris Salewicz, *McCartney* (New York: St. Martin's Press, 1986), p. 30.

16 *"never in a bootlicking way"*: Ibid., p. 29.

16 *"a conformist rebel"*: Ibid., p. 33.

16 *"What I didn't like"*: Beatles, *Anthology* (San Francisco: Chronicle Books, 2000), p. 18.

17 *"What's up, Mum"*: Michael McCartney, *The Macs* (New York: Putnam Books, 1981), unnumbered.

17 *"in case I don't"*: Bob Spitz, *The Beatles* (New York: Little, Brown, 2005), p. 89.

18 *"It was terrible"*: Barry Miles, *Paul McCartney: Many Years from Now* (New York: Henry Holt, 1997), p. 20.

18   *"I would have liked"*: McCartney, *Macs,* unnumbered.
19   *"What are we going to do"*: Hunter Davies, *The Beatles* (New York/London: W. W. Norton, 1968), p. 27.
19   *"It was a silly joke"*: Ibid.
19   *"That was the worst thing"*: Beatles, *Anthology,* p. 19.
19   *"See, the prayers"*: Davies, *Beatles,* p. 27.
20   *"I think it shattered"*: Salewicz, *McCartney,* p. 29.
20   *"I was determined"*: Beatles, *Anthology,* p. 19.
20   *"It'll go better"*: McCartney, *Macs,* unnumbered.
20   *"There was a lot"*: Miles, *Paul McCartney,* p. 22.
21   *"It was Ivan who"*: Dennis Ellam, *Daily Mirror,* "The Kid Who Started the Beatles," October 9, 2005.
22   *"It's him!"*: Beatles, *Anthology,* p. 21.
23   *"It was music,"*: Ibid., p. 21.
23   *"He was lost"*: Davies, *Beatles,* p. 31.
24   *"Something was making me"*: Miles, *Paul McCartney,* p. 23.
24   *"It's a funny, corny little song"*: Beatles, *Anthology,* p. 20.
26   *"I saw Ivan coming in"*: Author interview with Colin Hanton, 12/07.
27   *"a little sloshed"*: Beatles, *Anthology,* p. 20.
27   *"There's no way"*: Author interview with Rod Davis, 11/07.
27   *"It was uncanny"*: Spitz, *Beatles,* p. 97.
27   *"He could play and sing"*: Ibid., p. 97.
28   *"I'd been kingpin"*: Davies, *Beatles,* p. 33.

CHAPTER 3

29   *"He was a born leader"*: Chris Salewicz, *McCartney* (New York: St. Martin's Press, 1986), p. 66.
30   *"he displayed no qualms"*: Ibid., p. 32.
30   *"No way"*: Michael McCartney, *The Macs* (New York: Putnam Books, 1981), unnumbered.
31   *"John told me"*: Author interview with Rod Davis, 11/07.
31   *"He was very nice"*: Author interview with Colin Hanton, 12/07.
31   *"Paul was very intent"*: Ibid.
32   *"John did have a mean streak"*: Davis, 11/07.
32   *"If John didn't like him"*: Hanton, 12/07.
33   *"John was caustic"*: Barry Miles, *Paul McCartney: Many Years from Now* (New York, Henry Holt, 1997), p. 32.
34   *"Then somebody, probably John"*: Ibid.
35   *"We saw ourselves"*: Ibid., p. 36.
36   *"a complete idiot"*: Davis, 11/07.
36   *"It wasn't the life for me"*: Hunter Davies, *The Beatles* (New York/London: W. W. Norton, 1968), p. 33.
37   *"A terrible dump"*: Hanton, 12/07.

37   *"Paul gave me a list"*: Author interview with John "Duff" Lowe, 3/08.

38   *"The girls usually sat"*: Hanton, 12/07.

39   *"They were on the platform"*: Lowe, 3/08.

39   *"It was a dreadful noise"*: Ibid.

41   *"A lot of people lost their patience"*: Author interview with Bill Harry, 11/07.

41   *"special bond"*: Miles, *Paul McCartney*, p. 49.

41   *"I just called them the College Band"*: Harry, 4/08.

42   *"I never felt"*: Hanton, 12/07.

42   *"I rounded on Paul"*: Ibid.

CHAPTER 4

43   *"I was very conscious of gathering material"*: Beatles, *Anthology* (San Francisco: Chronicle Books, 2000), p. 42.

44   *"the greatest teacher"*: Barry Miles, *Paul McCartney: Many Years from Now* (New York: Henry Holt, 1997), p. 40.

44   *"I was trying to prepare myself"*: Ibid., p. 43.

45   *"I ruined Paul's life"*: Author interview with Ray Connolly, 11/07.

47   *"Welcome to the Casbah!"*: Pete and Rory Best, *The Beatles: The True Beginnings* (New York: Thomas Dunne Books, 2003), p. 31.

47   *"Are you all enjoying yourselves?"*: Ibid., p. 32.

48   *"We looked down on them"*: Author interview with Brian Griffiths, 3/08.

49   *"It's so vivid to me"*: Ibid.

50   *"Not an important chapter"*: Barry Miles, *The Beatles: A Diary* (New York: Omnibus Press, 1998), p. 24.

51   *"This is Pete"*: Pete Best with Bill Harry, *The Best Years of the Beatles* (London: Headline Book Publishing, 1996), p. 31.

52   *"I've had some amazing news"*: Michael McCartney, *The Macs* (New York: Putnam Books, 1981), unnumbered.

52   *"It was a 'that's more'"*: Beatles, *Anthology*, p. 45.

53   *"We were like carnival barkers"*: Ibid., p. 47.

54   *"We'd scoffed at them"*: Author interview with Howie Casey, 3/08.

55   *"He could play for more"*: Griffiths, 3/08.

56   *"It wasn't a good thing to go"*: Author interview with Astrid Kirchherr, 11/07.

57   *"They did anything I told them"*: Ibid.

58   *"There stood an emaciated skeleton"*: McCartney, *Macs*, unnumbered.

58   *"That's pretty good"*: Beatles, *Anthology*, 56.

59   *"We all knew"*: Author interview with Chas Newby, 12/07.

60   *"Well, it was a great gig"*: Ibid.

CHAPTER 5

62   *"Paul sometimes freaked"*: Author interview with Astrid Kirchherr, 11/07.
62   *"I've got cards"*: Author interview with Bill Harry, 4/08.
62   *"I don't remember"*: Author e-mail interview with Tony Sanders, 8/08.
63   *"Stu wore dark glasses"*: Ibid.
63   *"I was always practical"*: Barry Miles, *Paul McCartney: Many Years from Now* (New York: Henry Holt, 1997), p. 65.
65   *"They were just"*: Author interview with Mike Byrne, 4/08.
65   *"They would sing"*: David Jones, "He Loved Me, Yeah, Yeah, Yeah," *Daily Mail*, 10/11/97.
66   *"Paul said it looked"*: Ibid.
66   *"I'm a bit"*: Author interview with Iris Fenton (Caldwell), 5/08.
66   *"Being a girl of that"*: Ibid.
67   *"It made him very"*: Ibid.
68   *"It was as if"*: Sanders, 8/08.
70   *"He came and told me"*: Author interview with Peter Brown, 10/07.
70   *"You see, I'd lived"*: Author interview with Rex Makin, 12/07.
71   *"A bit of a drama-queen move"*: Author interview with Tony Barrow, 12/07.
71   *"And we'd do it"*: Miles, *Paul McCartney*, p. 96.
72   *"John was just laughing"*: Kirchherr, 11/07.
73   *"They really cared"*: Ibid.
74   *"He said, 'Will you walk'"*: Author interview with Sam Leach, 4/08.

CHAPTER 6

76   *"He looked slyly"*: Author e-mail exchange with Tony Sanders, 9/08.
77   *"I depended on him"*: Hunter Davies, *The Beatles* (New York/London: W. W. Norton, 1968), p. 111.
77   *"I knew that was where"*: Beatles, *Anthology* (San Francisco: Chronicle Books, 2000), p. 75.
78   *"It was a constant fight"*: Ibid.
78   *"There wasn't even a murmur"*: Alistair Taylor, *With the Beatles* (London: John Blake, 2003), pp. 32–33.
78   *"Paul was the one"*: George Martin with Jeremy Hornsby, *All You Need Is Ears* (New York: St. Martin's Press, 1979), pp. 137–38.
79   *"When they left"*: Mark Lewisohn, *The Beatles: Recording Sessions* (New York: Harmony Books, 1988), p. 17.
79   *"quite certain that their songwriting"*: Beatles, *Anthology*, p. 123.
80   *"The people down south"*: Martin with Hornsby, *All You Need Is Ears*, p. 127.
81   *"Congratulations, boys"*: Lewisohn, *Beatles*, p. 23.
82   *"An intimidating standard"*: Tim Riley, *Tell Me Why* (New York: Knopf, 1988), p. 60.
83   *"He had an intuitive understanding"*: Author interview with Tony Barrow, 12/07.

83   *"Brian! Two pounds, fifty-three!"*: Ibid.
83   *"The audience was always"*: Beatles, *Anthology,* p. 95.
84   *"But it could be"*: Ibid., p. 96
85   *"That'll do, they're on"*: Brian Southall with Rupert Perry, *Northern Songs* (London: Omnibus Press, 2006), p. 13.
85   *"A small office"*: Ibid.
85   *"John and I didn't know"*: Ibid., p. 17.
85   *"They'd taken a vow"*: Author interview with Bill Harry, 11/07.
85   *"I think [John] fixed things"*: Beatles, *Anthology,* p. 94.
87   *"That was really the birth"*: Author interview with Chris Hutchins, 4/08.
88   *"John, John. Stop it"*: Ibid.
88   *"I just saw both of them disappearing"*: Ibid.

CHAPTER 7

90   *"Paul always had this aura"*: Author interview with Billy Hatton, 8/08.
90   *"Oh, it wasn't a joke"*: Author interview with Rex Makin, 12/07.
90   *"I was going to rearrange his face"*: Hatton, 8/08.
93   *"Ta! Thank you!"*: Michael Braun, *Love Me Do! The Beatles' Progress* (Harmondsworth, UK: Penguin, 1964), p. 41.
93   *"I don't feel like I imagine"*: Ibid., p. 33.
93   *"we get the going show-business rates"*: Ibid., p. 32.
93   *"Like a dog"*: Hatton, 8/08.
94   *"That's just typical Paul"*: Braun, *Love Me Do!,* p. 82.
95   *"I think he saw his chance"*: Author interview with Chris Hutchins, 4/08.
95   *"Dick's face fell"*: Ibid.
95   *"He keeps saying he's not interested"*: Braun, *Love Me Do!,* p. 82.
96   *"Let's hope they're still"*: Ibid., p. 47.
97   *"They didn't care much"*: Author interview with Geoffrey Ellis, 11/07.
101 *"As soon as we got outside"*: Isla Blair interview with Fiona Moore, Faction Paradox Web site, http://www.kaldorcity.com/people/ibinterview.html, undated.
101 *"rollicking, madcap fun"*: Bosley Crowther, "Screen: The Four Beatles in 'A Hard Day's Night,'" *New York Times,* 8/12/64.
101 *"I think a lot of these songs"*: Barry Miles, *Paul McCartney: Many Years from Now* (New York: Henry Holt, 1997), p. 164.

CHAPTER 8

103 *"They were flying high"*: Author interview with Roy Corlett, 4/08.
104 *"They were so cocooned"*: Author interview with Tony Barrow, 12/07.
104 *"It was just madness"*: Author interview with Peter Brown, 10/07.
105 *"Just think of* Satyricon*"*: Jann Wenner, *Lennon Remembers* (Harmondsworth, UK: Penguin, 1970), p. 84.

105 *"Paul was wild"*: Author interview with Chris Hutchins, 4/08.

105 *"trawlers, trawling for sex"*: Barry Miles, *Paul McCartney: Many Years from Now* (New York: Henry Holt, 1997), p. 142.

105 *"He didn't speak to me"*: Hutchins, 4/08.

106 *"Well, can you fix that"*: Ibid.

106 *"I'm Donald O'Connor's daughter!"*: Ibid.

106 *"John, fucking hell!"*: Ibid.

107 *"It was like his career"*: Author interview with Nat Weiss, 10/07.

107 *"Lennon got looser"*: Hutchins, 4/08.

107 *"I discovered the Meaning"*: Miles, *Paul McCartney*, p. 189.

108 *"Paul was really the most"*: Barrow, 12/07.

108 *"They come to Elvis"*: Hutchins, 4/08.

108 *"He was dragging his heels"*: Ibid.

109 *"You tell the world"*: Ibid.

110 *"The audience rose"*: Author interview with Geoffrey Ellis, 11/07.

110 *"He'd coerce the others"*: Barrow, 12/07.

111 *"Neil Aspinall used to explain"*: Weiss, 10/07.

112 *"When this paper tears"*: Barry Miles, *In the Sixties* (London: Jonathan Cape, 2002), p. 72.

113 *"There was always something"*: Author interview with Gordon Waller, 4/08.

113 *"Coming through, Colonel!"*: Miles, *Paul McCartney*, p. 121.

114 *"That's it!"*: David Sheff, interview with John Lennon and Yoko Ono, *Playboy*, 1/81.

116 *"They were the kings"*: Author interview with Ray Connolly, 11/07.

118 *"In that respect"*: Bob Spitz, *The Beatles* (New York: Little, Brown, 2005), p. 560.

CHAPTER 9

121 *"It was stuff happening"*: Barry Miles, *Paul McCartney: Many Years from Now* (New York: Henry Holt, 1997), p. 121.

122 *"had a great little talk"*: Ibid., p. 126.

122 *"Jane was a teenaged"*: Author interview with Tony Bramwell, 3/08.

122 *"I must know"*: Beatles, *Anthology* (San Francisco: Chronicle Books, 2000), p. 210.

122 *"the other guys were sort of partying"*: Miles, *Paul McCartney*, p. 116.

122 *"a very rich avant-garde period"*: *Paul McCartney World Tour* program, 1989–90, p. 51.

123 *"He seemed to know nothing"*: Barry Miles, *In the Sixties* (London: Jonathan Cape, 2002), p. 76.

124 *"He was sure"*: Ibid.

125 *"It went on"*: Ibid., p. 102.

125 *"All you do"*: Ibid., p. 106.

126 *"the strangest briefing"*: *Paul McCartney World Tour* program, p. 53.

127 *"There was controlled chaos"*: Author interview with Tony Barrow, 12/07.

127 *"I was more ready"*: Miles, *Paul McCartney*, p. 381.
130 *"I don't have easy"*: Ibid., p. 289.
131 *"the environment thing"*: Barry Miles, "A Conversation with Paul McCartney," *International Times,* November 1966.
131 *"I can hear a whole"*: Hunter Davies, "Atticus," *Times* (London), 9/18/66.
133 *"his amused smile"*: Miles, *Paul McCartney,* p. 279.

CHAPTER 10

135 *"We Beatles are ready,"*: Reuters, "Paul McCartney Predicts Breakup of Beatles Soon," *New York Times,* 1/23/67.
136 *"The more drugs he took"*: Author interview with Chris Hutchins, 4/08.
139 *"Did you say, 'You've got to admit'"*: Hunter Davies, *The Beatles* (New York/London: W. W. Norton, 1968), p. 268.
141 *"Paul was upstaging him,"*: Geoff Emerick and Howard Massey, *Here, There and Everywhere* (New York: Gotham Books, 2006), p. 157.
142 *"I thought, 'Fucking hell!'"*: Barry Miles, *Paul McCartney: Many Years from Now* (New York: Henry Holt, 1997), p. 317.
142 *"Nobody knew exactly"*: Author interview with Tony Bramwell, 3/08.
143 *"You would want to look away"*: Miles, *Paul McCartney,* p. 383.
144 *"You just have to imagine"*: Author interview with Nat Weiss, 10/07.
144 *"It opened my eyes"*: Beatles, *Anthology* (San Francisco: Chronicle Books, 2000), 255.
145 *"We'd been trying"*: Ibid.
146 *"You cannot"*: Ibid., from contemporaneous media, p. 263.
147 *"He used the fact"*: Author interview with Tony Barrow, 12/07.
147 *"Paul was a problem"*: Weiss, 10/07.
147 *"Maybe Paul began"*: Ibid.
147 *"If you wanted something"*: Author interview with Peter Brown, 10/07.
148 *"We were almost"*: Beatles, *Anthology,* 268.
148 *"we've fuckin' had it"*: Jann Wenner, *Lennon Remembers* (Harmondsworth, UK: Penguin, 1970), p. 52.
149 *"You don't need scripts"*: Beatles, *Anthology,* p. 272.

CHAPTER 11

151 *"Tell you what, Ray"*: Author interview with Ray Connolly, 11/07.
153 *"He really expected"*: Author interview with Tony Barrow, 12/07.
154 *"Paul disliked the idea"*: Ibid.
154 *"I remember talking"*: Beatles, *Anthology* (San Francisco: Chronicle Books, 2000), p. 285.
156 *"an 'underground' company"*: Barry Miles, *Paul McCartney: Many Years from Now* (New York: Henry Holt, 1997), p. 441.

156 *"a shoplifter's paradise"*: Keith Badman, *The Beatles Off the Record* (London: Omnibus Press, 2000), p. 329.

156 *"just weren't our thingy"*: Ibid., p. 376.

158 *"She had never met"*: Author interview with Nat Weiss, 10/07.

158 *"They were definitely close"*: Ibid.

158 *"even when John's"*: Author interview with Ken Mansfield, 3/08.

159 *"He wanted to do things"*: Ibid.

160 *"I had no idea"*: Ibid.

161 *"really was like a Joe Orton play"*: Miles, *Paul McCartney*, p. 453.

162 *"Did somebody speak?"*: Tony Barrow, *John, Paul, George, Ringo and Me* (New York: Thunder's Mouth Press, 2005), p. 247.

163 *"I am fucking stoned!"*: Geoff Emerick and Howard Massey, *Here, There and Everywhere* (New York: Gotham Books, 2006), pp. 246–47.

164 *"One of his masterpieces"*: Beatles, *Anthology*, p. 297.

164 *You and your Jap tart*: Chet Flippo, *Yesterday* (New York: Doubleday, 1988), p. 263.

165 *"They were very playful"*: Author interview with Chris Thomas, 6/08.

166 *"It's too fuckin' much!"*: Flippo, *Yesterday*, p. 264.

CHAPTER 12

168 *"Yes, I suppose,"*: Linus Gregoriadis, "Beatle Paul's Secret Love Who Had to Let It Be" *The People*, 4/13/97.

168 *"I'd love to see you"*: Tony Bramwell, *Magical Mystery Tours* (New York: Thomas Dunne Books, 2005), p. 284.

169 *"She used to write"*: Author interview with Nat Weiss, 10/07.

170 *"I said, 'Yeah, babe!'"*: Author interview with David Dalton, 3/08.

170 *"They all wanted to fuck her!"*: Ibid.

171 *"You have to consider"*: Author interview with Danny Fields, 9/08.

171 *"Are you kidding?"*: Ibid.

171 *"They were very much into it"*: Author interview with Ken Mansfield, 3/08.

173 *"I'm not suggesting"*: Ibid.

177 *"Paul and Linda trashing"*: Dalton, 3/08.

177 *"John was the ne'er-do-well"*: Author interview with Ray Connolly, 12/07.

181 *"This is the first time"*: Peter Brown and Steven Gaines, *The Love You Make* (New York: Signet, 1983), p. 314.

181 *"Call back Monday!"*: Richard DiLello, *The Longest Cocktail Party* (New York: Playboy Press, 1972), p. 196.

182 *"I'm sure Lillian"*: Author interview with Danny Fields, 10/08.

182 *"you must come to dinner"*: Dalton, 3/08.

183 *"It feels fine"*: Keith Badman, *The Beatles Off the Record* (London: Omnibus Press, 2000), p. 427.

CHAPTER 13

186 *"Quite a good vibe"*: Author interview with John Kosh, 7/07.

186 *"It always surprised me"*: Barry Miles, *Paul McCartney: Many Years from Now* (New York: Henry Holt, 1997), p. 551.

186 *"The point is"*: Keith Badman, *The Beatles Off the Record* (London: Omnibus Press, 2000), p. 412.

186 *"Such a dreadful, dreadful feeling"*: Jann Wenner, *Lennon Remembers* (Harmondsworth, UK: Penguin, 1970), pp. 118–20.

187 *"just sort of morphed"*: Author interview with Chris Thomas, 6/08.

187 *"Everything is true"*: Author interview with John Kurlander, 7/08.

188 *"He'd be on his stool"*: Ibid.

191 *"The truth of it all"*: Roy Corlett interview with Paul McCartney, BBC-Merseyside, May 1969.

192 *"It's like he knew,"*: Wenner, *Lennon Remembers,* pp. 60–61.

192 *"Nobody quite knew"*: Beatles, *Anthology* (San Francisco: Chronicle Books, 2000), p. 349.

192 *"I think he felt"*: Author interview with Ray Connolly, 12/07.

193 *"It was really spooky"*: Bill De Young interview with Fred LaBour, Scripps-Howard News Service, 2004.

195 *"I could write songs"*: Miles, *Paul McCartney,* p. 569.

196 *"I remember lying awake"*: Ibid.

196 *"He was absolutely red"*: Author interview with Terry Spencer, 8/08.

197 *"I'm really very sorry"*: Ibid.

197 *"all bloody stupid"*: Dorothy Bacon, "Paul Is Still with Us," *Life,* 11/7/69.

197 *"To escape"*: QNP, "Surviving Beatles Mates Again—McCartney," *Courier-Mail,* 9/12/91.

198 *"I was a zombie"*: AP, "Linda Saved Beatle Paul from Heroin" *Advertiser,* 9/6/91.

198 *"Here I am living on a stone floor"*: Author interview with Danny Fields, 9/08.

CHAPTER 14

200 *"Paul was relaxed"*: Author interview with John Kurlander, 7/08.

200 *"He'd played everything"*: Author interview with Chris Thomas, 6/08.

201 *"I'll try and hustle"*: Keith Badman, *The Beatles Off the Record* (London: Omnibus Press, 2000), p. 485.

201 *"probably be a rebirth"*: Ibid., p. 487.

202 *"He went completely out of control"*: Richard Starkey testimony quoted by Peter McCabe and Robert D. Schonfeld, *Apple to the Core* (New York; Pocket Books, 1976) p. 170.

202 *"since he was our friend"*: Ibid.

203 *"I couldn't believe it"*: Ray Connolly, *Stardust Memories* (London: Pavilion, 1970), p. 99.

204 *"He's fuckin' trying"*: Author interview with Ray Connolly, 12/07.

204 *"I think what he was trying"*: Beatles, *Anthology* (San Francisco: Chronicle Books, 2000), p. 352.

204 *"Christ, what have I done?"*: Connolly, *Stardust Memories,* p. 93.

204 *"It wasn't like that!"*: Connolly, 12/07.

205 *"sheer banality"*: Richard Williams, "McCartney Review," *Melody Maker,* 4/17/70.

206 *"personal problems"*: Alvin Shuster, "McCartney Breaks Off with Beatles," *New York Times,* 4/11/70.

206 *"I'll see him"*: Jann Wenner, "Paul McCartney," *Rolling Stone,* 4/30/70.

207 *"fighting with myself"*: Richard Merryman, "Paul McCartney: The Ex-Beatle Tells His Story," *Life,* 4/16/71.

207 *"Oh, we've got to"*: Ibid.

208 *"the most big-headed"*: Jann Wenner, *Lennon Remembers* (Harmondsworth, UK: Penguin, 1970), p. 42.

208 *"I'd heard versions"*: Connolly, 12/07.

208 *"It was so far-out"*: Merryman, "Paul McCartney."

208 *"I sat down and pored"*: Paul Gambaccini, *Paul McCartney: In His Own Words* (New York: Flash, 1976), p. 32.

208 *"like a spoilt child"*: (and other testimony) Court documents cited by Keith Badman, *The Beatles Diary Volume 2: After the Break-up, 1970–2001* (London: Omnibus Press, 1999), 27.

209 *"thanks for getting us out of that,"*: Barry Miles, *Paul McCartney: Many Years from Now* (New York: Henry Holt, 1997), p. 581.

210 *"My husband would like"*: Dave Spinozza interview, *New Musical Express,* 5/28/71.

210 *"You're Paul McCartney!"*: Author interview with Denny Seiwell, 7/07.

211 *"He always put himself together"*: Ibid.

211 *"We were told exactly"*: Dave Spinozza interview.

211 *"He had great ideas"*: Seiwell, 7/07.

211 *"she thinks she's"*: Dave Spinozza interview.

211 *"I'm going to teach you"*: Merryman, "Paul McCartney."

CHAPTER 15

213 *"He loved to hang out"*: Author interview with Denny Seiwell, 7/07.

214 *"He seems to be wasting"*: Ringo Starr interview, *Melody Maker,* 7/31/71.

215 *"He just asked if I fancied"*: Author interview with Denny Laine, 10/08.

215 *"The band gelled"*: Ibid.

215 *"I'm gonna go with Linda"*: Seiwell, 7/07.

216 *"I was used to going"*: Laine, 10/08.

216 *"Ninety percent of it was playing"*: Seiwell, 7/07.

217 *"He wanted her to be with him"*: Author interview with Danny Fields, 10/08.

218 *"She could be difficult"*: Seiwell, 7/07.

218 *"I sheared the sheep"*: *Melody Maker,* 11/13/71.

219 *"He'd been away"*: Author interview with Henry McCullough, 5/08.
220 *"They'd step outside"*: Seiwell, 7/07.
220 *"It was literally"*: Ibid.
221 *"I had returned"*: Mary McCartney Donald's interviews of Paul McCartney, edited by Mark Lewisohn, *Wingspan* (New York: Bulfinch, 2002), unnumbered.
221 *"We've no managers"*: *Melody Maker*, 2/26/72.
221 *"We just rolled off"*: McCullough, 5/08.
221 *"Quite a mad thing"*: Donald, *Wingspan*, unnumbered.
222 *"Cover of the* Daily Express!*"*: Chris Salewicz, *McCartney* (New York: St. Martin's Press, 1986), p. 234.
222 *"It wasn't my style"*: McCullough, 5/08.
223 *"We went to a studio"*: Ibid.
224 *"I like being independent"*: Laine, 10/08.
224 *"Paul and Denny breaking out"*: Seiwell, 7/07.
225 *"We'd hear stuff"*: McCullough, 5/08.
225 *"It was seen as uncool"*: Seiwell, 7/07.

CHAPTER 16

228 *"John and Yoko are not cool"*: *Melody Maker*, 11/30/71.
228 *"I think I might"*: Author interview with Ray Connolly, 12/07.
228 *"It was too painful"*: Ben Fong-Torres, "Yesterday, Today and Paul," *Rolling Stone*, 6/17/76.
229 *"I don't think that'll ever happen"*: Paul Gambaccini, *Paul McCartney: In His Own Words* (New York: Flash, 1976), p. 37.
230 *"Paul could never talk"*: Author interview with Henry McCullough, 3/08.
231 *"He'd promised we'd participate"*: Author interview with Denny Seiwell, 7/07.
231 *"I just need you to play this!"*: Ibid.
231 *"If I don't get out of this"*: McCullough, 3/08.
232 *"I can't do this"*: Seiwell, 7/07.
232 *"I don't think he ever knew"*: McCullough, 3/08.
232 *"I don't know quite why"*: Gambaccini, *Paul McCartney*, pp. 73–74.
232 *"I was determined"*: Mary McCartney Donald's interviews of Paul McCartney, edited by Mark Lewisohn, *Wingspan* (New York: Bulfinch, 2002), unnumbered.
233 *"We all mucked in"*: Geoff Emerick and Howard Massey, *Here, There and Everywhere* (New York: Gotham Books, 2006), p. 340.
234 *"great album"*: *New Musical Express*, 1/19/74.
235 *"He didn't quite fit"*: Donald, *Wingspan*, p. 78.
236 *"He was absolutely demanding"*: Author interview with Alan O'Duffy, 4/08.
237 *"There was some thought"*: Ibid.
238 *"We had no clue"*: Author interview with May Pang, 4/08.
238 *"How'd you know?"*: Ibid.

239 *"It was like yesterday"*: Ibid.

239 *"She was very nice"*: Chris Salewicz, "Paul McCartney: An Innocent Man?" *Q*, October 1986.

239 *"I took him"*: Ibid.

240 *"Let's see each other"*: Pang, 4/08.

CHAPTER 17

243 *"You just had to be"*: Author interview with Howie Casey, 3/08.

243 *"And he did"*: Mary McCartney Donald's interviews of Paul McCartney, edited by Mark Lewisohn, *Wingspan* (New York: Bulfinch, 2002), unnumbered.

243 *"It's like having parents"*: Ben Fong-Torres, "Yesterday, Today and Paul," *Rolling Stone*, 6/17/76.

244 *"We were so tight"*: Author interview with Denny Laine, 10/08.

245 *"We almost went down"*: Coverage cited by Keith Badman, *The Beatles Diary Volume 2: After the Break-up, 1970–2001* (London: Omnibus Press, 1999), p. 182.

246 *"I'm saying to him"*: Fong-Torres, "Yesterday, Today and Paul."

246 *"you'll never want"*: David Gardner and Tim Miles, "Grieving Paul Gave Me a Great Big Hug," *Sunday Mirror*, 11/5/95.

248 *"I was a little put out"*: Donald, *Wingspan*, unnumbered.

248 *"Linda is a nice chick"*: Beatlefan, Spring 1978.

248 *"If someone didn't seem to fit"*: Donald, *Wingspan*, unnumbered.

250 *"I said, 'Are you joking?'"*: Author interview with Chris Thomas, 6/08.

250 *"I dunno"*: Author interview with Tony Bramwell, 3/08.

250 *"Paul was reluctant"*: Author interview with Steve Holly, 4/08.

251 *"He just followed"*: Author interview with Laurence Juber, 7/07.

252 *"I think the album"*: Thomas, 6/08.

252 *"Like this, not that"*: Ibid.

253 *"I remember thinking"*: Holly, 4/08.

253 *"a bloody great bag"*: Donald, *Wingspan*, unnumbered.

CHAPTER 18

257 *"awful blues bash"*: Beatlefan, Fall 1978.

258 *"It's ten years since"*: Newsweek, 9/29/80.

258 *"Anything I say"*: Good Morning America, ABC-TV, 11/27/80.

260 *"four need work"*: Paul Williams interview of George Martin, undated.

261 *"You know, John's dead"*: Author interview with Eric Stewart, 5/08.

262 *"People are printing"*: Hunter Davies, *The Beatles* (New York/London: W. W. Norton, 1968; 1996 ed.), p. 372.

263 *"A maneuvering swine"*: Ibid., pp. 368–74.

263 *"I've talked to Yoko"*: Richard Williams, "Paul McCartney Sets the Record Straight," *Globe and Mail*, 1/21/82.

264 *"I'm as intelligent"*: Richard Harrington, "Paul McCartney's Long and Winding Road," *Washington Post,* 10/29/84.

264 *"We just picked"*: Joan Goodman, "Paul and Linda McCartney Interview," *Playboy,* 12/84.

265 *"It begins with me in black tie"*: Author e-mail exchange with Peter Webb, 6–9/08.

265 *"What he described"*: Ibid.

267 *"He didn't make"*: Ibid.

267 *"It was almost completely"*: Author interview with Eric Stewart, 4/08.

268 *"We were both having"*: Ibid.

269 *"What a piece of shit"*: Author interview with Hugh Padgham, 4/08.

269 *"I didn't think"*: Ibid.

269 *"How many number one hits"*: Ibid.

269 *"He asked me who"*: Ibid.

269 *"he'd seen everything"*: Ibid.

270 *"Give that man"*: Stewart, 4/08.

270 *"He was all pissed"*: Padgham, 4/08.

271 *"I looked at it"*: Ibid.

CHAPTER 19

274 *"Too elevated to have"*: James Henke, "Can Paul McCartney Get Back?" *Rolling Stone,* 6/15/89.

278 *"I wrote 'em"*: Bill Flanagan, "Boy You're Gonna Carry That Weight," *Musician,* 5/90.

280 *"Fucking* cunt*"*: Author interview with Danny Fields, 10/08.

281 *"We can't do this"*: Henke, "Can Paul McCartney."

282 *"I thought critics"*: Ibid.

282 *"He didn't want to use"*: Author interview with Hamish Stuart, 4/08.

282 *"Paul has a clever"*: Flanagan, "Boy You're Gonna Carry."

283 *"it just wasn't working"*: Stuart, 4/08.

284 *"You could always hear"*: Ibid.

284 *"he came in one day"*: Ibid.

CHAPTER 20

286 *"The great thing"*: *Paul McCartney World Tour* program, 1989–90, p. 85.

287 *"Then I thought"*: David Fricke, "One for the Road," *Rolling Stone,* 2/8/90.

288 *"The first thing"*: Mat Snow, "Paul McCartney," *Mojo,* 11/95.

290 *"You could tell"*: Author interview with Hamish Stuart, 4/08.

292 *"She wanted to be"*: Author interview with Carla Lane, 5/08.

292 *"I had a double-barreled name"*: Author interview with Mark Featherstone-Witty, 4/08.

293 *"Then get up"*: Mark Featherstone-Witty, *Optimistic, Even Then* (London: The Schools for Performing Arts Press, 2000), p. 190.

293 *"It's wrong to scream"*: Featherstone-Witty, 4/08.

294 *"Lennonesque"*: *Paul McCartney New World Tour* program, 1993, p. 69.

295 *"Paul wanted togetherness"*: Stuart, 4/08.

296 *"Anyone can be made"*: Author interview with Hugh Padgham, 4/08.

296 *"She was the big cheerleader"*: David Lister, "McCartney Says Wings Retrospective Aims to Ease Hurt of Criticism of Linda's Singing," *Independent*, 5/29/01.

296 *"She was a little"*: Snow, "Paul McCartney."

297 *"I went over"*: Ibid.

297 *"I would have loved"*: Allan Kozinn, *New York Times,* unpublished interview excerpt.

297 *"So it was great"*: Ibid.

298 *"And you know"*: Ibid.

CHAPTER 21

303 *"We are improving"*: *Evening Standard,* 12/18/95.

304 *"Linda sat me down"*: Author interview with Carla Lane, 5/08.

304 *"Oh, they're daft"*: Ibid.

305 *"When everything is"*: *Daily Mail,* 12/8/97.

305 *"All the doctors"*: *Daily Mirror,* 9/4/96.

306 *"Yoko insisted"*: Bob Spitz, "McCartney Still Here, There, Everywhere; Keeper of the Beatles Flame Has New Album, Several Music Projects and a Knighthood," *New York Times,* 5/25/97.

307 *"[John] was the visionary"*: Ibid.

307 *"It was always"*: Author interview with Danny Fields, 8/08.

307 *"No, you don't!"*: Bob Spitz, "McCartney Still Here."

308 *"We've had a couple"*: Paul Bracchi, "The Tears I Wept for Linda, by McCartney," *Daily Mail,* 12/8/97.

308 *"One day she said"*: Lane, 5/08.

309 *"She called me"*: Ibid.

310 *"He kept saying"*: Alex Tresniowski et al., "Paul's Lovely Linda," *People,* 5/4/98.

310 *"He looked totally"*: Lane, 5/08.

311 *"I just let it"*: Simon Evans, "The Long and Winding Road to Recovery," *Birmingham Post,* 10/2/99.

312 *"He wasn't thinking"*: Author interview with Chris Thomas, 6/08.

312 *"These were just"*: Ibid.

CHAPTER 22

321 *"He kept yelling"*: Nadia Cohen, "Mystery of Sir Paul, Heather and the ring that went out the window," *Daily Mail*, 6/3/02.

322 *"I don't want"*: Louise Oswald and Annette Witheridge, "Macca Throws Heather's Ring out of Hotel Window," *Daily Mail*, 6/2/02.

322 *"Having a joke"*: Richard Simpson, "Paul refused to let me sign pre-nuptial pact, says Heather," *Evening Standard*, 9/4/02.

322 *"It's still not"*: Gary Wright, "It's Not Too Late to Call It Off, Dad," *The People*, 6/16/02.

323 *"The great thing"*: Paul Du Noyer, *Mojo*, July 2001.

324 *"He called back"*: Author interview with Denny Seiwell, 7/07.

325 *"[She] had just been"*: Interview by Johnny Black, 2003.

325 *"John had nothing"*: Ibid.

326 *" 'The fuck's he playing' "*: Ibid.

326 *"It was bare"*: Ibid.

327 *"People say, 'I never bothered' "*: Ibid.

328 *"After a while"*: Author interview with Mark Featherstone-Witty, 4/08.

329 *"His face was like"*: Author interview with Tony Bramwell, 3/08.

329 *"Fuck off!"*: Nicole Martin, "Foulmouthed Fracas as Sir Paul Visits Blaine Circus," *Daily Telegraph*, 9/20/03.

329 *"I was drunk"*: Laura Collins, "For 15 Years I Lied and Lied for Macca," *Mail on Sunday*, 5/13/07.

331 *"Is it because"*: Ben Todd, "They Won't Believe You Either, Heather," *Sunday Mirror*, 10/22/06.

332 *"She's just awful"*: David Litchfield, "Heather's Attitude Was That If the Kids . . . ," *Mail on Sunday*, 5/21/06.

ACKNOWLEDGMENTS

I spent nearly two years walking in Paul's footsteps, from Liverpool to London to New York to Los Angeles and beyond. Along the way I met, was befriended by, and abused the kindness of legions of people. They sat for interviews, sometimes repeatedly; they offered their memories, insights, and advice; they opened their homes, archives, and address books; they weathered my endless calls, e-mails, and visits; they were enormously generous and kind, and I owe more than I could ever say here.

For interviews, insights, and fact-checking: Peter Brown; Nat Weiss; Danny Fields; Tony Bramwell; Tony Barrow; Joe Flannery; Bill Harry; Astrid Kirchherr; Mike Byrne; Ray Connolly; Roy Corlett; Rod Davis; Colin Hanton; Denny Seiwell; Henry McCullough; Carla Lane; John "Duff" Lowe; Billy Hatton; Geoffrey Ellis; Don Short; Eric Stewart; Denny Laine; Howie Casey; Chris Hutchins; Iris Fenton; Laurence Juber; John Kosh; David Dalton; Alan O'Duffy; Brian Griffiths; Steve Holly; Rex Makin; Ken Mansfield; John Gustafson; Chas Newby; May Pang; Tony Sanders; Gordon Waller; John Kurlander; Robbie McIntosh; Hamish Stuart; Chris Thomas; Mark Featherstone-Witty; Hugh Padgham; Peter Webb; Terence Spencer; Spencer Leigh; Sam Leach; David Kahne; Peter Asher; Barry Miles; Larry Kane; Hanalei Perez-Lopez; Richard DiLello; Bob Gruen; Stuart Bell; Rosha Laine; Joe Boyd; Ray O'Brien and a few MPL veterans and other studio-and-road-tested veterans who know who they are, and a lot more, too.

For research guidance: Kevin Roche in the archive room of the Liverpool Public Library; Paul at Abbey Road; Jamie Bowman at the Beatles Story in Liverpool. Also the staffs at the British Library and the New York Public Library, and collector extraordinare Brenden Hyde.

Writers are supposed to be misanthropic and self-involved, so there's no accounting for the warmth and generosity of Bob Spitz; Mark Lewisohn; Allan Kozinn; Dave Marsh; Tim Riley; Spencer Leigh; Paul Du Noyer; Chris Salewicz; Keith Badman; Richard Stolley; Debbie Geller (RIP), Bill Flanagan; Blair Jackson; and Matt Hurwitz.

Employers, editors, colleagues, and friends, all long-suffering: Barry Johnson; Karen Brooks; Sandy Rowe; Peter Bhatia; and now Dennis Peck and Joany (no relation, she hastens to add) Carlin at the *Oregonian*; Lanny Jones; Cutler Durkee; Jamie Katz at *People*. And also Dan Conaway; Geoff Kloske; Shawn Levy; Dave

Walker; Geoff Edgers; Tim Goodman; Ryan White; and Rick Emerson. Also, many, many thanks to Brendan and Christe White, proprietors and sole underwriters of the Pacific City, Oregon, Writers' Colony.

Thanks also to Zachary Schisgal and his colleague Shawna Lietzke at Simon & Schuster; and to my agent, Simon Lipskar, and all his colleagues at Writers House.

And did I mention that I have a family? All the love in the world to Anna, Teddy, and Max; and all that and much more to my wife, Sarah.

INDEX